life, Money & Illusion

Living on Earth as if we want to stay

Well-being can be sustained when activities:

1 - use materials in continuous cycles;
2 - use continuously reliable sources of energy;
3 - come mainly from the qualities of being human
    (e.g. creativity, communication, movement, appreciation,
    and spiritual and intellectual development).

Long-term well-being is diminished when activities:

4 - require continual inputs of non-renewable resources;
5 - use renewable resources faster than their rate of renewal;
6 - cause cumulative degradation of the environment;
7 - require resources in quantities that undermine other people's well-being;
8 - lead to the extinction of other life forms.

(www.SustainWellBeing.net/challengeandgoal.html)

Editors: Sean Fordyce and Heather Hamilton
Cover Concept: Kim Ford, Moxie Media
Cover Prepress: Mary Ferguson, Carruthers Communications
Interior Design: Sean Fordyce

Order Information:
Seven Generations Publishing
2799 McDonald's Corners Road, RR# 3
Lanark, ON K0G 1K0 Canada
Phone: (613) 259-9988
www.SustainWellBeing.net

First Edition: October, 2006.

Library and Archives Canada Cataloguing in Publication

Nickerson, Mike, 1951-
        Life, money & illusion : living on earth as if we want to stay /
Mike Nickerson.

Includes bibliographical references and index.

ISBN 0-9780973-0-0
        1. Human ecology. 2. Economic policy. 3. Sustainable development.
I. Title.
II. Title: Life, money and illusion.

HD75.N53 2006   338.9   C2006-902665-3

Printed in Canada
On Old Growth Forest Free 100% Post Consumer Waste Paper

Life, Money & Illusion

& Illusion

Living on Earth as if we want to stay

Mike Nickerson

Seven Generations Publishing

Lanark, Ontario

2006

This book is dedicated to

Daniel

Eliza   Taegan

Lillian   Zephyr

and
all the children who will follow,
from whom our generation borrows the Earth.

Acknowledgments

This book would not have been possible without help of many kinds. First, thanks go to my mother, Betty Nickerson, for instilling in me a social conscience and an awareness and love for the natural world. In addition, she taught me, and countless others, that we can create our own world. To you, the reader, I relay her words: "Keep your eyes on the stars and do what's possible."

Credit is due to the International Development Resource Centre (IDRC), for the seed money that enabled me to overcome my hesitation and commit to the long writing task. Special thanks to Gisele Morin-Labatut who helped me make contact with IDRC.

Thanks to Richard Douthwaite, Marjorie Kelly, Rupert Sheldrake, Bernard Lietaer, Gregory Palast, and Brian Czech for their permission to use substantial quotations from their works.

As I set out to organize the notes from years of reading, I was living alone with my teenage daughter, Julia. Julia gave domestic purpose to my life, and occasional help around the house. I will always be grateful to our close friends, Stuart Jackson and Sheila Cook who helped keep me from getting lost in the doldrums of solitude. Others to whom I am grateful for moral support are David Laine and Alice Ayer, Randi Cherry and Robert D'Aoust, Keith Shackleton and Diane Ziegler, Joel LeBlanc and Martina Flanegan, Ann Mully, and Peter and Ann Bevan-Baker.

In August of 2002, at a Green Party Convention in Montreal, I met Donna Dillman. While there, we shared amusement around policy deliberations. Later we explored compatibilities, fell in love and married. Donna has since been my constant companion, and an invaluable help with edits to all manner of writing, long and short, including three drafts of this book. She also compiled its bibliography and index and acknowledges her gratitude to Roy Van der Mull, of VDMA Training and Consulting, Inc., for helping to make it possible for her to give this work the time and attention it required.

Both Sean Fordyce and Heather Hamilton edited comprehensively through the manuscript, providing corrections and countless suggestions for making it easier to read and understand.

John McMurtry, Linda Harvey and Richard Priestman also read entire drafts, pointing out ways to polish and embellish the text. Dr. Gray Merriam, Ray Purton, Ted Mosquin, Nancy Stegmayer, Robert

Rattle, Sam Noumoff, John Fisher, Adam Brierley and Chandler Davis all provided helpful comments on particular sections.

With deadlines closing in, a team of friends took on proofreading the 17 chapters. Thanks to Ileana Belanger, Robert Rattle, Wendolyn Nicholds, Fred Thompson, Mary Ferguson, Keith Shackleton, Carmen Penty, Ann Mully, Steve Nickerson, Lynn Daniluk, Jeff Woods, Randi Cherry, Ted Mosquin, Dave Seburn, Jackie and Bill Unitt, and Eleanor Drover for rising to the occasion, and completing the entire task in less than 48 hours.

Thanks, to Kim Ford of Moxie Media Studios for the cover design and to Mary Ferguson of Carruthers Communications for making the final touch ups, to Terra Nova Rubacha for her drawings of the shield and the governor, and to John Bianchi for the rope drawings.

Joe Jordan, Member of Parliament for Leeds-Grenville, (1997-2004) was the lead proponent for the *Canada Well-Being Measurement Act*. I am tremendously grateful for the opportunity he provided to develop and promote this important first step toward securing the future. I am also thankful for his having taught me some of the ropes of the legislative process and for taking the letterhead overrun with total grace.

Appreciation also to Alex Michalos, William Krehm, Ed Finn, Hazel Henderson, Richard Douthwright, Dr. Brian Czech and John McMurtry for providing volumes of their work for me to study. Years before I understood the significance, the late Brian Dolby explained to me how banks create money out of thin air. Thanks also to Ron Colman for his contagious enthusiasm about well-being measurement and for reliable help with related details. As well to Delores Dickey, Mark Anielski, John Baranyi, Frank De Jong, Bill Van Iterson, Jerry Heath, Eric Walton, Tom Kennedy and Douglas Jack for ideas that are woven into this text. Russell McOrmond, of Flora.org deserves a special mention for hosting our web site.

Others who have informed or encouraged this work are: Edwin Abbott, Peter Ajello, William Alexander, Pete Amyoony, Robert and Christine Anderman, John Anderson, Leonard Angel, Alan Appleby, Peter Au, Arnold and Joan Baker, Gordon Ball, Rex Barger, Richard Barre, Rick Barsky, Ardythe Basham, Barbara Beach, Michel Beauregard, Hugh Benevides, David Bennett, Desmond Berghofer, Robert Bigras, Brian Black, Michael Bloomfield, Bruce Bodiam, Greg Bonser, Helen and Andrew Brink, Bob Bromley, David Brown, Marvin Brown, Bruce Buchanan, Rita Burtch, Dana Bush, Charles

Caccia, John Calvert, Alf Cassidy, Alice Chambers, Greig Clark, Don Chisholm, John and Bobby Clarke, Dianne Clipsham, Stephanie Coburn, Richard Collier, Ron Conrad, Phyllis Creighton, Henry Dahle, Ann Dale, Lobie Daughton, June Davies, Caspar Davis, Dolores Dickey, Chas Dietrich, Marie Dion, Glenn Drover, Wally du Temple, Pat Duignan, Henry Dumouchel, Anna Dunkley, Kitty Dunn.

Doug Emmons, Bonnie Jayne Errett, David Faed, Paul Falvo, Jen and Stephen Fisher-Bradley, Paul Fitzgerald, Peter Fitzgerald-Moore, Judith Flannery, Alan Fox, Evelyn Frain, Jessica Fracassi, Javor Frajkor, Jim Fulton, Sylvia Furman, Robert Gairns, Maureen Geddes, Claude William Genest, Parm Gill, Orland Gingerich, Thomas Goff, Patricia Gordon, Morgan Grams, Bob Gray, Carol Greene.

David Hahn, Eric Hall, Clare Hallward, John Hanna, Shelley Hannah, Martin Hart, Robert Hay, Bob Henderson, Ole Hendrickson, William Henry, Jennifer Henstock, Barb Hicks, Marian Hindmarsh, Harry Holloway, Robert and Marilyn Horwood, Deborah Hudson, Bill Hulet, Vivian Hostetler, Daniela Jansson, Ann Jarnet, Howard Jerome, Bobbie Jordan, Walter Josephy, Eric Joss, Monica Kalistar, Michael Keating, Bryce Kendrick, Ruth Kennedy, Pat and Richard Kerr, Bev Kettle, Christine Kilgour, Lois Kivipelto, Ziggy Kleinau, Paul Kluchert, Harold Koehler, Wendy Kotilla, Anton Kuerti, Helmut Kuhn, Terry Kuny, Rob Kurdziel, Steve and Edith Kurtz.

Jeffrey Laine and Roxanne Heiden, Martha and Ken Laing, Peggy Land, Thomas and Patricia Lawson, Joe LeCoix, Eric Lilius, Carolyn Linden, Bernard Littlejohn, Don Lockhart, Bruce Lorie, Frances MacKeen, Dr. Paul MacKenzie, Gary Magwood, Tom Manley, Ted Manning, Gerry Masuda, Lea Matyuska, Paul Maurenbrecher, Don McAllister, Muriel McCaskill, Kenneth McCracken, Don and Louise McDiarmid, Janice McDougal, Brandy McPherson, Greta McGillivray, Tony McQuail, Gray Merriam, Doug Miller, Erik Millett, John Milton, Frank Mitchell, Jim Mitchell, Robert Monte, Rachel Moore, Gwen Morawetz, Linda Mosquin, Ray and Ruth Morris, Heather Mountain, Donald Munroe, Mari Naumovski, Keith Newman, Thomas Nichols, Lise Nickerson, the late Dr. Mark Nickerson, Marki Nickerson, Rain Nickerson, Sayo Nickerson, Steve Nickerson.

Lotus Nip-Bogrees, Sue Noakes, James O'Grady, David Oldford, Andrew Owens, Peter Padbury, Chris Paige, Don Page,

Noel Parrott, Joyce Paul, Paul and Tiina Payson, Charles Peacock, Frank Peddle, Laurel Pedersen, Dave Perceival, Christine Peringer, Arthur Petch, Roger Petry, Shirley Picknell, Blodwen Piercy, James Pine, Dr. Andre Piver.

Darrin Qualman, Angela Reid, John Rensenbrink, Brian Rich, Jim and Barb Riesberry, Jim Rogers, Andrea Roper, Britt Roscoe, Kendel Rust, Carl Ruttan, Jim Sanders, Pamela Schreiner, Gretchen Schwarz, Lucy Segatti, Nancy Shaver, David Sherwood, Jan Slakov, Judy Smith, Wilfred Sorensen, Julia and Steve Sparkes, Irene Spry, Nadine Steele, Lars Stuurop, Doris and James Sutherland, Nigel Tappin, Bill Tarman-Ramcheck, Amy Taylor, Barb Titerington, Ralph Torrie, Marja-Liisa and Ahti Tulvanen. Romy Turner and Otto Spika, Leon and Sandi Vandervalk, Stu Vickars, Gene Villeneuve, Blair Voyvodic, David Walsh, Shirley Walsh, Marilyn Waring, Randy Weekes, Anthea and Wesley Weese, Norma White, Dennis Whitfield, Ian and Karen Whyte, Tom Wilkinson, Ken Willis, Katherine Willow, Edward Wilson, Malcom Wrathwell, Colin Young, Wendy Zatylny.

Many thanks to the following organizations: the Atkinson Charitable Foundation for their encouragement and support and for their critical work animating experts in the field of genuine progress measurement to develop the Canadian Index of Well-Being (CIW); Web Networks for internet service; The Canadian Centre for Policy Alternatives; the Recycling Council of Ontario; the Green Party of Ontario; the Green Party of Canada and North West Environment Watch.

While the experience of human beings has changed drastically since I wrote *Planning for Seven Generations* (1993), the basic nature of life has not changed. It is under more stress than at that time, but the way it works is the same as it was long before humans emerged. That I could think of no better way to express many of the concepts in the "Life" sections of this new book is a tribute to the late George Mully. His well-seasoned talent molded my early work as he polished the script, and produced and directed the *Guideposts for a Sustainable Future* video for the popular-education discussion kit by that name.

Finally, to the many other people who have explained their views to me and whose names escape me, my apologies and gratitude.

Table of Contents

Foreword

Years of research and expression piled up before me as the second draft of this book passed through my ink jet printer. The International Development Research Centre (IDRC) had provided a grant to get me started and, after several extensions, they set a deadline to see what I had been up to.

On August 14, 2003, after an hour-long drive to Ottawa, with manuscript in hand I walked several blocks to the IDRC building. All seemed normal until, at the last intersection, cars were gridlocked and pedestrians had to wind their way between them with no guidance from the traffic lights. When I entered the building, the security staff were trying to figure out why their building had no power. By the time I left, they had learned that the whole city was down. In fact, all of north eastern North America had lost power. Huge lessons were learned from that blackout. While millions of people witnessed the abundance of stars above their cities for the first time, it had also become abundantly obvious how massively dependent we are on electricity.

More than two years and four drafts later, this book is in your hands and the lessons of the 2003 blackout are already all but forgotten. In their place is growing evidence of the larger energy challenges involving natural gas, oil and climate change. True appreciation of these challenges is held at bay by our natural tendency toward denial. Our minds are far too sensible to absorb information, which, with no solution in sight, would cripple us with despair. The problems of confronting planetary limits cannot be acknowledged without a goal, a plan, and the hope that we might overcome the trouble and, once again, imagine a secure future.

Clarifying the goal and outlining a plan is the purpose of this book. We are challenged as no previous generation has ever been, but, we also have unprecedented potentials for meeting the challenge. The answer lies in understanding the present situation and internalizing the vision of a sustainable future. In the chapters that follow, you will read about what makes life successful, how the human family has grown from an inconsequential presence on the planet, to a dominating influence, and how today's most serious problems are emerging from our success. While congratulations are in order for the robust formula that drives growth, we must now recognize that our size is stretching planetary limits and that the formula behind our previous success is now the source of our peril.

That we are in grave danger is the bad news. The good news is that the essential step for resolving the problem has been accomplished, on the scale of our individual lives, by practically every grown-up person. While the scale of civilization is six billion times larger, the problem is the same as that faced by each and every adolescent as he or she moves into adulthood.

To young people getting bigger is very important. Once each of us is big enough, however, we stop growing. As a civilization we are at the stage where we have grown large enough, yet, like many teenagers, we hesitate to take full responsibility for our strength.

On the scale of individual people, we live in communities where our parents, teachers, and the institutions of society define our responsibilities and reprimand us when we do not behave accordingly. As a civilization, we live within the community of species and the ecosystems that enable all life. Reprimands for irresponsible behaviour come in the form of environmental problems: depletion of resources, toxic waste effects and the disruption of life supporting systems.

The accountability of adulthood can be intimidating to a child grown large. In the end, however, almost all of us make the passage with more or less grace. As societies, it is time to accept the responsibility that comes with our mature form.

On the scale of civilization, the challenge is huge, but it is not beyond our collective abilities. Ours is a time of extraordinary opportunity for exciting, purposeful lives. Should we awaken to the task and shepherd our species successfully through this time of passage, our generation will be forever honoured by those who follow.

Understanding our nature as individuals and, collectively as societies, is intrinsic to understanding and accomplishing effective change. Essential for hope, is recognizing how fundamental cooperation is to being human. To be human is to work together. From the most ancient times, families and tribes cooperated to hold the natural world at bay and to provide for their young. Over the thousands of years through which our numbers have expanded, our talents and our techniques for cooperation have evolved. Starting with parental instincts and mutual dependency, and evolving through honour, tradition, barter, exchange currencies and monetary credit, the number of people who can work together for mutual benefit has greatly expanded. In today's global economy billions of people integrate their efforts toward common ends.

With the size and anonymity of the global economic system, however, personal experience of the enormous amount of cooperation involved has, to a large extent, been lost. At the same time, while the pursuit of self-interest, greed and competition can result in an abundance of goods and services available for the common good, those, sometimes unsavoury, characteristics have come to confuse our common purpose and distract us from genuine progress.

Chapters ahead will outline how the continued expansion of our cooperative ability to produce for human consumption has gone from making us ever more successful to threatening our future. As with a full-grown child, civilization has reached the point where its direction must change from simple expansion to a more sophisticated use of skills and abilities. While growing more "body mass" may still be in order for some less developed nations, overall, it is time to move toward sustainable relationships between nations and with the living Earth.

The few years I thought it would take to research and write this book stretched out to a decade as I discovered that ecological adaptation involved biological, technical, economic, social and spiritual change. Increased efficiency, renewable energy systems, the cyclic use of resources, and local food security are important parts of the picture. More illusive, yet ultimately more effective, however, is the necessary shift in purpose; from striving to produce and consume ever more, to enjoying life; from stimulating desire, to finding peace with enough.

As the spectrum of interrelated topics unfolded before my inquiry, I came to appreciate the process of learning to talk. To infants, none of the words they hear make any sense. Yet, simply by listening, without comprehension, to the words and sentences spoken around them, they do learn to communicate with words. So it was for me as

I delved into unfamiliar subject matters. Initially I lacked the background details to fully appreciate what I was reading. As I collected information, however, patterns became apparent. More satisfying, was when the patterns of one field started to integrate with those from other fields, and an overall congruence started to emerge.

Much effort has gone into ordering the present information so that less familiar details are introduced after providing supporting material. Even so, there remain circles of understanding where information "A" needs to be understood for detail "B" to make sense, yet, item "A" itself cannot be clear until item "B" is taken in and absorbed. Depending on how much you already know, the pages ahead may provide you with details for which full explanation has yet to be made.

Starting with Chapter 7, there are seven chapters explaining economic problems and solutions. They contain many details that can help one understand the modern crisis and some of its structural solutions. If you find they contain more detail than you are comfortable with, skip ahead to Chapter 14 — Cultural Foundations. From there on you can read about mechanisms for change, and you can always go back to the nuts and bolts as further interest develops.

Humans are hugely capable. We can easily master living on this bountiful planet, and thereby enable successive generations to live here for millions of years to come. Such a positive future requires that this generation accept responsibility for its mature strength. The essence of how we might meet this responsibility is outlined ahead. The direction is ours to choose.

1

Without Vision, the People Perish

Collecting the Vision

Events in the early 1990s caused me to realize that our economic system has passed its "best before" date. As the decade dawned, the volume of economic activity had been growing for years. Each year, new, all-time records were being set for the production and consumption of goods and services. Then, for a couple of years, the economy did not grow; it just churned away at the greatest volume ever known. I was astonished to discover that many people were experiencing serious hardship because the volume was not expanding.

The way the system is set up, it is not enough to produce huge amounts of goods and services. The volume must always be getting bigger. This is a critical problem on a finite planet where we are already stretching material limits.

Ever since realizing that increasing hardship can accompany record economic output, I have been studying economics, trying to understand why. What is it about the way we organize our mutual provision — the economy* — that causes hard times if we are not always producing greater total volumes? How might we recreate the system so that we can prosper without destroying ourselves? This book represents what I have found.

No person provides directly for all of his or her own needs. The economy is the process by which people exchange one sort of help —

---

* From the start, I want to demystify the term "economy." You will see it used interchangeably with the phrase "mutual provision." Economic exchange is a basic element of human life.

goods they make or services they perform — for those of others. Economic exchange need not be based on selfishness or exploitation. When two people love one another, the help they provide each other is a basic form of economics.

While economic exchange is the foundation of human communities, we are stuck in a model that is on a collision course with planetary limits. To adopt another model, we have to overcome the perception that the present structure is the only form possible. The human family has come to what is probably the most critical choice we will ever make. It is now necessary to question what we are trying to accomplish.

A Fundamental Change

...we have crossed a monumental historical threshold. Because of the fivefold economic expansion since 1950, the environmental demands of our economic system have filled up all the available environmental space on the planet. In other words, we now live in a "full world."

David Korten

Throughout our entire existence, until some time in the last century, humans were an insignificant presence on Earth. The Earth was almost "empty" of humans. There was huge potential for expansion. And expand we did. At the beginning of the third millennium, the Earth's ability to support humans is "full," or close to full. Some say it is more than full.

Until recently, it mattered little what we did to the Earth. There were not enough of us, and the tools we used were not powerful enough to cause ecological problems on anything but a local level. This is no longer so. With over six billion people using all manner of powerful equipment and chemical ingenuity we are having a huge impact on the foundations of our well-being. This is a fundamental change in circumstances, which, if we intend to maintain our well-being, requires an equally fundamental change in how we manage ourselves. The perceived need for continuous economic expansion is in direct conflict with the limitations of our planet.

As its title implies, this book looks at three main topics: "Life" refers to the biological perspective of what makes a species successful; "Money" encompasses the history of economic exchange; and "Illusion" looks at the apparent contradictions between the first two, in particular, around the assumption that the economic system must expand forever.

How I Got Involved

In the 1950s, nuclear bomb tests were raising mushroom clouds above the Arizona desert. I was a child and my mother was one of many women from Winnipeg and elsewhere across the Great Plains of North America, who collected their children's baby teeth and sent them for testing. Strontium-90 is a radioactive fallout from nuclear explosions. When it settles on grasslands and enters the food chain of grass, cows, milk and children, young growing bodies take it in and use it as they use calcium to grow teeth and bones. Strontium-90 was found in our baby teeth and the evidence made a strong argument for stopping the above-ground testing of nuclear weapons.

I remember my mother reading bedtime stories to us from Rachel Carson's biologically inspired, poetic narrative, *The Sea Around Us.* Years later, when I read Carson's better known book, *Silent Spring,* Mom told me about how Rachel Carson was harassed by the scientific community for her "alarmist ideas" about the dangers of broadcasting manufactured poisons into the environment and for suggesting that we should look to the natural world for our models of survival and well-being.

Having learned about natural resources and pollution at my mother's knee, it should come as no surprise that, when I finished my formal schooling, I wanted to do something to help.

While searching for my role, I came across the Encyclopædia Britannica's, 1952 edition of *The Great Ideas.* It talked about how ideas occur in the context of what is already known. Every now and then, someone makes a new connection or sees a new perspective and is able to express the evolving view in a way that others can then see more easily for themselves. Every individual has the potential, from their unique perspective, to see things in a new way and to have new realizations. My writing has since been inspired by the possibility that you, and other readers, might see the ideas I have been gathering and take them forward to better understanding. "Co-intelligence" is the term coming into use to describe the enhanced ability to think, comprehend, and innovate, which occurs when people open themselves to a free flow of ideas and information between them.

In 1971, I resolved to travel and ask people working on issues about the insights that inspired their efforts to make the world a better place. As a filter for sincerity, I focused on people who felt strongly enough about their work to carry on with little or no expectation of financial gain. (It's not that making money at what one does indicates insincerity, but when one works without personal gain, there is little besides sincerity for motivation.) I traveled across Canada and down the west coast of the U.S. looking for people working voluntarily or not-for-profit. I would arrive in a city, find the library, look up the community directory, call the contact people from a variety of citizens' groups and explain my interest in their work. On meeting, I would ask what they were trying to accomplish, what they were trying to overcome, and what they knew about the way society changes. It was a fascinating summer.

That informative journey was followed by joining with a number of other idealistic young people in Toronto and founding the Institute for the Study of Cultural Evolution (ISCE). Together, we continued the study of problems and solutions and how change takes place. The scope of the study was extended to include professional research into the issues that inspired voluntary and non-profit work. The Institute operated for four years and at one point involved more than 20 people.

Among other things, we were looking for cultural items that caused a minimum of problems. Cultural items are techniques people have devised for doing things. The knot used to tie shoes, different types of tools, clothing and shelter, the lullabies sung to help babies sleep, computer programs, forms of entertainment, and different ways of organizing projects, large and small, are examples of cultural items. While the cultural items used to provide for basic human needs differ from culture to culture, those basic needs — food, shelter, education, health care, personal fulfillment, etc. — remain the same. By looking at the spectrum of different techniques used and, where there are choices, selecting the ones with the least negative impacts, we could take a large step toward overcoming the problems arising around us.

The most significant outcome from the four years of the ISCE's work was the summary outline that emerged. When the organization disbanded in 1974, I took all the notes collected about solutions and problems and separated them into areas of common interest. After describing the subject of each category with a sentence, I began circulating the resulting guidelines as a citizens' view of the opportunities and challenges of our times.

Looking at them a year later, a friend noted that the outline defines what is, and what is not, sustainable.

That our study should culminate in an outline of sustainability made sense when I thought about it afterwards. Long-term well-being (another way to say sustainability) is a natural interest of those whose immediate needs are met. Once the basics are provided for, people aim to secure their well-being, and that of their families and communities, into the future. When something is sensed to be getting progressively worse, people become concerned, form organizations and take action. The focus of our study was three fold: the problems causing concern,

Well-being can be sustained when activities:

1 - use materials in continuous cycles.

2 - use continuously reliable sources of energy.

3 - come mainly from the qualities of being human
(i.e. creativity, communication, movement, appreciation, and spiritual and intellectual development).

Long-term well-being is diminished when activities:

4 - require continual inputs of non-renewable resources.

5 - use renewable resources faster than their rate of renewal.

6 - cause cumulative degradation of the environment.

7 - require resources in quantities that undermine other people's well-being.

8 - lead to the extinction of other life forms.

the visions being developed of an order that would not have such problems, and the work being done to get from the one to the other. It follows then, that the summary of a study looking at long-term problems and their solutions would encompass sustainability.

The problems were (and indeed remain) compelling, but the extent to which solutions had been worked out, filled me with hope and inspiration. In the years that followed, I produced numerous educational materials based on this eight-point outline and related details. Always, the outline has been presented as food for thought.

You too are encouraged to question it.

Does it make sense to you?

If it does not, upon what point or points do you disagree?

For what reasons?

Is there something missing?

Where, for example, does durability fit in? Recycling resources can be wasteful of energy when the same materials could provide many times as much service if the products made from them were designed to last.

If the basic eight-point framework makes sense, it can be used to assess what you see going on around you and for making decisions about what actions to take.

* * * * *

Even in the 1970s there were many thousands of people working on sustainability issues. As I met with people and read the material they suggested, it became clear that the challenge was broadly understood. Discovering that the overall concern was regularly rebuffed when decision-makers were called upon to take action, was disturbing.

Finally, in the Fall of 1983, a glimmer of hope appeared. The United Nations passed a resolution creating the World Commission on Environment and Development. In the words of the Commission's mandate, it was created "at a time of unprecedented pressure on the global environment, with grave predictions about the human future becoming commonplace." The Commission set out to investigate the pressures and predictions.

The chair of the Commission was the Prime Minster of Norway, Gro Brundtland. Her co-chair was the Deputy Prime Minister of the Sudan. The credentials of the 21 Commissioners were equally impressive. Among them were leaders in related ministries of government, research organizations and international, non-governmental organizations. The Commission traveled to every continent and met with governments, academics, industrial leaders, citizens' organizations and concerned individuals.

In April of 1987, its report, *Our Common Future,* was released to the world. The report confirmed that we are, indeed, faced with a crisis of proportions unparalleled in recorded history. The Commission wrote, "We are not forecasting a future; we are serving a notice, an urgent notice..."

SUSTAINABLE ACTIVITIES

1) Use materials in continuous cycles

Pictures from space show our blue and green planet as a small sphere orbiting with its moon in a vast emptiness. A closer look reveals that the layer of materials actually of use to living things is only a very thin film over the planet's surface.

Within this limited stock of materials, any substances needed regularly must, over time, be used again and again. The cycles, which bring the needed materials back for reuse, must either occur naturally, like the cycles of water and carbon, or they must be maintained through mindful recycling programs.

2) Use continuously reliable sources of energy

We are consuming supplies of coal and oil at a far greater rate than they are created. The dangers of releasing all the carbon in these resources aside, their massive use cannot be our habit if civilization is to be a permanent presence on Earth. There is simply not enough of these fuels in existence. The same is true of nuclear energy. The enormous costs and dangers might, perhaps, be overcome, but the raw fuel is, in the end, also limited in supply.

Energy sources that can be relied on over the thousands of years that await the human family include: heat from the Earth's core, tides, the Sun (nuclear fusion at a safe distance) and the wind and water, which the Sun sets in motion. These power sources are abundant, and can be harnessed practically anywhere. With the exception of the problems associated with large dams, these renewable sources of energy have relatively little or no negative environmental impacts.

3) Come mainly from the qualities of being human

Once we have secured the food and shelter necessary for healthy life, worlds of opportunity open up for personal growth and satisfaction. The three Ls — Learning, Love and Laughter — as well as art, music, dance, sport, communication, service, and appreciation of the universe, within and around ourselves, can all make life worthwhile. Without harming the Earth they can provide pleasure, purpose and meaning to our lives.

NON-SUSTAINABLE ACTIVITIES

4) Require continual inputs of non-renewable resources

Non-renewable resources are resources available only in limited quantity. Metals, coal, natural gas and oil are notable examples. They can be very useful, even essential, for building a sustainable society, but if our way of life always requires that more and more of these materials be extracted, we will eventually run out. Dependency on more at that point would be disastrous.

5) Use renewable resources faster than their rate of renewal

Renewable resources are resources that maintain themselves through natural processes. Some examples are forests, fish stocks, ground water and soil fertility. As long as the rate at which they are used is not greater than the rate at which they grow or accumulate, the situation can remain viable. When the rate of use exceeds the rate of renewal, the stock will become depleted and problems will follow.

6) Cause cumulative degradation of the environment

Certain amounts and types of pollution are cleansed by natural processes. When we create waste that nature cannot handle, or that cannot be absorbed as fast as we create it, pollution builds up, causing problems that become more and more serious as the activity continues. Some pollutants can create serious hazards even when thoroughly diluted. Small amounts of toxic materials, after being absorbed by tiny organisms, can accumulate in the flesh of the creatures that eat them. If these creatures are then food for larger ones, the accumulated toxins are concentrated even further. Through this biological accumulation, some poisons, although thinly dispersed, can be found in dangerous concentrations — for example, in fish from polluted water and in the humans that eat those fish.

7) Require resources in quantities that undermine other people's well-being

The cooperation needed to build a sustainable world order will not come about as long as some groups of people take unfair advantage of others. Inequity often leads to social strife and armed conflict. Furthermore, the people at the bottom of the pyramid of exploitation are often forced by desperation to degrade the environment around them for day-to-day survival. The degradation of their territories not only makes life worse for them, it undermines the global systems that provide for those at the top of the pyramid, as well as for those below.

8) Lead to the extinction of other life forms

The web of life is intricate and mutually supporting. However, it is weakened with each life form lost. If we maintain patterns of development that regularly destroy, or significantly diminish, the presence of other forms of life, we progressively undermine our own existence as a part of the global ecosystem. With the loss of species we also lose genetic possibilities for fighting disease, in people and in food crops, as well as potential new sources of food. In addition to the dangers and loss to people, fair play would acknowledge that other living things have their own right to exist.

Many present efforts to guard and maintain human progress, to meet human needs, and to realize human ambitions are simply unsustainable — in both the rich and poor nations. They draw too heavily, too quickly, on already overdrawn environmental resource accounts to be affordable far into the future without bankrupting those accounts. They may show profits on the balance sheets of our generation, but our children will inherit the losses.

Our Common Future, Report of the Brundtland Commission

The Brundtland Commission, as it came to be known, was not pessimistic. It coined the phrase "sustainable development,"* to identify "development that meets the needs of the present without compromising the ability of future generations to meet their own needs." Based on such development, it asserted that the human family

* While sustainable development has been used in good faith by many, it has been spun around to mean sustaining development — pursuing perpetual economic expansion. Critics of this phrase feel that corporate globalization came about while civil society was distracted by the rhetoric of sustainable development. Because they feel the time we have lost will cost us civilization, some of these critics are understandably angry. My use of the phrase is as originally coined by the Commission.

could yet secure the future if we acknowledge the challenge, and set our sights on resolving it. Social conditions were also highlighted: "Poverty is a major cause and effect of global environmental problems." The Commission wrote, "It is therefore futile to attempt to deal with environmental problems without a broader perspective that encompasses the factors underlying world poverty and international equality." The Commission called for "a vast campaign of education, debate and public participation." By confirming concerns about natural resources and pollution the Brundtland Report legitimized action. It was okay to respond. And people did. There was an enormous increase in environment related activity.

One example was the recycling program in the Canadian city of Kingston, Ontario. Some years before the Brundtland Report, while developing the *Guideposts for a Sustainable Future* discussion kit, I was invited to conduct a workshop at the inaugural meeting of the Kingston Environmental Action Project (KEAP). After opening the meeting with a "popular education" discussion, KEAP was founded and those present decided to make the institution of curbside recycling in Kingston its primary project.

They developed and submitted a proposal that was turned down by the Kingston City Council. In each of the next four years they presented ever more sophisticated proposals, with the same outcome. Then in 1987, with the Brundtland Report saying we really do have to deal with environmental problems, the KEAP proposal was accepted. (Within a few months, curbside recycling enjoyed upwards of 80% participation.)

We had all learned the 3 Rs — Reduce, Reuse, Recycle — as a key to easing the problems at hand. In the late 1980s, with legitimacy finally given to these concerns, recycling expanded rapidly. The Kingston example was one of many that achieved participation rates of 80% and 90% within months of program start-ups. The volume of materials being recycled skyrocketed.

Of the 3 Rs, it was clear that reduction of personal consumption and reuse — keeping items in use for longer periods of time — could be even more effective than recycling in the effort to reduce resource consumption and waste. The increase in recycling could be measured because it involved physical substance. Reduction and reuse, as acts of omission, could not be measured. It is, nevertheless, probable that they also increased substantially.

Whether or not the recession that followed was directly related to reduction and reuse efforts would be an interesting research topic.

From my perspective, it was "Reduce, Reuse, Recession." Reduction and reuse are directly opposed to the expansion of production and consumption. This is the moral dilemma of our times.

Was it this conflict of goals that triggered the October 19, 1987 stock market crash, known as "Black Monday?" The October 19th date for the discussion of the "urgent notice" at the United Nations had been set six months earlier when the Brundtland Report was released. The discussion took place, but it was obscured from public view by extensive coverage of that day's stock market crisis. Could sales of shares in offending industries have triggered the computer enhanced crash that erased one-third of the stock market and shook the financial world? This would be another topic worthy of a doctoral thesis. Whatever the causes, the events that followed illustrate a point of critical importance.

Popular concern for environmental adaptation was starting to transform civilization. Once the cause gained legitimacy, momentum grew rapidly. It is, and was, well within our knowledge and ability to develop satisfying ways of living that fit within ecological bounds. People were ready! Why did we stop?

When our "leaders" recognized the direct interference reduction and reuse posed to the goal of perpetual economic expansion, legitimacy was quietly diverted away from them.

Whether consciously, in support of recognized interests, or subconsciously, as a result of deep allegiance to familiar goals, reduction and reuse were seldom mentioned in official circles after that. Efforts to solve the problems of poverty no longer looked at moderating consumption in the over-consuming world so that present production could be shared more equitably. The emphasis shifted back to solving the problem by promoting massive expansion of the global economy.

For the established order, this solved the moral dilemma. We could not reduce and reuse in good conscience when the goal of society is to expand production and consumption. Recycling is okay because it expands commerce and provides resources for ever-hungry production machinery. Reduction and reuse clearly inhibit growth. Stimulating a review of the values that are at odds here is a central goal of this book.

This is the conflict of values that compelled me to study economics. How can a system that effectively enables thousands of millions of people to cooperate in mutual provision not be sensitive to the resource limits and pollution problems that threaten the foundation of its existence? Why must we forever struggle to expand, rather than enjoy our success?

This study soon confirmed the astonishing discovery identified at the beginning of this chapter: for society to remain healthy under the present economic structure, the volume of economic activity must always get bigger.

Two contrasting views became apparent. Those who see human well-being from the ecological perspective say we have to establish food security for a stabilized population and halt the accumulation of toxic chemicals in the environment. They suspect that perpetual economic expansion, like perpetual motion, is impossible and that, sooner or later, we will have to address our economy's addiction to "growth." Better to do so before resources are further depleted and the planet even more overwhelmed with waste.

On the other hand, those with faith in the present economic system counter by asserting that we can, and will, always be able to expand economic activity. We need only accept their faith, eliminate public control over services and remove any regulations that inhibit the effective functioning of self-interest, markets and money. In other words, people, trying to get as much as possible for themselves, will provide ample motivation to accomplish anything necessary and, because a growing economy will make us rich, we will have money to spend on solving problems.

The ecological and the conventional economic perspectives are very different. Each will be detailed in the chapters ahead. Following that, are proposed solutions that would combine what remains helpful from the conventional economic perspective with the new understanding of (what David Korten identified above as) our "full" world. As you will see, there is enough vision to make the world work for all who live here, and for the generations to follow. First, however, a look at some of the dynamics with which we have to work.

Hope and Hindrance

People are remarkably perceptive, intelligent and creative. Creatures with far less ability have lived on Earth for hundreds of millions of years. Humans should expect far more. While we wield enough power to destroy the Earth's ability to support us, we can, instead, use our knowledge and skills to establish satisfying ways to live that can evolve for as long as the Sun shines.

The extent to which people are aware of the problems and can see where solutions lie, has given me enormous faith in human ability. By extension, I have a strong faith in democracy. Not democracy as in having an opportunity every four years or so to choose rulers, but democracy where issues of concern are considered by all who are interested, and where the thoughts arising are shared and discussed. If we can tap into the huge awareness available in the population and the good will of those who care about the future, we can secure our place on this planet for countless generations to come.

But the problems are huge. They are far greater than any individual or organization can grasp, let alone deal with. Yet, if we can align the collective ability of the hundreds of thousands of people who care enough to work towards solving them, we are up to the task.

Why We Will Succeed

The human species is extraordinary, a prime candidate for a long stay on Earth. We have thumbs with which to hold, carry and otherwise manipulate objects. Our senses of sight, hearing, touch, smell, and taste are well developed. When aided by telescopes, microscopes, Geiger counters, spectrometers, thermometers and other technical extensions, our ability to notice what is going on around us is spectacular. We have a highly developed ability to intuitively recognize patterns in the observations we make, leading to understanding and the ability to predict the consequences of events and actions. We have memory, both individually and through recorded information, with which to bring a vast accumulation of past observations into consideration for problem-solving. We can communicate by speech and through print and other media. Huge numbers of people can share information and pass it forward through time. We also have the creative ability to use the information to plan actions, and the skills with which to make things. These qualities are present in each one of us, and our ability to team-up for projects is legendary.

We have applied our talents long enough to know a great deal about how this planet works, what we need and how to provide for those needs from what the Earth offers. We were well able to provide for ourselves a hundred years ago, and since then we have developed countless new capabilities. There have been very helpful advances in health care, psychology, communication, understanding of ecological systems, physics, cybernetics, and the knowledge of techniques by which to grow, design and manufacture useful items.

Uncertainty about the future is not because we lack ability. We are more than capable of providing for our needs without undermining long-term well-being. Why then are we getting into so much trouble? Why do we threaten the integrity of whole ecosystems and see huge numbers of people living in desperate poverty while more wealth is created each year than has been seen in most centuries past?

These dangers arise because those in control cling to management principles from very different times. In our infancy and youth as a species, we needed only to look after immediate needs: food for tomorrow and to get us through cold or dry seasons; shelter; clothing; and the tools to maintain these. We were incapable of significantly disrupting the vast continents of life that surrounded and nurtured us. This has changed. We now significantly impact on practically everything that lives — the atmosphere, soils, lakes, rivers and even oceans. This is the fundamental change of circumstances that requires a fundamental change in how we manage ourselves and our planet. This point cannot be over-emphasized. It is now necessary to pay attention to the repercussions of our acts. Our customs, traditions and economic system developed during a period when the thought that we might disrupt planetary balance was absurd. Consequently, these institutions give few clues for solving today's problems, yet, they provide the patterns by which most of our activities are determined. Restructuring these institutions to help us find and maintain balance with the rest of life needs to be a top priority.

A Percian Shield

In seeking solutions, we have to look closely at the problems. The danger here is that because some of the problems have been neglected for too long, they have become frightening.

I find it helpful to remember a story from Greek mythology. The hero was Perseus and, the villain, Medusa. Medusa was a monster, so horrible to look at, that, anyone who dared do so would turn to stone from sheer fright. By polishing his shield, and only looking at the paralyzing problem via the reflection he found there, Perseus was able to get close enough to kill Medusa and rid the world of the problems she caused.

Because we are faced with problems that can be paralyzing to look at, we need a shield like that of Perseus. We have to avoid paralysis, yet keep a clear enough view of the problems to deal with them directly.

Two factors can help us face the great challenge. One is the extraordinary nature of human beings described above. The other is our connectedness with others. Strong relationships in one's life multiply one's strength. Personal bonds reinforce the reality that we are not alone. I've frequently reflected on an observation made by John Daveikis, illustrator of my first book, *Bakavi; Change the World I Want to Stay On.* After having traveled in a poor Asian country back in the early 1970s, John observed that, no matter how hard things became for those people, they just huddled closer together in the great love they had for each other and it was okay.

Primary relationships stabilize us. They are testimony to the web of relationships that bond us together as communities and nations making us extraordinarily capable of meeting the present challenge. We are an extraordinary species capable of long-term success on Earth. We need only to visualize the task before us and proceed.

2 Vision for the 21st Century

Since 1968 I've been searching out insights into the challenges and solutions of our times. Like the colours in a paint set that enable an artist to make pictures, these insights, clustered into topics, provide pools of perspective from which a vision can be illustrated. The chapters ahead will use the assembled images to compose a vision of where we are, how we got here, where we could be and some of the steps for getting from here to there. The following topics will be helpful as we proceed.

Conventional Wisdom

Conventional wisdom is a product of what people think and what we think other people think — beliefs, customs, laws and shared images. It is the underlying assumptions upon which we build our world-views.

As new ideas spread through a population, conventional wisdom evolves. In his book, *The Phenomenon of Man,* Tielhard de Chardin identified the sphere where this takes place as the "noosphere." It is similar in scope to the biosphere. The biosphere is the layer of life that surrounds the planet, interconnected by the flows of nutrients and energy between living things. "Noos" is Greek for mind. The noosphere is the layer of consciousness that is interconnected by ideas and information flowing between people.

Most people have a tremendous respect for convention, if not consciously, on a subtle level. It has taken thousands of years to assemble today's world-view with its understanding of what is good and what is not. Flavoured with our individual experiences, conventional wisdom forms the foundation of who and what we think we are. Sharing a common perspective of: right and wrong, what we can expect, what to aspire toward, and what to avoid, enhances the ability of a population to act together in mutual provision.

Problems arise, however, when circumstances in the world change and conventional wisdom does not. With its multitude of individual components, and its roots reaching back centuries and millennia, conventional wisdom does not shift easily.

One well-known shift took place when the accepted view — that the Earth was the center of the universe — changed to one where we understood that we are only inhabitants on one planet orbiting around the Sun. With each person who grasped the solar system view, it became easier for the next person to do so. So it is with the notion that the world revolves around the human economy. This is slowly being replaced by the view that the economy is a part of the larger system of material flows that connect all living things. When this perspective shifts into place, it will be obvious that our economic well-being requires that we account for, and respond to, factors of ecological health. Unfortunately we do not have a century or two to make the change. By clarifying the nature of the old and new perspectives, and by identifying actions on which we might co-operate to move the process along, we can help accelerate the shift.

Most people seek only to lead good lives. Without dedicating a lot of time to re-imagining the world, they accept the conventional wisdom and use it to make judgments. At present, the broad perception of what is good and proper is thoroughly saturated with conventional economic views. For effective change to take place, the goal of growth, which has been primary since ancient times, must move to second place, behind living within planetary limits.

In this communication age it is possible for ideas to spread rapidly. A great deal of information about sustainability is flowing through the Internet and other media, but at this point, it seems to make little headway against the torrents of powerfully produced commercial messages. Advertising keeps the consumer ethic ever present. Almost all mass media has been purchased by accomplished adherents of the management school that judges success by the measure of money. Their editorial comment saturates the noosphere with justification and encouragement for pressing on with perpetual economic expansion.

Governments have come to sing the same tune through a combination of factors: accepting the established formula for success;

dealing with an electorate informed by the commercial media; busy lobbyists; and in some cases, generous campaign contributions. Governments simply reflect the collective world-view on which they depend for survival. This is a source of hope because, as powerful as governments are, they will change when we do.

If we recognize the need to transform society in order to regain social and ecological balance, there is only one power available to us that does not require great wealth or the use of violence. It is the power of collective persuasion. It works on the subtle levels of thought and conversation and it works directly through democracy.

A change in society's goals may be widely understood as necessary, but until that change is recognized as legitimate, the actual shift in how things are managed will be delayed.

A parallel to this exists in the physics of freezing water. If water is very still it can be chilled to well below the freezing point before it turns to ice. When crystallization does start in such "supercooled" water, the entire sample can turn to ice in a few moments. I witnessed this once with some very cold beer. Sitting motionless in a freezer for too long, it became supercooled. When I retrieved it, the impact of setting it down on a table was enough to trigger crystallization. Crystals formed before my eyes and the entire contents turned to ice in a few seconds.

Rapid social transformations have taken place on regional levels three times since I've been following world news: in Iran in 1979; in the Soviet Union in 1990, after the fall of the Berlin Wall the year before; and in South Africa in 1994. None of these events was anticipated, even though, in at least the first two cases, substantial intelligence forces were deployed to keep track of the situation.

Iran had been a key U.S. stronghold in the Middle Eastern oil lands. The ruling Shah was well equipped with military equipment, yet, one day, with the return of an exiled religious leader, the Shah was deposed and a new social order began. In the Soviet Union, it took longer, but the effect was the same. Regardless of its superpower status, the established order was washed away by widespread popular sentiment. In each case, popular sentiment developed first, and structural change followed the conventional wisdom.

After 30 years of bad news and dire warnings about social and environmental stress, enough people are aware of the need for change to shift the conventional wisdom and establish the legitimacy of new goals. Thousands of organizations are prepared to provide details about specific concerns and how changes can be made. This supercooled situation is possible because we are immersed in mass media images that endlessly assert that consuming more is the purpose of life and that there is no alternative to perpetually expanding production to feed that consumption. What we need is a social equivalent to tapping the beer bottle on the table. Is it possible that presenting a blunt question about what the population feels our goals should be would provide the necessary impact to tip the balance? The fundamental change described in this book is ready to happen, we are attending only on a catalytic signal.

The Pace of Change

It makes a big difference whether change is imposed or evolves. Extremes tend to carry within them the essence of their opposites. Action begets reaction. Aggressive actions beget aggressive reactions. With sensitivity and inclusiveness, however, change begets new ways of doing things. As the conventional wisdom evolves to recognize human activity as a part of our planet's ecology, actions will increasingly be taken to align the things we do with the new vision.

That said, we don't have a lot of time. Fortunately public awareness of the environmental imperative has been spreading at least since the first global environment conference in Stockholm in 1972. Issues of social justice have been known for much longer.

Acknowledging these issues and discussing them publicly would lead to a general understanding. Instead of having policies thrust upon society with the almost inevitable backlash, action would be seen to emerge from society and would, therefore, slide more naturally into place with minimal reaction.

Nothing Practical Will Come from Attacking People

Although attitudes and actions can be mistaken, individuals deserve respect. While people seldom see themselves as bad, actions taken without considering the impact they have on other people or the environment can have negative results. Those results can indeed be bad. The chances are, however, that the person who took the actions had other goals in mind and perhaps even achieved the "positive" result anticipated.

If the people causing negative impacts by their actions are verbally or physically attacked, they are not likely to think, "I have done something wrong and deserve to be hurt." They are more likely going to defend themselves. Their actions may have been thoughtlessly self-serving, but attackers will be seen as "enemies," willfully trying to do them harm. Through aggressive actions, people often take on the characteristics of those they despise.

If our intent is to solve problems, we need as much insight and cooperation as possible, particularly from those who are in positions where the decisions are made that cause the problems.

Mahatma Gandhi set the example of principled, determined, non-violent action for change. The British Empire was the most powerful force the world had ever known, yet, by clearly stating what the problems were, detailing solutions and building popular understanding and support, Gandhi catalyzed the end of British rule in India. We can do the same for replacing our non-sustainable culture with one that fosters healthy communities and ecosystems.

Later I will say more about my suspicion that we are conditioned to be confrontational and thereby rendered much less effective at challenging the obsolete aspects of the conventional order.

Working Together

There are two distinct models that people use to accomplish large tasks. They are embodied in their respective meeting formats. In one, someone is in charge, there is a head table or podium from where information comes and toward which everyone else looks to be instructed. In the other, participants meet as equals. Seating is usually in a circle, so that everyone can see and hear everyone else and be seen and heard in return.

The head table approach is the way of kings who ruled by "divine right," and of governments that implement the will of their leaders. As long as the situations being dealt with are not too complex, this can be effective. Information is channeled to one person who makes the decisions and everyone else does what they are told. However, when power corrupts, or when the world turns out to be more complex than what the rulers imagine, things can go terribly wrong.

If the authorities at society's head table were inspired to lead us toward a healthy balance between communities and with the Earth, we might move resolutely in that direction. Unfortunately, concerns of sustainability have not been part of the methods that brought them their positions of authority. Reinforced by their personal success, they are convinced that directing our many efforts toward the expansion of wealth will put everything right.

In the circle of equals model, deliberations are not so simple. While a lot of time can be taken up considering the many points of view, a wide range of perspectives can illuminate issues in ways that top-down management can seldom approximate. The circle approach has synergetic bonuses.

Synergy is the tendency of whole things to be greater than the sum of their parts. For example, we each have two eyes. Each eye sees the world in a slightly different way. When the two views are combined in our brain we can see how far away things are. This is depth-perception, a perspective not obvious to either eye on its own. Similarly, a group of people has a far greater depth of insight than all the individuals by themselves.

While knowledge and intelligence vary considerably between individuals, these are not the only things that count. Each of us has a unique perspective and sees the world a little bit differently. Anyone considering an issue may notice and comment on particular details, triggering new insights throughout the group. That person might not be familiar with the body of knowledge already assembled on the issue, but, in an open discussion, there is the possibility that they would have insights that can enlighten those who have studied the topic for years.

This is particularly true of young adults. While their experience is restricted by their years, their minds are often sharp and fast. Unencumbered by masses of information, previously drawn conclusions, and the wear and tear of decades of use, keen young minds are a great asset to any group. Young people, like everyone else, should be welcomed to the task with enthusiasm and respect. By all means, draw on expert knowledge, but remember that the human condition has undergone a fundamental change and that the challenges of our time require new perspectives.

The following are ideas whose importance has become increasingly clear as a result of such open interaction. They will help to clarify the topics ahead.

Unfolding Ideas

"There is a tradition in some societies, whenever decisions are being made, to consider the interests of the next seven generations. For the modern world to do the same would mark our passage to maturity." Thus begins my 1993 publication, *Planning for Seven Generations*. The statement implies that our decisions should reflect long-term considerations, rather than just immediate interests. That book refers to a Native American tradition. Some may ask: why *seven* generations?

As individuals, at birth, some of us have great-grandparents to marvel at our arrival. Most often we know our grandparents and our parents. We know ourselves, and as time passes, our children, our grandchildren and, in some cases, our great-grandchildren. These seven generations are the longest, subjective, "yardstick" available to human experience.

If work is, indeed, "love made manifest," as Kahlil Gibran suggests, there is no greater love than that of parents for their children. Grandparents usually have great affection for their grandchildren, and great-grandchildren are a wonder and sign of great good fortune for the parents of their parents' parents. Not only does seven generations measure a significant period of time, it is a time frame distinguished by compassion.

This book is also written with the interests of the next seven generations in mind. The impulse to care for the young is ancient, far older than the human species. Human culture itself is far older than the cultivation of greed and self-interest as stimulants for economic expansion. Greed may be a controlling passion at present, but the urge to make the world work for our children provides a strong lever for lifting ourselves out of that rut.

Fractals

The notion of "fractals" can help illuminate the similarities between an individual person and society. Fractals are the similarities in patterns observed at various levels of detail. The pattern of major bays and peninsulas along a continental coastline are a good example. They are similar to the smaller bays and peninsulas that make up local coastlines and again, similar to the bumps and crevasses of rocks and sand where they meet the water. Ice crystals provide another example. Large crystals will form across a freezing pond, with branches made of smaller crystals resembling the larger ones, growing off of them. In turn, the smaller crystals have similar crystals, smaller still, forming off of them.

Similarly, a society exhibits many of the characteristics of an individual human. Specialized human cells, which serve as organs, parallel workers grouped in industries, specializing in various sorts of work. Transportation systems move goods through various stages, from raw materials to end uses, in a manner similar to how one's digestive system moves food through various organs, refining it and assembling the parts into all manner of useful substances to be delivered by blood flow to where they are needed.

When comparing the maturation of a child with the evolution of society, a promising possibility arises. As children grow and become strong enough to hurt others, they are expected to become responsible with their strength. Most children do accept this responsibility as they become adults. Where they hesitate, they are obliged, first by social pressure and then by law, to live within responsible bounds.

As a civilization, we have reached physical maturity, only recently becoming big enough and strong enough to do serious damage to our planet. It is now time to take responsibility for the effects of our actions. Social pressure is mounting as more and more people witness changing climate, falling water tables, extinguished species and increasing numbers of people stricken by pollution related diseases. If our societies do not act responsibly by taking effective action to stop such damage, we will be judged and dealt with by the laws of nature.

> *Negligence begins today; now that we know.*
> William McDonough

The Hubbert Peak

Another idea that filled out with detail, thanks to feedback, started with the quotation:

> *Our ignorance is not so vast as our failure to use what we know.*
> M. K. Hubbert

M. K. Hubbert was a geophysicist who made a significant contribution in his field by identifying the pattern of resource discovery, exploitation, and depletion. I don't recall where I first saw the above quote, but I reproduced it in an earlier writing to highlight the general thesis that we know we are facing environmental limits, yet continue to accelerate our activity. A person working with Dr. Hubbert's legacy read the quote and contacted me to explain what the man had discovered.

In essence, when a resource is discovered and uses found for it, production of that resource begins. With the resource available on the market, more uses are found and increasing quantities are produced for that market. Demand and production grow, hand-in-hand, until the easy-to-exploit sources of the resource are used up and production moves to reserves that are harder to exploit. Production strains to keep up with rising demand and then, usually around half way through the exploitation of the overall supply, it is no longer possible to produce as much as people want. As production diminishes, the price goes up and use declines from then on. When charted on a graph, the rise and fall in the level of production has come to be known as the "Hubbert Curve." The high point is called the "Hubbert Peak." The Hubbert Curve is explained in more detail in Chapter 16 on Motor Culture.

Cognitive Dissonance and Denial

Once we have passed the Hubbert Peak of petroleum production, adapting to the decline will be one of our biggest challenges. For several generations we have always had the potential to draw up more oil to power the ever greater number of engines we have been building to provide for our needs, and to service our expanding ambitions and pleasures. The prospect of not always having more convenient energy on hand to fuel our growth is problematic. Not having as much as we have become accustomed to will be disrupting.

When faced with big problems without clear solutions it is natural either to despair or to put the matter out of our minds. Since despair inhibits all manner of action, when hope is scarce most of us settle into denial. The human mind is well equipped to be aware of problems, yet carry on without acknowledging them. This is not unique to problems of sustainability. It is a regular part of human experience. Psychologists call the underlying dynamic "cognitive dissonance."

When people receive new information that is contrary to what they already believe, they become uncomfortable. The distress, great or small, causes them to seek release from the tension and anxiety. If little of consequence is attached to the issue, it is simple enough to adapt our vision of reality to include the new perspective and the tension is released. On the other hand, if one has a personal investment in the matter in question, he or she will search for other information that supports the original view or that discredits the new information. The more heavily one is invested, emotionally or financially, in the original perspective, the more effort goes into maintaining it. If millions of dollars or a lifetime of work are invested, it is possible for the people involved to turn new information inside out so that they hear the opposite of what is expressed, or simply, to block it out of consciousness entirely.

A familiar (and politically neutral) example of cognitive dissonance frequently happens when preparing for a trip. There are often many things that need to be done before departure. As departure time approaches, a sense often arises that there is more on the "to do" list than can be accomplished. This creates uncomfortable dissonance. We want to get it all done and, therefore, ignore evidence that it may be impossible. As time passes and the impossibility becomes harder and harder to ignore, the discomfort grows. Eventually when the impossibility can no longer be denied, we will drop some items to make the list manageable. This can be a great relief, but if the list is still longer than reality allows, dissonance may arise again.

Once the trip starts, the issue of what can be done before leaving is finally resolved. Things either got done or they did not. With any luck, the residual anxiety from the preparations will fade quickly enough so as not to spoil the trip itself.

A more serious illustration can be found in the debate over the connection between carbon dioxide emissions and climate change. The connection has been substantiated by innumerable scientific studies, some conducted a century ago. The heat retaining nature of CO_2 is a reproducible physics experiment. While the scientific evidence is shifting the conventional wisdom, decisive leadership is scarce. The dissonance of those with interests vested in carbon fuels is too strong for them to admit that the world that has worked so well for them has, in fact, changed.

The products and services provided by fossil-fuels are integrated so thoroughly into everyday life that there are few among us who have managed even to imagine how we might live with less of it. Inappropriate and counterproductive here are shame and blame. We are all immersed in a system that has, since before any of us were alive, made the expansion of fuel consumption a central part of cultural evolution. Most of us have long established addictions to the energy from carbon fuels and are only now awakening to this problem. Although feeling legitimate shame can lead to personal change, when the steps to take are unclear, it is far more likely to trigger denial.

We need to feel positive about ourselves and the human prospect so that we can duck around the screen of denial and gently take action in the direction we know is essential. At the very least, when the democratic opportunity arises, we need to steer clear of our psychological protections, in order to put our mark in the box that says yes to sustainability.

The Economic Quandary:

> *Whatever is normal appears natural.*
> Anon.

Most of today's economic decisions are based on assumptions that proved successful decades, or even centuries ago, and continue to be systematically applied. The patterns and inertia of the management system continue to be immensely successful in their own terms. The overall volume of production and consumption continues to rise. The process has been progressively refined and applied up to this day, enabling the human presence to multiply many times over. It is a story of extraordinary success. Great wealth and power continues to accumulate to those in charge, further reinforcing their belief that the system is working. They feel good about their accomplishments, making it very difficult for them to see that our present crisis is a product of that success. They are to be congratulated, then gently urged to acknowledge the new challenges.

I have a strong recollection from my childhood of a poem my Grandfather wrote. I would print it here, but no one in the family has been able to find a copy. It spoke in rhyming couplets of numerous difficult circumstances that nations have found themselves in over the centuries and how, through the cooperative application of skills and ingenuity, huge obstacles were overcome. Then came the clincher. When we are faced with success accompanied by unintended side effects, we tend to be disinterested, self-absorbed and otherwise unprepared to address the situation. We can deal with adversity, but success may get us in the end.

The true belief of the present leadership in "solutions" that increase present problems brings to mind a popular joke:

> *One dark evening a man was on his hands and knees under a street light looking through the grass. A pedestrian asked what he was looking for. "The keys to my car," replied the man. Having some time and feeling helpful, the pedestrian joined the man in his search. After a while, with no success, the pedestrian asked, "Where were you when you lost your keys?"*

"Over there by my car," the man gestured.
The pedestrian was puzzled. "Why are you looking for them here?"
The man without keys explained, "The light s better!"

When the solution to a problem is based on growth it can find acceptance within the present order. Conventional economics has become, in the broadest sense of the word, the "religion" of the modern world. To question this faith has become heresy. If pressed politically, such questions can arouse outright hostility. The light is indeed much better if we look for solutions within the dominant paradigm of perpetual economic expansion.

Be that as it may, expansion is now at the root of some serious problems. Effective solutions to the modern crisis lie elsewhere.

A Question of Direction

Might the goal of sustainability serve the needs of human kind better than the goal of perpetual economic expansion?

There are only two schools of thought about how to meet the challenge of our times. One is the biological approach, which sees humans as just one part of the life processes on the planet. Long-term well-being from this perspective requires stabilizing the overall throughput of energy and natural resources within the regular availability and tolerances of the Earth's life supporting systems. Environmental sustainability also requires social justice. If the system does not include everyone, those left out will have no choices for supporting their lives besides taking from others or encroaching further on already stressed ecosystems.

The other perspective is the financial one, which seeks long-term well-being through economic growth. The dynamics of supply and demand in the market place will detect most problems and adjust prices in ways that will solve them. This perspective contends that as long as our economic system is expanding we will have the financial means to address any problems that are not automatically corrected by the market.

These two perspectives are symbolized in the title of this book by the words "Life" and "Money." Since these perspectives have very different suggestions for solving serious problems, the "Question of Direction" asks: Which of these world-views should public policy be based on? Upon which assumption do taxpayers want their tax money spent? Upon which do citizens want their public lands to be used?

In some ways, these two perspectives can be complimentary. *Natural Capitalism* by Paul Hawken, Amory Lovins and Hunter Lovins, and *Eco-Economy* by Lester Brown provide abundant examples where profits can increase by reducing natural resource requirements and waste. It is where economic expansion requires increased waste and ecological disruption that the question becomes relevant: in particular, when obsolescence is planned to make way for more production. In such cases, we have a moral requirement to determine which value has priority over the other.

The Solution of Living

The one area in which we can grow indefinitely is through the development of ourselves. There is no doubt that we need concrete material goods in the form of food, clothing and shelter. When these are not available their provision is totally preoccupying. However, once we have enough of those material basics to be healthy and to have the sense that we will not be wanting for them next week or next month, there are other possibilities for personal fulfillment that do not involve more "things." Once necessities are covered, there is reason to believe that an afternoon with a good friend can be more rewarding than another basket of consumer goods.

Beyond the environmental degradation of endlessly increasing material consumption, the materialistic focus that perpetual growth of production and consumption requires, robs us of ourselves and impoverishes our lives and communities. To fill the void, the media is ever present with assertions that if you are wanting in your life, the glamorous product before you is just the thing, and the cycle continues. Friendship and creativity are the real thing!

With few exceptions, each manufactured product is a bite out of the Earth and requires carbon to be released into the atmosphere. Beyond the basics, we don't need a lot of material goods to secure healthy lives. Satisfaction from that point is more a product of enjoying life than it is of accumulating more stuff. Unfortunately, with our present system, the media won't earn its pay by saying that friendship and creativity are "the real thing." Nonetheless, our well-being thrives on the things that come from exercising our own living selves: our senses, our relationships, our creativity, our understanding and our imagination. These things are the stuff from which our selves are made.

* * * * *

The collage of ideas that follow aims to further illuminate the world-views of "life" and "money," their nature, how they have changed, the problems emerging and solutions that we can implement if we so choose.

Our situation today is not unlike that of a butterfly in its caterpillar form. In the generations past we have chomped our way across the planet consuming forests, soils, fisheries and mineral deposits. We have grown very large. It is not the caterpillar's role to grow forever. At a certain point, it has enough wealth within its skin to take a rest, allowing other possibilities to arise and to metamorphose the material resources it has mobilized and become something more appropriate for its adult stage in life. At some point, as societies, we must recognize that we have harnessed enough wealth to last for generations and think about what form might be more appropriate for the centuries ahead. We know what the Earth offers and what we need for healthy lives. A secure, fulfilling future is possible if we make it our primary goal. Security won't be found under the street light of perpetual economic expansion, but the option of a secure future exists as surely as life has thrived on this planet for thousands of millions of years.

3 Life: How it Thrives Thrives

Amidst the vast emptiness of space our blue and green planet provides a rare oasis of opportunity. Orbiting at a prime distance from its star, the Earth is neither too hot nor too cold. Water exists here in abundance. The elements of carbon, oxygen, nitrogen and various others are present in quantities sufficient for life to thrive. The Sun's energy animates the land and moves the water and the air. Daily and seasonal cycles of heating and cooling help to break down rocks. Countless waves and rains wash elements free from exposed surfaces. Since ancient times, these basic substances have mixed and matched where the Sun's rays meet the Earth.

Within this incubator of possibilities, the line between spontaneous chemical reaction and self-reproducing life was crossed, and the first magical combination of Earth substances began to live. As inconsequential as they might seem today, these tiny lives had dominion for a thousand million years. During that time, they engineered the basic building blocks of life as we know it. Among their greatest creations, were flagella, chloroplasts and mitochondria.

Flagella brought the gift of motion. Their characteristic anatomy of two central, fibrous strands with nine similar strands encircling those, enable the whip-like motion that propels most single celled creatures to this day. Descendants of the original flagella are present in almost everything that moves. They live on, within ourselves, cleaning our lungs and helping to move food through our intestines.

The chloroplasts, which make plants green, are also entities with a separate past. The functionality they developed for trapping energy from the Sun within the chemical bonds of a simple sugar proved so useful that practically all of life has evolved around the service they provide.

Mitochondria completed the dynamic trio by achieving a major breakthrough with the process they developed for retrieving Sun energy from organic matter. Biologists speculate that somewhere in the ancient seas, an amoeba-like cell ingested a mitochondrion and, rather than digesting it, formed a symbiotic relationship. The mitochondrion provided energy in exchange for protection and organic bits, which it processed for their mutual benefit. This primeval act was an early fractal of economic exchange. The symbiotic relationship with mitochondria, pioneered so long ago, is inherent today in all but the most primitive of life forms.

Within each of our bodies, mitochondria reliably release the energy we use to function. The mitochondria in our cells are too big to travel with a sperm so they are passed through the generations with the mothers' eggs. When an egg is fertilized and begins to multiply, the mitochondria also reproduce and become enmeshed in the new life, at the cellular level, to provide for the whole. They are essential to our lives, yet they are not directly related to us.

So closely have these "power plants" been associated with the plants and animals they serve, that we long assumed they were human, mouse or maple tree, depending on where they were found. As with chloroplasts, their independent nature was known in the 1960s, but it was not until genetic profiling became reliable in the late 1980s that it was confirmed that, in fact, they have their own genetic code.

If we read the fossil record correctly, the dynamic trio of flagella, mitochondria and chloroplasts succeeded in establishing these key capacities of life two and a half billion years ago. From these profoundly vital symbiotic arrangements, made in ancient times, the entirety of both the plant and animal kingdoms have emerged. Evolving together they have converted the substance of this planet into a splendid web of life, of which we are fortunate to be a part.

It has taken eons for life, and weather, to extract from the atmosphere and bare rocks the masses of nutrients that comprise the ecosphere. Fresh nutrients entering the sea enriched the cycles there. On the land, loose material accumulated and various organisms found safe habitat in it. The more organisms that lived and died in the evolving soils, the more nutrients there were for plants to feed on. The more plants there were and the greater their diversity, the more animals they could support. Practically everything taken from the soil by plants and animals was returned, and soils became richer and more abundant. Thus, the total of all the substances passing in and out of living things — the biomass — expanded.

This order of life continues. Living things grow, reproduce and pass away. Old organisms decompose to provide nourishment for the new; leaves return in the Spring and seeds sprout.

Over three thousand million years passed with life becoming ever more abundant and ever more sophisticated in its individual and cooperative enterprises. Very recently, on this time scale, one-one thousandth of the time since life began, humans appeared.

Each human is made up of 30 to 70 trillion individual, self-reproducing cells. In addition to these human cells, tens of millions of additional micro-organisms, flagella, mitochondria, and others that aid digestion and synthesize vitamins, are integral parts of the magnificent organisms we think of as ourselves. In all, as many as 100 trillion cells are joined in an intricate, cooperative venture to make each one of us.

The news that a sizable portion of our physical form is not genetically related to our human selves could shock some who imagine themselves as independent and self-contained. Others may be reassured to know that we are not alone in our efforts to survive and that cooperation has been a fact of life for thousands of millions of years.

We have long known about the symbiosis between more obviously separate organisms. The case of lichens, where an alga and a fungus grow together, is well-known. The alga captures sunshine and shares that energy with the fungus. The fungus secures the joint venture to the rock, provides nutrients and holds moisture, to share with the alga. Together, when their lives are spent, their remains often provide the first organic matter for rocky ground that is starting to become soil.

Even though we know that two (sometimes three) species are involved, lichen appear to be a single form of life. More overtly cooperative is the Acacia tree in the African savanna. In trying times, when most of the other vegetation has been eaten back by animals, this tree alone is full with leaves. On examining the branches, a species of ant can be found that lives nowhere else. Any creature that tries to eat leaves off the Acacia tree is attacked by the ants and soon changes its mind. For its part, the tree has nodular growths that excrete a liquid, which is the primary food for the ants.

Sharing the Substances of Life

Like lichens, we are composed of different organisms, but we tend to think of ourselves, if not as independent beings, at least as cooperative entities, separated from the rest of the world by our skin. This boundary, however, is very porous. Look at this knot.

As the knot moves along the rope, material passes continuously in at one end, and out the other. Before long, the material that originally made up the knot is entirely replaced by new material, yet the basic pattern of the knot does not change. It is the same with our bodies. Bodily materials change completely every seven years, most of them within a single year. With the exception of the aging process, the basic pattern of our bodies, and of ourselves, remains the same.

Most of the materials from which our bodies compose themselves over the course of our lives, are outside of our skin right now. A person of average size and life expectancy will, over a lifetime, pass well over one hundred thousand pounds of life substances through his or her physical form. This mass of substances, which makes up our body throughout infancy, childhood, adolescence and the decades before our last breath, is identified, in the Navaho tradition, as the "long body." For each of us materially, all that we have been and all that we will be, our long body, is in the soil, water and air about us — our environment. Thus, we are literally dumping on ourselves when we release toxins into the environment. On the same basis, if we are to care for ourselves, we need also to care for the environment, which contains all the stuff of our ongoing forms.

Among the substances flowing between life forms, water, oxygen and carbon are the most dynamic.

Most of the water molecules present on Earth today are the same molecules that were here when the planet first cooled billions of years ago. Water makes up most of our body and continuously cycles all over the Earth. The next time you drink something, look closely at the liquid. Molecules in the water you are about to drink have been to every part of the globe. They've come from oceans, lakes, quiet swamps and rushing rivers; from glaciers, forests, frost, fog and dew. They've been in clouds, high in the atmosphere and in vast reservoirs deep in the Earth. Most of the water molecules present in your drink have also been in and out of countless other living things. In fact, you may well have shared your drink with every form of life that has ever lived on Earth. Through water alone, we are bound together with everything else that lives, yet we share far more.

Our interrelationship with the rest of the living world becomes more intertwined as we share carbon through the wonder of plant photosynthesis. Carbon dioxide, and water (CO_2 and H_2O) provide this process with carbon (C), oxygen (O), and hydrogen (H). Sun energy is captured in the chemical bonds as these elements are joined together into glucose ($C_6 H_{12} O_6$), a simple sugar. In the process, six molecules of CO_2, plus six molecules of H_2O, plus energy, combine into one glucose molecule ($C_6 H_{12} O_6$), plus 6 oxygen molecules (O_2).

The oxygen, which is not incorporated in the glucose, is released into the atmosphere and the sugar becomes the source of energy for the plant's life. Whether the captured sunshine remains stored as glucose in the plant, or is transformed into the starches, fats and other substances of the plant's new growth, most of it is available to animals and decomposes when they eat the plants. As the energy moves through the food chain from the chlorophyll to the plant, to the animals that eat the plants, to the animals that eat those animals and to the decomposers that eat all the waste and any of the participants that fall out of life, a perfect symmetry exists. In the process, every bit of energy originally captured by photosynthesis is released. As the organic matter, from all the various life forms, is metabolized, the same amounts of carbon dioxide and water are formed as was originally involved in the photosynthesis.

The cycle is interrupted only in circumstances where the remains of plants and animals accumulate in locations where decomposers cannot do their work. Those deposits become the peat, coal, oil and natural gas that now power our "cultural metabolism." That is, they power the mining, harvesting, processing and assembly of materials into tools, transport, and the multitude of manufactured items that make up the collective entity (society), which we inhabit and from which we draw the things we need.

Powered by the energy cycle initiated with photosynthesis, life has come to thrive in every territory, climate and food niche. Tens of millions of different species have developed ever more sophisticated ways to move and to sense, to think and to feel, to ward off illness and to heal. From the molecular interactions within and between cells, to the relationships between creatures, those who study life and life processes are discovering extraordinary complex interdependencies everywhere they look.

Essential to the system are the decomposers. Mold, fungus and other decomposers do not deserve their bad reputation. They are singled out here because their service is often not appreciated. While we don't want them to consume our food, the foundations of our homes, or our bodies before we die, the role of decomposers is indispensable. Indeed, if it were not for their tireless work breaking down the dead and discarded substances from living things, life would all but end. The Earth would be littered with the remains of things that were once alive and the only nutrients available for new life would be those slowly eroding from the Earth's crust.

Huge volumes of water, gasses and nutrient elements flowing between life forms integrate the biomass. The exchanges of matter and energy within cells is a fractal of the flows between cells, the flows between organs, and the flows between organisms. The list of essential life-sustaining services provided within and between all that lives could fill many books. So thoroughly are living things intertwined that all life on Earth can be pictured as a single living organism.

The Living Earth

As individuals, we are largely unaware of the functioning of our many specialized organs and metabolic processes. We are even less aware of the individuality of the trillions of cells that provide those services. It seems equally probable that few, if any, of those cells are aware of who we are or what we think.

Could it be that for every level of organization of matter there is a corresponding level of consciousness? Could life as a whole be conscious? If it were, we would be no more likely to sense its awareness than our big toes are able to sense our awareness. If we felt for the Earth as a living, conscious being, it would be as easy to love her as it is to love the people who care for us. In a very broad sense, the Earth "is" our Mother. From the first living cell that emerged from her bulk, to today's continents and oceans abounding with life, the Earth has provided all with the physical substances to make living possible.

Recent studies of the atmosphere have enriched our understanding of the relationship between the planet and the life it supports. The atmosphere acts like the feathers of a bird or an animal's fur, in that it makes adjustments that maintain a suitable and protective environment for the life it enfolds.

The Gaia Hypothesis, named after the Greek Goddess of the Earth, was formulated by James Lovelock and Lynn Margulis. Lovelock had been working for the National Aeronautics and Space Administration (NASA) on a project to develop equipment for detecting life on other planets. NASA did this by studying Earth to find signs of life that could be sensed from far away. The behaviour of atmospheric gases in various combinations can normally be predicted by the rules of steady state chemistry. In studying Earth's atmosphere, however, scientists discovered that it extensively violates the laws of chemistry. The predicted behaviour of the gases in the atmosphere should make our planet too hot for any but the most primitive of life forms.

Closer investigations indicate that the gases of the atmosphere are only a part of the global ecosystem. The rock of the Earth's crust, the oceans, the atmosphere, and the life forms they encompass, have evolved as a single, tightly-integrated system. The system compensates for changes in the global climate by adjusting the rates at which gases such as oxygen, methane and carbon-dioxide are produced and removed from the atmosphere. The observation of this "self-management" led to the Gaia Hypothesis: the hypothesis that the Earth actively maintains conditions suitable for the growth and well-being of living things. James Lovelock's book, *Gaia: A New Look at Life on Earth,* explores these ideas.

For some, viewing the Earth as actively nurturing life is a retrieval of ancient wisdom. For others, it is a new concept with the power to change the way we treat the planet and ourselves.

Life Science

The life process has long been a matter of interest and study for curious minds. At the dawn of our scientific age, the Belgian doctor, Jean Baptiste Van Helmont conducted an experiment. In 1652, he wrote:

> *I took an earthen vessel in which I put 200 pounds of soil dried in an oven, then I moistened it and pressed into it a shoot of willow weighing five pounds. After exactly five years the tree that had grown weighed 169*

pounds and about three ounces, but the vessel had never received anything but rain water or distilled water... in the end I dried the soil once more, weighed it and got the same 200 pounds I started with, less about two ounces.

This experiment provides hope for today. It showed that most of the substance that made up the willow tree's mass (169 pounds) came from air and water only. Air and water can be found practically every place on Earth. This means that, if what we want from the Earth is a good, healthy life for ourselves and our children, the basic demands we make on the planet are minimal and can be managed. The sophistication of what life does with carbon, hydrogen, oxygen, nitrogen, potassium, phosphorus and a handful of other elements is extraordinary, and the cycles, which keep these essential elements within reach, have served reliably for thousands of millions of years.

The basics of human security need not detract from the health of the living Earth. Provided our numbers stay within the Earth's carrying capacity, food, clothing, shelter, education, health care, companionship and challenge can all be provided for from within the natural cycles of the Earth's substance.

Maintaining ourselves in good health is not what causes most of the problems outlined in the next chapter. Rather, it is the "cultural metabolism" that we create to satisfy our vivid imaginations and complex ambitions. Like the metabolism of biological life, the manufacturing processes created by humans constitute another sort of metabolism. While this cultural metabolism results from applying our consciousness and is intended to serve our distinctly human needs, all the products and by-products resulting from it come to exist within the same biosphere that is home to all of life. Once we create material substances, it is nearly impossible to keep them out of life's flows.

Ecology

In 1869, Ernest Haeckel coined the word "ecology" to represent the study of the relationships between different organisms and between organisms and their surroundings. Although studies of the structures and functions of nature had been conducted earlier, they had not previously been identified as a collective science. Ecology includes the flow of materials between organisms, mutual dependencies and the factors that limit growth. Of particular significance are the following two categories of limitations.

The first is the limitations of resource supply caused by the depletion or absence of some nutrient, or other material, needed to maintain a way of life. This can also include limited space and access to sunshine.

The second is the limitations of tolerance — tolerance to climatic differences, tolerance to toxic substances, and tolerance to competition.

These limitations determine why some creatures can live in one place and others can't, why a particular life form is abundant in one location and only occasionally found in another, and why some creatures pass from existence altogether. These two limitations are sometimes referred to as "laws" of nature: the "law of the minimum" and the "law of tolerance."

The law of the minimum refers to situations where organisms are limited in areas because some substance or circumstance, among those it needs, is not available in sufficient quantity. Only one required condition need be lacking to keep the numbers of that organism low, or absent, even when all the other necessary conditions are met in abundance. A striking example was a problem with sheep in part of New Zealand. All the conditions seemed right for the sheep, and they grew well, but they would not reproduce. An analysis of the soil revealed an absence of the trace element cobalt. When cobalt was added to the sheep's rations, they soon began producing healthy lambs.

Koala bears provide another example. Koalas eat only eucalyptus leaves. Where there are no eucalyptus trees, there are no Koala bears. Limiting situations can also rise and fall. If conditions are right, the population of many organisms will grow until they have consumed almost all of the essential food. At that point, the scarce food becomes a limiting factor. The population then drops off until the food source recovers and the cycle begins again. Depending on how gentle or how drastic the overshoot of optimum population was before the numbers collapsed, the population might rise again to similar heights, or the organism might find that conditions had been changed by the excess and that only a partial recovery is possible.

The law of tolerance asserts the obvious. If conditions in an area are intolerable for particular organisms, those organisms won't be able to live there. There are things that live in hot springs that cannot live in colder water, while the creatures that thrive in near-by lakes and streams would find the hot springs intolerable. Communities of plants and animals that do well in the cool, under diffuse light, live in the shade of forests. If the trees are all cut away, much of the life below will find the direct sun intolerable. New plants and animals that do well in direct sunshine will populate the area. Over the years, if a new generation of trees grows up, the Sun-loving creatures will find the territory increasingly intolerable, and a new community of shade-adapted life will move in.

Wine confirms one threshold of tolerance. Yeast digests the sugar in juice to get what it needs to grow and multiply. The by-products are alcohol and carbon dioxide. The CO_2 bubbles away and the alcohol accumulates in the confined container until its concentration exceeds what yeast can tolerate. When that point is reached, somewhere between 12% and 14%, the yeast goes dormant or dies and the wine is ready for bottling. Check the next wine bottle you see. If you find an alcohol content higher than 14%, it is the result of further processing by the people involved.

Obeying these "laws" of nature is not a matter of choice. They shape the entire biological world. Within these bounds, however, the vast diversity of life has evolved. The total volume of life in any particular area cannot expand beyond the volume of the nutrients and/or energy available. Any growth in overall volume would require an increase in the availability of essential substances, or a change of climate bringing more heat or moisture.

Carrying Capacity

Carrying capacity is the amount of life that a territory can sustainably support.

For any particular area, carrying capacity can refer to the population of a single organism, a community of organisms, or to the amount of life overall. The territory can be a particular field or forest, a continent, or the planet as a whole.

Maximum carrying capacity is directly related to limiting factors. The number of deer that an area can support is limited by the amount of open fields and meadows available for food, and the proximity of forests where they can hide. The carrying capacity will go up as more areas are cleared, until the point is reached where shelter becomes scarce and exposure to weather and predators becomes a limiting factor.

Moisture is often a factor limiting carrying capacity. Deserts contain entire ecosystems, but their carrying capacity is far less than would be the case in a similar sized territory with more water. If the rainfall in a desert area were to increase slowly over several thousand years, a succession of ecosystems would evolve. As rainfall increased, the desert plants and animals would find conditions increasingly intolerable and they would be replaced by plants and animals common to grasslands. With more moisture, trees would grow, crowding out the grasslands, and those forests with their flora and fauna would eventually be replaced by the thriving communities of a rainforest. As the carrying capacity increased, most of the substance composing the increased biomass would be from the air and water. The other materials involved — potassium, phosphorous and other trace elements — would, for the most part, be the same nutrient elements that were present in the original dry-land soils.

At any stage along the way, the total volume of life would be limited. The sophistication of how life uses the resources available, however, could evolve. The volume of life — the biomass — is limited by the amount of energy and resources available, but the sophistication of how that endowment can be used is open ended.

I had a fascinating opportunity to witness the arrival of two new insects to a piece of land where I camped for two decades. The first to arrive was the Gypsy moth. It had been brought to Boston from Europe in the late 1860s, to be bred with silkworms in the hope of starting a northern silk industry. Some of them escaped. I saw a picture of a dozen men up in a big tree trying to catch the escapees in an effort to prevent their spread into the wild. They were not successful.

That was in the late 1800s. The Gypsy moth has been spreading very slowly ever since. In the 1980s, Gypsy moth caterpillars arrived at my camp in eastern Ontario. With no predators, they multiplied rapidly and in a couple of years were eating all the leaves off the apple, oak and poplar trees. Entire hillsides of shade were consumed, leaving parts of the landscape looking like Winter. Then the caterpillars would stop eating and make their cocoons. The trees produced a new set of leaves on a reduced scale that maximized the capture of energy while supporting a minimum of foliage. (This was in contrast to the normal bushy array, which maximizes the amount of foliage a tree can support, a circumstance enabled by the better placed leaves subsidizing those in the under-layers.)

The pattern was repeated several years in a row. Although the recently planted apple trees were not strong enough to survive, the oak and poplar came back each Spring, lost their leaves and then grew new sets after the caterpillars retired into their cocoons.

At the peak of one season, I was sitting at a picnic table listening to the sound of caterpillar droppings, and the odd caterpillar, falling like rain. It struck me that none of the biomass was being lost. The leaves were consumed, digested and dropped to the forest floor where they decomposed and were taken back up by the trees the next year to be made into leaves again. Even the caterpillars would leave their skins behind and, after they had laid their eggs, the moths would die, and decompose.

One year, I noticed a black bug that I had never seen before. It had a Gypsy moth caterpillar in its mouth. This welcome fellow made us glad we had not sprayed poisons to kill the caterpillars. The next year there were many more of the black bugs and after another few years, the Gypsy moth caterpillars, while still common, were greatly reduced in numbers and the leaf cover was not visibly compromised. The same amount of nutritional elements were present in the area as always. The only difference was that there were now two new insects sharing the biomass and taking their turns under the Sun.

Life's Chemistry

Most, if not all, of the chemical compounds utilized in life's metabolic processes have been in use for many millions of years. They have been sufficient to maintain all of life's many forms and they enable the continued evolution of new forms. All are fully recyclable. In conditions of warmth, moisture and oxygen, everything that has lived can be disassembled into the basic elemental components that other life can use to build its various forms. Even the potent poisons produced by some insects, snakes, and fungi are rendered harmless and useful when the decomposers get through with them.

This steady biochemical state became disrupted as the ingenuity of human beings diversified. With mental capacities far in excess of what we need to keep fed and to raise our offspring, we long for ways to apply our genius and satisfy our boundless curiosity. Our excess capacity finds expression in two different domains. We create new ways of doing things with matter and energy and we develop new ways of being in our consciousness and interactions.

While we have little ability to sense changes in the quality of life experienced by other living things, material innovations can be seen and therefore compared. Eyes, legs, roots, leaves, and claws have evolved gradually. The evolution of such diverse functional parts of multicellular organisms is common to all species. In humans, however, such development has taken on a new dimension and flourishes in the cultural sphere. Other creatures touch on this realm when they build homes and fabricate simple tools, but the capacity to rearrange the material world to suit the will is most pronounced with humans.

Where many creatures, through biological, metabolic means, came to extract calcium and phosphorus from their food and assemble them into teeth, humans learned to "digest" rock and extract copper and tin to assemble into bronze spear points and arrowheads. These products of our cultural metabolism provided an extension to our biological form. They gave us "teeth," as it were, that we could propel through space to "bite" creatures that we wanted to eat (or perhaps, which wanted to eat us.)

For thousands of years, the cultural extensions to our biological metabolism consisted of shelter, some clothes, a handful of tools and utensils, and ritual objects. Slowly, we learned more tricks to expand our capabilities. Then, in the last few centuries, the expansion of our cultural metabolism accelerated rapidly. To the older technologies for using wood and metals to expand our domestic, hunting and agricultural endeavours, we now add all manner of other earth substances and produce hundreds of thousands of different products.

Of particular note are the discoveries that have enabled us to metabolize fossil-fuel. At first, coal was used simply to provide heat to warm our dwellings, and then for refining metals. With the more recent invention of engines, we broke through the limitations of muscle power, and then, with the clever applications of electricity...

Today, uncounted millions of motors run all manner of equipment, providing a flood of goods and services such that an observer from another planet might even mistake the human being as an extension of the technosphere, rather than the other way around.

Emerging amidst our rapidly diversifying mechanical technology has been the revolution in chemistry. The alchemists of the Middle Ages were the forerunners to today's chemists. While they did not succeed in their mission of turning lead into gold, they did discover that by grinding clay and limestone into a fine powder and heating the mixture to a high temperature, they could create cement. With cement for mortar, stones could be laid, one upon the other, to make buildings and fortifications of never before experienced size and strength.

The quest for knowledge by the alchemists was institutionalized when the cement they had invented was used to build the first universities. Still today, formal graduates wear the flat topped hat called a "mortarboard" to commemorate the mortar boards that held the cement-based mortar used in building those early campuses.

While universities and scholarship offer a smooth passage to the topic of non-material applications of our extraordinary mental capacities, the thread of chemistry needs further exposure. Far beyond working with clay and lime, today's chemists have discovered the secrets of chemical bonding, and can make all manner of substances to perform a huge variety of tasks. Many of these creations have never before existed on Earth. Some of the products and by-products are harmless. Some, such as dioxin are extremely dangerous. As with everything we create, these substances can easily become enmeshed in the material flows of the biosphere. None of our novel chemical creations has been around long enough to see whether or not, as a species releasing these substances, we can still pass evolution's tests in the court of natural selection.

Life-based Pursuits

The other plane on which we exercise our genius is the experience and utilization of the life inside our individual physical forms. Amidst all the material cycles and limitations, consciousness emerged that was sophisticated enough to be self-aware. We feel, think and create. While our spirits and their ability to create are thoroughly enmeshed in the stuff of the Earth, once our physical needs are met there are limitless possibilities for what we can do with life. We can pursue many of these possibilities to our heart's content without substantially increasing what we need from the material world. In fact, if we choose to concentrate more on life and less on stuff, we could substantially reduce our material consumption and, at the same time increase our well-being.

Life-based activities are things we can do because we are alive. They include, for example, appreciation, empathy, friendship, love, art, music, dance, sport, parenting, looking, listening, smelling, touching, tasting, thinking, meditating, scholarship, service, etc.

Rather than diminishing with use, life-based activities tend to become stronger and more rewarding through use. Furthermore, one person's participation in one or another of these activities, given due respect for other people's sensitivities, does not diminish anyone else's opportunities. The opposite is more often true. The better someone gets at a life-based activity, the greater their ability to entertain others, or to teach them to develop in a similar manner.

It is interesting, even exciting, to contemplate how our society would be different if life-based pursuits were encouraged with a vigour comparable to that employed in the promotion of material consumption and accumulation. With accumulation and consumption, once someone collects more than their share of material resources, someone else will have to make do with less. That our neighbour's success may be at our expense or that our nation's prosperity may be at the expense of other nations can be found at the root of much personal and international tension.

While industry is always eager to sell material accessories, life-based development tends not to require much material resources, and is not likely to inspire organized conflict. Quite the contrary. By developing human potentials, we increase our personal satisfaction and simultaneously reduce our territorial and material needs, thereby reducing the threat we might pose to others. The more we develop our skills and abilities, the more we can help others to do the same. Sports, music and other creative activities give pleasure to both participants and observers. As we develop our own inner calm, we can help others find calm in their lives. As we increase our understanding, we can help others to understand.

The satisfaction derived from life-based activities is far greater, proportional to the material required, than from inessential material consumption. The prospects for the future improve when we place more value on what we can do with our lives, rather than on the quantity of the goods we consume. If the material accessories can be avoided, a shift to life-based activities would go a long way to ease environmental distress and enable the restoration of ecosystem health.

> *If only people could see each other as agents of each others happiness, they could occupy the Earth, their common habitation, in peace, and move forward confidently together to their common goal. The prospect changes when they regard each other as obstacles; soon they have no choice left but to flee or be forever fighting. Humankind then seems nothing but a gigantic error of nature.*
>
> Abbé Sieyes, Prelude to the Constitution 1789, France

The desire to grow is firmly rooted in our characters. Throughout our formative years and well beyond, growth is a preoccupation. To be able to crawl, to reach the water tap or to have our own way, all require getting bigger. The residual urge to grow has been deliberately harnessed to stimulate the expansion of material consumption. The dilemma is that, while each of us wants to grow, collectively we have already grown to confront the limits of our planet. The solution has a well-established precedent in each of our individual lives. For the most part, as we become adults, our physical growth comes to an end. As physical maturity is established, more attention goes into developing our understanding, skills, relationships and appreciation for life and the world around us.

Conserver lifestyles are easier to promote when it is clear that they offer abundant opportunities for improving one's condition. Life-based pursuits, or the 3 Ls — Learning, Love and Laughter — as they are referred to for our sound bite world, offer boundless frontiers. The development of our human abilities was the essence of human culture before the commercial era pushed acquisition to its current place of prominence. The saturation of landfill space, problems with pollution and painful experiences with finite natural resources bid us reconsider the emphasis we place on the pursuit of our human potentials.

In the same way that a growing embryo goes through the stages of evolution, civilization will likely follow the pattern of individual maturation.

As a culture we are in late adolescence. We have grown big enough to accomplish anything that life requires of us. Now, as self-centeredness gives way to responsibility, our rapid physical growth can transmute into the development of the remarkable qualities that make humans unique among life forms. The vast richness that is available to people in this realm suggests that, perhaps, such activity is the purpose of being human. The endless possibilities for personal satisfaction that being alive offers, provide the reflective polish for our Percian shields.

4 Problems with Life: Human Impacts on a Full Planet

Life doesn't have a problem. Much of the world freezes solid every year and life carries on, or waits underground, in its roots, burrows, and seeds, until things warm up. The same happens in places with extreme droughts. Some seeds can wait for decades in parched ground. When rain comes, they pick up where they left off and continue with their cycle. There are so many types of living things adapted to so many different circumstances, that no matter what sort of changes come about, something will find it suitable and will thrive and evolve. Forest fires, hurricanes, earthquakes: life takes them all in stride.

Biodiversity

At the present time, however, an increasing number of species face an uncertain future. Their resilience for dealing with natural change is compromised by unnatural change. As humans clear forests, drain wetlands and plow up remaining prairies to plant crops and build cities, the plants and animals that used to live in those places lose suitable habitat. In many places, after persistent human expansion, agricultural lands and built-up areas stretch from the ocean up over the hills and mountains and beyond. Nothing natural of adequate size or condition remain. Without suitable habitat, whole ranges of species perish, never again to tread the Earth or open their leaves up to the Sun.

Pollution also alters habitat quality to the point beyond the tolerance of some species, as does rapidly changing climate. Mobility can save only a few as they try to move away from polluted areas or search for climatic zones that match their needs. Some will succeed, others will not.

With all the changes humans are making to the ecosphere, biodiversity, the sum total of all the different life forms that make up ecosystems, is shrinking. Extinctions have not taken place at the present rate since the end of the Cretaceous era, 65 million years ago, when the dinosaurs disappeared, along with an estimated one fifth of all life forms present at that time.

While extinction is a natural part of evolution, as less well-adapted species make way for new life forms, the present rate of extinctions is calculated to be a thousand times faster than the normal level. Each life form is a marvel and its extinction reduces the wonder of our planet in a way that any open heart can sense.

When making room for expanding human enterprise, the disappearance of life forms diminishes even the narrow interests of our own species. Some of the species lost might have come to serve our ends directly as food, or to breed into existing crop varieties, reinvigorating their genetic makeup and increasing their resistance to disease, as has been the case for ages. Even when we do not eat a species ourselves, their termination can disrupt food chains and cause other species, which may play a greater role in human well-being, to become scarce. Wild plants have often served as medicines, or have provided the initial compounds for developing healing drugs. Many of the plant species disappearing presently haven't even been identified, let alone tested for healing qualities. Other disruptions of natural balances can end up disrupting our lives. For example, if the forests, in which insect-eating birds build their nests, are cut down, those birds must live elsewhere, or die. The insects, which they would have eaten previously, can then multiply, uninhibited, to levels that can threaten crops, human comfort and health. With each thread lost from the web of life, the whole fabric becomes weaker and less resilient. It is not possible to determine at what points the weakened fabric might start a chain reaction that would breach ecosystem integrity and lead to conditions favouring a very different order of life.

Indeed, there are places on Earth where human activity has already triggered such transformations. Even so, life, in general, is not threatened. Remember, the entire planet is thought to have been populated from a single living cell. Life recovered, magnificently, from the mass extinctions of the late Cretaceous era, and from other troubled periods in the distant past. With three quarters of the planet's surface covered with water and thousands of millions of years left in our Sun, life in some form will endure.

Human Prospects

As a species, humankind is unlikely to become extinct. We have extraordinary capabilities, we can eat almost anything, and we are extremely adaptable in the short-term.

Where cause for concern does lie, however, is in our civilization. (The organized masses of humanity, which I refer to as the Collective Human Organism.) To a large extent, who we are as individuals is a direct result of our cultural circumstances. Most of the food and material goods we consume are the products of complex and far-flung systems. The way we see the world, and most of what we do with our lives, is tied directly into the massive, cooperative networks of civilization. If we disrupt the life process, much of how we maintain ourselves and much upon which our characters are based could be lost in the confusion. The Earth's ability to maintain human beings in our present numbers, at the present level of intensity, is becoming increasingly precarious.

This is where the Percian Shield can again be useful. In facing this danger, recall again the amazing potentials of being human. We are in trouble, but never before has there been an organism as competent as humans. We have what it takes to succeed on this planet over the long-term. Whether or not we respect ecological limits will be the deciding factor.

Beneficial discoveries in health care and in technology have enabled our numbers to grow exponentially. While it took a million years, until the early 1800s, to reach a population of one billion people, the second billion took little more than a century. Since then, we have added four billion, the last billion taking only 12 years. More people are alive today than had lived throughout all time up until the last century.

Humans are not the first creature to experience rapidly growing numbers. Populations of organisms rise and fall in response to opportunities and the limitations of tolerance and minimum supply.

The miracle of the first cell's emergence would have been followed by its growth and division into two cells. Each of these was destined to divide and those four cells became 8, 16, 32, 64, and on and on. Except where limited by temperature or other tolerance issues, with nothing else to eat them, that first life form would have spread to fill all locations, there to multiply, until at least one essential nutrient was depleted. Other nutrients might still be abundant, but once one was no longer available in minimum supply, some cells, unable to get what they needed, would die. Their bodies would break down and release the nutrients they were made of, enabling other cells to grow in their place. The population of that one life form would have found a steady state that could only increase as new nutrients entered the system from the surrounding rock.

In a world with millions of life forms, the unbalanced expansion of any one organism can cause trouble. Duckweed provides an example. Duckweed is a small plant that floats on ponds and streams. It has a single oval leaf less than a quarter of an inch in length, and a tiny root (or two) that hangs down into the water. In suitable conditions, each leaf will grow another, which, when mature, separates and drifts off on its own to grow yet another like itself.

As long as the population of these plants is small, a doubling of their numbers is of little consequence to the living community. However, as the area covered in duckweed expands, a crucial change takes place. Let us say, for this illustration, that it takes one day of summer sun for the duckweed population to double. It has been growing all summer and covers just one sixty-fourth of a pond's surface. That's not much, but in less than a week, that small area becomes a thirty-second, a sixteenth, an eighth, a quarter, a half and on the last day the population of duckweed goes from where half of the pond is open, to where the entire surface is covered over. At that point, sunlight and oxygen are cut off from life below the surface. The exponential speed with which this change is taking place helps explain why, all of a sudden, by historical standards, human beings are plagued by environmental problems when, throughout time, the possibility of disrupting planetary life was unimaginable.

Historical Limits

Two types of limitations were identified in the previous chapter. Limitations of resource supply and limitations of tolerance. All of our environmental challenges fall into these two categories. Prehistoric evidence suggests that we have brushed up against these limitations on numerous occasions in the past.

Mesopotamia had been a vibrant civilization. While providing for its expanding population and pursuing great works, that people eliminated their local forests and those in surrounding lands. Following the removal of the trees from the northern mountain area, erosion exposed salt-laden sediment. The salt washed into the rivers and when irrigation water from those rivers evaporated, it left behind enough salt to render the soil unfit for crops. Fifteen hundred years of successful agriculture atrophied to where it could only support a small fraction of the previous population.

The Mayan empire suffered a similar fate. While their lands once supported population densities equivalent to those of Los Angeles County, today little remains but ruins and a small native population. Much effort has gone into explaining why that civilization failed. The pollen in lake bed sediments indicated that there was an abundance of trees up until 1200 years ago. Studies of skeletons preserved from the period shortly after the trees disappeared revealed signs of severe malnutrition. Computer modelling of the situation by climate scientists indicated that the loss of tree cover likely resulted in less rain and a seven degree increase in average temperatures. The ability to grow food would have been greatly reduced and the inclination for conflict increased. By the time the Spaniards arrived, the population had already crashed and those who remained had little resistance to European diseases. The Spanish conquest was no contest.

Viking history provides another example of the tolerance problem. Carbon dating of tree remains, found far north of the Canadian tree line, reveals that there was a warm period between 880 and 1140 AD. During that period of relative warmth, Viking settlements were established along the edge of their climatic tolerance. Eric the Red (Erikur Raude) settled in Greenland in 982. Around 1000 AD, another settlement was established on the northern peninsula of Newfoundland. As the climate cooled again, however, these settlements died out or were abandoned, leading to speculation that conditions had become intolerable.

Because we are so clever and adaptable, response to limitations is more complex with humans than with other creatures. Again and again, when we have come up against limitations that might otherwise end our expansion, we have found ways to get around them. Minor set backs aside, we have done an extraordinary job of providing for the steady expansion of our population. When the mammoths and other large animals were gone, we got by hunting other creatures. When our numbers grew beyond what we could feed by hunting and gathering, we learned to cultivate crops. As we have depleted soil fertility, we have replaced natural fertility with industrially processed fertilizers.

When ecosystems became intolerably degraded, like the expanding southern boundary of the Sahara Desert, or the radiation-poisoned lands around the Chernobyl nuclear accident, some possibilities for moving elsewhere remained. Migration isn't always successful, but, even so, we have yet to face a limitation that has done much more than temporarily slow the expansion of our population as a whole.

Civilizations in the past that lost their ability to grow sufficient food have disappeared. Today, where a territory cannot provide sufficient food, transportation networks bring food in to trade for other goods that the people there produce. This adaptive cleverness by which we have stretched the Earth's human carrying capacity has enabled us to reach planetary limits. At the same time, it has resulted in a complacency on the part of some. They feel that we need not worry about limitations; that we will always be able to develop our way around them.

On the contrary, it is important that we pay attention to specific circumstances. In particular, we need to consider the basic nutrient elements. There will never be substitutes for nitrogen, potassium and phosphorus. Of these three essential ingredients for plant growth, potassium is quite common and is seldom a limiting factor. Nitrogen and phosphorus are more problematic. Following the components of the carbon cycle — oxygen, carbon and hydrogen — nitrogen is the largest elemental requirement of life. It constitutes 16% of protein. While the majority of the atmosphere is nitrogen, plants cannot use it in the gaseous form. Microorganisms in the soil, and lightening, transform nitrogen from the air into usable forms. Over millions of years, these processes built up the volumes of fixed nitrogen in soils, from which they are slowly released to cycle through the life process. Intensive modern agriculture has diminished this natural fertility to the point that natural processes cannot keep up with our nitrogen requirements. We have overcome this limitation by discovering ways to fix nitrogen by bonding it chemically with the hydrogen from natural gas. While this is very clever and has enabled a vast expansion of agricultural production, it depends on the availability of natural gas and additional energy, which are themselves subject to limitations.

Phosphorus is more complicated. When it is exported from an area in the form of food products, it must be replenished. Phosphorus is water soluble and tends to find its way to the oceans where it gets deposited on the ocean floor. The cycle that brings it back for use on land is geologic in duration. Eventually, given millions of years, the Earth's crust folds and heaves and the phosphorus-rich sediments rise up to where fresh water can rinse it out for plants to use again. There are large deposits of this nutrient, which we presently mine, crush and distribute to agricultural operations around the globe. While these deposits are vast, they are not infinite and the process makes us, yet again, more dependent on energy.

If we were to achieve a stable population around the numbers that can be supported by low-input agriculture, our skills and ability to provide for each other could serve us for millions of years to come. However, the present system is addicted to continuous expansion and the ideology that justifies that addiction is pursued with religious conviction. Unless this changes, we will repeatedly confront limitations until we come across a situation around which we cannot stretch our expanding demands. Our mushrooming presence threatens our foundations in the living world. If we allow that foundation to crumble, civilization will be a thing of the past and human life much less common and very different.

Over the last few decades, some of the limitations we have confronted have become global in scale. Our numbers are now so large, and our technologies so powerful, that we affect the entire planet, rather than just isolated parts. There are no new frontiers, and few places to go when serious damage is done. In the year 2000, 39 million people — more than the population of Canada — were living and dying in refugee camps. A growing proportion of these — around half — are environmental refugees, that is, people forced to leave lands that can no longer support them because of flooding, desertification, loss of forest cover or other intolerable circumstances brought on by excessive human activities. The rest are escaping wars, that, in addition to degrading local ecosystems, are, more often than not, fought over limited resources.

Too often we overcome one resource limitation by stretching another. The effect, overall, can be likened to a rubber band that can stretch and then stretch some more. Frequently, our solution to local resource shortages is to transport the limited resource from an area where it is more abundant, or to manufacture alternatives using additional energy and other resources. While this process gives the impression of increasing abundance, like the rubber band that appears longer when stretched, continued expansion puts more tension on remaining resources. At the present time, our capacity for moving resources around and for powering industrial processes is enormous, but, like the rubber band, there will be a point where further expansion will fail.

Why would we want to grow until we meet a limit that defeats us?

Our repeated triumph over limits has lead to a faith that we will always find ways to overcome them. This is a dangerous illusion. What is the point of pushing the limits? A touch of humility could be the measure needed to save civilization from the overconfidence our narrowly defined "success" has brought about.

Problems We Face

At the beginning of the third millennium, a number of limitations loom on the horizon. Some are being dealt with, others denied. From the perspective of the seventh generation, they must all be resolved.

Limitations of Tolerance

In the category of tolerance limitations, we face issues of ozone depletion, acidification (acid precipitation), accumulation of solid waste and persistent toxins, and the concentration in the atmosphere of gases that cause climate change.

Ozone Depletion

Coordinated international action to address this problem makes it a hopeful precedent and a good place to start.

When it was revealed, in May of 1985, that industrially produced CFCs, (chlorofluorocarbons) were drifting into the upper atmosphere and causing ozone molecules to break down, there was cause for concern. In addition to circulating in refrigerators and air conditioners, CFCs were also being used to wash newly manufactured circuit boards and as a propellant in spray cans. These last two uses were expanding steadily and resulted in large-scale, regular, and direct release of the compound.

Ozone is a molecule with three oxygen atoms rather than the two oxygen atoms that are normal in the air we breath. Ozone is a hazard to health when we breathe it, but in the upper atmosphere it stops much of the Sun's ultraviolet radiation from reaching the Earth.

Decreased ozone in the upper atmosphere increases ultraviolet radiation, which in turn, can damage plants, increase instances of sunburn, and cause eye problems and skin cancer.

The ozone hole was a surprise and a fortuitous discovery, first observed using a device invented by the same James Lovelock who formulated the Gaia Hypothesis. Lovelock invented the device to study the atmosphere for the NASA project described earlier. Had the ozone hole not been observed, and had the exponential growth in the production and release of CFCs continued, we might today, be in a situation where everything under the Sun would be seared by ultraviolet radiation. One might wonder what other damage is going unnoticed.

The data, from which the ozone hole was eventually noticed, had been collected for other purposes. It was around for two or three years before the discovery was made. Once the hole was recognized, the world reacted remarkably quickly. As an environmental issue, it had the advantage that the problem affected everyone, right in their own backyard, and the industries producing the harmful substances were relatively few in number and there were profitable substitutes to be manufactured, not to mention a bonus from the sale of sun screen.

Only two years after the ozone hole was discovered, delegates from a 150 countries met in Montreal to formulate *The Montreal Protocol on Substances that Deplete the Ozone Layer.* The protocol was ratified in countries around the world, and by the year 2000, production of the dangerous substances had been reduced by 90%.

It will be decades before natural processes can correct the damage done, but expansion of the cause has been reversed.

Acidification

Although it is taking longer to agree on action plans, a similar process is taking place around sulfur dioxide (SO_2) emissions from the burning of fossil-fuels. Coal and oil often have sulfur in them. When this burns, it forms sulfur dioxide that combines with water in the atmosphere and returns to Earth as dilute sulfuric acid — acid precipitation. By 1983, when the *Convention on Long-Range Trans-boundary Air Pollution* finally came into force, all life in thousands of lakes had died as a result of intolerable levels of acidity, and large tracts of forests were degenerating.

Part of the reason it took much longer to negotiate an agreement to reduce SO_2 emissions from fossil-fuel burning power plants and automobiles was that the problem wasn't directly affecting those causing it. The damage was mostly downwind from the major sources. Also, the vested interests of the fossil-fuel, power generation and automobile industries reacted with classic denial behaviour and used their power in an effort to prevent change.

Eventually, regulations and procedures were adopted and acid release levels dropped to about half of what they had been. As the targets for these programs were reached in the mid 1990s, studies of the most effected regions revealed that a large portion of the affected lakes were not responding. New agreements on further reductions were reached in Canada in October of 1998, and the U.S. is being encouraged to take additional steps. The long-term problem is that, while the amount of sulfur in gasoline had been reduced by half, the amount of gasoline being burned has doubled, largely counteracting the gains made by the regulations.

Other Toxic Waste

The eruption of manufactured chemicals into our cultural metabolism spun off from a strategic effort during the Second World War. Supplies of natural rubber from the Far East were terminated and an acute rubber shortage followed. The intensive effort by chemists to produce synthetic rubber unlocked new secrets of chemical synthesis, and with it a vast potential for creating other substances, almost at will. The widespread use of synthetic fertilizers, pesticides and all manner of other chemical products began after WW II, when the chemical industry started looking for commercial applications for their new-found capabilities.

Tens of thousands of chemicals, never before existing on Earth, are presently being produced by industrial processes, and more are created every year. Once created, these new substances inevitably find their way into the environment where they can present totally new challenges to the complex chemistry of life. Many of the new substances cause no obvious problems. Some are poisonous, but break down into harmless components fairly quickly. Others cause problems and remain in the biosphere long after they escape human use. Most of the thousands of newly created substances have never been tested individually, let alone in combination, to see what effects they may have on different living things and on the life process.

DDT was an early example and one of the first toxic chemicals to be noticed concentrating through the food chain. This "bioaccumulation," happens when small amounts of a substance are taken in by small creatures at the base of the food chain. The toxin persists in their bodies and, when numbers of them are eaten by a predator, the accumulated toxins are concentrated in the predator's body. In the DDT case, caterpillars, having eaten leaves sprayed with the poison, were being eaten by birds. If the birds didn't die outright, the DDT disrupted hormonal processes and caused eggs to be produced with shells too thin to bear their mother's weight as she incubated them.

The fight to ban DDT, initiated by Rachel Carson's *Silent Spring,* was one of the first environmental battles. DDT is no longer used in North America or Europe, but the manufacturers continue making it to sell to the developing world.

In the global environment, there is no "away." DDT is chemically stable. That is, it takes a long time to break down and even then some of its by-products are toxic. The same dangers that led to its being banned here are problems where it is still used. On top of that, it circulates all over the Earth. The "boomerang effect" brings it back to the Northern countries on the produce from countries where it is used, as well as via global air and water circulation. Steps can be taken to minimize its presence on food products, but little can be done to keep it from circulating with the air and water. Pesticides and numerous other industrially produced toxins vaporize into the air or blow about suspended in water particles or as dust. These circulating chemicals can settle out anywhere. In particular, large quantities of pollutants are found in the Arctic where the air cools and many of the substances it is carrying precipitate out. Practically every person on Earth today has traces of DDT, and dozens of other industrially produced chemicals, in their bodies.

The process of bio-accumulation became widely recognized following the mercury poisoning in Minimata, Japan. Although small amounts of mercury had been released from industrial processes into the water there, it was not thought to be a problem until 1956 when mercury was identified as the cause of serious nervous disorders afflicting people living in Minimata. It was discovered that the mercury released was absorbed by microscopic creatures and remained in their body tissues. The mercury became increasingly concentrated as big fish ate little fish up the food chain. The people who caught and ate the bigger fish, particularly those for whom fish was a regular part of their diets, accumulated enough mercury to cause serious illness and death. The same problem was experienced in Western Ontario when a paper company dumped mercury from its bleaching operation into the English River. The native community 320 kilometers downstream also exhibited "Minimata disease" and had to stop eating the fish that had been their staple diet for centuries.

Dilution is no solution to pollution. I have heard stories about Snapping turtles and Beluga whales caught downstream from all the industrial activity along the St. Lawrence River. They were found to be so full of chemicals, as a result of bioaccumulation, that they could not be simply buried. They had to be disposed of as toxic waste.

In a detailed study conducted by Mount Sinai School of Medicine in New York City, a group of volunteers were found to have, on average, over 100 industrial chemicals within their bodies. Among those tested was media personality Bill Moyers, who turned 70 in 2004. Within his body they found "only" 84 industrial chemicals. That he was full grown by the time industrial chemistry went into full swing in the 1950s was presumed to be the reason that his "body burden" was less than that of many of the younger volunteers.

A body burden of industrial chemicals sounds like it could cause problems. For most of the substances we cannot say, "This one is harmless, that one causes asthma, and this other one causes cancer." While many such links have been established, the effects of the vast majority are unknown. Circumstantially, however, when I was in grade school in the 1960s, I knew of no one with asthma or other allergies and the chances of getting cancer were far less than today's one in three odds.

While the majority of the chemicals produced by humans have not been tested for ecological impacts or their effects in combination with other chemicals, some are known to be very dangerous, yet little is done to eliminate them. Dioxin, for example, is notorious. Studies have identified it as one of the most carcinogenic chemicals known. Dioxin can form spontaneously in the smoke from fires that burn items containing chlorine. Chlorine is manufactured in large quantities and distributed as a component in household bleach and many plastic products. It is also extensively used to bleach paper and purify tap water.

Dioxin is among the persistent organic pollutants (POPs). As the name suggests, these toxins do not break down easily and are subject to bioaccumulation. (The family includes: aldrin, chlordane, DDT, furans, hexachlorobenzene and polychlorinated biphenyls (PCBs) among others.) Many of them include chlorine.

From the life perspective, it is abusive and suicidal to introduce substances that are persistently toxic into the interconnected flows of the biosphere.

Climate Change

The biggest tolerance issue we are facing today is climate change.

All substances of biological origin are held together with energy originally captured through photosynthesis and shared through countless food chains. This energy is released when organic matter is digested, or its fossilized remains, fossil-fuels, burned. The carbon dioxide (CO_2) that was taken out of the atmosphere when the energy was captured by photosynthesis returns to the atmosphere when the energy is released.

As we extract coal and oil and burn them in massive quantities, huge amounts of CO_2 are produced. Although plants and sea creatures steadily take CO_2 out of the air, the rate at which we are releasing carbon has become greater than nature's ability to absorb it. This results in increasing concentrations of CO_2 in the atmosphere, which cause the "greenhouse effect." In a greenhouse, once sunlight passes through the glass, the soil and building materials become heated. These solid objects then warm the inside air. The heat from the air can only escape slowly as it warms the glass, and the glass, in turn, is cooled by the outside air. In the atmosphere, CO_2 and several other gases, act like greenhouse glass by slowing down the rate at which the Sun's energy, which is absorbed by the land, life and water, is able to return into space. Increasing heat retention causes changes in the weather, making northern areas warmer, melting glaciers and ice caps, and causing heavier rains in some places and increased drought in others.

Climate change is now a familiar issue. Like the ozone issue it gets people's attention because it affects almost everyone, wherever they live. Unfortunately, the parallel with the ozone problem ends there. While public pressure is mounting to deal with this problem, the sources of CO_2 are far more diverse than ozone. Every car, truck and chainsaw contributes to the problem. The number of industries with vested interests in the way things are is huge, and the amount of money involved, staggering. It has been estimated that one out of every six jobs in North America works on the production, use and maintenance of gas and diesel burning vehicles, their fuel and the roadways they use. Add to this most metal products, agricultural activity, food processing, manufacturing and electrical generation from coal, oil and gas and we find that practically everyone is presently dependent on the continued massive release of CO_2. On top of all this is an economic system programmed, and extensively subsidized, always to expand.

With dependency comes denial, and with massive investments, outright obstruction. The obstacles are immense, but there are solutions. The problems have to be accepted as real, and the decision made to solve them, before the way we manage mutual provision can be adjusted to accommodate those solutions.

Coming chapters will look at how the economic system works, and how it can be adjusted to help deal with these, and other problems. First, however, we will look at the other range of environmental limits, those of resource supplies.

Limitations of Resource Supply

The collapse of Canada's east coast fishery was a resource management wake-up call. The first European visitors to the Grand Banks described the fish there as being so numerous that one could "walk across the water on their backs." Although over-stated, the comment indicated massive abundance.

In 1975, I visited a fishing community up the northern peninsula of Newfoundland. Until ten years previously, all travel there had been up and down the coast by boat. An old-timer talked with me about fishing when he was young. They used cod traps. A cod trap consisted of two nets held vertically between weights on the ocean floor and floats at the water's surface. One net, called the straight net, ran from shore out to another net, which formed an enclosure. The cod, swimming along the coast, feeding on smaller fish, would come to the straight net and follow it out to the enclosure. The fishermen would then hit the water with their paddles as they went to close the gate. This served to hasten the fish into the trap ahead of them. After the opening was closed, the fishermen netted out as many fish as they could salt and pack in a couple of hours, keeping the others alive and fresh in the trap. When they needed more fish, they would go to the trap and net some more, and when the enclosed fish were all gone, the gate would be opened and the process started again.

As the cod population dropped, this procedure became less effective, resulting in the change to gill nets. Stretched between weights and floats like the cod trap nets, the gill nets had mesh, sized so that when fish swam into them they got stuck there until the fishermen hauled in the catch. At first, the gill nets were eight-inch mesh, but when these weren't catching enough fish, six-inch mesh became the norm.

By the time of my visit even these were drawing meagre catches. Most of the fish were being caught by big, expensive, subsidized factory ships, dragging mile-long nets through schools of fish and processing the catch on board without even docking at a Newfoundland port. Along with industrial quantities of the target species, bycatch species were being caught by the ton, and thrown, dead, back into the sea.

Despite abundant warnings from scientists and fishermen that fish were being taken faster than they grew, little was done until the amount of cod fish available dropped below what was practical even for the factory ships. When the fishery was closed in 1992, tens of thousands of Newfoundland fishermen lost the livelihood that had been the foundation of their communities for 500 years. The factory harvesters sailed off to other locations to help deplete other fish stocks.

By 1992, according to the United Nation's Food and Agriculture Organization (FAO) all of the world's 17 major fisheries were being harvested at or beyond their sustainable capacity, and nine were in a state of decline, including those for Atlantic Cod, Blue-fin Tuna, many tropical grouper species, Marlin, and California Sardine. One study conducted by oceanographers from Dalhousie University in Nova Scotia, estimated that once serious exploitation of mature fish in the open ocean begins, commercial fishing techniques regularly deplete the biomass of those fish by 80-90% within 15 years.

Proof of Fundamental Change

There has been a fundamental change in the relationship between people and the Earth. This change requires an equally fundamental change in how we manage ourselves.

Throughout history, the amount of fish that people could catch was limited only by how much time and equipment we invested in fishing. More time or more equipment meant more fish would be caught. This is no longer the case. Today, the amount of fish we catch is limited by the number of fish in the sea. This is a fundamental change with far-reaching implications. The situation with fish is not unique. We face similar limitations with forests, soil fertility, fresh water and fossil-fuels. The significance is enormous. It affects the entire relationship between people and these essential resources. It also

77

affects the relationships between people. No longer can we necessarily provide for expanding human need (or desire) by expanding production. In the areas already affected, when an individual consumes more than his or her share, less is available for others. Economic programs have always aimed to increase supplies. That's what the present system is designed to do. But supplies in some areas are no longer expandable and, in certain cases, they are diminishing.

This fundamental change is proof that we are physically mature as a species. As such, we are called upon to take full responsibility for our actions.

There are some promising signs that we are rising to that challenge, the *Montreal Protocol* being a prime example. However, like the measures taken to stop acid precipitation, the solutions will be tenuous until we metamorphose the basic structures of society to harmonize with our physical maturity. It has become critical that we develop an economic system based, not on growth, but on sustainability.

Forests

Besides the normal process of maintaining and reproducing themselves, forests fill many roles in their ecosystems. Their roots hold soil together, they moderate the climate and they provide habitat for other plants and forest creatures. They cushion the impact of falling rain, and enable much of it to evaporate from their leaves so that it can travel further inland with the air.

Rather than selectively removing some trees and leaving the forest, profit motivated forest harvesters often cut everything. After clear-cutting, creatures depending on forest conditions can no longer exist there. The soil, exposed to sun, wind and rain, often erodes, clogging waterways and filling in reservoirs with silt. The water, previously held and shunted inland, floods downstream instead, leaving some inland territories increasingly arid.

Throughout most of the world, forests are still being cut faster than they can regrow. In the rich Northern countries, however, between abandoned agricultural and rangeland reverting to forest cover, tree plantations, and the importation of forest products, the proportion of forested lands is starting to expand. Even so, problems still remain with the limited ability of single species plantations to do a forest's job, and with the decline of forest cover. Nevertheless, there is some hope in the recognition that because forest cover is valuable, it should be maintained.

Soil

As a result of intensive and sometimes careless use, the natural fertility of agricultural soils has been declining. Since life began, the tendency has been for fertility to accumulate in soils. Drawn up by plants, eaten by animals and returned to the soil countless times, the soil nutrients in an area have tended to stay local. Except where glaciers scraped by or where oceans or volcanoes covered the land, little was ever lost and slowly, steadily, new materials from rock and biological activity were added. Studies of past civilizations have found that in many of the places where large numbers of people have lived, this two billion year trend of increasing fertility has reversed. Over the last century, with civilization's spread over most of the Earth, natural soil fertility is in decline practically everywhere.

Intensive cultivation has been extracting nutrients and hauling them away to feed expanding and ever more urban populations. After the food is eaten, the resulting human manure is seldom returned to the soils that provided the harvest. Usually, it is considered "waste" and discarded, with or without treatment, sometimes in ways that remove it indefinitely from the nutrient cycles. The limitation of available soil fertility is held at bay with synthetic fertilizers produced and transported at great energy expense.

Removing the protective cover of forests and grasses exposes the soil. Repeated plowing exposes the soil structure to the elements. Oxygen, sun and weather can cause exposed soil life and organic matter to die and break down, and for the soil to erode. The weight of big agricultural machinery can also damage soil by compacting it so that water, roots and other soil life have trouble penetrating it. Artificial fertilizer can damage soil microflora and other organisms that nurture and support plant roots and maintain healthy soil structure. Excessive irrigation can also degrade soil. When the water evaporates, it leaves behind dissolved salts that can accumulate to intolerable levels. The result of these various problems is the loss of thousands of acres of arable land each year.

In some places, this problem is recognized and efforts are being made to slow or reverse the process. The most encouraging efforts are in the rediscovery and expansion of natural "organic" farming. Organic agriculture endeavours to reproduce the conditions of nature, whereby humans share the substances of life without depleting the soil, or requiring manufactured fertilizers and toxic pesticides. Although it is still a small portion of overall production, the volume of organic produce is doubling every few years. This is very encouraging, because, not only does it reduce degradation of the soil and minimize toxic residue on food, organic agriculture tends to be local and can, thereby, insulate us from some of the dangers that would arise in the event that massive scale, cross-continental transportation becomes unreliable.

Two changing numbers used to be the centerpiece of an entire wall in the lobby of the International Development Research Centre (IDRC) in Ottawa. One kept a running count of the human population, the other, of the total area of arable land. A person could watch as the numbers changed every few seconds. The population counter was rising steadily, adding around seventy million people each year. The one displaying the amount of productive land, on the other hand, showed a steady decrease of around five million hectares annually. The mathematics needed to reveal the problems here are not complex. The implications are bracing. It was an impressive reminder of the challenges at hand. It also testified to the tenacity of the growth ideology. In many official circles there is still no acknowledgment that expanding population is a problem.

Fresh Water

Of the renewable resources, fresh water has the greatest potential for limiting our growth.

Although the planet is covered with water, only a small portion is fresh. All living things need water. Around 70% of all the water humans take from lakes, rivers, streams and wells is used for agriculture. Two-thirds of the balance is used in industry. The remaining 10% is used in our homes.

The rate of extraction is already creating problems with rivers around the world. In China, the USA and Eurasia, there are previously great rivers that no longer make it to the sea during the irrigation seasons.

Of further concern are the underground reservoirs of water called aquifers. The water available from them is often remnant from past ages when the climate was wetter, or it has collected over long periods of time. In some cases, the water has moved a long distance underground to get to where it is drawn up through wells. In many dry regions, such aquifers are used to water crops, and because they take a long time to refill, they are easily overdrawn. In parts of China, India, the United States, Saudi Arabia and North Africa, wells have to be drilled deeper and deeper to maintain sufficient supplies. One-quarter of China's grain harvest and large quantities in India and the USA, are dependent on this "fossil" water. In the event that the water is depleted in any of these locations, the availability of food will diminish, and prices will, undoubtedly, rise around the world.

Water continues to evaporate from the oceans and fall on the land. By becoming accustomed to food crops that do not need as much water, using irrigation techniques that minimize evaporation, and by installing reduced-flow toilets, shower heads and the like, we can get more of what we need from the water that is renewably available. The first step toward living with any limitation is to acknowledge that the limit exists, and then to respect and include that consideration in planning and decision-making.

Metals

The resources so far discussed have all been renewable. That is, they keep growing, or cycling, by themselves. If we are patient, live within the limited amounts renewably available, and preserve the natural systems that keep the cycles moving, they can provide for us forever.

There is a town in China that was renamed hundreds of years before the birth of Christ. The new name, literally translated, is "No Tin." There had been a tin mine nearby, but the mine was exhausted. No tin is available there and there hasn't been any for more than two thousand years. Hence the name.

Metals and other mined minerals are different from renewable resources in that their quantities do not increase and they have no natural circulation. They can, however, be available indefinitely if we design for durability and recycle responsibly.

We do recycle metals with considerably more intent than we presently apply to preserving nutrient cycles. Gold and silver have been carefully recycled for thousands of years. In the 1960s, Buckminster Fuller's *World Resources Inventory* calculated that, with minor losses, all the copper that has ever been mined was being reused every 44 years. A good portion of the tin from No Tin is likely still in use today.

Both out of respect for finite supplies of metals, and because mining operations are among the most energy-intensive and polluting things that people do, care and attention are in order when we use them. While recycling keeps these valuable resources available for new uses, the energy-intensive nature of remelting them makes design for durability and easy repair prime considerations.

Energy

Trumping water as a limiting factor overall is the fossil energy with which we pump water and with which we do an enormous amount, and variety, of other work. While both water and energy resources are limited, water recirculates after use, whereas, after most uses, fossil energy resources are gone.

While nuclear, wind and biofuels are filling a small portion of the need, for the most part, today's civilization runs on fossil-fuels. Quite apart from the problems of climate change, these fuels are finite in quantity. Estimates put the period over which they were created at between four hundred million and eight hundred million years. Fossil-fuels did not replace wood and animal power as the prime mover of human activity until late in the nineteenth century. Optimistic projections suggest that we will have practically exhausted them within a 400 year period. According to a variety of predictions, the most versatile and portable of the fossil-fuels, petroleum, will not be available in sufficient quantities to meet demand within a decade. Long-term dependency on fossil-fuels is not an option.

Investments in fossil-fuels are enormous and the power of those controlling the industry is among the greatest on Earth. There is little interest within that sector to acknowledge the limitations of supply. Yet, what little there is, is telling. While bringing in record profits from conventional oil sales, British Petroleum is starting to say that "BP" stands for "Beyond Petroleum." It has become a major manufacturer of solar electric panels. Over the last few years, around the globe, more wind generated electricity production capacity has been installed than any other form of electrical power generation. In Germany, wind power now provides 10% of their electricity.

Enormous savings in energy can be realized through conservation. In *Natural Capitalism,* Paul Hawkin, Hunter Lovins and Amory Lovins, show how we could reduce our material and energy consumption by 75% to 90%, with no drop in our "quality of life." As we shall see, the economic incentives for doing this have been tested, but are not yet widely applied.

The prospects for reducing our level of resource dependency even further, by changing our priorities from expanding material consumption to the enjoyment of life, has hardly even been touched upon in official circles.

Humans are tremendously resourceful when it comes to overcoming limitations. In the end, however, we are totally enmeshed in the life processes and, therefore, subject to the "laws" of nature – the limitations of resource supplies and the impacts of waste. What we call the economy operates totally within the planetary ecosystem. Traditional economics may account only for the interactions between people, and see itself as independent from nature, but this illusion was acceptable only when people were few, like duckweed covering less than 1% of a pond. Although humankind is extraordinary, there is a need to acknowledge our place as part of the natural order. We need to expand economic accounts to include interactions with our ecological foundations. Market prices must include considerations for the security of resource supplies and the impacts of fabrication, transport use and the disposal of products. If we use our ingenuity to work limiting factors into our long-term plans, we may yet avoid disaster.

5 Mutual Provision: Money, Markets and an Orderly World

Work is love made manifest.
Kahlil Gibran

When two people love each other, the help they share is economic exchange. Money need not be involved. Simple or complex, economics is the study of mutual provision – the work people give, trade or sell for mutual benefit.

Money didn't come into the picture until people had been taking care of each other for a very long time. The process has become complex, and under the cover of that complexity, some unsavoury advantages are being taken. Nevertheless, economics looks at how we cooperate en masse to keep the human family going. By clarifying the basic operating processes and how they have evolved, it will be easier to picture how the economic system accomplishes the remarkable task of integrating the work of billions of people into a massive web of mutual provision. (The phrases "economic system" and "system of mutual provision" will continue to be used interchangeably to prevent losing sight of what an economy is for.)

Commercial media gives us few details about the economic process. Most people hear next to nothing besides the reverent and frequent quotation of stock market levels, unemployment figures, interest rates and the rate of economic growth. By the time you have read the next few chapters, the logic employed by those making economic decisions should make more sense. This look at how things are working, or not working, will provide a context for viewing the solutions presented in Chapters 11, 12 and 13. These solutions would be obvious if economists looked beyond money and markets and integrated into their work the understanding developed by ecologists and sociologists.

We cooperate in mutual provision because we can produce a lot more when different people take on different tasks and trade, rather than when each individual tries to do everything for his or her self. An elementary example would be when one parent goes out to catch food while the other maintains the living space and keeps the children from getting hurt or lost. The mind boggles at the thought of trying to sneak up on an animal while, at the same time, keeping a toddler satisfied and safe. With more people involved, it becomes possible to take care of children, find food, build shelter, make clothing and tools and maintain social harmony simultaneously, and with a measure of quality.

As our economic interactions become more sophisticated and our support activities are divided up among more and more people, direct exchange between participants diminishes. Individuals are less likely to know those with whom they are trading. Services could be accepted and the reciprocal service forgotten or avoided. Questions arise about the balance between individual contributions, and how much of which products and services are needed. In response, we have developed trading techniques that help resolve these concerns. Prime among these are money and markets. Through these innovations, the number of people cooperating in mutual provision has expanded from families and clans to practically the entire human race.

While there are many problems with the way this process has evolved, particularly with its recent, rapid integration at the global level, there is, nonetheless, merit remaining in the basic process. Please resist the urge to discount the basic mechanisms because of the problems that have evolved from them. We will come back to look at those problems in later chapters. If we can first understand the fundamental processes, we can use what works to recreate an economic structure that is sensitive to today's challenges. There is a baby of genuine value in the bathwater of recent economic history. It is one that enables an enormous synergy for the human race. We will have time enough to look at the dirt that can be washed off the baby before we throw out the bathwater and proceed to dress the child in clothes that suit the brilliant species it represents.

Division of Labour

It is hard to imagine any one person producing everything that he or she needs. It would be hard enough even if one were able to start out with the necessary tools, rather than having to design and fabricate them before doing each new task. Remember, everything that can be bought, with the exception of unimproved land, is produced by other people's efforts. Try for a moment to imagine living entirely from your own work producing food, shelter, clothing, education, amusement, health care, sanity, etc.

I think it is safe to assume that people have always cooperated to survive. From as far back as we have evidence, people have lived in groups. When a number of people (as few as two) start working together, the tendency is for the individuals to take on different tasks.

When someone does something many times over, ways of holding the tools, what to expect from the materials, hand motions, trouble spots to look out for, and many other aspects of the task become second nature. A person specializing in a particular set of tasks can learn to do them much faster and better than someone new to the work. Practice improves our ability to do whatever we do.

If the scale of a survival/trading group reaches the point where each person can become excellent at a few tasks, far more will be produced by the whole community than by the same number of people working separately with each doing a larger variety of different tasks. In addition to the expertise that comes from practice, not having to put one set of tools away and pick up another set increases production. Cooperation can keep all tools in skilled hands throughout the working day, resulting in more to go around and the possibility of everyone being better off.

Up to a point, division of labour becomes more and more effective the larger the number of people involved in the trading group. Such dividing up of tasks ceases to be beneficial where an individual's part in the process becomes so small that they no longer feel the satisfaction of accomplishment or recognize the greater good toward which their effort is being directed. At this point, morale declines.

Economies of Scale

Division of labour is the first stage in achieving "economies of scale." Further gains can be achieved by making several of something when the material and tools have been assembled to make a single item. When sandwiches are being made, for example, by the time bread, butter, mayonnaise, cheese, lettuce or whatever, are assembled, along with the appropriate knives and a cutting board, it would take almost no additional time to make two or three sandwiches, rather than just one. Cleaning up afterward would take only slightly longer and, overall, the time involved per sandwich would be much less.

Up to a point, the greater the volume of a product being produced, the greater the economies of scale. At a certain level, it becomes practical to develop specialized tools for very specific tasks, making that part of a process even quicker and more precise. Assembly lines take this efficiency to another level, by breaking the procedures down into individual steps and assigning someone different to each step. This means that assembly line workers seldom or never have to change their position or the tools in hand, and every bit of their activity can be concentrated on swiftly passing the product through their stage of production.

In a large, productive facility, the cost of specialized tools for hundreds or thousands of workers doing a wide variety of tasks can be very high, particularly when highly technical equipment is required. Extremely large volumes of output are necessary to pay back the expense of setting up. Nevertheless, such expenditures are made and products, which would have cost a fortune to make on a small scale, can be provided at remarkably low cost.

The "limited liability corporation," indicated by "Ltd." at the end of a company name, is testament to the extent to which economies of scale are pursued. "Limited liability" becomes useful in an organization when the scale of operation is so vast that it is beyond the means of any individual or organization to finance its creation. More importantly, it would cost so much to set up that, if there were a problem, those involved would be ruined financially. In the face of such danger, people naturally want to avoid the responsibility of huge-scale operations, despite the potential gains for society as a whole. To enable the social benefit, without requiring excessive risk, the institution of limited liability was created in law. With limited liability, investors and board members are protected, within some guidelines, from losing anything more than their own personal financial investment. With this safeguard, people can be recruited to organize and direct enormous tasks of potentially great advantage like canals, cross-continental railways, global trading operations and international communications systems. The downside of such an arrangement is that it can enable such organizations to sidestep the collateral damage their operations may cause. We will come back to the nature of large and enormous operations further on.

Development

With division of labour comes the notion of "development." One example, for me, was getting a stroke sander for my woodworking shop. A stroke sander is a stationary tool with a table that rolls back and forth under a long, moving sanding belt. It has a paddle with which one can press the sandpaper down on to the woodwork as desired. Mine enables sanding flat wooden items up to the size of a big door. I had managed to get ahead enough to purchase one, and with my next cabinet job, I appreciated that it took only two hours to sand its flat surfaces. Previously, with a hand-held sander, the job had required eight hours of labour. The stroke sander did a better job and I was in much better humour when the task was over. This tool increased my productivity, making it easier to support myself and, if I wanted, to get ahead again and develop further.

A more rudimentary example of the development process would be that which might start an agrarian society moving toward industrialization. If a group of farmers were able to feed one more worker than it took to grow its food, that extra person could take on the task of raising and training a work animal. When the animal was ready to join in the efforts of mutual provision, it could do enough work to compensate for the food needs of its trainer and probably another person. A second person, not needed for food-production may, perhaps, take up tool-making and improving the farmers' tools. Improved tools could then free up still more labour for other things. This freeing up of labour from time-consuming tasks to build tools and systems that enable more efficient production, which, in turn, enables still more people to take on other tasks, is development.

Presumably, the purpose of the improvements and increased efficiency is the betterment of society. As long as people lack adequate food, clothing, shelter, cooking utensils or other basic goods, the goal and purpose of development is clear. When sufficient goods are available for all of a society's material needs, the goals being served by further development become less clear and the purpose becomes a legitimate question for discussion.

Managing Exchange

The advantages of different people taking on different sorts of work and sharing what they produce is obvious to participants in a family, clan or tribe. For a long time these relatively small human groups existed in isolation from each other and worked to provide all

89

that they needed. As long as the group was small enough for its members to recognize each other, trade could be maintained on a familiar basis, everyone doing their tasks, and drawing what they needed from the community. Necessity, custom, duty, peer pressure and familiarity were sufficient to ensure that each member did his or her share. When everyone participated, the community was strong and the individuals secure. If capable individuals did not do their part, all were put at risk. Under these conditions, terms of trade could be as loose as personal relationships were strong.

Mutually supporting groups were successful and our communities grew. As the number of people in a trading unit expands, the heartfelt sense of providing for and being provided for by one's own, becomes weaker. It becomes difficult to keep track of who is helping out and who is not. More clearly defined terms of trade become necessary to assure participants that they are not being taken advantage of by people they do not know. The need for a clear way to measure the value of individual contributions was one of the inspirations from which money arose. There were several stages, however, before money came to be what it seems today.

The Market

When communities grew beyond the scope of personal relations, markets became central to mutual provision.

Traditionally, a market was the physical location where people came together to trade their goods. Instead of people carrying their goods to the many places where others lived, everyone with things to trade would bring their wares to a single place on Market Day. There they would bargain and trade. Acquaintances were made, old friendships renewed, news shared and a good time had by many.

The word "market" has now come to refer to the entire spectrum of channels through which goods and services are traded. This includes the local market, stores, mail order operations, stock exchanges, and Internet trading sites.

Markets have had positive impacts on efficiency. By making it easier for people to specialize and live from a single type of work, markets accommodate division of labour and efficiencies of scale.

The market system of the Roman Empire collapsed with that empire. As market trading reemerged in the towns and cities of medieval Europe, the feudal system was stuck in an awkward, tradition bound, form.

Across Europe and elsewhere, feudal systems gave a privileged class of nobles ownership of the land. They exchanged use of the land with the peasants for a portion of the harvest and other specific services that they might choose. A problem for the nobles, who received large amounts of food was, what to do with it? Without international markets for food products or even refrigeration, there was little they could do with food except feed people.

According to Adam Smith, the first philosopher to recognize the methodology of the market and write about its evolution, feudal nobles would host huge banquets to "give" the food away. It was not exactly given away, however, because those invited to the feast were obliged by custom to make some gesture in exchange. They could be asked for allegiance in dealings with the king or to wage battle in case of attack. The web of obligation was strong and far reaching. The noble couldn't enjoy his wealth totally because he had to give it away, and those who received it were encumbered by obligations.

Supporting artisans was another way in which those receiving large amounts of food used their abundance. Artists, musicians, dancers, playwrights and trades people would be retained to entertain and enrich life in the court. The craftspeople were dependent on the nobles and the nobles shared the creative output of those they retained with others to further the obligation cycle.

This medieval cycle of obligations was relieved when money started to circulate again. With money, a person of wealth had the means to employ others directly, to produce things they wanted. Adam Smith used the example of a fancy buckle. Numerous crafts people might be involved in refining the metal, forming it into the desired shape, preparing precious stones and then using the stones to decorate the piece. In the end, the person paying for all the work had a fancy buckle that no one else could wear. The craftspeople had some money to purchase what they needed and no residual obligations. All were free to take the next steps in their lives without baggage from the last. This was a distinct liberation for participants. It made the market system appealing and accommodated the expansion of trade.

Tools for Trade

Trading between people is the essence of economy. Money is a tool created to make it easier for strangers to trade. Before paper money and credit came into being, trade was accommodated by barter, commodity-based currencies, coins and receipts for coins in storage.

Barter

As the scale of a trading community expanded past that of personal relations, barter provided a means of assuring fairness. One person would have a surplus of their product or produce and they would offer it in trade for things produced by others; a share of the harvest for someone's help bringing it in, a bag of grain for a pair of shoes. Whatever the exchange, both parties had the option of declining if they felt it was unfair.

Barter can get complex, however. If one had chickens to trade and wanted a pair of shoes, the person with chickens had to find a shoemaker who wanted chickens. Alternatively, he or she could find a baker who wanted chickens and was willing to trade bread for chickens, thereby enabling the chicken producer to trade with the shoe maker who was "in the market" for bread. Such exchanges could be difficult to find and carry out. As the number of different products and services available in a community increased, the potential complexity and consequent difficulty in finding the trades necessary to get what one wanted, multiplied.

Commodity Currency

Early on, commodities came into use as currency. The exchange is still barter, but the commodity is also a rudimentary form of money. Some items such as cows or wheat, were recognized as particularly useful in trade because most people could use them. If they did not need wheat themselves, it wasn't hard to find someone who did. As a result, the grain could be used as an intermediary in trades. If you had chickens and wanted a pair of shoes, but the shoemaker didn't want chickens, you could trade your chickens for wheat. The cobbler would take the wheat for the shoes since, even if he didn't need wheat at that time, he would know that he could find someone who did, or at least someone who would take the wheat in the expectation that they, too, could trade it. A residual testimony to this process is our word "pecuniary," which refers to things of, or related to, money. It comes from the Latin word for money, "pecunin," which, itself, is derived from "pecus," which means "paying in cattle."

Over the years, many different commodities have been used as "exchange currencies," including grains, cattle, shells, whisky and firewood. Tobacco was legal tender in Virginia, U.S.A., for over 150 years and was used as currency in Germany following the Second World War.

Coins

As people became accustomed to refining metals, these came into use as exchange commodities. Copper, brass, zinc, tin, nickel, gold and silver have all been used. One advantage of using metal for exchange is that it does not rot. If you had a surplus and left it sitting for a year, it would likely still be usable for trade. The same might not be said for a quantity of wheat. With good storage it might be okay, but there was also a danger that it would become mouldy and unfit to eat, or that you would find a bunch of fat mice where your "money" had been.

Metal doesn't rot or get eaten, particularly gold and silver, which don't even rust. Another advantage of metals, again gold and silver in particular, is that, because of their scarcity, a small amount could be traded for a substantial volume of other commodities. Using precious metals in exchange avoided the necessity, in the case of a major purchase/sale, of having to involve cartloads of an exchange commodity.

Receipt Currency

Gold and silver were convenient enough to move and valuable enough to be subject to theft, yet, they too could be bulky when very large transactions took place. As a result, the practice evolved of storing precious metal coins in places where they would be safe. Goldsmiths were known to have vaults where they stored their raw materials. For a fee, the goldsmiths would also store coins for people concerned about security. Those depositing gold with the goldsmiths would get receipts stating how much gold they had on deposit. They could retrieve the gold by presenting their receipt.

These receipts were among the earliest forms of paper money. Someone realized that they could pass along their receipts for stored gold, instead of retrieving the gold, and giving it, in trade, to someone who would likely just take it back to the goldsmith for redeposit. With this discovery, a whole new convenience arose that helped expand commerce by making it much easier to complete transactions. Paper, representing deposits of any commodity, be it gold, wheat or cattle, became currency – receipt currency.

The further evolution of paper currency into "fractional reserve currency," where more receipts are issued than the amount of gold/money being stored with goldsmiths/bankers, and of "fait" money, which are paper bills that have nothing of material substance backing them up, will be explained later.

Supply, Demand and Price

Much of the legendary greatness by which "the market" efficiently allocates resources to maximize benefits comes from the way it automatically balances supply, demand and price. Herman Daly and John Cobb note in *For the Common Good:**

> *One big lesson we have learned from recent history is about the vigor and resilience of the open market system of economics. The most important insight that economists have to convey about the market is how independent, decentralized decisions give rise, not to chaos, but to a spontaneous order... Individual consumers know their preferences better than anyone else and act directly to satisfy them in the marketplace. Individual producers know their own capacities and options better than anyone else and they too act on this information in the market. This essential feature of decentralized decision-making is what permits all this knowledge to be used.*

The order, spontaneously maintained by markets, comes from the way in which supply of, and demand for, goods and services establish prices and how prices, in turn, lead to productive resources being used to provide what people want. This fundamental process is central to the modern economic faith. Understandably so, as the creative abilities of literally billions of people and provision for their needs are thereby managed. Coordinating this enormous amount of activity is an organizational feat beyond the capacity of any individual or institution, yet it takes place, relatively effectively, on an ongoing basis.

In essence it works like this. Supply is the available amount of a good or service. Demand is the amount of goods or services that people want, relative to how much they are willing to pay for them. In a competitive market, free from manipulation, supply and demand are balanced through the way they interact to establish prices for each good or service. (For the sake of brevity, I will refer here to "goods or services" as "widgets.")

When there are fewer widgets than people want, some people will pay more to get the ones available. The price rises. As the price rises, it becomes more attractive for other people to go into the business of producing widgets and the supply increases.

*For the *Common Good; Redefining the Economy Toward Community, the Environment and a Sustainable Future,* published in 1993, has been a formative inspiration for many who have become interested in ecological economics, including myself.

When there are more widgets produced than there are people willing to pay for them at a given price, the price will drop, making widgets affordable to more people.

If the volume of widgets produced gets too high, producers have to lower their prices to make the products more appealing and to avoid being caught with unsold goods. Some producers will find the price too low to compensate for their efforts and will go out of business. The supply is thereby reduced, causing the price to rise to where it can sustain the remaining producers.

In the event that some material needed in the production of goods becomes scarce, the price will rise until demand drops to the point that it can be met by the available supply. This rise in price can eventually make more expensive, alternative materials, competitive, thereby expanding the supply of products that can meet particular demands.

Over time, open markets, using money for exchange, and allowing the interplay of supply and demand to set the prices of goods and services supplied by specialized producers, proved advantageous. It has become the established pattern of mutual provision.

The result has been impressive. The volume and variety of goods and services available has mushroomed. Multitudes of paying jobs have been created making it possible for people to purchase what they need and more. Most of the world has adopted this system or is in the process of doing so. By the measure of its spread and by the increases in productivity that it stimulates, open market systems are an enormous success.

There is, however, a tendency for things that grow to great proportions to contain within them the essence of their opposite. So it is with the market system. From its success comes problems. The "free from manipulation" criteria for effective markets can be overrun when some participants become powerful enough to usurp the price-setting function to serve their own ends. There are also some threats to long-term well-being that exist in a time frame beyond that to which markets respond. In such cases, it appears necessary to pay some direct attention and establish guidelines to "manipulate" markets toward solutions, rather than letting the problems grow unattended. Such problems may eventually come close enough for the market to respond, but by then they could be too big to solve without widespread hardship.

Competition

Implicit to the price setting mechanism of supply and demand is competition. Individual producers, providing similar widgets, compete with each other to make less costly or better quality widgets, so that people will buy from them first. If one producer discovers a technique for cheaper production or better quality, that producer will have an advantage in the market. It will be the other producers who go out of business if supply is greater than demand.

Through this sort of competition, the market also encourages innovations, resulting in higher quality and lower price. These benefits are among the first casualties when the market formula is undermined by producers who control a large enough portion of one market or another to set prices independent of the market process.

Self-interest

At the time when the cultural pattern of market economics was first clearly identified, "self-interest" was recognized as a primary stimulant for economic growth. Adam Smith, a moral philosopher working in the latter part of the 1700s, identified the positive effects of people working for their own self-interest. By closely observing people's decisions and actions about earning and spending money, Smith identified the underlying patterns of behaviour that had evolved around the use of markets and money. It was a remarkable feat of pattern recognition. His book, *The Wealth of Nations,* published in 1776, is seen as the revelation of the capitalist system. The process had been evolving for centuries, but this was its first clear enunciation.

Capitalism, in essence, is a system of mutual provision operating on the basis of private ownership, individual and corporate, with decisions about resources and production being made by those owners, and informed by supply, demand and price signals from open markets.

The legitimacy of this way of organizing economic activity is, to this day, frequently justified by Adam Smith's work from over two centuries ago. One concept in particular, and often the only one referred to, is his analogy of "the invisible hand."

As ever greater numbers of people were integrated into systems of mutual provision, they became less and less connected to each other. With this shift, the motivation to work for one's community for love, loyalty or duty, gives way to working from the perspective of one's personal self-interest. Smith pointed out that when people try to improve their personal lot by working hard at their specialty, they do more good for society than if they intentionally set out to do good. It is, he wrote, as if they were "guided by an invisible hand."

In the earliest mutual support groups, one's activities were defined by custom and necessity. Once one's obligations were fulfilled and the community's basic needs met, there was little incentive for producing more until the customary cycles came around again.

When people began trading as individuals, there was more incentive for producing a surplus. After providing what they could for themselves and their dependents, any surplus could be taken to the market and traded for other things they needed or wanted. The more surplus they produced, the more they could get for themselves. If the interest of having more for themselves could be stimulated, they would produce more.

As this attitude of wanting more for oneself became more prevalent across a trading community, the volume of goods and services available in that community also increased.

In Adam Smith's time, this "invisible hand" of the market was particularly helpful. Mass production was just beginning and food, clothing, pots, pans and other goods were often not available in the abundance people needed, or at prices they could afford. Almost all economic activity was in the production of goods and services that people needed. If someone wanted to make a lot of money, they did so by providing more of the goods and services in demand. The willingness of others to pay was evidence that the products and services offered were desirable. The harder people worked, the more there was to go around, and the hard workers did well for themselves. As a stimulant for economic production, self-interest is very effective. Promoting self-interest has become, perhaps, the most dynamic element of the capitalist system.

Today, advertising ceaselessly encourages us to want more. Our children are encouraged to strive for high paying jobs so that they can buy lots of stuff. The class structure in our society emphasizes possessions and the display of possessions is seen as testimonial to our rank. While ostentatious display of wealth has long been practised by kings and nobility, historically, in many cultures the esteem with which a person was regarded was based on the service they provided directly to their community. The transformation, from the extent of service provided to the amount of personal wealth accumulated as a measure of status, was the work of the "invisible hand." If improving one's personal lot resulted in doing good for society, it followed that the richer one became, the more good he or she is presumed to have done. This might have been true at one point, but, as I will discuss, along with other problems arising from the scale and abstraction of today's gigantic system, personal financial advancement is no longer directly connected to the well-being of society. Where individuals see themselves as entirely separate from the rest of the world and where their interests contradict the common good, serious problems can arise.

Before moving on to matters of magnitude and abstraction, there are three more fundamental elements of our economic system to identify: interest, gross domestic product and growth.

Interest

Nothing makes money grow more directly, or uncompromisingly, than loaning it at interest. Interest is a fee that a borrower pays for the use of someone else's money. It is similar to the rent that a tenant pays for the use of someone else's building.

Interest has roots in early agricultural times. If someone wanted to grow food but didn't have seed or livestock to start with, they could borrow enough to get started on the understanding that, after they had grown the crop or raised the animals, they would return the amount of seed or livestock they had borrowed, along with a portion of the natural increase.

Interest is also seen as compensation for the foregone enjoyment of one's money. When a person earns money they are entitled to spend it any way they wish, within the confines of the law. If they choose to make it available for someone else to use, they are not enjoying what it might have brought to them. In exchange for missing that pleasure and making the buying power available to someone else, they take compensation in a percentage interest charge. At the same time, the money made available enables people with skills and time to undertake enterprises that they would not otherwise have been able to attempt.

Charging interest on loans was considered a form of usury and had been against the law in many social orders since ancient times. It is still considered a sin in some societies today. The service that interest can provide, in terms of coaxing savings out of non-productive storage and into productive development, as well as for stimulating the powerful motivation of self-interest, made its removal from the list of deadly sins a matter of contention for centuries.

Today, charging interest is a well-established right in the capitalist system. Not only is it within the law, it is at the very heart of the system. Much more will be said about interest in the chapters ahead, and about the repercussions of its rise, from deadly sin to its present position of primary duty.

Gross Domestic Product

Gross Domestic Product (GDP) is an extension of the idea that the more money individuals make the better off society is. If this premise of the invisible hand is accepted, then it seems to follow that the more money a nation makes, the better off everyone is.

GDP, previously GNP ("N" for national) is a measure made by adding together the financial transactions that take place in a territory over a period of time — the total cash flow of the economy. The difference between GDP and GNP lies in which activities are to be included. The change was a large and unnoticed step taken to prepare the way for corporate globalization and will be elaborated on when that topic is discussed in Chapter 10, The Monopoly End Game.

While the pursuit of personal gain has been justified for more than 200 years, and a person's worth has long since come to be measured by their income level, it took until after the Second World War for GNP to be adopted as a goal for public policy. This was done in response to the problem of how to finance that war. It started as an inventory of where money was being made in order that taxes could be collected to pay off the war debt. One of its first expressions was in a 1939 paper by John Maynard Keynes and Richard Stone titled, *The National Income and Expenditure of the United Kingdom, and How to Pay for the War.*

Up to that time, government policies had been formulated around specific targets such as building houses, improving sanitation, developing industries, expanding educational facilities, or other works of practical description. The notion of pursuing the expansion of overall economic activity for its own sake was novel. When it was announced, in 1954, at a Conservative party conference, R. A. Butler, the British Chancellor of the Exchequer, (equivalent to our Minister of Finance, or the U.S. Secretary of the Treasury) explained that if growth were to average 3% a year, production would double in 25 years, thereby doubling the amount of goods and services available to everyone.

Since that time, expanding GNP has increasingly become the primary goal of public policy. GDP (or GNP) has the seductive advantage of being easier to measure than wealth, happiness, or other specifics of well-being. It has come to be the measure of government success replacing real, but harder to measure aspects of the human condition. This completed the abstraction of the economic process. No longer were the goals of society to be framed in terms of material or social goals. The goal was to expand monetary activity. This expansion is called "growth" and all good is assumed to flow from its continuation.

Growth

With the vision of progress bound to the expansion of monetary economic activity, growth in gross production was enthroned as the goal of economic life. The goal is not just to increase the amount of economic activity, but to do so proportionally to its expanding size. That is, the larger an economy becomes, the larger the increases must be to maintain the same rate of growth. Expansion by an amount proportional to something's expanding size is the formula for exponential growth. It is the formula illustrated by the duckweed example in Chapter 4.

The difference between arithmetic growth and exponential growth is the difference between:

Arithmetic growth (+ 10)

| 100 | 110 | 120 | 130 | 140 | 150 | 160 | 170 |

and

Exponential growth (+ 10%)

| 100 | 110 | 121 | 133 | 146 | 161 | 177 | 195 |

The difference starts out subtly enough, but after 40 increments the subtlety is long gone.

Arithmetic growth

| 510 | 520 | 530 | 540 | 550 | 560 | 570 | 580 |

and

Exponential growth

| 4979 | 5476 | 6024 | 6626 | 7289 | 8018 | 8820 | 9702 |

With this perspective in mind, it is not hard to imagine how problems might arise from pursuing exponential growth for seven generations. Perpetual expansion by modest arithmetic growth could be problematic enough on a finite planet, exponential growth is frightening. The motivation for writing this book, as I mentioned, was that, the way our economic system is presently structured, society is not healthy unless exponential growth is maintained. I hope you feel as keen to understand this dilemma as I did.

Herman Daly pointed out that, "The growth ideology is extremely attractive politically because it offers a solution to poverty without requiring the moral disciplines of sharing and population control."

It is an article of faith to proponents of growth that when more money is being made everyone is better off. This faith is expressed by the "Trickle-down theory," which suggests it doesn't matter if money-making enterprises have little to do with particular human needs. With more money circulating in society, for whatever reasons, it is supposed to automatically trickle down to where it is needed. Those of the "Capitalist Faith" believe that increasing the amount of money in circulation will lift everyone in the economy toward greater affluence.

Faithfully, we endeavour to grow out of our problems rather than face them directly. With soaring technical capacity, there were lots of reasons to hope for having more, up until we started to seriously confront planetary limitations. These limits have repeatedly been pushed back by technical innovations, often inspired by the profitability of implementing the new technology. So effective have been the technical fixes that many in the economics profession truly believe that we will always be able to overcome limitations through innovation and growth. This article of faith is among the greatest obstacles to finding an enduring balance with the life processes of our planet.

With these observations, we will now move on to the more complex aspects of our economic system and the problems that have evolved with its success. They include the disadvantages that arise as the system grows beyond comprehension, the temptations of power that have possessed some of those faced with the opportunity to tap into large scale money flows, and the ultimate problem of how to resolve a "Global Monopoly Game" that has essentially been won.

6
Magnitude and Abstraction: When We Grow Very Large

Size and Scale

A tale is told about the invention of the game of chess. It was in Persia and so grateful was the King for the wonderful game, that he offered the inventor anything in his kingdom as a reward. The inventor asked for one grain of wheat for the first square on the chess board, two grains for the second, four for the third, eight, sixteen and so on, doubling for each square. The King was amazed to discover that this seemingly modest request would, through the wonder of exponential growth, have cost him his entire kingdom. The wheat, for the last square alone, would have filled a train of boxcars wrapping around the Earth at the equator 25 times.

Both the human population and our economic activity have been growing exponentially for centuries. It is little wonder that we have come to stretch the Earth's ability to support us. The magnitude of our presence is at once testimony to our extraordinary success and a harbinger of danger.

For over 30 years we have heard news about environmental limitations, yet our political and economic leaders seem only able to imagine solving problems by making agreements and changing laws in order to accommodate further growth.

There are ways to maintain mutual provision that do not undermine the foundations upon which they operate. These are the topics of the Economic Solutions Chapters 11, 12 and 13. The purpose of this chapter, however, is to look at how faithful application of the fundamental principles described in the last chapter, have transformed the world.

In our current world, the cultural factors that form the character of society and influence who our children will become, are very different from what they were when the present era emerged from feudalism. Technical activity dominates our experience, obscuring our view of the natural world. That same technical activity has grown to a size capable of disturbing the balance between humans and other living things. The main participants in the economic process are no longer individuals and small firms responding to market signals in the dance of mutual provision. Instead, gigantic corporations operate around the globe with a power greater than that of most nations. These entities impel markets to serve their interests. With these changes, the fundamental principles of economics, unchanged though they may be in expression, acquire new attributes and have different effects in terms of the well-being of the human family.

Development

Development has been the name of the game for centuries. Ever larger productive operations have produced economies of scale that greatly reduce the cost of goods. Along the way development has routinely freed up workers for new and expanding enterprises. The promotion of self-interest, mechanization, investment, mass production, sales, profit and reinvestment have expanded capital exponentially.

With the growth in capital and the availability of workers, the number and size of new enterprises have grown. Innovations that improve productivity can so reward the inventors as to launch them into the stratosphere of riches. While most new inventions today are owned by large corporations, the stories of the few individuals who are able to profit from their creations are spread far and wide, inspiring tens of thousands of bright minds to occupy themselves looking for ways to further increase production and thereby make their fortunes.

With the harnessing of fossil energy and electricity, motors could be attached to any sort of machine. Networks of factories are dedicated to the production of motors that, as fast as they are made, are hooked up to machines to further expand production, or to enable the consumption of energy in the provision of services, great and small. The flow of fuel into mechanized systems has increased steadily ever since machine technology became available. At the turn of the millennium, global consumption of oil alone exceeded 80 million barrels a day — over 84 million as we prepare to go to press — a rate at which, if drawn solely from Kuwait's oil reserves (over which the Gulf War was fought in 1991) would have, within four years, exhausted that source. The vast oil reserves of Iraq could only feed the collective global demand for three-and-a-half to ten years, depending on whose reserve estimates are accurate. For a short while, in the early 1970s, overall demand diminished as the world responded to the first "oil crisis." For that brief period only, the finite nature of fossil-fuel reserves was legitimized in the public consciousness.

Parallel to mechanization has been the emergence of modern science. Its intense, deliberate search into every corner of the material world for clues about how things work has enabled many of those aspects to be turned to human service. Science has fed the steady flow of innovation.

In the realm of public health, the discovery of germs and how to avoid them, followed by massive public spending on sewer and water systems, prevented millions of premature deaths. The discovery of antibiotics and the basics of nutrition extended human life. As industrial production increased, infant mortality dropped and the human population began to rise rapidly. Our population had risen by several billion before anyone even thought of balancing the widespread practice of death control with birth control. Even today, powerful forces block the stabilization of population, informed as they are by fundamentals from an earlier age when the Earth was practically empty of humans, a large portion of children died before the age of five, and elders were dependent on their descendants for the help they needed in their declining years. The human presence today is very different than it was in Adam Smith's day.

Abstraction

One need only remember scenes from Alice in Wonderland to know that the scale from which one looks at something can make a huge difference in how it appears. To a human, a mowed lawn is easy to walk across, but, for a creature the size of an ant, the same lawn would seem like a dense forest. Whereas the human would see the broad overview of the territory where the lawn was located, the ant would be aware of countless fine details in its immediate vicinity. The difference is significant.

One summer day, I was cutting back the plants around my garden with a scythe. A scythe is a three-foot blade on a long handle that will cut down a large swath of plants with each swing. It was invented hundreds of years ago to extend a person's reach so they didn't have to bend over to cut hay or grain crops. That tool removed me sufficiently from my work that I was unable to save a nest of song birds in a comfrey plant. By the time I saw the nest, the swing was already underway. It sliced through the nest, destroyed the eggs, and assured that there would be more bugs and less bird song in the months to come.

If one is working with a mechanically powered machine, the thoroughness with which one surveys the larger territory being worked is further diminished. The time it takes for reflexes to activate mechanical controls and for the machine then to change course is longer so the whole operation is less likely to respond to unexpected changes.

Automated machinery removes us one step further. Unless a system is specifically programmed to look out for, and respond to, particular variations in its course of activity, it has no sensitivity to potential impacts. Bottom draggers, large-scale fishing operations that draw fishing nets along the ocean floor, are notorious for disrupting various habitats there, and with them the life processes of bottom dwellers and other species that depend on them.

When the work of mechanized enterprises are owned and directed by people who neither live in the area nor work the equipment, sensitivity to unfolding circumstances is even further diminished. Many consequences are practically invisible to decision-makers.

In today's thoroughly industrialized world, there are networks of factories filled with automated and semi-automated production machinery. With various levels of detachment, these systems are supplied with raw materials via complex networks of other organizations directing resource extraction, processing and transportation equipment.

As the contemporary economic process unfolds in the manner inherent in the presently accepted formula of perpetual expansion, organizations that are already unimaginably big are merging with others as large as themselves, producing entities of ever greater proportions. Control of the collective activity of the global industrial process is directed by fewer and fewer people, further and further removed from the effects that their decisions have on the lives of people and on the natural world. The impacts that those decisions have are enormous.

As corporate entities get bigger, there is little place for input from employees, and decisions are made with less consideration for individuals. Productivity is high, so the number of jobs is lower. With lots of workers to choose from, most individuals are expendable. Thousands can be cut loose and replaced by others who will work for less, or their jobs may be replaced entirely by further automation, leaving only a handful of workers to maintain the equipment. As individuals in a large corporation, most workers are as insignificant as the tiny cells that make up one's fingers or toes. In some ways they are less significant. Our cells are integrated with our whole selves by a nervous system that provides an open line of communication, and the individual cells are assured basic support in all but the most life threatening circumstances.

All is not downhill with complexity. While we humans are further removed from our circumstances than single-celled creatures, we have more capabilities with which to assess what we notice and a great many more options in the ways we might react. Large organizations are also capable of bringing additional capabilities to bear in the sensing and assessment of what they are doing, if they so choose. Unfortunately, the present goal, focussed almost exclusively on accelerating economic expansion, seldom includes increasing sensitivity to impacts. As a civilization, at present, we have little empathy for the natural world, or even for our own future.

All entities need sense organs. Many modern productive enterprises have large numbers of intricate sensors testing their internal metabolism and making adjustments to maintain appropriate temperatures, thickness, rates of flow, conductivity and so on, depending on the processes they use and products they make. When it comes to their participation in the greater metabolism of society and the environment, however, custom has it that all they have to account for are income and expenses. Money in and money out are all that matter if their only external focus is monetary gain. This narrow view has more in common with single-celled organisms than with the humans who keep the accounts. In addition to being able to count money, humans are sensitive to light, sound, temperature, taste, motion and, for those of a clear heart and open mind, character, beauty, justice and sustainability. Hope would grow from engaging these sensitivities in corporate life.

The accounting systems used today are far from the end of their evolutionary potential. Some corporations are pioneering environmental accounting with an eye to increasing natural resource and energy efficiency, as well as on reducing waste. The objective is still profitability, but the expanding focus promises increased sensitivity to matters critical to long-term well-being.

Corporate sensitivity evolves quickly when required to by law. Emissions of pollution into the air or water are now regulated in many places. Under such conditions, great ingenuity has been demonstrated as producers build in measuring processes and adjust their production techniques to operate within regulations.

While regulations, or market-based equivalents such as emissions trading, can be effective at encouraging corporate sensitivity, they are indirect. The corporate entities, for the most part, are still looking with only one sense and that sense sees only money. Balancing the costs of complying with regulations against the costs of paying fines, buying permits or relocating the operation where regulations don't apply, misses the point. Clean air and water are needed by everything that lives, from fish and trees to the children of the most powerful financial autocrat.

A number of factors contribute to the tendency for corporate entities not to expand their sensitivities. On the moral level is the fundamentalist belief that the invisible hand maximizes well-being through market activity. If money is being made, the greater good is being served and, if there is a problem, the market will send the necessary signals. Upon these justifications, corporate culture has narrowly defined its purpose to be the maximization of return to shareholders. Through common law — law as interpreted by judges — the directors of corporations have "fiduciary duty," meaning they are obliged, by law, to look after the financial interests of shareholders. If they do not, they can be sued. On another flank, if they do not maximize the potential of the company to make money, they face the possibility of a hostile takeover by people who will focus on maximizing profit.

With these considerations, it is not surprising that if someone on the corporate ladder has a conscience for values that go beyond the financial bottom line, they will, almost surely, be detected and passed over when promotions are made. Those already in decision-making positions would correctly suspect that such a person would dilute the singleness of purpose that is the tradition.

In contrast, some companies, such as the Body Shop and Interface Flooring, have Chief Executive Officers who have either built the companies up from the start with a broader perspective in mind, or have had a revelation when they were already at the top. These are excellent examples of companies sensitive to the impacts they make. Their success demonstrates public appreciation of social and environmental values.

Ethical investment is a possible vehicle for engaging corporate sensitivity. Citizens with social and environmental values can put their savings into funds that screen companies for signs of applied environmental and social conscience. It's a start. Investment capital is a lure that is visible to conventional profit-oriented companies and can motivate them towards evolving their sensitivity. Dangling ethical funds in the corporate sea catches the attention of some. The more capital invested through such schemes, the better the bait and the greater the influence.

The Fallacy of Misplaced Concreteness

In Adam Smith's time, the common good may, indeed, have been served by making money. If a person or company could profit through open markets, it was because its product was wanted. The market made sure that quality products were offered at the lowest price for which they could be produced. Smith correctly observed that markets were only effective as long as no single actor, or association of actors, had enough power to influence prices by themselves. Today, there are many players in the economy that can, and do, distort prices, ending the openness of markets and eliminating their efficiency. Furthermore, it is not clear whether profits made through intense, persuasive advertising, or through speculative trading of currencies and abstract financial assets, leave societies better off or worse.

The discipline of economics evolved as a means to analyse what was happening in our widespread and diverse system of mutual provision. Economics has developed predictive methodologies that have proven to be a powerful tool for maximizing monetary gain. It is also used extensively to justify the expansion of productivity and increasing profits. In its quest to claim status as a science with accurate predictive ability, however, economics has created, what some call, a fallacy of misplaced concreteness.

Herman Daly and John Cobb describe this problem in great detail in the opening chapters of *For the Common Good*. Daly and Cobb trace the history of modern science in the West, pointing out that physics was the model because of the reliable way in which inanimate matter adhered to observed "laws." Once the laws of physics are understood and the nature of the component substances and forces quantified, it is possible, through mathematics, to make accurate predictions of what will happen under various conditions. This predictive quality is immensely useful in designing and producing things that provide wonderful new opportunities for people.

A gram of a particular carbon fuel will always produce the same amount of heat when it burns (given similar conditions of ventilation, background temperature, etc.). The relationship can be traced to the number and strength of the energy bonds between atoms and all is very predictable. However, in the biological sciences, predictable cause and effect relationships are common, but not always reliable. Given certain conditions, most creatures will respond in predictable ways. The "law of the minimum" and the "law of tolerance" mentioned earlier, provide useful ways of looking at biological interactions. There are, however, enough anomalies that in biology "laws" are understood to be approximations.

If certainty is compromised in the biological sciences, it is almost nonexistent in the social sciences. When large numbers of people are involved, polling firms can determine what people's preferences are, "19 times out of 20." Such information is then used to make educated guesses about future interests. This is "soft" science. "Hard" science is much more certain about what it studies. Nevertheless, humans are a part of the world, complete with our unpredictable eccentricities. It is important to try to understand what we are about. Nutrition, health care, psychology, and communications are all disciplines that have expanded our understanding of ourselves, enabling us to plan and develop ways of being that improve our lot. The advertising industry applies some findings of social science very profitably, but occasionally their campaigns fail. As individuals, people can act as they will, regardless of what is expected. It is a good thing too. Within our capacity for unexpected actions lies hope for the future.

Two hundred years ago, most of the decisions about what to produce were the result of personal observations about what was in short supply and, consequently, was generating a price high enough to warrant developing a business to supply the market. Today these observations are refined to a "science."

Among the things that economic "science" assumes about people are one, that we care only about our personal self-interests, and two, that we will always want more. With the human character so defined, conventional economics goes on to assume that the receipts from transactions — how much people actually pay for things — are indisputable evidence of what people value and how much they value them. Other factors — the environment, non-paid work, community bonds, non-commercial entertainment and other things for which no hard data exists — are assumed to be of no value and perhaps ignored. Working from these assumptions, formulas are created to analyse supply and demand, to determine what ought to be produced, how much to produce, and what prices might be expected for producing those things.

The reputation that the economics profession ascribes to itself, as a "hard science" with accurate predictive power, is more the product of its ability to increase the wealth and power of those who apply it, than to its effectiveness at assessing the well-being of our system of mutual provision. Indeed, one might think that the purpose of economics is to enable those with money to make more money, rather than to track the most efficient way to manage resources for the common good. Because there is more involved in mutual provision than just what is paid for, the claim to concreteness by economics is misplaced. (Despite the "scientific" rhetoric, at universities economics is taught in the Faculty of Arts not Science.)

Daly and Cobb tell of early economists who were inspired by the ideal of hard science. In their search for "laws" that could be applied to understand and work with the market, they abstracted the human experience and disregarded elements that did not fit neatly into their formulas. Other economists expressed concern about the direction economics was taking. As far back as 1827, Swiss economist J. C. L. Simonde de Sismondi wrote: "Humanity should be on guard against all generalization of ideas that causes us to lose sight of the facts, and above all against the error of identifying the public good with wealth, abstracted from the sufferings of the human beings who created it."

Such warnings are still being ignored. The mainstream of the economics profession aimed to refine human behaviour into formulas as concise as those Isaac Newton developed to predict the movement of the planets. In so doing, facts and circumstances that cannot be resolved into clear numbers have been disregarded. By assuming that the only things of value are those for which people pay directly with money, the process fails us.

Externalities

Other things, like natural resources, which are taken from nature without paying, and pollution, which is put into the environment without a fee to correct the damage, are called "externalities." The impacts of these things on the natural world, on people alive today and on those who will be alive in the future, are simply ignored, as are the social consequences of the externalities associated with low wages, layoffs, plant closures, reliance on long-distance transportation and other economic decisions. As social and environmental problems become more and more serious, deficiencies in the present economic system are increasingly apparent.

Among the social payouts of doing business are the wages and benefits that workers receive. These are specific expenses that are paid and accounted for by economists. However, if profits are increased by holding down wages, eliminating jobs or moving entire operations to where wages are lower or environmental regulations less stringent, there are social costs incurred that do not have to be paid or accounted for by the company making the decisions. The stress arising from inadequate income has well documented health effects, and aggravates other social problems. The costs that producers avoid are eventually paid, either through the pain and chaos of unattended problems, or through social programs. With mounting expenses in health care, social services, police, judicial and correctional costs, municipal budgets can become stressed. This can result in increased taxes and reduced services that compounds difficulties and spreads physical and emotional distress through whole communities.

Because these costs are not paid by the company whose decisions brought them on, they are not accounted for and, therefore, are not included in the price of the goods involved. This is a market failure that is exported around the world through "Free Trade" regimes. Efforts by any producer to include external costs would make their products more expensive and therefore less competitive. The result is a "race to the bottom" as producers manipulate circumstances in order to pay the lowest wages and externalize as many costs as they can.

The market cannot produce the result of efficiently allocating resources to maximize benefits if prices don't represent all the costs of production. When the externalized costs are paid by people who do not receive the benefits of the products, those people are subsidizing the production and consumption of those products. There is then no financial inspiration for customers to consider less destructive products or for companies to improve performance. If, on the other hand, companies had to pay external costs, the price consumers pay for those goods would increase. Along with the economic justice of people paying all the costs of the products they enjoy, producers would be inspired to look at their operations with increased sensitivity to social and environmental impacts.

Local economies are much more likely to pay attention to external impacts of production, since the people involved have to live with the consequences of their activities. In the 1930s, the Irish were tired of seeing large portions of their population emigrate for lack of work. Looking toward self-sufficiency, they elected a government that promised to put them to work making things that Ireland needed. This goal was criticized by orthodox economists; maximizing monetary return was the proper way to run an economy. In April 1933, John Maynard Keynes gave a lecture at University College in Dublin praising Ireland's bold experiment. Keynes was, perhaps, the most influential economist of the 20th century. Richard Douthwaite notes in his book, *The Growth Illusion,* that Keynes "attacked the paying of too much attention to what today we would call the 'bottom line'." Douthwaite goes on to quote from Keynes' Dublin lecture:

> *This whole conduct of life was made into a sort of parody of an accountant s nightmare. Instead of using their vastly increased material and technical resources to build a wonder-city they built slums, and they thought it right and proper to build slums because slums, on the test of private enterprise, "paid," whereas a wonder-city would, they thought, have been an act of foolish extravagance which would, in the imbecile idiom of the financial fashion, have"mortgaged the future"; though how the construction today of great and glorious works can impoverish the future, no man can see until his mind is beset by* **false analogies from an irrelevant accountancy**... *The nation as a whole will assuredly be richer if unemployed men and machines are used to build much needed houses than if they are supported in idleness.*
>
> *The same rule of self-destructive financial calculation governs every walk of life. We destroy the beauty of the countryside because the unappropriated splendors of the countryside have no economic value ... London is one of the richest cities in the history of civilization but it cannot afford the highest standard of achievement of which its own living citizens are capable because they do not"pay."*

When we discuss monetary systems further on, we will look at what Keynes proposed to solve the economic crisis of the 1930s.

Abstract Growth

If you want to be a designer, you have to make up your mind as to whether you want to make sense or make money.

Victor Papanek, *Design for the Real World*

Along with dismissing environmental and social contributions and consequences, illusions are nurtured in economics by the extensive use of mathematics to explain economic processes. By looking at numbers without keeping an eye on the things they represent, a veil separates the theoreticians from society. Numbers are able to follow mathematical formulas and, among other things, they can grow forever. It is then assumed that economic activity can also grow forever. With tongue in cheek, Daly and Cobb make the observation that, "if money balances can grow forever at compound interest, then so can real GNP, and so can pigs and cars and hair cuts." Aiming for the impossible goal of perpetual exponential expansion of economic activity is leading us into extreme danger.

However, striving for perpetual economic expansion is just one example of where misplaced concreteness is leading us astray. When theories are based on abstractions, further abstractions can result. The expanding spiral of ideology can produce amazing results.

Daly and Cobb quote two contemporary economists. George Gilder writes:

"The United States must overcome the materialistic fallacy: the illusion that resources and capital are essentially things, which can run out, rather than products of the human will and imagination which in freedom are inexhaustible."

And then to make his point as clearly as possible, Gilder adds: "Because economies are governed by thoughts, they reflect not the laws of matter but the laws of mind."

Julian Simon tops that by saying, "You see in the end copper and oil come out of our minds. That's really where they are."

The logic is that, without the application of human ingenuity, creativity and will, copper and oil would never come out of the ground, or be put to any use practical to humans. While this is true, it does not follow that our minds create the substances that our creativity and efforts draw out.

Aleister Crowley, who has written extensively on the subject, describes magic as "causing things to happen in accordance with one's will." Making a sandwich is magic in that the creative process starts in the imagination. Once there is a mental image, we can assemble the necessary ingredients and process them in the ways necessary to make, Shazam! a sandwich. The economic system overflows with such magic on enormous scales. For anyone not familiar with the techniques involved in collecting, processing, assembling and distributing things, a great deal of awe and wonder is inspired. Given our capacity for denial and self-deception, it is not hard to see how the thought that oil and copper are products of our minds might be accepted to justify personal interests. According to Daly and Cobb, Gilder and Simon "are very influential in Washington."

The sentiments of Gilder and Simon are reflected in hopeful reports that we are using less materials and energy to achieve each unit of productive output. This is a good thing and should be encouraged, but it is premature to celebrate the trend as a solution to our problems with diminishing resources and pollution. Such efficiency innovations have only slowed the rate at which material consumption is expanding. They have not eliminated the exponential expansion of our annual impacts, let alone eased the cumulative effects of persistently adding the present year's impacts to that remaining from all previous years. To date, the only time resource consumption has diminished overall is when economies have collapsed. Collapsing economies is a final solution we should be trying to avoid by improving how we view the human project.

A Problem with Supply and Demand Setting Prices

The economics profession is pleased with its accomplishments. Sitting at the right hand of wealth and power is bound to instill confidence and pride. Again quoting Daly and Cobb: "Such elaborate and beautiful logical structures heighten the tendency to prize theory over fact and to reinterpret fact to fit theory."

Through my involvement with the promotion of expanded measures of well-being here in Canada, I had the opportunity to sit in on some meetings of a government sponsored program with a mandate to develop indicators of environmental well-being. The meetings were co-chaired by true believers in economic convention. I was intrigued by how they saw the world.

The way in which supply and demand determine prices is central to the market faith. One of the co-chairs, a practising economist, had written a paper reassuring those who were concerned about resource supplies that the market was fully able to take care of any such problems and that, indeed, the signals from the market indicated that all was well. His paper was peer-reviewed and published in the reputable *Resource Policy Journal.*

Near the beginning of the paper was a reference to the Club of Rome's 1972 publication *Limits to Growth.* In that report there were strong warnings about natural resource limitations, how we were approaching them at accelerating speed and how decision-makers ought to bear this information in mind when planning and making decisions.

After referring to that report, the *Resource Policy Journal* article presented two assumptions:
  a) If scarcity is reflected in high prices, raw materials have become less scarce.
  b) If scarcity is reflected in meagre production, we are driven to the same opposite conclusion; that production had accelerated.

The authors don't definitively say that these assumptions are accurate, but their acceptance is implicit throughout the article.

The first assumption is based on the accepted relationship of supply to demand. As the supply of something falls behind demand, people are willing to pay more to have some of what is available. The second assumption is based on the notion that the less there is of something, the smaller the volume that will be produced. Since the volume of many basic commodities arriving on the international market has increased steadily since the Club of Rome's report, and since the price paid for many of those commodities has fallen during the same period, using these assumptions, the article concludes that the *Limits to Growth* was fundamentally mistaken.

After reading the article, I was amazed that the applied logic of supply, demand and price could create such an illusion in this obviously intelligent person. As I described earlier, the basic interaction of supply and demand in open markets provides an enormous benefit. Even so, some of the conclusions that economic theory draws from those price signals call for more detailed investigation.

In the Fraser Institute's 1999 *Critical Issues Bulletin on Environmental Indicators,* these same assumptions are taken to their logical conclusion. True belief is revealed in the quote, "energy resources are not being depleted." At the time, the price of oil had remained relatively constant, in inflation-adjusted terms, for decades. It follows, in the above line of reasoning, that there has been no change in the amount of oil available. With receipts in existence for tens of millions of barrels of oil every day (over 84 million each day at present) this claim contradicts basic mathematics. The result of subtracting any amount from even a very large number, results in a reduction of the number.

The precepts of supply and demand are misleading in this context. It is likely, since our industrial economic structure has grown in lockstep with oil consumption, that the value of our money is determined by the availability of oil, rather than the availability of oil being revealed by its price. When comparing the evidence of basic mathematics with a faithful application of economic precepts, I am inclined to accept the mathematical conclusion that oil reserves are indeed being depleted.

The following biological model explains the situation of resource draw-down in a way that the two economic precepts cannot. Consider a slice of bread with a spot of mold growing on it. Under warm, moist circumstances the mold will grow to cover and ultimately consume the entire slice. As its growth progresses, it sinks "roots" into the bread to absorb the carbohydrates and other nutrients needed to feed its growth. Other structures transport the nutrients to where they are needed. With the bread mold, the greatest rate of resource extraction is achieved just before the supply of the resource is exhausted.

The metabolization of carbohydrates and the controlled combustion of fossil-fuels are practically identical. Our oil wells and pipelines; mines, crops and transportation systems supply hydrocarbons and other resources to human culture very much like the structures of the bread mold serve its own culture. Could it be that what we presently call economic growth is synonymous with accelerating decay? If so, the future of civilization depends on our recognizing information outside the normal perspective of established economic theory.

The increased availability of commodities that is evidenced in steady or falling prices, results from our expanded capacity to extract these resources worldwide. The explosion of commodity production that followed the oil price increases of the 1970s is detailed further on. In brief, the petroleum exporting countries had a great deal of money to invest. Numerous countries borrowed that money to develop their capacity to bring basic commodities to market, only to discover when they got there that there were many other new producers, and that they were all in competition with each other. The market was flooded with their product and prices fell. It wasn't because there was more of the commodities overall, it was because the same natural resources that had always been around were being exploited faster than ever before.

Much has changed from when the precepts of classical economics were identified. Relatively small, local businesses have been replaced, to a large extent, by enormous international enterprises. The power of people and animals has been augmented by billions of motors and engines powered by inanimate energy. A world with boundless new frontiers has filled up to the point where people are found in great numbers practically everywhere. Economic activity has evolved from an almost exclusive focus on the direct provision of human needs — food, housing, clothes and tools — to where, by far, the greatest volume of economic exchanges involve abstract financial trading in currencies, bonds, stocks and derivatives. The disproportionate size of abstract finance has shifted the focus of economic policy away from securing human needs, while the expansion of our population and material impacts require, more than ever, that we focus on material resources and planetary life-supporting systems.

The economic precepts that were practically sound at the time of their conception are fast losing their relevance. As in the supply, demand and price example above, where the precepts conclude that we need not worry about natural resource depletion, applied theory can give an opposite message from what we need to understand to make effective decisions. Given the larger picture, we can conclude that economics as presently practised is short-sighted. It sees little beyond the immediate present and is dangerously inadequate when it comes to helping the human family chart its course into the future.

Substitution

Substitution is another precept mentioned in the *Resource Policy Journal* article on supply and demand. It aims to further reassure us that there is nothing to worry about regarding natural resource supplies. Substitution is where, when resources become scarce and prices rise, a substitute for the resource is found. Tin was used for making cans at one time, but as a relatively scarce resource, it came to be substituted for by zinc plating on steel and, more recently, by a plastic coating inside the cans. Fibre optic cables made of silicone now replace copper in some applications for transmitting communications signals. Silicon is more abundant than copper and it can provide more and better signals. Such cases of substitution are abundant. They are testimony to the ingenuity of humankind. However, as we navigate our way into the future, the faith that substitution will always solve problems of resource supply could be disastrous.

The dangers arising from the assumption of substitutability are worrisome in several regards. Of particular note is when it comes to substituting people with money. Machines are frequently bought to substitute for labour. How much money does it take to replace a worker? How much money would you trade for your spouse or your child? While this may seem extreme, in the end, every person replaced by financial capital is the child, spouse or parent of someone.

Replacing people with machines depreciates more than the lives of those who lose their jobs. The substitution is often made when calculations suggest that it is less expensive to buy a machine than to continue paying a person. The conversion has the effect of depreciating the value of the work of everyone doing similar jobs. The lower rate for which a machine can do the job sets a competitive wage in the same way that workers willing to work for less would. Wage rates fall, or more jobs are lost. In addition, as automation continues, the money being paid for work is redirected away from workers and back to those providing capital, further increasing the divide between rich and poor.

The theory supporting the substitution of people with machines is that of "development," where machines liberate people from menial tasks, enabling them to find more fulfilling work in other jobs. As noted earlier, this theory has worked, particularly in circumstances where the culture involved was still struggling to provide for basic needs. On the other hand (in recent times) there are large numbers of cases where replacing people with machines has led to personal tragedy for workers, their families and, sometimes, whole communities.

On another front, no matter how sophisticated our technology becomes, there will never be substitutes for nitrogen, potassium, phosphorus or any of the other elements that constitute nutrition. The building blocks of physical life are common to all creatures and are not likely to change. Basic nutritional elements are crucial. It is irresponsible to assume that, in the long-term, there can be an effective substitute for agricultural fertility.

Naturally occurring nitrogen, potassium and phosphorus have been wasted because we are slow to grasp full-cycle nutrient management. Manufactured fertilizers have substituted for natural fertility, but only with considerable increase in the energy required to produce them. Substitutions dependent on increased energy use are common and subject to the problem of diminishing energy supply. It is assumed that we can substitute alternative sources of energy (solar, wind, tidal) for the dwindling reserves of fossil-fuels. Such substitution is possible to an extent, but there is little evidence suggesting we could meet current demand, let alone produce additional volumes, to solve every other shortage for which additional energy might be used to manufacture substitutes. The maintenance of the processes by which our essential nutrition is assured, including the energy systems they depend on, should be the focus of active, intelligent attention rather than abstract calculations based on economic theory. Generalizations are where the danger lies. It is worth paying attention to what is actually going on.

Elasticity of Demand

I have long been amazed that all products are lumped together in the one category of things for sale. It seems to me that there is a critical difference between things that are essential for living, and everything else. There is an indirect recognition of this when economists talk about "elasticity of demand." Potential customers balance what items are worth to them, compared to the prices asked. When an item is not necessary, people lose interest in the item as the price goes up. Things that people are willing to do without, after a relatively small price increase, are said to have an elastic demand — demand goes down quickly as prices rise. It is very different with essentials. If a person does not have anything to eat, they will pay whatever they have to get food. This is inelastic demand. While food has a low elasticity, electric toothbrushes are not so difficult to do without.

Matters affecting food, shelter, education and health care should not be left to the same automatic and speculative processes that govern the supplies of hair dye, computer games and whatever the latest gadget is, "as seen on TV."

Problems With Our Market Economy

Socialism collapsed because it did not allow prices to tell the economic truth. Capitalism may collapse because it does not allow prices to tell the ecological truth.

> Oystein Dahle, former Exxon VP
> For Norway and the North Sea

Civilization has flourished and become something quite different from what it was in the early days of market capitalism. Human impacts on the natural world have multiplied many times over, and the methods by which we observe and interpret our presence have become abstract and removed from the billions of actions that daily shape our world. Nevertheless, the economic theories derived from observations made two centuries ago have changed very little. The faith remains that if something makes money, it is good.

With our changed circumstances, the market system is failing on numerous fronts. Problems with resource supplies and pollution are scarcely noticed. People without money, other living things and future generations are disregarded. Land, money and labour, upon which everyone's well-being depends, are treated like poker chips in a gambling hall. Short-term self-interest has grown out of proportion. The sort of competition between producers, upon which the market system depends in order to best serve the common good, has practically disappeared in many sectors. What it means to be efficient has changed and the institutions of interest, money and economic growth have taken on new qualities. These changes bring huge repercussions and require a fresh approach to how we structure our mutual provision.

7
Where Value is Neglected

In *The Green Economy,* Michael Jacobs describes the "invisible elbow." The "invisible hand" turns individual self-interest to the service of society through market activity. The invisible elbow represents other aspects of the market that do not serve the common good. Jacobs chose the image of the elbow because elbows "are sometimes used to push people aside in the desire to get ahead. But more often elbows are not used deliberately at all; they knock things over inadvertently."

Being damaged are those things that are invisible to economic observation because they do not have prices. People following their self-interest will often waste resources and pollute, fully aware, or blissfully unaware, of the damage they are causing. They can even rationalize that personal benefit outweighs the costs. The benefits are theirs and the costs fall to others, presently or in the future.

The Tragedy of the Commons

The "tragedy of the commons" was popularized by Garrett Hardin in his 1968 book by that name. The classic example is from 16th century England where peasants worked land belonging to the hereditary landowners. Each family had a plot for growing crops and they had land in common on which to graze livestock. The commons, where the animals grazed, had a carrying capacity capable of supporting a certain number of animals. When that many animals were present, the scene was set for the tragedy to unfold.

Some individual would get an additional animal and turn it out to graze on the commons. None of the animals then got quite as much grass as it needed, but the individual with the extra grazer got the entire benefit of that animal, while the disadvantage of the overgrazing was spread among everyone with animals on the commons. With advantage to be gained personally and disadvantages shared among many, others were tempted to increase their well-being by grazing extra animals. The tragedy was overgrazing, which leaves pastures vulnerable to erosion. With the loss of topsoil, the land could no longer produce as much for animals to eat and, even with a return to responsible management, the commons could not support as many animals as it had before.

The commons of our era are things of common benefit for which there are no sales slips to identify their value and thereby make it possible to work them into economic calculations. They are called externalities because they are external to accounts. Among the things ignored are natural resource stocks and the effects of pollution.

Economics is Three-fifths of Ecology

Economics =   *Materials / Processing / Distribution*
_____
Ecology = *Natural Resources / Materials / Processing / Distribution / Waste*

Nowhere is the fallacy of misplaced concreteness clearer than where economics meets ecology. It will also be one of the easiest places to correct the system once the will emerges to return it to health.

Throughout the billions of years that life has existed, the waste from every life form has provided nourishment for others. With minor, localized exceptions, human beings did not break this pattern until the industrial revolution. Today, we disrupt it enormously, but traditional economic practices have yet to catch on.

The evolution that modern accounting must accomplish can easily be remembered with the formula, "economics is only three-fifths of ecology." Economics is human ecology except that, at present, it assumes that natural resources and waste absorption are unlimited.

To the extent that conventional economics keeps accounts, human activity can be divided into three basic steps: assembling materials, processing and distribution.

1) Assembly of materials:
   Locating or gathering raw materials, for example, soil and seed, metallic rocks and energy or, information and images.
2) Processing the assembled materials:
   Planting, cultivation and harvesting, extracting metal from the ore and forming it into useful items, or organizing information into a coherent, useful or entertaining format.
3) Distribution of the end product:
   Getting the produce, manufactured goods, or the reports, films or whatever has been produced, to people and places where they can be traded for use and appreciation.

In a complex economy, the raw material for one economic activity is often the product of one or several other activities. However, the three steps are basic to them all.

In the "economy of nature," these same three steps are followed. Plants and animals gather nutrients, process (digest) them into useful forms, and distribute them to organs and limbs for use in their growth and activity. Sometimes, creatures even gather materials and form them into "artifacts" for specific purposes, such as nests and honeycombs.

In nature, these steps of assembling materials, processing and distribution are accompanied by two further considerations: the natural resource base and waste absorption. In the human economy, with the exception of minimal waste disposal costs, and the mechanical costs of resource extraction, few fees are paid for these additional considerations and, therefore, they receive little attention. They are the subjects of the "law of the minimum" and the "law of tolerance." In today's circumstances, it is a huge mistake not to account for the whole process.

If Mother Nature were to present invoices for resources extracted and wastes absorbed, conventional economic accounting would help keep human activity in balance with the rest of the natural world. Unfortunately, the only notice nature gives on outstanding accounts, is foreclosure. Species that consistently overstep ecological bounds simply disappear. To avoid this drastic result, we have to extend our own accounting systems to include considerations of waste and resource supplies. Consistent recognition of these bounds through accounting requirements would put all businesses in the same boat. The competitive edge would fall to those who could find ways of producing their goods and services with minimal pollution or resource depletion. This would contribute far more to our overall well-being than the present situation where the competitive advantage often goes to those who take the least responsibility.

It's not just the natural cycling of life substances that is overlooked by the present system. Many people and other living things also fall through the cracks.

Overlooking the Poor

The service provided by the market system — to organize human activity for the common good — depends on people having money with which to cast their "economic votes," as it were. The needs of people with little or no money are invisible. This includes today's poor, people in less developed countries whose mutual provision is not centred around internationally tradable currency, and the unborn descendants of everyone, rich and poor alike.

The unmet needs of today's poor are not inconsequential to the well-being of the whole. Short of desperation, poverty can lead to deteriorating health, contagion and stress on health care systems. The depressed living conditions of people without means can sour the overall mood of society, or instill debilitating insensitivity. Those who fortify their good fortune by denying this market failure, and block their perception so that they can manage not to care, are diminished thereby. When need becomes desperate in urban areas, the repercussions can affect more than just the disadvantaged. Minimal means cause people to resort to low quality goods and the consequent waste. In rural societies, disenfranchised people often have no choice but to accelerate ecological deterioration by clearing forests and cultivating fragile lands in the effort to grow food for their families.

"A rising tide lifts all boats" is the explanation given for how economic growth will deal with the plight of the poor. Expand the amount of wealth in society and it will "trickle down" to provide for everyone. Unfortunately, the continued growth of the economy is being accomplished, in part, by tightening up corporate activity so that as little as possible leaks out to trickle down. The proportion of corporate earnings that goes to directors and shareholders is rising rapidly, but a growing percentage of the workforce has less to take home today than they did a decade ago.

A century ago, the legendary financier, J. P. Morgan stated that a company's top executives should not make more than 20 times as much as their lowest paid worker. Today, in the U.S., the average CEO makes over 400 times the income of the average worker. Increasing numbers of people are paid less than a "living wage." That is, their pay for full-time work is less than what is needed to cover the costs of living. While the Dow Jones Industrial Average advanced 300% between 1987 and 1997, the average hourly wage in the U.S. dropped by 7%. In Canada, Statistics Canada reports that young couples with children experienced a 30% drop in their wealth between 1984 and 1999 while the top 10% of families saw theirs increase 35% over the same period.

As for the fate of the poorer nations, the Northern banks and financial institutions have extracted several times as much money from southern countries through interest payments than has been loaned to them or given as aid. It is hard to trust the sincerity of the rich world's interest in "raising all boats" when it drives the process by which terms of trade are determined so as to advance its own interests while ignoring the interests of those without wealth.

Justice would require structuring the rules of the economic game so as to provide equal opportunities for everyone. Some argue that terms of trade should favour the less advantaged in order to incline the world toward equilibrium. It is no secret that wealthy interests use the power that comes with wealth to increase their advantage. They lobby for, and get, lower taxes, subsidies to their businesses, government contracts, bailouts when their speculative ventures run amiss, and influence of various sorts over political decision-making.

Clever arguments abound about how, if wealthy interests are not provided with more advantages, there will be dire consequences for employees, depositors or the entire economy. The power of those interests is sufficient to make the rest of the world hostage to their demands. They are capable and willing to precipitate the dire consequences of which they warn if they do not get their way. The reason is less often their precarious circumstances than it is their wish for additional power and prestige. Jobs and the economy are endangered the way a playground ball game is endangered when the player whose equipment is being used threatens to take his ball and bat and go home. If the ranks of the wealthy were not so dedicated to trying to win the "Global Monopoly Game," and were, instead, genuinely interested in "raising all boats," they have the means at their disposal to empower the human family to realize its extraordinary potential.

Mahatma Gandhi said, "Take care first of the least among you." Were his vision respected, we would remove the distress of having to earn foreign exchange to pay interest to those already rich, and let that money earned by poor nations be used to provide education and basic health care for those most in need. The product would not be chaos or unchecked population growth, but positive development. Rather than producing goods to sell outside their countries, the people would go to work producing food, clothing, tools, education and elder care for each other and then they would no longer be poor. With such means of livelihood comes the dignity of participation and the real goods needed to sustain themselves.

Gandhi's solution differs markedly from the present regime, which encourages large, world-scale industries to produce commodities for sale to countries with the means to pay for them. Around the world, developing countries are caught in the debt trap, borrowing money to produce inexpensive goods for wealthy countries, and then returning the money earned to the richest people in those countries as loan and interest payments. Global GDP is rising, but few boats that are not already floating high are rising with it. Were the same resources used to build export industries used instead to employ those in need to produce basic goods for local markets, those markets would again show their effectiveness at accommodating mutual provision.

Education (particularly of women), health care, and the confidence that one's community can care for one in old age have proven again and again to be the recipe for stabilizing population. It does not require being wealthy. It requires making local well-being the priority and focussing available resources on that goal. The state of Kerala, on the west coast of Southern India, took this course of action, achieving literacy and population-stabilizing birth rates similar to those of North America. They didn't become "rich" — their average income remains close to that of the rest of India — yet their quality of life improved significantly.

Education and health care, unlike roads, copper and oil, are almost without cost from an environmental perspective. For the most part, they do come from our minds. Sharing information is primarily a process of good will. When someone shares information with someone else, it costs both people some time, but the person passing the information along does not have any less information for having given it away. Education is almost entirely information, and health care is mostly information and attention when provided at the preventative level where it is most effective.

If goodwill and the free flow of information in these two areas were to take precedence over competitive self-interest, population numbers would stabilize in poor regions, and the people there could move forward on a development path that would free them from needing outside support. Enticing them into the global economy to compete with the most powerful commercial interests in the world is a trap. Some well-placed individuals in poor countries are admitted to the rich world's club in exchange for providing access to natural resources and cheap labour, but their personal success is often at the expense of their countries and the people living there. The present style of globalization is about opening the doors of nations so that international corporations can set up shop and extract profits. Such dealings seldom improve the circumstances of the local population in the way that local production for local needs would.

Overlooking Future Generations

We don t inherit the Earth from our parents,
we borrow it from our children.

Traditional African wisdom

If the exclusion of billions of people alive today is the cause of unnecessary hardship, social disruption, and environmental degradation, excluding the interests of people not yet born will prove even more so. The costs of activities that are externalized on to communities and the environment will, cumulatively, be our legacy to future generations. Many of those who will be living in the future will have money with which to "vote" in the markets when their time comes. Unfortunately, for them, the value of the money that they would be willing to pay is presently ignored because of a practice called "discounting," or "forward discounting."

Discounting assumes that things are more valuable today than they will be in the future. The assumption is based on the mathematical model of exponential growth. Numbers, growing by a percentage of their increasing size, become very large. (Remember the King of Persia's chess board and the duckweed?) Discounting assumes that it makes more sense to exploit a resource now, unless the future value of the resource will be more than the money that the resource can bring in today, PLUS the amount that can be made investing that money at compound interest until that future date. There is nothing to slow the growth of numbers besides the amount of paper or computer memory needed to record them. Money invested is assumed to follow this same abstract mathematical pattern. In some cases it does, for periods of time, but to assume that it always will, is dangerously misplaced concreteness.

Along with the seeds of disaster, there is an element of truth behind the practice of discounting. Throughout the industrialization process, capital has been in demand. When invested in productive enterprise it has been seen to produce great benefits in the form of needed goods and services. When sold, these products provided additional capital for investing in the production of more, necessary goods. In the context of the material scarcities of the early industrial era, money invested and managed to expand the industrial base may have lived up to exponential expectations. The resulting material abundance was impressive enough to support the hypothesis of discounting.

By assuming that continued material expansion will provide similar benefits for the future, and by ignoring the mounting ecological and social costs associated with the huge task of maintaining exponential growth, discounting may still seem appropriate. Unfortunately, while money may continue to grow, it cannot be counted on to substitute for necessities. One may make more money investing in cosmetics and the fashion industry than they would investing in soil conservation, but if the soil is lost, all the glamour in the world won't prevent calamity. While the rich fashion magnate might be able to afford scarce food, a world of desperation would be the fate of his or her offspring.

There is a qualitative difference between the value of food security and the value of the fashion industry. As long as our accounting practices assume that the capital from one can be substituted for the value of the other, future generations will be cut loose to fend for themselves. In the meantime, the cumulative activity of humankind has crossed the threshold between an empty world and a full world. The accumulating costs of externalities are unaccounted for, yet the accompanying problems are becoming increasingly obvious.

If money is spent on conservation instead of being invested for profit, that money is assumed to depreciate by the amount that it does not grow through compound interest. Understanding that interest rates are always set higher than inflation, $100 not invested today at a 5% return, will only be worth $95 next year, $90.25 the second year, $85.74 the third, and so on. Within 25 years, the value of the $100 would be accounted for at less than one-third of its present value. At this rate,

$1,000,000 worth of trees or petroleum today would be accounted for as if it were worth under $7,000 in 100 years. Hardly worth considering. Certainly not the sort of prospect that would inspire forgoing the pleasures or opportunities of using a million dollars today. Conversely, if a forest is cut down and sold, every $100 made and invested at 5% is assumed to multiply 130 times in one century.

Through this accounting magic, relatively small amounts of natural resources liquidated today and invested to gain interest would be worth millions of dollars in the form of financial resources in a hundred years. Yet, the people living 100 years from now may not feel that we have done them a service by turning those resources into cash. If they were to participate in today's markets, they would bid the price of diminishing resources up, not down.

Before we approached the peak of oil production, we seldom gave more value to a barrel of oil than what it costs to pump it out of the ground, process it and ship it to market with a bit of profit and tax. To people a hundred years from now, petroleum would have the value of the enormous service it could provide them, if our generation had not consumed it all. People 100 years hence will also have a far greater appreciation of the debilitating effects of accumulating pollution. They would know that stopping that accumulation at the production stage would be far less expensive than having to live with the effects, or to attempt the, often impossible, feat of removing contaminants from the environment once dispersed. As the Brundtland Commission stated in *Our Common Future,* "[future generations] may damn us for our spendthrift ways, but they can never collect on our debt to them."

The spirit of discounting was expressed clearly by the Malaysian minister responsible for that nation's forests. He said that Malaysia should cut down all of its trees, sell them, and invest the money, because money grows faster than trees. When he heard this, David Korten, author of *When Corporations Rule the World,* said, "the image flashed through my mind of a barren and lifeless Malaysian landscape populated only by branches of international banks, with their computers faithfully and endlessly compounding the interest on the profits from Malaysia's timber sales." King Midas, with his golden touch, would have recognized the devastation.

The trees are valued in this perspective only for the money that can be made when they are sold for lumber or pulp. Other services that forests provide are not visible until rivers flood, waterways are blocked with displaced top soil, wells run dry, inland areas become drought stricken, native species disappear and tourists lose interest. Even then, the lost values of the forest would not be accounted for unless they had to be paid for at public expense, or possibly if the loss disturbed the ability of some other business to make money.

Proof that money accounts don't necessarily grow forever is not hard to find. My parents told me stories about how, with the onset of the 1930s depression, fortunes that had been growing for decades disappeared overnight. In North America, the stock market periodically takes substantial dives causing vast amounts of money to disappear. In the last couple of decades, Mexico, Thailand, Malaysia, Indonesia, the Philippines, Hong Kong, South Korea, Brazil, Russia and Argentina have all gone through financial shocks that have left their money greatly reduced in value. In all these cases, the assumption upon which the practice of discounting is founded — that wealth will increase uninterrupted — has been discredited.

Meanwhile, we don't bother to secure local food systems or other resource supplies, eliminate pollution, or invest in preserving community cohesion, because the theory of discounting says it is not economically rational to put wealth into activities that do not produce constant, measurable financial returns.

While conventional calculations like discounting may have a role to play in decision-making, we owe it to our children to pay active attention to tangible circumstances, and projections thereof, when making decisions that will affect their lives.

Because the market has no "eyes" to "see" the legitimate interests of generations yet to come, its magic becomes slight of hand, taking unfair advantage of those who will follow. If we are to leave the world in as good a condition as we found it, or even in the considerably worn state we have brought it to today, we will have to soon, and dramatically, increase our economic system's sensitivity to the future.

Overlooking Other Living Things

The other group not recognized by markets is everything alive that is not human. The "Golden Rule" — "Do as we would be done by" — is presumed to govern relationships between people only. In light of the interdependence of all life, its broader application is warranted.

Every form of life has struggled to maintain its place under the Sun; most have been at it for far longer than humans. In a broad view, they have as much right to well-being as we do, and their extinction should draw as much outrage as a genocide against humans.

Moral considerations are, however, deemed irrational by the economics profession. They consider the only rational view of people to be that we are concerned only for ourselves, that our wants are infinite and that we seek to satisfy them. Even within this questionable assumption, massive extermination of other living things is ill-advised as we are not sure at what point undermining the web of life will pull the rug out from under our own ecological life support. Market driven activities have extensive repercussions that affect the productivity and health of the natural world.

Human psychology makes it easy to block the sense of loss that can come with news of extinctions or lesser harms done to other living things. We have our priorities, and when they conflict with the well-being of others, it is our nature to put our own immediate interests first. Without other living things, our prospects diminish. We are well advised to pay attention to their fate.

Some things should not be bought and sold:
Land, Money and Labour as Commodities

In its enthusiasm for making money, capitalism encourages the buying and selling of everything. Sarcastically, the most exuberant enthusiasts are said to be willing to "sell their own mothers." Fortunately, there are some laws that override economic interests and prevent the buying and selling of people, but it is not that far back in our history that trade in humans was acceptable for wealth creation. Perhaps someday there will be guidelines regulating speculation in land, money and labour.

Land (including natural resources), money and labour are not the same as wheat, shoes and laundry services. Their qualities are of far greater depth and breadth and require greater respect.

Problems with the Commodification of Land

Land was here long before people showed up to use it. It is the foundation for all terrestrial life. We may work on it, clear the forest or drain the water so that we can grow food or build buildings, but we do not create it in the way we create other goods and services. To claim ourselves as sole possessors is opportunistic.

Many fortunes have been made buying land and leaving it vacant until expanding human activity increases its "site opportunity value." When a rail-line, road or subway is built, or development pressures increase, land values rise. The value increases because the land can be used more effectively to serve more human needs. This is the opportunity value of the site, and a substantial profit can be made when it increases. The increased value, however, is not the result of the speculator's efforts. Rather, in most cases, it is the efforts of others organizing, building and paying for transportation systems, sewers, water lines or other buildings nearby, that make the plot in question more valuable. Such increases in site opportunity value are the focus of "Georgian taxes." First popularized by Henry George in the late 1800s, these taxes seek to derive the money needed to maintain society from the benefits that arise thanks to nature, and to the value built up by others in surrounding areas. At the same time, the amount of taxes would be decreased on buildings, and other creative developments undertaken by people on their properties, thereby encouraging these activities because they make the area more valuable for everyone. Georgian taxes will be described in more detail in Chapter 11.

Greater recognition of the service provided by land would prevent much potential grief. Respect is in order for the eons over which the land has developed its capacity for food-production. That cities around the world are built upon the best of agricultural land is an unfortunate fact. Why we do this is clear. People prosper on fertile land. They invest the wealth produced from the soil in buildings and activities that are similarly wealth producing. The cycle provides more opportunities for more people. Expanding businesses need space to grow and workers need places to live. Increasingly, non-agricultural uses spread over the best land on the planet, taking it away from farms and pushing food-production on to less suitable soils.

Some progress has been made in some jurisdictions to stop "urban sprawl," but such guidance is often subject to growing urban pressure. It just takes the election of one government that believes money can substitute for fertile soil and building permits get issued, overriding earlier conservation efforts. Once built upon, it is practically impossible to reclaim land for agricultural use.

Even where land is being used for food-production, treating it as a commodity for exploitation produces a variety of problems. Pressures to increase productivity lead to economies of scale with ever greater areas being worked by fewer people, leading to reduced sensitivity to the needs of the soil and a depopulated countryside. Parallel to this is the emphasis on maximizing financial returns within the narrow definition of conventional accounting. With environmental costs externalized, farming practices are pushed toward those that diminish fertility and pollute streams, rivers and ground-water. Furthermore, making soil productivity a part of global trading regimes, leads to specialization with large areas of single crops being produced for export. Large areas of single crops are more susceptible to pest infestation and the need for broadcasting poisons to control them. Nutrients contained in crops are shipped far away from their origins and the capacity for maintaining soil fertility and long-term food self-sufficiency is diminished.

Soil will be the foundation of human communities for seven, seventy and seven hundred generations. To leave it to market forces, which recognize only immediate interests, is not appropriate. As long as people or corporate entities see it as a commodity to be exploited like any other for wealth maximization, it will be subject to having its essential elements converted into money and lost forever to those who might inhabit the territories in the future. We will have killed the goose that laid the golden eggs.

Problems with the Commodification of Money

Money is to civilization what the circulatory system is to an individual. Money connects billions of people in mutual provision in the same way that blood flow connects billions of cells toward the same end for an organism. Money was invented for this critical task. Unlike with our mothers and would-be slaves, however, there are no rules stating that it cannot be bought and sold.

Trafficking in money intensifies the boom/bust cycle of business and causes a lot of problems for people who have done nothing to warrant such trouble.

Currencies change in value compared to each other as a result of variations in how well different countries are doing and speculation about possible variations. If a people are blessed with valuable natural resources, are working hard and/or innovating new and better products and production techniques, they will have much to sell at competitive rates. With their products in demand, the value of their money will increase, as it underlies the prosperity and is the medium for which their goods are ultimately traded. If a nation is having a hard time — bad weather has affected its crops, it's industries have become obsolete, or a natural resource it has been trading is running out — the value of its currency will drop. It has less to offer that others want to buy. Those speculating in currency see less potential for gain from such countries and consequently, will only buy their currencies at a cut rate.

135

Official devaluation of a currency lowers the cost of the work done in the country and makes the products of its labour more appealing to people in other countries. It also makes imported goods more expensive, reducing demand for those goods and thereby reducing the flow of local money out of the country. Without interference, devaluation can stimulate economic recovery. People get work making goods that sell overseas and money comes into the country enabling it to improve its production facilities.

Official devaluation, however, can also cause nightmares. If speculative traders sense trouble in the devaluation, they may sell off their holdings of that currency. With the currency being sold for less and less as speculators flee, the unfortunate country may then have to raise its interest rates to encourage capital to return. Higher rates provide increased returns for speculators owning/using the money, but it is the opposite of what is needed within the country. Low rates would encourage new businesses, employment and export potential. High interest rates create additional hardship when farms and businesses can't service their loans and go bankrupt, further reducing employment and delivering another blow to the confidence upon which social, as well as economic, harmony depend.

With nothing governing the purchase and sale of money, the management of national economies moves out of the hands of elected representatives, who are responsible for the well-being of their electorate, and into the hands of moneyed interests, whose only goal is to make money for themselves. The invisible hand of self-interest loses the justification of serving society when money is traded as a commodity. In Chapter 12, among the practical changes described there, we will see how the institution of a very small tax on speculative monetary transactions could significantly reduce the damage caused by buying and selling money.

Problems with Commodification of Labour

The one thing that almost everyone has to trade is his or her ability to work. Trading this ability is the only means that many have to survive. If there is no place for individuals to contribute their work, or they cannot make enough from the work they have to cover expenses, desperation lurks. Trading one's own labour for pay is dignified. Having the value of one's labour manipulated by large-scale economic processes is only a step short of slavery. The actual purchase and sale of people stopped (in the developed world) when fossil energy and motors became readily available, yet the value of labour continues to be manipulated by people who have little knowledge or interest in the lives of the people involved.

People trading their labour are the essence of mutual provision, but the market's tendency to abstraction separates the labour from the people who provide it. Commodification of labour commodifies human beings. As a commodity, labour is an expense to be minimized. If a job can be eliminated or the labour purchased for a cut rate, the bottom line improves. This view provides another aspect of misplaced concreteness. Labour is not separable from human beings. Minimizing labour costs creates other costs. Unemployment, and jobs that pay less than a living wage, have serious consequences in terms of depression and desperate action. The economy does not recognize the human suffering involved. The costs that arise, including law enforcement, legal fees, medical expenses, alcohol sales and rehabilitation, are added to the GDP total, and mistaken as contributing to the health of the economy.

In his book, *The Growth Illusion; How Economic Growth has Enriched the Few, Impoverished the Many and Endangered the Planet,* Richard Douthwaite explains how the abstract accounting of conventional economics overlooks the serious hardships caused by unemployment. In fact, markets welcome unemployment because it helps increase profits. Stock prices drop when most people are employed and they tend to rise as unemployment rates go up. Douthwaite writes:

> In 1958, a professor at the London School of Economics, A. W. Phillips, published a paper that was to have a profoundly damaging effect on millions of lives. By plotting the annual rate at which wages in Britain rose against the percentage of people unemployed for each year from 1867 to 1913 he produced what came to be known as the Phillips Curve.

From his investigation, Phillips concluded, "the level of unemployment might explain the level of inflation." He hypothesized that by maintaining a certain level of unemployment it might be possible to control inflation. The idea is that when people are desperate for work, they are willing to work for less pay, thereby lowering the cost of production. Douthwaite continues that this reasoning:

... proved enormously attractive to politicians who immediately forgot the author s caveats... They were excited, because Phillips work made it entirely defensible for them to let unemployment figures rise, as, the higher the figures were, the more downward pressure they could say they were placing on the inflation rate. Lower inflation, of course, meant more competitive exports, and hence better prospects for growth, quite apart from preserving the wealth of those with monetary assets.

At the time, an increase of unemployment to 1.5 % was thought to be enough to control inflation. We have since been slowly conditioned to accept ever higher rates. At the time *The Growth Illusion* was published in 1992, levels of 10% were reported as a condition we ought to expect. As we look with reverence to the "greater good" of economic growth, we are supposed to overlook the trauma that unemployment causes in individual lives and the social problems that result.

8 Where Value is Overstated

Problems with Self-interest

As a stimulant for economic growth, self-interest is very effective. We feel our own needs directly, and have the best vantage point from which to see how they might be fulfilled. When inspiration and opportunity come together, things get done.

Beyond wanting what was needed to get by, the desire for personal gain was a taste that had to be cultivated. The history of industrialization contains many confrontations between traditional lifestyles of local self-sufficiency, and the needs of industry producing for distant markets. At first it was difficult to find people who would work long and hard at repetitive tasks, and then want to consume all the things that were produced through those efforts.

Having been encouraged to want more so persistently, and for so long, most people today feel that they never quite have enough. Yet, there have been people in many places and times who were content with their lot. Once their basic needs were met, they would invest what remained of their time in the cultural riches of their society, rather than seek to expand their material consumption. People satisfied with "enough" were a problem for industrial development. Where local trading had been the custom, it was sometimes hard to get the people to work for money. An effective tactic of colonial authorities was to establish taxes that had to be paid in money, thereby forcing people to work at jobs that paid money.

It was not uncommon for early industrial facilities to be built and then to find that the locals were not interested in working all day, every day. After countless generations working the land, they were accustomed to working at a familiar series of tasks to meet immediate needs and those of the coming season of drought or cold. They would work hard at those tasks and then take it easy until the next stage in the annual cycle came around. In Medieval Europe, there were more than 150 religious holidays to help the peasantry fill in their time.

As the industrial revolution took root in England, "Highland Clearances" served a two-fold purpose for the woolen industry. As mechanized processes were invented for carding, spinning and weaving wool, the cost of production, and therefore the cost of products, dropped. With the entire British Empire as a market for their low-cost, quality woolen products, the demand for wool to feed the expanding industry was high. However, tenant farmers inhabited much of the land that could have been raising sheep. The tenants had lived there for generations, trading a portion of their harvest and some labour on the landlords' farms in exchange for the right to work a small plot and use the commons for grazing. As the woolen trade took off, landowners found they could make more money, with less effort, grazing sheep and harvesting wool, than by collecting rent.

Forcing the tenants off the land made it available for grazing and, without their traditional livelihoods, the former tenants had little choice but to seek work in the factories. Even so, the labour problems were not solved. In many cases, the tenant farmers in England, as elsewhere, would only work until their basic needs were met. How could workers be enticed to keep working at repetitive, boring and sometimes dangerous jobs? In some cases, more money was offered to tempt them to work longer hours, but that just enabled them to stop working sooner. The practice of paying less was found to be more effective at keeping them on the job longer.

Needless to say, by persuasion, or through the destitution and demise of those who could not adapt to urban ways, growing cities came to be populated by people who wanted more. People have become remarkably self-interested, willing to work long hours at narrowly defined jobs and eager to spend everything earned — and more.

With the adoption of money as the medium of trade, a focus on monetary gain enabled the satisfaction of almost any need and desire one might have. Money was an ascending value before Adam Smith drew attention to how pursuing self-interest could serve the common good. In Smith's time, the value of self-interest was moderated by traditional values. Smith himself was best known in his own day for his book on moral philosophy, *The Theory of Moral Sentiments*.

Even in a world steeped in other values, the pursuit of self-interest has proved to be extremely powerful. Not only have people been pleased with the goods and services the system makes affordable, those becoming rich from the process are extremely pleased and work hard to press the values of self-interest and the market to ever greater heights. Selfishness has gone from a merely tolerated behaviour to become the foundation of economic thought and planning. Greed and materially covetous behaviour are now handsomely rewarded for stimulating economic growth. The greedier people are, the more they want, the more they will do to make money to acquire things and the more the economy grows.

In Smith's day, the population was familiar with the traditional mix of values that gave order to society — Do unto others... love thy neighbour, thou shalt not kill, steal, covet, bear false witness... and the like. These kept self-interest within bounds. As wider and wider circles adopted market values, the older values faded. Each generation has been a little more familiar with prices and a little less familiar with compassion and altruism. Two centuries later, the dominance of market economics is heralded as "The New World Order." Traditional values have all but disappeared from the decisions made by business and government and from a lot of individual choices as well. The majority of decisions are now based solely on monetary costs and returns. In his book, *The Rich and the Super Rich,* Ferdinand Lundberg identified the standard doctrine of our age: "Always pay the lowest possible wages and taxes, charge the highest possible prices and rents, and never give anything away unless the gift confers some hidden, possibly over compensatory personal benefit."

Calculating one's monetary self-interest has become almost second nature. Parents today, faced with the choice of seeking employment or staying home to care for their children, might use economic math to see which option makes financial sense. If it costs X dollars to pay for child care and one can make 3 X dollars working, market logic holds that it is better to pay for child care.

Greed is still widely thought to be an unbecoming trait. It is given legitimacy, however, by the ascension of market values and their enthusiastic promotion by the people who rise to power through the system. Status is measured by wealth. Some influential publications rank the effectiveness of different societies by how many millionaires and billionaires they produce. They don't ask about what those people have done to bring so much money to themselves. Wealth comes from working with natural resources and labour. It is possible for someone to enable the provision of so many goods and services that great wealth is their reward. It is also possible that a swath of depleted resources, pollution and human exploitation lies in their wake. In this era of electronic financial trading, wealth can also be made buying and selling parts of companies, future production, national currencies and other financial instruments without substantially increasing the amount of goods or services anywhere. With accounts that look only at how much money is made, it all appears the same.

In 1985, in a commencement speech at the School of Business Administration, University of California, Berkeley, Ivan Boesky clearly stated the sentiment of our times: "Greed is all right, by the way. I want you to know that I think greed is healthy. You can be greedy and still feel good about yourself." Not long after, he was convicted for conspiring to file false documents and for having made millions of dollars trading on inside knowledge of the stock market.

Pursuing self-interest has been at the heart of much of the reorganization of the political economy in recent years. It takes money to make money, so laws are being made, and old ones adjusted, to accommodate the interests of people and corporations that already have money. They can be counted on to want more. Accommodate their interests, locally and internationally, and the volumes of money being used will grow. In theory, everyone will be better off. Unfortunately, money being made is no longer a sure sign that society is receiving benefits. Are we really better off when money is made through the psychological leverage of high powered advertisements convincing people to purchase things that they otherwise might never have imagined wanting? Is it really "better" for people to spend more money on products that can only be used once, that wear out quickly, or soon go out of style? Are we better off with products that sell for less because jobs were eliminated and/or wages held at low levels, or because resource drawdown and pollution are left out of accounts?

Fast food, cheap goods and the latest gimmick being intensely promoted on TV accelerate the dollar flow. Compared to these private enterprises, the remaining commons of education, health care, and old age security are not as prone to financial acceleration and appear, using the GDP measure, less useful to well-being. It sometimes appears that the invisible hand has evolved with the morality of our day and is maximizing its competitive advantage by picking pockets.

Along with eagerness to serve oneself to the greatest possible extent, is often found a willingness to overlook other considerations. This is where "the invisible elbow" comes into play. Wanting a lot may be effective at stimulating economic activity, but it is also an unsavoury characteristic to encourage. Actions taken to satisfy greed can easily cross the line between serving society, and hurting others or disrupting the ecological balance. Add the human capacity for denial and we have a dangerous cultural trend.

The genie of self-interest has been released from the confines of traditional morality. We are challenged to return some balance between it and other aspects of human nature.

Self-interest at the Corporate Scale

History is full of stories about people who have pursued their personal interests without regard for others. The actions of one person can cause a lot of trouble. How much greater are the stakes when an organization pursues self-interest ignoring the common good? This danger exists at an enormous scale in the modern limited corporation.

Originally created to take on large tasks for the benefit of society, these legal entities were controlled by the governments that granted their charters. Over the last two centuries, however, the legal structure has mutated and the bonds of social responsibility have been broken. Indeed, as Marjorie Kelly documents in her inspiring book, *The Divine Right of Capital,* corporate entities have so affected the legal structure that operating for personal gain has become their duty.

The transformation took many steps, but a number of court cases are notable. In the 1819 case of *The Trustees of Dartmouth College v. Woodward,* the U.S. Supreme Court ruled that contracts of a corporation cannot be altered by government. This has subsequently been interpreted to mean that corporations are private businesses. Kelly points out that it is bizarre to use the word "private," which normally refers to things belonging to individuals or small groups, to identify organizations that "have more investors than a state has persons, have revenues larger than the gross domestic product of nations, and employ legions of lobbyists intent on bending public legislatures to their will."

Another landmark decision was the 1886 decision of *Santa Clara County v. Southern Pacific Railway,* where the U.S. Supreme Court ruled that corporations are persons. This is now used to assert the right of corporations to freedom of speech, to lobby governments and to make political contributions. Then, in 1919, the Michigan Supreme Court cemented the privilege of capital into place. They ruled in the case of *Dodge v. Ford Motor Company* that, "A business corporation is organized and carried on primarily for the profits of the stockholders. The powers of the directors are to be employed for that end." Based on this latter ruling, it is now against the law for a publicly traded company to serve any end besides making as much money as possible.

Ben and Jerry's Ice Cream was famous for its quality product and enlightened employment practices. When it was forced to sell to the highest bidder it found that it could not make its labour relations polices a part of what it was selling.

A person can spend her or his entire life making a product, proud that quality is of primary concern. If that person then sought to expand the business with money raised by selling public shares, the day the first dollar was accepted from the stock market, that person would find that, by law, the business was obliged to make money.

Marjorie Kelly says it is time for a new enlightenment. In the Middle Ages, nations were understood to be the property of kings and the word of kings was law by divine right. Lords and nobles were entitled to huge territories and all the plants, animals and people that grew and lived there. At one point in that order, the king and nobles were obligated to protect the people and settle disputes, but the sense of duty fell away, leaving only the right to a continuous stream of income from the people they lorded over. This continuous stream of income was considered socially acceptable until Voltaire, and others, challenged the "divine right of kings" and democracy began its slow assent to legitimacy. Similarly, today, it is accepted that shareholders are entitled to a steady stream of income, regardless of what they contribute to society, or draw out of it.

Kelly doesn't lay blame. She opens our eyes to the unconscious prejudice that favours concentrated wealth, so that balance can be restored to the system. Markets are supposed to balance the creativity of producers with what people want, and with the availability of natural and financial resources. Supply and demand, competition, profit, self-interest, wealth creation and so forth... she finds beneficial and worth keeping. Maximizing returns to shareholders, however, systematically favours the interests of one group over others, thereby interfering with the operations of free markets.

Companies, especially new ones, sell stock to the public to raise money for productive activity. Overall, however, money tends to flow from productive enterprises to their stockholders. In 1998, according to the U.S. Department of Commerce, companies buying back their stock exceeded new stock sales by $267 billion. In addition, dividends paid to stockholders extracted another $238 billion. This sort of net drain of capital has been going on for decades.

Stockholders warrant a stake in the overall process, but surely the people who manage the productive activity, those who do the physical and mental work, the communities in which companies operate, and that educate their workers, and others affected by corporate activities also have a stake. Marjorie Kelly writes: "Concern for the public good is the animating force of the democratic order — and it must become the animating force of our emerging democratic economy. We must have a conscious and deliberate concern for the public good built into the system design."

The idea that corporations belong exclusively to the shareholders is as mistaken as the notion that all the land and people of a nation belong to the king. The decision of *Dodge v. Ford Motor Company* was made when the shareholders had recently pooled their personal savings to physically build the company. The situation is far different today where only one out every hundred dollars invested in stock actually goes toward productive investment and disproportionately more wealth is extracted from companies by shareholders than the amount they invest.

The change in focus that Kelly proposes is revealed elegantly in how she analyses the basic statement of income and expenses.

Profit = Revenue − Costs

This is commonly broken down as:

Income from capital + Retained earnings =

Revenue − (Employee income + Cost of materials, insurance, taxes etc.)

implying that the income of employees is a cost to be minimized.

The statement could read:

Employee income + Retained earnings =

Revenue − (Capital income + Cost of materials etc.)

suggesting that providing employees with money to live and to purchase products is the purpose of a company, and that the cost of capital is a cost to be minimized.

In fairness to all productive inputs, the equation might best be written:

Capital income + Employee income =

Revenue − Cost of materials

Coming to see a corporation in this way would lead to a natural partnership. Employees would stand to gain if the company does well, as they would stand to lose if it does poorly. Such interests inspire creativity and quality performance. It would also be a watershed step toward returning some of the most powerful entities on Earth to the service of the common good.

The Divine Right of Capital concludes with suggestions for how to begin this change. Kelly suggests:

> *Employees on boards, profit-sharing, a public service mandate embodied in corporate chartering law, new kinds of social-benefit statements, new mechanisms of accountability to the public, ways to impeach CEOs: in short, we need a democratic economic Constitution. We need well-thought-out checks and balances of the sort first imagined in the U.S. Constitution, but recrafted for today s economic realm. If the framers democratized government, our task is to democratize economics.*

Problems With Competition

Competition is a key element in a market economy. With competition, producers work hard to keep their prices as low as possible and/or to make their goods better than the others offered. The assumption that the market provides quality goods at the best possible price is where it gets its legitimacy.

When one producer or association of producers has the power to directly influence prices, this function of the market is defeated. When producers control prices, they set them to maximize profits rather than to serve the common good. While we are regularly told that mergers, layoffs and reduction of employee benefits are necessary to increase competitiveness, we seldom hear about how far away we are from gaining the benefits of competitive markets.

Competition is self-eliminating. Successful companies grow. Unsuccessful ones disappear. The winners buy up smaller companies and merge with other large companies to become huge. Buying out the competition is so profitable that large loans can be arranged for such projects. As corporations expand and merge there is less and less real competition. Frequently, supposedly competing brands are made by the same companies or by different companies whose directors attend the same clubs.

As long as production costs are within the range affordable to new enterprises, prices cannot be set too high or the traditional market process will take over. Adding too much profit to a price would make it possible for a new organization to set up production and offer the product at a lower price. Unfortunately, as the complexity of the technology and scale of production reach enormous proportions, it becomes less and less likely that any but the most thoroughly financed institutions will be able to participate. This is a big change from the days when Adam Smith observed the market and saw a process where, for the most part, small-scale local producers competed with each other to provide goods for local consumption.

Today there are many situations where price setting eliminates the ability of free markets to produce "quality goods at the best possible price." The extent to which the process of concentrating economic control had already progressed 50 years ago is quite surprising. John Porter's, *The Vertical Mosaic* (1965), and Ferdinand Lundberg's, *The Rich and the Super Rich* (1968), provide detail on this from a Canadian and U.S. perspective, respectively.

The control of prices by producers has been an issue at least since the 1600s when European businessmen tried to break up Crown monopolies. In 1623, the British Parliament passed legislation making nearly all monopolies illegal. Anti-combines and trust-busting legislation, aimed at maintaining competition, have been on the law books throughout the capitalist world ever since.

The effectiveness of this legislation has, however, been questionable. Thurman Arnold, author of *The Folklore of Capitalism,* was the Assistant Attorney General in charge of the Antitrust Division of the U.S. Department of Justice from 1938-1943. In his book, Lundberg paraphrases Arnold:

> *The purpose of the Act governing conspiracy to fix prices... is to make possible from time to time ceremonial observances of the American belief in competition. These ceremonial observances take the form of criminal prosecutions so that a concerned fraction of the public may believe the competitive situation is being defended. Meanwhile, concentration and monopoly advance in rapid strides from decade to decade...*

Lundberg describes the prosecution of General Electric. With 39 anti-trust actions against it and 29 convictions from 1941 to 1961:

> *Many of the defendants... looked upon themselves as the fall guys of U.S. business. They protested that they should no more be held up to*

> *blame than many another businessman, for conspiracy is just as much "a way of life" in other fields as it was in electrical equipment. "Why pick on us?" was the attitude. A former vice president of General Electric recorded his belief that a third of the American economy - automobiles, steel, cigarettes, cement, oil products, chemicals, roofing materials and machinery - is price-stabilized through agreements of the leading companies.*

The number of antitrust suits in the U.S. peaked in 1960. There were fewer under President Kennedy and, according to Lundberg:

> *...came to a virtual halt under President Johnson. The Johnson Administration... apparently* [gave] *Big Business the green light on mergers and regulation in general, in return for... its full endorsement of Mr. Johnson s personally engineered disastrous Vietnam War.*

With most government activity dependent on computer programs to manage its work, the monopolistic practices of Microsoft stare it in the face daily. Because Microsoft's operating system is made to favour programs that make profits for the company, people find that they are restricted in what they can use their computers for. Whether the Microsoft antitrust case is an attempt to revive competition or a practicality of government management, the power of that corporation is such that the changes ordered along with the initial guilty ruling will likely be tied up in the courts for years to come.

In their Global Economy Project, the Institute of Policy Studies found that the world's 200 largest corporations account for over 27% of the entire world's economic activity. These giant entities, with their abundant financing and international reach, are in little danger of being pushed out of business. Individuals and small producers, on the other hand, are being hurt. In sports and scholastic achievement, competition encourages people to perform at their very best. Competition also stimulates economic performance. There is nothing like a little (or a lot) of fear, that one might be beaten out of the market and face the possibility of not being able to afford food and shelter to get people moving. Those who win often get wealthy. The picture is not so bright for those who lose. Winners are few, losers many. Much fuss is made about winners, however, giving them a far higher profile than their numbers warrant. At the same time, there are a lot of damaged lives that go unnoticed or are soon forgotten.

In recent decades, the drive for international competitiveness has increasingly influenced national policies. There is strong motivation for this, brought about by our system of creating money through debt. This will be explained in Chapter 9. International competitiveness is said to be necessary so that our companies can prevail over companies operating out of other countries. Winning the competitiveness race is often given as the reason why jobs are being automated and wages and benefits restrained. This results in our own people being defeated in an effort to defeat other people. In a global community, defeating our neighbours is a self-contradicting goal. If our success must come at the expense of our neighbours, international "community" is a misnomer.

Theory has it that those who lose out in economic competition get involved in other forms of business, thereby expanding the volume and variety of goods and services available. This is an assumption preserved from an earlier time. We have long since passed the stage where important tasks could not be done for lack of human labour. The world is full. The only frontiers remaining where much additional productivity is required are the needs of the poor, but since they have no money, those opportunities are ignored. As a result, the growth of economic activity has to be maintained through artificial obsolescence, abstract financial trading and creative (deceptive) accounting. There are exceptions. From time to time, new types of activity do open up, but, like winners, they receive a lot of coverage in the media and seem more common than they are.

It is particularly naive to expect poor, newly industrializing countries to produce in a manner that can compete with sophisticated, highly capitalized, transnational companies. These countries can provide raw materials and lower labour and environmental standards, but they are ill equipped to compete on any other grounds. The big businesses that are successful in the developing world are often extensions of the existing order from the North. The few local individuals who do prosper may as well be from the North as, in most cases, their good fortune comes from serving Northern interests.

Global competition is not like the competition in the board game Monopoly where losers can go to the fridge and make a sandwich. If one is pushed out of the "world game" of mutual provision, one's children go hungry. Hardship and fear can turn into rage and terror. What we are seeing is predatory self-interest of powerful organizations, dressed in the abstract ideology of economic science, seeking to feed their addiction to growth on the resources and cheap labour of disadvantaged people. Assertions that the greatest good will come from giving the giant producers free reign to compete in markets everywhere, are narrowly informed. They come either from the fundamentalism of eighteenth century, free-market ideology, or they are made through the self-deception that springs from having too much to gain, or lose, to notice social and environmental effects while exploiting opportunities.

In many cases the giant corporations can only deliver goods more cheaply if external costs are ignored. The extensive costs of transportation are subsidized by others — as are the costs resulting from pollution, resource depletion and undermining local livelihoods.

This was the message from Chiapas, Mexico at the beginning of 1994 when the Zapatista movement voiced its objection to the North American Free Trade Agreement (NAFTA). Among other things, NAFTA required Mexico to allow the import of inexpensive corn, produced industrially in the U.S., with highly subsidized energy. To rural Mexican communities supporting themselves selling corn produced with human labour this imposition meant disaster. Perhaps some of them could find work in the Maquiladora, where U.S. and Canadian companies were setting up huge factories to take advantage of low Mexican wages, but this was not their custom, nor the lifestyle they wanted. Their livelihoods, communities and traditions were being sacrificed to a system that respects only the value of money. "Enough" they said, as they stood up to face the government troops sent in to defend the corporate interests who wanted to compete "freely" in the markets of Mexico.

Adam Smith is honoured as a luminary for his clear explanations about how well competitive markets serve the common good. Smith also warned of the dangers of letting control of society fall into the hands of the moneyed interests that operate through profit-making companies. Workers, he pointed out, have little energy left after their hard labours to try to understand and direct the operation of society. The aristocracy, living off their hereditary incomes, tended to be too comfortable to trouble themselves deeply with matters of state. The rising business class, in contrast, was accustomed to working with the many elements that make up society, and it was only too eager to take the reins of power and direct the ship of state. Smith warned that:

...any new law or regulation of commerce which comes from this order ought always to be listened to with great precaution, and ought never to

be adopted till after having been long and carefully examined, not only with the most scrupulous, but with the most suspicious attention. It comes from an order of men whose interests is never exactly the same with that of the public, and who accordingly have upon many occasions, both deceived and oppressed it.

When "free markets" are invoked to justify painful decisions being made to accommodate corporate globalization, given the loss of the competitive and local aspects of the market economy, we are well advised to heed Smith's warning.

It would take a major restructuring to return the system of mutual provision to where local producers competed in local markets to provide for the needs of their communities. Huge economic players are the reality of our age. For those powers to spontaneously adopt compassion and responsibility for values other than profit would seem a miracle. Toward that end, however, an effort to open each other's eyes to the impacts that large operations have on social and ecological realities is a step any of us can cooperate on.

Widespread economic exploitation breeds rebellion and ecological exploitation undermines the resilience of the life supporting process. These can be very costly side effects. If the present order could see these impacts in terms they understand, as costs they have to pay, our collective self-interest could be invoked. Monitoring externalities, and assigning monetary values to them, would bring those considerations into the market process. Given the unavoidable consequences of not doing so, and the increasing visibility of those consequences, it is reasonable to expect that this aspect of the system might be upgraded in the foreseeable future.

Problems with Trade Based on Comparative Advantage

It has always been clear that trade is advantageous when two countries have an absolute advantage in the production of different goods. That is, when they produce particular goods more easily than other nations. We could grow bananas in Canada, for example, by building greenhouses and pumping heat and light into them. Honduras could, perhaps, grow enough wheat for its needs. However, since the Canadian prairies are so much better suited for growing wheat and bananas can grow wild in Honduras, it makes sense for each country to specialize where our absolute advantages lie, and to trade with each other.

Trading for the benefits inherent in "comparative advantage" is a different matter. Comparative advantage is often cited as a primary reason for encouraging international trade. The principle was first explained by David Ricardo in 1817. Comparative advantage identifies the mutual benefit to be realized from trade, even if one nation has an absolute advantage in both goods that might be traded. An example, adapted from Ricardo, explains that Portugal has an absolute advantage over England in producing both wine and cloth. Comparatively, however, Portugal produces wine more efficiently than it produces cloth. Although neither product can be produced as efficiently in England as in Portugal, England, within its borders, produces cloth more efficiently than it produces wine.

Because England can produce twice as much cloth, with a given effort, than it can wine, if it moves the effort used to produce one unit of wine into the production of cloth, it will get two additional units of cloth. Portugal, on the other hand, can produce 1.5 units of wine with the amount of work that it takes to produce a single unit of cloth. In this example, each country gives up one unit of production but ends up with a greater volume of the product for which it has the comparative advantage. Each country can then trade for the production units foregone, and the trading community will be better off by one unit of cloth and a half unit of wine.

England	Portugal
1 unit effort = 2 units cloth	1 unit effort = 1 unit cloth
1 unit effort = 1 unit wine	1 unit effort = 1.5 units wine
Total production for both countries: 3 units cloth and 2.5 units wine	

If one unit of effort in each country is moved from the less advantageous product, to the one for which it has the comparative advantage, the results would be:

England	Portugal
2 units effort = 4 units cloth	2 units effort = 3 units wine
(Note: Because climate and other circumstances differ in these two countries, "one unit of effort" has a different value in each country.)	

In Ricardo's time, money seldom travelled to other countries. Without communications systems for staying in touch, it would be risky to send money away for investment. One could move to another country, but most investors choose to pursue local opportunities over the uncertainty of becoming a stranger in a community with different laws, customs and language. Back then, when capital was not internationally mobile, it made good economic sense to invest where one's own country had a comparative advantage and seek gain by trading one's surplus with another country that had a comparative advantage in another product.

Explaining the principle of comparative advantage, Ricardo pointed out that it does not work within a single country because capital can move easily within a country. Suppose two provinces within one country produced the same two products described above and that one province could produce both products for less cost than the other. Because capital can move anywhere within the country, investors will invest in the province where the products can be produced for the least cost and sell to the other province. It would breach the standard doctrine to invest where the costs are greater.

Today, money moves between countries with far more ease than it used to move within a single country. For the same reasons that comparative advantage has never been relevant within a country, it is no longer relevant today at the global level. If China could produce both cloth and wine at less cost than anywhere else, investors who wanted to produce those goods, would invest in China. Why then do the proponents of "free trade" argue for the unrestricted flow of capital between nations by citing the gains of comparative advantage? Comparative advantage is dependent on the very same barriers to capital movement that they are seeking to remove? The oddity here brings to mind Adam Smith's caution that such proposals ought to be examined with "long,... careful... and suspicious attention."

The past utility of comparative advantage is further complicated by variations in the costs of labour. In Ricardo's time, almost all labour was paid at a subsistence level, so the comparison of production costs could easily be made in terms of how many person days were involved. Today, with some people receiving far less pay in some countries than in others, comparative advantage tends to be heavily weighted by wage rates. When capital is internationally mobile, it will employ cheap labour. In theory, this will lead to an equalization of wages between countries over time, but in the short-term it results in greatly increased profits. Over the long-term, the problems resulting when people accustomed to high wages find themselves trying to live on a Third World income have to be factored in.

When we add to these considerations the rising cost of transportation, the policy of disassembling the structure of nations to accommodate "Free Trade" cries out for review.

Efficiency is Not What it Used to Be

Something is efficient when it produces the desired effect with a minimum of waste and undesirable side effects.

Efficiency is an important consideration in most decisions.

With the fundamental change in the relationship between people and the Earth has come a fundamental change in what "effects" might be desired. There are people who argue at length that "efficient" refers only to getting the most result for the least monetary cost, reflecting the contemporary bias as to why we produce things. The dictionary definition, however, makes no mention of getting the best return for money spent, saying, rather, that efficiency is about producing the desired effect with a minimum of work. What if, rather than the expansion of money, the desired effect was long-term well-being?

The stated objective of economic activities has always been the well-being of society. If questioned, increasing wealth is always justified by the invisible hand's ability to turn money-making into social benefit. I've yet to hear anyone challenge this by asserting that increasing wealth is the ultimate goal. Since the decline of feudalism, expanding wealth has, indeed, frequently served the common good. It would be interesting, however, to see how long the legitimacy of the privileges that come with wealth could be maintained if the expansion of wealth was asserted as a primary goal without the claim that society's well-being is the end result.

Efficiency and Wealth

When industrialization took root, it offered a great increase in material goods. By organizing mechanized production on a large-scale, the cost of acquiring clothing, food and tools fell considerably. Easier access to these things improved people's lives. In order to set up large-scale operations, it was necessary to have enough money on hand to build the buildings, purchase or make the machinery, buy raw materials, produce products and ship them to market, all before there was any income from the operation to pay expenses. Having this sort of money available in advance requires accumulated wealth. As the benefits of industrial scale production became broadly recognized, there would have been far more opportunities for expansion than there was capital available. Built-up capital was not only a means for better serving human need, it was a limiting factor and, therefore, well worth cultivating for the common good.

That this was the case when industrialization got under way doesn't mean that it is the case today, or that expanding wealth is the most appropriate goal for the future. There are reasons to believe that there is enough wealth existing in the world, perhaps even too much. It is not so evident that there is enough employment or that the environment is in a state of health that can assure well-being for present and future generations.

The idea that there is enough, or even too much, wealth may seem strange in a world where so many people seem constantly in need of more. Needing money, however, is not so much a matter of insufficient wealth in the world, as it is a factor of how that wealth is distributed and used, and how we feel about the wealth we have.

We are at an advanced stage in the Global Monopoly Game. Most of the property on the "board" has been "purchased" and the gap between rich winners and poor losers is growing ever wider. Dedicated to the standard doctrine of paying as little as necessary and charging as much as possible, and reinforced by the thrill of their success, the winners can be counted upon to put their expanding fortunes into additional investments to further increase their wealth. Investing in large enterprises takes far less effort than loaning to small ones. A handful of loans, worth hundreds of millions of dollars each, is easier to manage than thousands of loans in the hundred thousand dollar range. You might imagine how much interest there is in loaning startup money to a custom woodworking shop, such as I support myself with, where $20,000 can buy all the necessary tools.

The sense of "needing" more money is as much cultural as it is a state of poverty. Most people in the industrialized world confuse needing with wanting. Enormous effort goes into encouraging us to want more, both through advertising and the lifestyles portrayed in the visual media. People can be attracted by advertising's magnetism to buy frivolous items only to find themselves short when they have to pay for necessities. One study found that, no matter how much money the people questioned were making, they all felt they needed around 20% more to get by comfortably. Indeed, thanks to easy credit, many now spend beyond their incomes to meet that desire. Throughout the industrialized world, all but the very poorest are fabulously wealthy compared with the average human being of 300 years ago.

The following story from the Internet reveals some of the illusions arising from our modern notion of progress:

A Fast Track to Prosperity

An American tourist visiting a tiny Mexican village complimented a fisherman there on the quality of his fish and asked how long it took him to catch them.

"Not very long," answered the Mexican.

"Why didn't you stay out longer and catch more?" asked the American.

The Mexican explained that his small catch was sufficient to meet his needs and those of his family.

The American asked, "But what do you do with the rest of your time?"

"I sleep late, fish a little, play with my children, and take a siesta with my wife. In the evenings, I go into the village to see my friends, have a few drinks, play the guitar, and sing a few songs...I have a full life."

The American interrupted, "I have a business degree from Harvard and I can help you! You should start by fishing longer every day. You can then sell the extra fish you catch. With the extra revenue, you can buy a bigger boat. With the extra money the larger boat will bring, you can buy a second one and a third one and so on until you have an entire fleet of trawlers. Instead of selling your fish to a middle man, you can negotiate directly with the processing plants and maybe even open your own plant. You can then leave this little village and move to Mexico City, Los Angeles, or even New York City! From there you can direct your huge enterprise."

"How long would that take?" asked the Mexican. "Twenty, perhaps twenty-five years," replied the American.

"And after that?"

"Afterwards? That's when it gets really interesting," answered the American, laughing. "When your business gets really big, you can start selling stocks and make millions!"

"Millions? Really? And after that?"

"After that you'll be able to retire, live in a tiny village near the coast, sleep late, play with your children, catch a few fish, take a siesta, and spend your evenings drinking and enjoying your friends!"

It may be that we have succeeded in creating enough wealth to serve human need and that it is no longer appropriate to view continued wealth creation as the best way to serve the well-being of society. The subsidies and advantages that are presently awarded to wealth-expanding operations, might more efficiently serve well-being if they were put directly into education, distributing employment opportunities, preventative health care and the preservation and enhancement of soil health and environmental stability.

What is the appropriate goal for civilization as we proceed into the 21st century? Do we want continued expansion of wealth or improved quality of life through full employment and environmental health? This points again to the Question of Direction, which is described in detail in Chapter 15.

Efficiency and Work

Up until the end of the 1800s, along with raising enough capital to build new factories, finding enough labour to work in those factories was a major challenge of progress. Long working hours were necessary to keep the machinery running. This changed as the 20th century dawned. Benjamin Kline Hunnicutt wrote in *The End of Shorter Hours* of how, early in the 1900s, technological innovations had increased productivity to the point where one commentator suggested we were suffering from "consumptive indigestion resulting from the outright satiation of human wants." Events from the era demonstrated, Hunnicutt wrote "that free time was the natural result of technological advance and that workers had a choice only as to the form that free time would take: leisure or unemployment."

Over the previous century, the work week was shortened from 70 to 60 to 50 to 40 hours. However, levels of productivity continued to rise and unemployment persisted.

In the latter part of the 1920s, proposals were coming forward for a 30-hour week, not just because spreading the available employment around enabled more people to work, but also for the benefits shorter hours provided for life outside of work. Free time was valuable in its own right. When all one's energy went into wage labour, time to fix up the house, play with the children, picnic by the river and to develop some personal qualities never saw the light of day. Such proposals, Hunnicutt continued, brought about strong opposition because "labour's shorter hour cause involved basic questions about the purpose of work and economic growth, the future of capitalism, and the very course of progress." The managers of industry and public opinion felt threatened by the possibility of people finding value in their lives that was not based in the jobs they were supplying.

These business leaders believed free time to be the result of market saturation, but they vehemently opposed further reduction of work hours and searched about for alternatives, such as foreign markets and increased "standard of living." Thus was born "the new economic gospel of consumption." If human need could be satiated, then the champions of growth would cultivate desire. In order to maintain the quest for efficiency, in terms of expanding (their) wealth, they went on the offensive. Hunnicutt reported that:

> *Serious advertising got under way and the public relations machinery went to work to convince people that it was unmanly, even antisocial to want to work less than 40 hours a week.*

The public relations effort, aiming to freeze the work week at 40 hours, was a success. We have since seen the "Brave New World" of media-induced desire expand into an all-pervasive enterprise. In a 1959 edition of *The New York Journal of Retailing,* Victor Lebow summed it up eloquently:

> *Our enormously productive economy... demands that we make consumption our way of life, that we convert the buying and use of goods into rituals, that we seek our spiritual satisfaction, our ego satisfaction, in consumption... We need things consumed, burned up, worn out, replaced and discarded at an ever increasing rate.*

We have boldly walked this path of expanding consumption ever since, leaving behind us a tragedy of depleted resources, saturated garbage dumps and widespread environmental degradation. Had the other course been taken, we could have created an ultimate material security for the human family with abundant time to celebrate life and to refine the culture into which our children grow. With enormous effort going into convincing people to buy more, and with cunning design causing much of what we buy to be discarded as soon as possible, can we still say that expanding production is efficient? What, and whose goal does it serve? It contributes to growth, yes. But what does growth, of that sort, contribute to?

Some would answer — employment — people need work. Unfortunately, this isn't the result of the goals pursued by the gigantic corporations. Technological innovations continue to reduce the labour needed for production and unemployment continues to degrade the lives of millions. Those 200 largest corporations, referred to earlier, that produce 27% of the world's economic activity, employ less than 1% of the world's workers. Since people need work to enable them to participate in some form of mutual provision, it is not efficient to deploy labour saving devices. The inability of decision-makers to grasp this fundamental change in the nature of efficiency causes enormous amounts of suffering.

When governments come to recognize this connection, we will see taxation systems based on the ratio of employees to profit. Large profits made utilizing little labour would be taxed more heavily than profits made while paying a greater proportion of earnings to the workforce. Either the inefficient businesses would improve their employment ratios or they would help pay for employment programs.

E. F. Schumacher, the Chief Economic Advisor to the National Coal Board in Britain for 20 years, retired in 1970. Having overseen the work of 800,000 employees, he knew the nature of big business. In 1973, he published *Small is Beautiful; A Study of Economics as if People Mattered*. I consider it among the most inspiring books I have ever read. It is even more relevant today than when it was written.

One of the points Schumacher makes lays the foundation for the shift in efficiency being proposed here. Using the traditional sense of the term, he said that we should reduce the "efficiency" with which we produce goods. He said that after we consider the people who don't work, those who don't actively produce things, and the time people normally spend in personal maintenance and leisure, only about 4% of our collective time as a society is actually spent at materially productive work. Schumacher argues that if we increase this percentage six-fold there would be

> ...*enough time to make a really good job of* [one's work], *to enjoy oneself, to produce real quality, even to make things beautiful... No one would want to raise the school leaving age or to lower retirement age, so as to keep people off the labour market. Everybody would be admitted to what is now the rarest privilege, the opportunity of working usefully, creatively, with his own hands and brains, in his own time, at his own pace — and with excellent tools.*

Ours is a challenging time in history. It offers enormous potential for satisfying human need and setting civilization on a course that could provide countless generations with secure, satisfying lives. Upgrading our understanding of efficiency is one clear, low-cost step in that direction.

The Institution of Interest/Usury

As a young teen, I remember opening my first bank account and having the interest payments I was to receive explained to me. Every month I would be paid a certain amount for leaving my money in the account. If I left the interest payments in the account, I would also be paid interest on them. I did some calculations and saw how my money would double, and double again and again, over time. I was keen to keep my money in the bank, until a few years later when I started thinking of things I wanted to buy.

I didn't realize that my bit of money was part of the reserves the bank used to create money to loan to others. Still, the interest I received was serving one of its purposes. It caught my interest and got my money to where it could be used by others, rather than my keeping it in a sock, or spending it right away.

Loaning money played a key role in transforming civilization from a multitude of locally based subsistence economies, to today's system of industrial production serving global markets. Having money available for loans is a key part of our present economic system. It takes money to make things happen. A loan can make it possible for a person with a good idea to develop that idea to the point that he or she has goods or services for sale. If all goes well, the loan can be repaid and the person will end up with his or her own tools and the experience to stay in business. Interest payments are the rental fee entrepreneurs pay until they can own their own businesses.

Those who earn more than they spend have capital, that is, money available for investment. The more capital invested in productive economic activity, the more goods and services will be available and the more work there will be for people to earn money for what they need and want. With goods, services and opportunities resulting from capital investment, increasing capital has, for many, become a primary focus of attention. To expand capital is the goal of capitalism.

Investing to make shoes or to provide a cleaning service is different from investing to make money. Aristotle identified the difference in the 4th century BC. He identified *oekonomia*, from which our word economics comes, as the art of household management. It refers to activities conducted to accomplish ends like producing food, shelter, tools or entertainment. *Chrematistike*, on the other hand, refers to economic activity that is carried on for the purpose of economic gain independent of whatever practical results might come of it. Aristotle approved of *oekonomia* but not *chrematistike*.

While money can be loaned at interest for either of these goals, the goal of economic gain is abstract. Indeed, the money itself becomes abstract; after a certain point it is seldom seen as anything more than numbers printed in an account book, or viewed online. Through the narrow focus on monetary costs and gain, investors can become insensitive to the troubles and grief that their moneymaking might cause. It is because of the troubles often caused when money is loaned for no purpose besides getting more money in return, that charging interest on loans has been condemned as usury (considered for centuries to be one of the deadly sins.)

It is the dire consequences that can befall those who cannot make their interest payments that gave usury its bad reputation. The problem, however, expands massively when practically the entire money supply with which societies do business is created through debt with associated interest demands. We will see below how paying interest, not just on our houses, cars and credit card balances, but on money itself, makes the "rat race" vicious.

Charging interest on loans is not necessarily usury, however. As mentioned earlier, when seed or livestock are loaned and returned with a share of the growing season's natural increase, it is not usury. How much different is that from loaning money and asking in return for some of the increase, along with repayment of the principal? There is no difference, as long as the money does in fact expand with use. If the venture, for which the money was loaned, goes broke, the expectation of the lender makes the difference. Lenders who insist on repayment in full, complete with interest charges, are guilty of usury. Lenders who accept a share of the misfortune, as they would have accepted a share of the good fortune, are acting in partnership and within traditional moral bounds.

The tension between the good that interest-paying loans can enable and the harm they can cause has been ongoing for millennium. The opportunities that access to investment capital provides are undeniable. Equally certain is the advantage that lenders have over borrowers. The greater the borrower's need, the greater the advantage of the lender. The temptation to exploit such advantage is older than recorded history. Enough farms were taken over by lenders and enough debtors sold into slavery by the time the *Old Testament* was written for that text to prescribe a Jubilee every 50 years. During the Jubilee year, all debts were to be forgiven and lands returned to their original owners. The purpose was to regularly rebalance society by counteracting the tendency of wealth to multiply, even as the disadvantaged became desperate.

The early prohibition of usury was aimed at protecting small farmers and craftspeople. The details about how much a loan will end up costing are not necessarily understood when farmers and craftspeople mortgage their farms and businesses to buy seed, materials or food for their families. What is found in the fine print of a truly usurious loan is that, if the loan is not paid back as agreed, the farm or business named as collateral would become the possession of the lender. By the time their house, farm or business is claimed by the lender for missing payments, it is too late. Charging interest on such loans was discouraged. The large-scale borrowing by kings, popes and nobles was seldom called into question.

As Europe emerged from the Middle Ages and business dealings began to replace the system of obligations that characterized feudalism, loaning money became a more common practice. This prompted the Church of Rome to reassert the rules against usury at its Third Lateran Council in 1175. A century later, in 1274, the assertion was reinforced at the Council of Lyons. Under threat of excommunication, landlords were forbidden to rent to usurers and, where they had already been provided accommodation, they were to be evicted within three months. Usurers were refused Christian burial and their wills were declared invalid. At the Council of Vienne in 1312, the prohibitions were extended to include the excommunication of rulers and magistrates who maintained laws supporting usury and any such laws were to be revoked within three months. Any person arguing that usury is not a sin was to be turned over to the inquisitors and punished as a heretic.

These were harsh laws, but so too was getting caught in the debt trap. When a person is in need, borrowing money can be their only hope. To lose one's land or business because of the substantial sums that interest-bearing loans come to demand could mean destitution, or even death, for debtors and their families. The moneylender, on the other hand, could make substantial gains by seizing the borrowers assets. In the eyes of the Church, moving wealth from people in need to people with more than they needed was unfair and immoral.

Taking unfair advantage of others — usury — referred to more than charging interest on loans. In a 13th century manual on the topic, written by St. Raymond, usury included raising the price of something because one has a monopoly on supply, hard bargaining to lower a price, charging excessive rent, subletting at a higher rate than a renter was paying, cutting wages, lack of lenience with a debtor behind on payments, requiring too much collateral on a loan and excessive profits by middlemen. All were denounced as sinful.

Charging interest on loans of money is the practice most often identified as usurious, yet it is not making a profit from loaning money that is the essence of the sin. Payment for loss incurred or gain forgone by the lender was considered legitimate. Compensation for late repayment was okay. Annuity investment, where the amount of return is based on the actual performance of the investment, and investment in trade journeys where profitable returns are expected but not certain, were acceptable. What was considered unlawful was to loan money at an interest rate identified in advance to be paid, come what may, with no risk to the lender.

During a 16th century parliamentary debate in Britain, usury was described as "any bargain, in which one party obviously gained more advantage than the other, and used his power to the full." Ironically this definition of usury comes from a debate that ended with the removal of British laws that forbade charging interest.

Compound Interest

The accumulation of interest charges can come as a surprise to borrowers. A typical mortgage for $100,000 at 10% interest, for 30 years, will cost the borrower $300,000 by the time it is paid off. This assumes that no payments are missed and that the home buyer does not end up paying interest on the interest. If payments on such a loan were deferred so that the interest was added to the principal and interest charged each month on the new total, the borrower would be paying "compound interest." The same $100,000 loan at 10% compound interest, if no payments had been made at the end of 30 years would cost a little less than two million dollars — equivalent on average — to paying back the entire principal every 18 months.

Most lenders would foreclose if a borrower were not paying the interest charges, therefore the massive gains of compounded interest would not come from a single borrower. Nevertheless, the interest income would likely be lent out through other loans, thereby gaining interest on the interest. The cumulative result for the lender would be the massive returns of compounded interest.

With loans to poor countries, the same pattern takes an enormous toll. Because these countries have an entire population to tax to pay off loans, lenders are more willing to loan additional moneys to cover the interest when payments get behind. Subsequent loans are often delivered with the requirement that publicly owned properties be sold to private interests. State run businesses, transport and communications systems, water works, health care and other such public institutions are removed from public control. While a price may be paid for the public enterprise, it is often less than full value, and the ongoing benefits are lost just the same. Unlike a private borrower whose debt is cancelled when their farm or house is confiscated, the poor countries gain only a temporary respite from the demands of their loans.

Difficulties arising from money loaned at interest led philosophers and statesmen to brand the practice as anti-social. By contrast, in the early 1990s, when concern for government deficits was being stirred up, the priorities expressed in editorials were almost the opposite. Governments were reported to be spending too much and had to cut back social services, job creation, education, health care, old age pensions, the arts, amateur sport and even the military. These calls for reduced spending were echoed throughout the media, but never, in the intense process of molding public opinion, was there any suggestion that we might reduce the deficit by cutting back on interest payments. This suggests that of all the things we do as a society, paying interest charges is the most sacred. This is an impressive rise to prominence for a practice that was once condemned as a deadly sin.

Restoring Balance

As mentioned earlier, the custom of the Jubilee year comes to us from ancient times as a way to rebalance society. The biblical reference is more widely known than the following example from Greek history. In his book *Voltair s Bastards; the Dictatorship of Reason in the West,* John Ralston Saul tells how Western civilization can trace its origins back to 6th century BC. At the time, Athens was in the wrapping-up stage of the money begets money process. The hereditary rich and ruling class had been exploiting their advantage to the fullest. When their debtors could not pay, they took possession of farms and, in some cases, sold the dispossessed into slavery to recover their money. With the loss of property came loss of citizenship, and as well, power was further concentrated in the ruling class. Athens was not well. Apprehension and discontent soured the civic mood and revolution seemed possible. A citizen named Solon was called to public office. He had held a year-long post as ruler 20 years earlier and was Athens' leading poet.

Solon's first acts were to eliminate debts, return confiscated lands and free the enslaved citizens. The End Game was replaced with a clean slate, and the Greece we read about in our history texts flourished, producing great art, architecture, democracy and the ongoing legacy upon which western civilization is based. Henry IV of France, with the help of his chief minister, Sully, did the same thing in the early 1600s.

The idea of cancelling loans is met with gasps of horror, not unlike the cries of heresy that greeted challenges to the divine right of kings in days past. We have to ask ourselves why this would be. Why is there such commitment to maintaining payments on mathematically intensified debts that are causing immense hardship and could, perhaps, push civilization into chaos? In the U.S., the excesses of debt-based money creation were neutralized by stock market crashes in 1837, 1857, 1892-93, 1907 and 1929. In each of these instances enormous amounts of debt evaporated. The difference was that in Athens and France, the process was orderly. In the U.S., before providing the foundations for new beginnings, the crashes produced chaos and hardship in great measure. Of the 1892-93 panic, John Ralston Saul writes: "four thousand banks and fourteen thousand commercial enterprises collapsed."

In ancient Greece and 17th century France, the thrill of gain was likely very much as it is today. People who were winning likely wanted to keep winning. It is unlikely that these qualities of being human have changed. Then as now, the winners would have overlooked evidence showing that their great success was causing harm. How did the end game of the past become obvious enough to enable an orderly transformation and yet, today the possibility is vigorously ignored? Saul attributes it, in part, to "the attachment of moral value, with a vaguely religious origin, to the repayment of debts."

Besides the psychological tendencies to ignore the unfortunate consequences of success and the deep level at which capitalist values have been accepted as personal and societal principles, there are technical factors that inhibit our ability to recognize the need for a rebalancing of accounts. Electronic banking and control of the media enable the winners of today's Global Monopoly Game to keep the game going in ways that were not possible before. When wealth was embodied in land, or in gold and silver coins, it was much more obvious when the game was drawing to a close. All the tokens could be seen to be in one camp. In today's cyberworld, accounts are kept in electronic files that fly from place to place at the speed of light. In the past, if one were sold into slavery, the change of status would have been obvious. In today's debt game, it is not as clear when one's lot has changed. How many alive today will work most of their lives, paying the proceeds of their labour into the accounts of moneylenders? Such debt "slavery" can be self-inflicted when people borrow for themselves, or it can be the result of entire countries being obliged to reorganize their economies to earn foreign exchange for paying off international debts. The chains of debt slavery can be velveteen, but the product of people's labours is claimed by others nonetheless.

Another advantage enjoyed by today's big winners is that we are a world informed by mass media. Radio and television stations, newspapers, and movie studios are expensive enterprises. Those who can afford to own mass media have technological access to people's thoughts and beliefs in a way that never existed before. Most of North America's mass media is controlled by a handful of wealthy interests. It is no surprise that their editorial policies and comments promote strategies that accommodate their continued winning.

As we move into the final stage of the present Global Monopoly Game, strategic plans are being implemented to open the entire world up to the process. This will enable the winners to go another round or two, before they own everything available. Wherever there is financial wealth to be made, there is the opportunity to help meet the next increment of exponential growth. Unexploited natural resources, inexpensive labour, the economies of developing countries, or the education, health care, water and waste systems of the developed world, all tie up money that could be tapped to maintain the present round of the money game. When those resources have been gathered, what will the next step be?

The institution of loaning money at interest offers great opportunities. We have built a complex industrial civilization on the opportunities. Now we face some dangers. More follows on the problems emerging from basing our system of mutual provision on the abstract expansion of wealth. First, however, more detail about how the institutions of money and growth will expand the context of the economic problem.

9
Money: Its Creation, Management and Growth

I confess; I'm thrilled when I receive a cheque or a handful of cash. It's an uplifting experience for most of us. Whether it comes in return for work, as an inheritance, as a gift, or winnings from a lottery, money in-hand means food, clothes, entertainment, transportation, tools and much, much more. Money gives us the power to select from all the goods and services produced throughout the vast system of mutual provision that encircles the globe. Money gives us command over the labour, skills and tools of others. It can make anyone a wizard. Dropping a two dollar coin on a checkout counter can pull a tuna fish out of the ocean, clean it, wrap it in steel and make it appear in your food basket ready for lunch. Money is indeed thrilling to have.

Money is the lifeblood of civilization. Without money it would be impossible for any but small communities to work together in mutual provision. By enabling millions of people to cooperate, money provides a great service. With this service, however, comes danger. Money gathers and flows in economic streams. The greater the flow, the greater the temptation to tap in and drink deeply.

Money is like sugar. Sugar and starch — which turns to sugar in our saliva as we chew — are basic energy sources for our bodies. Our sense of hunger is directly related to caloric intake, primarily from these sources. Because they satisfy hunger, most people like them.

For the first million years that people fed themselves on the variety of unprocessed foods, it was difficult to satisfy hunger without getting the vitamins and minerals our bodies required. One nutritional indicator (hunger) was sufficient: when our bodies sensed that we had eaten enough calories, the hunger stopped. However, when we learned to extract pure sugar and refine white flour, it became possible to extinguish hunger without meeting other nutritional needs. Hence, many people today are overfed, yet undernourished.

In the same way that sugar is taken to represent adequate nutrition, money is taken to represent economic health. While in the past there has been a close correlation between the amount of money being spent and the well-being of society, we are now finding otherwise. As human activity becomes ever more intense in the service of GDP expansion, this relationship has been lost.

Economic Health and the Money Supply

When you or I spend our money, it is gone. The view is very different for society as a whole. From society's perspective, when money is spent, it doesn't disappear, it becomes someone else's money. Our challenge, as individuals, is to keep getting more money to spend. For society, the challenge is to make sure that the right amount of money is in circulation and that it keeps circulating. Money serves three main functions:

1) It is a measure for identifying the relative value of different things.
2) It provides a medium of exchange that enables people to conveniently trade what they have to offer for what they need.
3) It provides a medium for storing value.

These purposes are best served when the value of the monetary units remains constant. The value of money depends on the relationship between the amount of money in circulation relative to the amount of goods and services available for sale.

The Quantity Theory of Money

The Quantity Theory of Money outlines the relationship between money and productive activity. Three factors influence the balance:

1) The amount of goods and services available for sale.
2) The amount of money in circulation, i.e. the money supply.
3) The average length of time that people hold on to money between when they get it and when they spend it.

How long people hold on to their money has the effect of increasing or decreasing money supply. If people are nervous about the future and hold on to their money, the speed at which the money circulates slows. This has the effect of reducing the money supply. If things are looking good, people are more likely to spend their money faster, creating the effect of more money in circulation.

The relationship between the amount of goods and services and the amount of money available to buy them is a critical one. These days, with only about 3% of the money supply existing as bills and coins, very little "money" is stored out of circulation when people's confidence is down. However, by not taking out new loans, while other loans are repaid, the amount of money in circulation is affected. For practical purposes, when the money supply contracts, there is less in circulation to pay for work or for the goods and services work provides.

The Quantity Theory of Money can help explain economic history. There are two main perspectives. One is that when the amount of money in circulation increases, given a consistent rate of circulation and stable prices, the amount of economic activity will increase. This is the mechanism by which governments, by spending money into the economy, can stimulate economic activity. The other is that when the amount of money in circulation increases, if there is not a corresponding increase in the amount of goods and services available, prices will increase. The resulting inflation is experienced as a reduction in what a given amount of money can buy.

The first Quantity Theory perspective — adjusting the money supply as a means of maintaining economic health — was well illustrated by the work of John Maynard Keynes. His theories about money supply and the economy were the foundation upon which the "New Deal" was designed to help end the Great Depression of the '30s.

The thriving economy of the 1920s produced lots of wealth and the holders of that wealth wanted more. Like today, there were limited opportunities to invest in new productive enterprises. Practically everything people needed was already being produced. (The needs of people without money were not seen as useful.) In place of productive investment, excess money went to speculation. Real estate and stocks were bought and sold repeatedly. At each step, the money-people fulfilled their own prophesies of perpetually expanding wealth by charging and paying higher prices for the same items each time they changed hands. Eventually the items involved were sensed to be over-priced and investors decided it was time to get out of that market. Some found that, in order to sell what they offered, they had to accept a lower price than they had originally paid. Others quickly interpreted the lower price as a signal to sell before prices fell further. The speculative bubble burst. Soon the feedback of falling prices created a panic. The crash wiped out much of the speculative economy and then continued on to wreck what had been a sound, productive economy.

With the exception of drought-stricken areas, food could still be grown in abundance; there were no physical shortages of energy or other natural resource supplies, no shortage of skilled workers or equipment to work with. What was different was that people were spooked by the thousands of bank and business failures and the soaring unemployment. The potential was still present for abundant mutual provision, but repercussions from the speculative toying disrupted the process and destroyed the confidence that is crucial to any sort of cooperation. People held on to whatever money they had. Any enterprise producing non-essentials was in danger. It seemed too risky to start or expand a business. Without business investment, capital was held out of circulation. Prices fell as producers tried to sell what they had, but spending stayed low. The magic of unassisted markets was gone. Something had to be done.

The New Deal was based on the Quantity Theory that economic activity will increase if the amount of money in circulation increases. Interest rates had been lowered to increase borrowing, but, unlike with the lowered interest rates following the September 11th, 2001 event, which helped to keep money moving, people were too cautious in the 1930s to take many chances with loans. Keynes observed that it was not sufficient to make money available; it was also necessary to make sure that it was spent.

With this in mind, government spending programs were initiated by the Roosevelt administration. Initially, relief money was distributed to prevent the starvation of those whose situation had become desperate — one in seven during the bleakest period. This was followed by farm loans and subsidies, programs for building schools, roads, parks, hospitals, renewing slums, and encouragement for art, theatre and writing. These moneys were paid to people who needed work and could be counted on to spend the money on living expenses. As the money was spent, it maintained and created other jobs for people supplying the increased demand.

Unfortunately, the substantial holdings of the well-to-do were not coaxed out of storage. Business interests, as today, were wary of government spending more than it brought in through taxes. Without the investment of that stored money, recovery was only partial. The employment situation improved and the economy revived a little, but it was still far short of the pre-30s level.

Full recovery waited until the U.S. entered WW II. The resistance that investors feel compelled to exercise around government spending did not apply to military spending. With vast amounts of money made available to the war effort, everyone had work. When the war was over, industry was in full swing. Manufacturers converted to civilian production and the people, with their confidence up and savings accumulated from wartime jobs, were out spending again.

At this point, the corollary of the second perspective of the Quantity Theory came into play. Too much money was circulating compared to what was available for purchase. Prices were bid up and within 12 years of the war's end, inflation claimed one-third of the U.S. dollar's purchasing power.

An early experience with the money supply, as exemplified by the following, provides some of the evidence from which the Quantity Theory has emerged. When the Spanish moved into the Americas in the early 1500s, they captured an Incan king and demanded ransom. They were paid with a large volume of gold and silver. Realizing that the Incas must have mines, they soon found the source and began serious mining and export of the metals back to Spain.

Gold and silver made its way into the European economy via the Spanish mints and the Dutch trading houses. Economic activity flourished. Money was spent into the economy and then, as there was no sustained increase in the amount of goods and services available, inflation struck, eventually reducing the value of gold and silver to the point that the overall purchasing power of the total money supply was about equal to what it had been before the new money was introduced.

Money Creation

[It is a] *mighty privilege, for a man to create a hundred pounds with the stroke of a pen.*   Bishop Berkeley, 1793

Historically, expanding population and increased productive ability have led to increasing volumes of goods and services. As the volume has increased, the amount of money circulating to pay for it must increase proportionately, otherwise, deflation will set in. For much of the time between the Renaissance and the capitalist era, gold and silver were the primary forms of money. With the exception of when there are large, sudden increases of gold and silver, as in the example above, the rate at which gold and silver came out of the mines more or less kept pace with economic expansion. As the value of gold and silver increased or decreased with the amount of goods and services being offered, investment in mining was encouraged or discouraged accordingly. This feedback process kept the volume of money available in balance with economic activity.

The right of "seigniorage" is the right to issue "money." Coins, clay tablets, notched sticks, tobacco, shells and carved stones, among other things, have been used as mediums of exchange. As long as money was made out of tangible objects, seigniorage was relatively straightforward.

Before providing more detail on how money is created through debt on the national level, I want to look at the basic process of providing a medium of exchange to facilitate mutual provision. The most basic process of money creation is demonstrated by numerous communities presently involved in Local Economic Trading Systems (LETS), and other enhanced barter projects. These systems are created in situations where the federal money system is failing; places where there are things that need to get done and people who have the skills to do those jobs, but where they cannot do the work because there is not enough money available to pay for their services.

A LETS system sets up accounts for participants, and distributes information about the skills that different members have and of the jobs they want done. When a match is found and a job done, a credit is added to the worker's account and subtracted from the account of the person who commissioned the job. These accounts are frequently managed by a computer program, with a coordinator entering the credits and debits regularly, so that everyone knows where they stand. The system might be described as computer-assisted barter.

An Ontario LETS program coordinator told of a single mother with young children who needed firewood and some repairs to her house for which she had no money. These needs were taken care of through the local LETS system, leaving her in a deficit situation for a while. Eventually, however, she realized that she could help care for other children and do some mending from her home, enabling her to maintain her balance within the system.

Not only did the local trading system solve her immediate needs, but in the process it removed the malaise of her predicament. She regained the dignity of participating as an equal in mutual provision and became integrated within her community at the same time. This is what an economy is for. Unfortunately, when economic policy is preoccupied dealing with challenges from enormous international players, individuals and local communities can be overlooked.

Of note is that, through the LETS program, this woman's community essentially gave her an interest-free loan. There is almost no chance that a bank would have loaned her money, and if one had, the interest payments would have added to her hardship. Further, there would have been no effort by the bank to help her integrate into the local community.

One community on the West Coast uses LETS to help save their forest. The ancient trees around them could be cut down and sold to get money to circulate, but many of the people live in the area because they love the forest. Removing the trees was not an agreeable option, so, instead, they created their own currency.

In some instances, these local trading systems have produced their own paper currency. Such bills physically represent a person's credit and automatically maintain the system's accounts. The number of "community dollars" in a pocket, or dresser drawer, represents their positive balance. These notes are sometimes called "hours" because they represent people's time. When someone buys something, their balance goes down automatically as they hand over so many "hours" in exchange for the hours of service supplied to them.

It's interesting to note that across North America, up until 1935, just about every bank and many communities issued their own paper currency. There were enough different notes issued by Canadian banks alone, from the first money printed in the French colonies of the 1680s, to the last notes printed in 1943, to fill 400 pages of the large format *Charlton Standard Catalogue of Canadian Bank Notes*.

When the Bank of Canada was established in 1935, it was given sole authority to issue bills and coins for the entire country. A gradual withdrawal of all other currencies was ordered, with outstanding currencies being purchased with Bank of Canada money. The last private bank note issue was of $5 bills produced by the Royal Bank of Canada in 1943. By 1950, the only legal tender in Canada was that issued by the Bank of Canada.

Creating Money from Nothing

The process of printing bills and minting coins presently creates only about three percent of the money supply. (It is significant that there is no debt involved in manufacturing coins and bills.) The rest of the money supply is created by large private banks. These private banks don't make coins or bills; they "create" money through credit/loans. For example, imagine that you have a business proposal and you need $100,000 to start up. You have convinced the bank that it is a sound proposal and they agree to loan the money. The bank doesn't give you the $100,000 from their depositor's savings. They create the money, out of nothing, by writing a credit line in your account book. "Presto!" With the stroke of a pen you can start withdrawing cash and writing cheques on that line of credit. The people you pay can spend the money you give them, or deposit it into their personal bank accounts, just like any other money they might receive. When you pay back the loan, the credit line is removed. The money the loan was paid back with is subtracted from the credit line and disappears. There is a catch, however. The bank wants interest on their loan. It created the principal, but it did not create any extra money from which the expense of interest charges could be paid. This is the cause of much hardship throughout society and around the world.

While the system is complex, the basic problem is not.

Consider four cowboys heading home after a long day on the range. Hot and tired, they drop by the local saloon to drink beer and play some cards. After ordering their beer, they ask the bartender if they can borrow some cards. "Of course," says the bartender. "But I'll need some collateral to make sure you return the cards; your horse or your saddle will do." To this he adds, "When you finish playing, I want you each to return 14 cards; one extra for interest."

You can imagine what happens when the card game is over.

In the economic parallel, as long as new loans are being taken out, more money is going into circulation, enabling earlier borrowers to earn enough to pay their interest charges. It is as if, back in the saloon, other people were borrowing additional decks of cards and the games they played intermingled with the other games in progress, in a way that enabled individuals to end up with more cards than they started with. While this would enable the first players to pay off their debts, it would leave an increased deficit for the players that followed, requiring even more people to borrow cards if collateral losses are to be avoided.

As we shall see later on, this mechanism, when applied to lending money rather than cards, is a principal reason why our economic system is compelled to grow.

Changes in the Value of Money

Both inflation — a decrease in the value of money reflected as increasing prices and deflation — an increase in the value of money accompanied by decreasing prices, can be destabilizing.

Inflation: More Money than Goods

As with Spanish gold or wartime spending, when too much money is moved into an economy, the value of the currency drops. There is "too much money chasing too few goods." If left alone, the value of money will find an appropriate balance with the products of the economy. Prices rise as the value of money falls until a balance is reached. The problem with higher prices is that, through no fault of their own, people on fixed incomes, all of a sudden, have to make do with less and people with savings find that their fortunes are systematically devalued.

Deflation: More Goods than Money

On the other hand, if the amount of money in circulation is insufficient for purchasing the goods and services available, the price of goods can fall, making every dollar worth more. Such "deflation" favours those with savings, but makes life more expensive for those with fixed expenses, such as rent, mortgages, or other loans.

Adjusting the Money Supply

Keeping the value of a nation's currency at close to a consistent value is the government's responsibility and a major concern of financial policy. It can be done in a number of ways. One means used to maintain the value of a country's money is to buy and sell it in financial markets. If the value is dropping, the government will buy all that is offered for sale at the lowest price it is willing to let it fall to. As long as that price is paid, it doesn't make sense for anyone to sell for less. The limitation to this is the amount of foreign exchange currency available with which to buy. Buying Canadian dollars with Canadian dollars does not work. The loss of foreign exchange currency reserves inhibits international trade and leaves a country vulnerable to further speculation. On the other hand, if the price of a country's money is rising higher than is desired, the central bank can offer up more and more to the market, until demand is satisfied and the price stabilizes. Significant amounts of foreign exchange can be gathered, thereby keeping the value of a currency down.

Operations in the money markets can counteract small fluctuations in currency value, but if there is a sizable imbalance between economic activity and the money supply, the tendency toward inflation or deflation will continue until balance is restored. Increasing or decreasing the overall money supply can restore balance.

If more money is needed in an economy, government can increase the supply by printing money and spending it into circulation, by borrowing it for the same purpose, or by making it easier for businesses and individuals to borrow it into existence through banks. In the past, when there has been too much money in circulation, the volume has been reduced through taxation, by selling government bonds, by raising the fractional reserve requirement or by increasing the prime interest rate. These approaches vary in their effectiveness and can have substantial impacts throughout a country.

When taxation is used to reduce the money supply, tax legislation is passed, people pay their taxes and that money goes out of circulation, until the government has cause to spend it. Selling bonds is similarly effective. An issue of bonds is printed, people buy them, and that money goes out of circulation. When it comes time to buy back the bonds, if the money is to stay out of circulation, a new bond issue is produced to reabsorb the money paid out redeeming the earlier issue.

Over the past few decades, because of the constant pressure to meet the demands of interest bearing loans, governments' flexibility has been limited to the point where it is no longer practical to take in money and not use it. Consequently, adjusting credit conditions, and thereby the amount of money being created through loans, is now the primary means of managing the money supply.

Making it harder to borrow effectively reduces the money supply. Two methods have been used: changing the amount of reserves the private banks are required to keep on deposit with the central bank and changing the prime interest rate, which affects the cost of borrowing. These are explained below.

Fractional Reserve Currency

A "reserve requirement" is the amount of money that banks must keep on hand in case people want to withdraw their deposits. Such reserves date back to the innovation of receipt currency. It had become customary to keep gold and silver safe in the vaults of goldsmiths, and to trade using the receipts for such deposits. Initially, the value of the receipts was the same as the value of the gold stored in the vaults. This is a 100% reserve. The goldsmiths had become bankers in their capacity to store gold and issue and redeem receipts, which were used as paper money. Eventually, bankers realized that most of the gold never left their possession. Accordingly, if someone wanted a loan, they were able to issue additional receipts in relative confidence that all the receipts would not be redeemed at the same time. Business opportunities that might have been impossible otherwise could be accommodated in this way and the banker was compensated for the service and risk, by the interest payments received from the outstanding loans.

With this ability to create money out of nothing came the perennial temptation to make more — much more — with proportionally less and less gold on hand. If the banks issued receipts totaling twice as much as the gold on deposit, they had a 50% reserve. These kinds of receipts became known as "fractional reserve currency." If the reserve was only 25%, banks could loan four times as much money into circulation as they had on deposit.

It may not have been considered ethical in the early days, but as long as people were confident that they could get gold for their receipts, it worked smoothly. It enabled economic enterprise to expand more quickly than if potential entrepreneurs had to wait upon the availability of "hard cash."

Fractional reserve banking has come to be not only legal, but also the norm. In Canada, the *Bank Act* set reserve requirements at 5%, although, with additional interest-bearing reserves also being required, 10% was more the norm. As recently as 1970, this limited the amount of money banks could create to under 10 times the amount they had on deposit with the central bank. By 1990, reserve requirements were reduced to 4% — a 25-to-1 money creation ratio. Three years later, reserve requirements had dropped to practically nothing.

A Danger of Fractional Reserve Currency

Throughout the history of reserve-based money, the most frequent cause of a loss of confidence has been over enthusiastic production. If the people producing credit, coins or bills cannot resist producing money faster than it can be absorbed, eventually there will be more money around than goods to be purchased, and prices rise.

Fractional reserve money always carries the risk of a confidence crisis. Various circumstances can inspire individuals to retrieve their money from banks and if there is sufficient cash in reserve to give to those who want their money, there is no problem. They may even decide to turn around and put that money directly back into the bank, knowing that it is, in fact, available to them. However, if many people

177

are influenced by the same circumstances and all start removing their money at the same time, the situation can accelerate into a "run on the bank." Confidence goes down, people are withdrawing their money, and it looks like there may not be enough cash for everyone wanting to make withdrawals, so many more people become worried and also try to withdraw their money. If the bank runs out of money it has to close its doors. In the past, depositors who did not get their money out before the doors closed might never have seen their savings again. Panic spreads under such circumstances and all the banks can find themselves flooded with claims. This contributed to the Great Depression, starting in 1929, and numerous similar crises after fractional reserve money became the norm. In the recent past, this pattern has been repeated in Russia, Argentina, Thailand, South Korea, Indonesia and Mexico.

Today, to reduce the risk of runs on banks, rich countries maintain a system of deposit insurance. Such insurance guarantees depositors that, if the banks get caught overextending themselves, subject to some stipulations, up to $60,000 for each account in Canada and up to $100,000 per account in the U.S., will be refunded by the respective governments. People with savings in excess of the limits can have all their money secured by maintaining more than one account. More later on how this eliminates the need for caution and guarantees extraordinary bank profits, courtesy of taxpayers.

Adjusting the Fractional Reserve Requirement

It was not long ago that raising the fractional reserve requirement was an effective way to limit money creation. By requiring private banks to keep a greater proportion of their deposits in reserves, they could not create as much new money. Raising the reserve requirement from 5 to 10% for example, would mean that the banks could only loan half as much money into circulation. Raising the requirement to 20% would cut in half again the amount of new money they could create.

In 1988 the Bank for International Settlements (BIS) adopted a policy saying it was unnecessary for banks to have any reserves when they made loans to the Organization for Economic Cooperation and Development (OECD) governments. The BIS is an international organization made up of private bankers. Its purpose is to balance accounts between countries involved in international trade, in the same way a central bank balances transactions between local banks within a country. It considers loaning to rich governments to be without risk because governments have entire populations that can be taxed in order to make payments.

In practice, the 1988 policy allowed making loans on a fractional reserve requirement of somewhat less than one-quarter of one percent. In 1991, following this recommendation, the Canadian government quietly amended the *Bank of Canada Act* to allow banks to create money for buying government debt without putting up any of their own money. Other industrial nations did the same. As of 1998, banks could lend up to 363 times as much money as they have on deposit. With interest payments guaranteed by taxpayers, it is surely a lucrative business and one that can flood the world with money.

This adjusted legislation was timely because a huge amount of bank capital had been lost as a result of speculation prior to the October 1987 stock market crash. The central role that banks played creating money for that failed gambling spree left them precariously close to insolvency. The new rules have restored bank profits and their ability to again pump money into the speculative economy.

Controlling Inflation by Raising Interest Rates

Having forsaken the adjustment of reserve requirements as a means to manage the money supply, the most readily available means is to raise or lower the prime interest rate. The prime interest rate is what the central bank charges for short-term loans to private banks. These loans are used daily to settle differences in accounts resulting from transactions between clients using different banks. The interest rates charged by private banks is the prime rate plus whatever additional charges they want to add. If the prime rate goes up, private bank rates go up and the cost of borrowing money increases. When the cost of borrowing goes up, fewer people take out loans.

Money loses value when inflation takes place; hence, those with large amounts of money encourage a strong government response to inflation. Governments respond by raising interest rates to discourage the creation of additional money through loans. As other loans are paid back, with fewer people taking out new loans, money disappears from circulation, reducing the ability of people to buy things and, thereby, reducing the inflationary pressure. For people and businesses with outstanding loans, the increased cost that results can be disastrous. Increased expenses and bankruptcies lead to job loss and, consequently, more people unable to pay for their homes, cars and other loans. This leads to another round of defaults and subsequent contraction in the money supply. This cure for inflation may bring as much, or more hardship than the inflation, but the hardship falls on people with little power to influence policy.

Controlling Deflation

Deflation can take place when there is a general drop in spending, or when production, and/or imports get significantly ahead of consumption. With unsold goods, producers are compelled to lower their prices to find buyers. Deflation may be caused by an excessive restriction of the money supply, by a crisis in confidence that causes consumers to refrain from spending their money, or from an expansion of production, which outstrips a population's interest in consuming. (In recent decades, a growing number of people have been finding that consuming more than they need actually reduces quality of life. Hence, the possibility of production outpacing demand.)

The problems that arise when deflation occurs are the same as those caused by high interest rates. The value of goods goes down as the purchasing power of individual dollars goes up. For example, when the value of money increases by 10%, the cost of a loan payment goes up by 10% in terms of what one has to trade to manage one's payments. Imagine the impact that three consecutive years of 10% deflation had on farm loans and household mortgages during the first years of the Great Depression. It is no wonder so many properties were lost. Whether the cost of credit increases because interest rates have been raised, or because the value of money has increased through deflation, the results are the same; increased expenses for everyone with outstanding loans, and bankruptcy and foreclosure for those living at the edge of their means.

Turning deflation around is thought to be less challenging than dealing with inflation. The first line of defence is to lower interest rates. In the Great Depression, even with interest rates near zero, people were too wary to borrow. The New Deal was necessary to get money into circulation. There are lots of places where injections of money are gratefully received into an economy. Between 1932 and 1934, the change in value of the U.S. dollar went from a decline of 10.3 %, to an increase of 3.4 %.

As interest rates reached the near zero level following September 11th, 2001, the head of the Federal Reserve, Alan Greenspan, mentioned the possibility that deflation might come to be experienced again in the U.S. His comment was met with such incredulity that he soon made a pointed apology for having even mentioned the "D" word. Effort has since gone into reassuring the financial community that "It can't happen here." That said, deflation has troubled the economy of Japan for more than a decade. Interest rates have been near zero there since 1995, but until recently, they had not been able to shake the deflationary conditions that started with the collapse of their speculative boom in 1989.

At present, the world is facing a combination of inflation and deflation. The costs of necessities — fuel, food, housing — are increasing, while the prices of non-essential goods are falling as a result of diminishing demand. For the affluent, increases and decreases have cancelled each other out. The poor, however, gain little relief with the decreasing cost of luxury goods. Their limited resources are almost all spent on ever more expensive essentials.

Problems with Debt-based Money

For the purposes of expanding the money supply, letting private banks create money with interest charges has some drawbacks. In his book about "modern money, debt slavery and destructive economics," Michael Rowbotham describes the hazards in detail. He identifies the practice of letting a nation's money supply be created by private interests through debt, as a "highly dubious practice [that] has been allowed to act as the foundation of our economies." And he points out the injustice of managing the money supply in a way that "people and businesses with outstanding debts can be suddenly hit with huge extra charges on their debts, simply as a management device to deter other borrowers." His warning, however, tells of a far deeper problem.

Many of us know the stress of a household mortgage. Rowbotham titled his book, *The Grip of Death*, citing the literal translation of "mortgage": "when the owner of a house pledges his or her house to another with a handshake ... until death." With the prices of houses moving upward, the proportion of people who do not own their homes outright — but pay for them at length through mortgages — has increased steadily. In 1960, mortgage loans, alone, created almost one-third of the entire money supply. Since then the proportion has risen to nearly two-thirds.

The availability of money with which you and I can trade is thanks in large part to people borrowing money into existence through loans for housing, yet those providing that service are under constant pressure to earn enough to pay off those debts. If interest rates get pushed up, or if they lose their jobs or are unable to work, dire consequences await. Millions struggle with work they despise, because they do not dare interrupt the steady earning necessary to keep their homes. With loan contracts demanding more money in return than the amount created by the loans, the competition for cash to repay loans with interest is intense.

The repercussions of debt also depreciate the commercial sector. The "pay your debts or suffer dire consequences" pressure so many are under has disabled the market process by turning competition from a stimulus to produce better goods for less cost, into a desperate struggle that has the opposite effect. Everywhere that money is borrowed, there is intense competition to gather enough to pay it back with interest. Wherever a cost can be cut or market share gained there is an opportunity to get ahead, too often at the expense of quality, workers and the environment. Second-rate materials and poorly paid workers are employed to provide low cost goods for cash strapped consumers. Often, goods are produced that no one would think to look for if it were not for the sophisticated advertising, which constantly coaxes people to part with their money.

Ever increasing economies of scale are used to increase profits. Fewer, bigger, more automated factories mass produce goods and distribute them over ever larger territories in search of the advantage that might bring in profits and pay off loans. In Britain, the 9% growth in GDP between 1985 and 1990, involved a 30% increase in transport.

When debt bondage extends into agriculture, the same considerations of increasing size and cutting corners to expand profits rise to the top of the priority list. Small-scale and family farms provide more employment per acre than large-scale operations, and they provide a range of produce close to where their customers live. Families working for generations on small farms are sensitive to the needs of the soil upon which their ongoing livelihoods depend. Without the pressures of debt they are inclined to take care of that soil. Unfortunately, farm debt is widespread. Competition drives produce prices down and producers are pressured into specialized and large-scale operations that depend on the intense production, packaging, transportation and middlemen that mass marketing requires. In turn, the necessary land and equipment require massive debt, and before long, concerns about soil fertility, nutritional quality and farming techniques that don't abuse the land or require poisons, lose out to the demand for return on investment.

Internationally, the debt trap takes on a new dimension. While practically all nations are using debt-based money, the obligations to repay debt are local to where the debt was assumed. This means that when the money created is used to purchase goods from another country, the debt remains behind and the country selling the goods receives the money, debt-free. With every nation struggling with the scarce money problem, receipts for sales overseas are very attractive. Consequently, heavy emphasis is placed on production for export. Rowbotham calls it "export warfare." The nations that appear the wealthiest also have the biggest debts and are under enormous pressure to sell abroad. It is no wonder that they take every advantage they can find.

Subsidized exports, barriers to foreign products and efforts to break down trade barriers in other countries are among the measures taken to gain an upper hand.

"Foreign aid" loans earmarked for buying the lender's products serve to cleanse money of debt. Such loans shift the interest burden from the lender to the borrower and the money involved returns directly to its country of origin. The borrower receives some of the lenders excess produce and the debt obligations of the loan, the lender gets its money back, debt-free.

While citizens, companies and nations struggle at the impossible task of earning more money than is available, the banking establishment is doing very well. In Australia, the Commonwealth Bank, which was established in 1912 with total assets of $20,000 had, by 1984, reached a net worth of $30,496,000,000. The Australian Institute for Economic Democracy points out that this process has accrued to the bank's credit.

> [Assets]... *equal to about one-third of the entire wealth of Australia... Does it not strike you as preposterous,* [it asks] *that an institution that produces nothing more than figures in books, can acquire the ownership of assets more vast than our greatest industries which employ thousands of people in all states, and upon whose physical production the entire economy of Australia depends?*

It works the same in all capitalist countries. Lord Josiah Stamp, a former director of the Bank of England, issued a clear warning in a public address in 1937. He said:

The modern banking system manufactures money out of nothing. The process is perhaps the most astounding piece of sleight of hand that was ever invented. Banking was conceived in iniquity and born in sin. Bankers own the earth; take it away from them, but leave them with the power to create credit, and with the stroke of a pen they will create enough money to buy it back again... If you want to be slaves to the bankers, and pay the costs of your own slavery, then let the banks create money.

It is a "mighty privilege," wrote Bishop Berkeley back in 1763, "for a man to create a hundred pounds with the stroke of a pen." With our global economy crippled by debt, and seeking relief from its bottomless obligations by expanding the volumes of resources it turns into garbage, it is perhaps time to ask if this privilege is well-appointed.

Debt-Money and Inflation

The classic cause of inflation is more money in circulation than is necessary to purchase available goods and services. People push prices up as they compete to buy limited stocks. While excess money in circulation has received the blame for recent bouts of inflation, when that money is laden by debt another factor takes over.

Looking back on the big deficit/inflation scare of the early 1980s, do you recall stores with empty shelves or car dealerships unable to find vehicles for eager customers? Goods, rather than being too few, remained abundant.

Do you recall anyone with the problem of having plenty of money, but nothing to buy with it? If inflation is no longer the result of the classic circumstance of more money than goods, what might have caused the inflationary pressure during that time?

When nearly all money is created as debt, every dollar, euro, pound or yen has somebody behind it compelled to pay back the equivalent, plus interest, to discharge their debt. Individuals strive for higher pay and manufacturers look for opportunities to raise their prices to enable debt repayment. Failure to repay debts can destroy a business or a family, so the underlying pressure toward inflationary wages and prices is constant and imperative.

We tend to think that whatever is standard practice is natural but, as we reassess the human project in light of the full Earth problem, the validity of the debt money system is ripe for review.

Government Created Money

It is as natural for a government to create and manage the money that enables its citizens to cooperate as it is for an organism to produce the blood that enables its cells to cooperate. A growing organism has to produce more blood to provide for the needs of its expanding community of cells, just as more money has to be put into circulation to keep the operations of a growing economy in balance. A traditional procedure for introducing new money into a growing economy has been deficit spending. That is, for governments to spend more money than they take in through taxes. Governments are often accused of mismanagement when they do this.

We hear that deficit spending is the cause of inflation, yet the commercial media fails to mention, let alone criticize, the role private banks play in inflationary money creation. They receive much of the government deficit spending as deposits. The private banks can then use that money as a fractional reserve and multiply it many times over through loans, exerting many times as much inflationary pressure. The bias of this reporting is more apparent when we consider that government spending is primarily for public services through accounts that are open for public scrutiny, while the private bank income from multiplying the deficit are all funnelled directly into their private interests. No questions are asked. Why is there less concern voiced about the actions of institutions that are unreservedly committed to serving their private interests than there is for a public institution that is obliged to serve ours? In seeking to answer this question one might come to suspect the manipulation of public opinion.

The money needed to expand the money supply through deficit spending can be created by the government itself through a national bank — like the Bank of Canada — or the government can borrow from private banks and let the private institutions create the money. Since 1975, government borrowing has increasingly been through the private banks. Because private banks charge interest for their loans, and keep that interest for their private dealings, creating money through them is costly. Canadian taxpayers provide billions of dollars annually in interest payments to private banks and their shareholders. We paid $37 billion on interest at the federal level in 2002. Not bad pay for bookkeeping, but Canadians have to wonder if they are getting as much value for this expenditure as they might. Over the years, these interest payments, along with interest on unpaid interest, have added up to hundreds of billions of dollars — an amount almost equal to the

185

entire national debt. It is to pay the interest on this debt that health care, education, social services and other programs were cut back.

It is worth noting also, that it would be a disaster if a government were to significantly pay down the national debt. Whether it is owed to private interests, or to our national bank, the money we use to trade is almost all created through debt. A great deal of money would disappear from circulation if those debts were paid back and a depression would likely follow. We could, however, borrow money from the Bank of Canada and use that money to pay back the loans from private banks. While the loans would continue to be outstanding, and money, therefore, still in circulation, the interest paid to the Bank of Canada instead of to private interests, would be returned to the public accounts less only the costs of accounting for the loans.

Canada did create its own money when dealing with the challenges of World War II. Money was created by the Bank of Canada and lent to the government at 1.5 – 2% interest. This credit financed Canada's war effort, housed a flood of immigrants, rejuvenated infrastructure, encouraged new technology, and financed the transition from being a rural, agricultural country to an urban, industrial one.

If the Bank of Canada had been used as intended — to finance the country's deficit spending — the hundreds of billions of dollars that have been paid as interest to private banks would have been paid instead to Canada's general revenue. The national debt, instead of being an expensive crisis, would be viewed as a significant portion of the nation's money supply. No extreme measures would be required. What was not spent on interest payments could be used to improve the quality of education, health care and environmental protection and to reduce taxes.

Around the time the Bank of Canada was established, Prime Minister Mackenzie King said,

> *Once a nation parts with the control of its currency and credit, it matters not who makes the nations laws. Usury, once in control, will wreck any nation. Until the control of the issue of currency and credit is restored to government and recognized as its most sacred responsibility, all talk of the sovereignty of parliament and of democracy is idle and futile.*

Regaining Control of a Nation's Money

Andrew Jackson, the seventh president of the United States made it his business to wrestle control of the money supply away from private control and return it to the nation it was intended to serve. When Jackson was elected in 1828, he set about removing personnel from within the civil service who served the interests of the Second Bank of the U.S. In his first term he fired two thousand of the federal government's eleven thousand employees. In 1832, President Jackson vetoed a bill to re-charter that privately owned bank, four years before its 20-year charter was due to expire.

Outraged, the Second Bank contributed $3,000,000 to the campaign of Jackson's challenger in the next election: a huge sum in 1832 dollars. Nevertheless, after campaigning on the promise to restore control of the money supply to the state, Jackson was re-elected by a landslide and, using money created through public institutions, began buying back the national debt held by the Second Bank.

Fighting back, Nicholas Biddle, the head of the Second Bank of the U.S., began shrinking the money supply so as to create economic hardship and thereby turn the American people against Jackson before he could close the bank by vetoing another bill to renew its charter. With surprising honesty, Biddle stated that,

> Nothing but widespread suffering will produce any effect on Congress... Our only safety is in pursuing a steady course of firm [monetary] restriction — and I have no doubt that such a course will ultimately lead to restoration of the currency and the re-charter of the Bank.

In *The Money Masters,* by Bill Still and Patrick Carmack, it is reported that:

> Nicholas Biddle made good on his threat. The Bank sharply contracted the money supply by calling in old loans and refusing to extend new ones. A financial panic ensued, followed by a deep economic depression. Predictably, Biddle blamed Jackson for the crash saying that it was caused by the withdrawal of federal funds from the Bank. Unfortunately, his plan worked well. Wages and prices sagged. Unemployment soared along with business bankruptcies. The nation quickly went into an uproar.

Newspaper editors joined the opposition in the campaign, blaming Jackson for the nation's troubles. Were it not for the surprise support of the Governor of Pennsylvania, where the Second Bank was based, and Biddle's careless boasting about his plans to crash the economy in order to have his way, the Bank might have had its charter restored. As it was, the House of Representatives voted in 1834 not to renew and the bank disappeared when its charter expired two years later.

In 1835, Andrew Jackson became the only President ever to pay off the national debt. Other efforts to create currency in the name of the USA did not fare as well.

An Offer We Can't Refuse?

Why do we pay interest to private banks when the nation's business could be conducted with money created by the nation for its own use?

The answer might have to do with two other experiments conducted in the United States with nationally created money. Abraham Lincoln had a lot of expenses associated with the American Civil War, which ran from 1861-1865. Near the end of that conflict, he issued an order to print a paper currency known as "Greenbacks." Lincoln explained his policy like this:

> *The Government should create, issue and circulate all the currency and credit needed to satisfy the spending power of the Government and the buying power of consumers... The privilege of creating and issuing money is not only the supreme prerogative of Government, but is the Government s greatest creative opportunity... By the adoption of these principles, the long-felt want for a uniform medium will be satisfied. The taxpayers will be saved immense sums of interest. The financing of all public enterprises, and the conduct of the treasury will become matters of practical administration. Money will cease to be master and become the servant of humanity.*

This policy inspired an editorial in the *London Times* explaining the Bank of England's attitude towards it:

> *If this mischievous financial policy, which has its origin in North America, shall become indurated down to a fixture, then the Government will furnish its own money without cost. It will pay off debts and be without debt. It will have all the money necessary to carry on its commerce. It will become prosperous without precedent in the history of the world. The brains, and wealth of all countries will go to North America. That country must be destroyed or it will destroy every monarchy on the globe.*

Five days after the Civil War was over, President Lincoln was assassinated. There were no further issues of Greenbacks, and they were eventually removed from circulation. The next time that money creation was tried in the name of the U.S. was by President Kennedy. He ordered the printing of United States Notes. These differed from the standard Federal Reserve Notes. The Federal Reserve, although its name suggests otherwise, is a private operation created and controlled by the richest financial operators in the U.S. Rescinding Kennedy's order to print money in the name of the U.S. was among the first things that President Johnson did after Kennedy was assassinated.

Whether or not private banking interests had anything to do with the untimely deaths of those two presidents, the fact remains that it is within the power of nations to create their own money. Letting private interests charge for creating the money supply essentially gives them a cut from everyone's business. One has to wonder how one group got the privilege to tax the blood that flows between all people and makes civilization possible? Unnatural dangers aside, it makes sense for nations to manage the creation of their money, and to oversee the way in which credit is allocated so that the life blood be directed sufficiently towards those organs and functions of society that contribute to the health and well-being of the whole.

Problems with Growth

Growth is generally considered to be good. Everything grows in the early stages of life. It is a sign of vigour and health. In our own early years, getting bigger was a preoccupation. We are encouraged by our parents, who eagerly anticipate our being able to care for ourselves, and by our own frustration with personal limitations. We keenly anticipate being able to reach the light switch and the water tap, and drive the car. It is no wonder that growth has a positive feel to it.

As individuals, however, we grow to a certain size and there we stay, (give or take a few pounds a year). We are big enough to do what humans do. To double our adult size would be of little advantage and it would create problems in terms of clothes, furniture and getting in and out of buildings and cars. Another doubling after that would be disastrous. While physical growth comes to an end, we continue to grow emotionally, spiritually and intellectually as well as in our skills and relationships.

Likewise, perpetual physical growth does not exist on the level of ecosystems. The natural growth and expansion of plants and animals in any region only continues until circumstances of space, fertility and climate put a cap on how much material can be involved in life. Ecosystems, like individual people, can become more sophisticated after they reach physical maturity. While the territory may evolve more species, and more complex interrelationships within the ecosystem, there is a natural limit to the volume of life that can exist there.

There are close parallels between this pattern and the economic reality we have created. There are also significant differences. Young economies grow as they adopt efficiencies of scale, the use of money and mechanization. There is much that people can use and a great deal of inspiration focuses on the production of those things. Our economic tradition has long exhibited the characteristics of exuberant youthful and adolescent growth. Unfortunately, as societies we have yet to accept, and find an effective way to manage, the mature stage of economic life at which we have arrived.

Human economies don't consume everything on Earth at this point. In their paper, *Human Appropriation of the Products of Photosynthesis,* Peter Vitousek, and others, calculated that, although we are only one of between 5,000,000 and 30,000,000 species, we already consume 40% of all the net products of photosynthesis on Earth, excluding the oceans (25% if the oceans are included). This was in 1986, when the human population was around 5 billion.

There is abundant evidence that we are disturbing life processes at our present volume of activity. As with the physical growth of an individual, another doubling of human activity would be disastrous, and another after that, simply impossible, even for abstract mathematics. This impossibility stands, even before we consider that most of our present energy needs are met by reserves that are the legacy of past ages.

Life patterns and planetary limits are not taken seriously by most. In official circles where big decisions are made, the policy is to grow and grow, and then grow some more. If we have poverty, we are supposed to grow so that there is more wealth to raise people out of their difficulties. If there are environmental problems, we are supposed to grow a richer economy so we have the financial resources to repair the problem. If we are depleting a natural resource, expanding extraction of that resource from lower quality reserves is prescribed. Whatever the problem, growth is the solution. When growth stops or when the economy shrinks, widespread hardship seems to support the thesis that we have to grow to be well. If our well-being depends on the impossible we are indeed in trouble.

Some true believers in "Growth Everlasting" will assert that we are learning to expand economic activity without increasing the amount of natural resources we need or the waste we create. We are becoming more efficient and getting considerably more service from natural resources than we did a few decades ago. Such improvements deserve applause and should be encouraged. But our enthusiasm should not obscure that, overall, our consumption of natural resources and production of waste has continued to rise without a pause. Expansion is built into the very structure of the present system.

Sustainable Investment Opportunities

When the Brundtland Commission popularized the notion of sustainability in 1987, numerous interpretations began to appear. I was surprised by one in particular, but it has since helped me to understand the perspective from which it comes. To see sustainability as requiring sustainable investment opportunities is to see the world from within the "money" paradigm. That paradigm assumes that well-being depends on continuous growth. With that as a given, the challenge of finding new places to invest the exponentially growing volume of money is a matter of much concern.

The following are assumed:

1) Money is created through loans rather than resources or work.
2) People who lend money have to receive more money in return for their capital than the amount they lend out.
3) Without new investment opportunities, money earned by wealthy investors would stay in savings and be lost to circulation, causing a depressed economic state.

Therefore, the economy must grow. While volumes of capital can evaporate with the collapse of companies, stock markets and whole economies, there is no official plan for rationally bringing the system to a stable state. The only goal is to grow — forever.

How then to accomplish the enormous amount of wealth expansion that is necessary? There are a number of processes underway that contribute in their own ways. They include encouraging higher levels of consumption, expanding throughput by encouraging waste, redundancy and obsolescence, and increasing the size of the speculative economy. Individual entities within the system can also accommodate their expansion by triumphing over competitors and absorbing what is left behind.

To increase individual consumption, advertising persistently uses sophisticated persuasive techniques to encourage us to buy more and more. Children are targeted as soon as they can lift their heads toward a television screen and the pitch continues throughout life. Every year, $450 billion is spent on psychological studies, creative talent, and mass distribution advertising through every form of media. In thousands of different ways, the same message is repeatedly impressed on our minds. If you want to be happy/lovable/worthy/respected, you need to buy X. It doesn't matter what the product or service promoted is, the message is the same. Acquire! It is the sort of omni-pervasive persuasion that George Orwell warned of in his book, *Nineteen Eighty Four.* Large portions of the population have taken the message to heart and have come to live under the stress of increasingly unmanageable personal debt.

Planned obsolescence helps. By making products to be used only once, to wear out quickly, to be incompatible with the next version of related equipment, or to go out of style, the length of time that they take up space in the consumer's life is diminished. The sooner they are thrown away, the sooner the individual is likely to buy more. (Landfills are assumed to be limitless.)

Although mass marketing techniques and planned waste are far more sophisticated and lead to far greater levels of consumption than was the norm in the 1920s, investment capital faces the same problem that it did in that era. There isn't enough that needs producing for local markets to occupy the capital that wants to grow. There are abundant needs for which increasing production could provide critical benefits, of course, but as mentioned earlier, the poor cannot help with the problem under which the wealthy labour.

The other standard option for investment capital is speculation. Any asset that might go up in value can be used. Stocks, bonds, national currencies, real estate, art, antiques and other collectibles are the most sought after. As long as the system is stable, there is a good chance that someone else with money to invest will pay a higher price tomorrow, or next month, for something bought today. With enormous amounts of money looking for investment opportunities, holders of capital are continuously bidding prices up and up. It is similar to the classic inflation pattern of too much money chasing too few goods, except that it is selective about which prices it drives up. With the exception of some real estate and national currencies, the items involved are of interest primarily to those with more money than they need.

Such inflation does not pose a problem. Indeed, it is inflating prices that speculators count on to make their money grow.

Making fortunes grow through real estate causes housing prices to rise beyond the reach of many who need homes. Here we see another failure of the GDP measure and the goal of expanding it. The expenses of those who cannot afford the security of owning their own homes and of those whose financial means are dangerously stretched by the costs of paying for homes, are misrepresented. The increase in the cost of each house sold registers as a positive step towards the goal of expanding economic volume, yet, the stress and other repercussions associated with the lack of a basic necessity never register.

Stocks provide vast investment opportunities. Originally, stocks provided a means to raise money to build large expensive industrial projects. Stock markets exist to enable investors to retrieve their money. Without a market where stocks can be resold, it might be necessary for companies to sell off their productive assets to reimburse investors who wanted, or needed, their money back. Without the "liquidity" of being able to retrieve investments through resale of stock, it would be far harder to find people who would loan their money and hence, help create large enterprises. While the stock markets are justified by this service, the vast majority of money changing hands in stock markets today is between people speculating that the price of the stocks they buy will inflate and provide them with a profit when they sell to other speculators. New issues of stocks are still sold on occasion for the purpose of creating new businesses, but the vast majority of stock sales contribute nothing to practical development.

Speculative transactions are purchase-and-sale agreements between willing partners. For the most part those directly involved are aware of the dangers and opportunities of what they are doing. The danger for society as a whole comes from the situation where more and more money is diverted into speculative trading and is thereby lost to the goods and services economy. In addition, since financial speculation has become the larger part of the economic process, decisions about managing the economy are increasingly influenced by the needs and desires of the speculative community, rather than by the needs of those dependent on jobs for their income.

By far the greatest part of our modern economy is the purchase and sale of real estate, currencies, stocks, bonds and other papers representing a commitment to pay the owner in the future. While these speculative items help meet the expectation that the economy should grow, they do so without contributing much of use to mutual provision. When applied to real estate and national currencies, speculative activity can lead to the degradation of families, businesses and sometimes entire countries.

Why is There Never Enough?

I grew up thinking that if a person needed a house they would arrange a mortgage, work to pay it off and eventually have the house as their own. I thought, too, that a business would borrow money to buy tools and materials, make and sell its products, pay off its loans, and then be in business for the long-term, making goods for the market, and income for the ongoing sustenance of owners and workers. Surely, with our immense ingenuity and productivity we could arrive, have enough, and enjoy life. Alas, this is not yet the way that our economic system works.

If only people with substantial wealth could perceive the enormous gains that would come from investing where real investment is needed today. In the developed world our level of productivity was high enough in the 1920s to produce everything people needed. Rather than pioneer a world without need by helping the poorer nations to match our accomplishments, we developed a culture of waste. To maintain investment opportunities, people were conditioned away from the frugality, which had been a virtue since ancient times, and encouraged to be free-spending, wasteful consumers. Now, we produce all that we need, and all we can waste, only to find that there are even larger volumes of money around seeking opportunities to grow.

We are acting like the proverbial boiling frog. A frog will jump out immediately if put into hot water. If it is set into cool water, however, and the water slowly heated, it will sit, unaware of the temperature change, until it cooks. Even as human activity breaches limits of tolerance and resource supply, we maintain the course, collectively supporting, and working to achieve, the goal of perpetual growth.

As massive, expanding volumes of wealth look for additional opportunities to continue growing, where is the economy heading? Why is "enough" such a difficult concept to grasp? Why do we have to grow? These were the questions that started me thinking about and studying economics.

While some of the answers are different perspectives of the same problem, together they provide insight into this most critical question.

One cause cited for the need to grow is about confidence. If the statistics don't show growth, people become nervous and start saving instead of buying. The resulting drop in demand depreciates the market and with it, people's confidence. The feedback loop is depressing.

It is difficult to tell how much popular confidence is actually the result of the media always reporting growth in positive terms and recession in negative terms. The impact might be different were expansion reported to be impinging on planetary limits and recession said to be stabilizing the economy. While this alternate interpretation may be more accurate in the "life" perspective, the points below have to be dealt with before that view becomes comfortable.

Another reason the economy, as presently structured, has to grow has to do with the money supply. When money is brought into circulation through interest-bearing loans, there must always be more loans made to create the money needed to pay the interest. Without new loans to increase the money supply, payment of interest fees would contract the money supply. With less money around, economic activity would shrink.

The third explanation has to do with the amount of money it takes to purchase the total product of everyone's labour. Taken together, the price of all goods and services produced, over a given period of time, consists of:

1) the wages of all the people involved, from the extraction of resources to the completion of purchase transactions;
2) the profits included along the way; and
3) the cost of capital borrowed to finance various steps.

Of these expenses, most of the wages earned will be spent buying from the total package of goods and services produced — the "gross product." Much of the profits will be spent the same way. Some of the profits, however, and much of the return on capital will go to people who are already consuming as much as they want.

Additional income, for the wealthy, does not necessarily lead to increased consumption.

For the sake of this illustration, let us say that the total price of the goods and services for a year is $1,000,000 (It is closer to a million times that — one trillion — in Canada and over ten times larger still in the U.S., but I'm trying to make this understandable.) If, of the $1,000,000 gross product, $100,000 goes to people for whom the additional income will not result in additional consumption, that money will not be available to purchase from the $1,000,000 worth of goods and services. If only $900,000 is available to purchase $1,000,000 worth of product, a tenth of that product will remain unsold. With unsold product, companies will cut back on production, less wages will get paid, reducing what workers can buy, and a downward spiral is likely.

If, on the other hand, the missing 10% is invested in new enterprises (growth), that money is spent back into circulation where it is available to purchase the balance of the initial round of production. Contraction is thus avoided by expanding overall activity.

Another reason that money has to grow to avoid hard times, is that the really big money is well invested, receiving its 5% or 10% interest, no matter what. If the economy does not grow to provide that increase, the returns on those investments reduce the money supply and diminish the economic opportunities of others.

One final reason for continued expansion is that if the number of people sharing an economy grows and the economy stays the same size, there is less available for each person. While population growth is not a sole cause of the problem, it is sometimes used to deflect scrutiny from other causes. Wherever human impacts are felt, it is important to recognize population growth as an aggravating factor. It is equally, or more important, to look at other factors. The evidence shows that populations stop growing of their own accord when local economies are managed in a way that provides people with basic education, health care and old age security (See Kerala, p128).

10 The Monopoly End Game

For many generations, we have had little experience with anything besides expansion as an economic goal. While the inertia of the present system is immense, the scope of the damage it is causing is more so. The time has come to find a steady state. Much thought has gone into how to make the shift from a growth-based system to one based on long-term well-being. Some of the techniques developed are the topic of the three chapters in the section, Economic Solutions. Before we move on to those solutions, however, we will first look at the excesses that seem necessary in order to continue with expansion at this late stage of the game.

Today's economic system evolved around the advantages provided by division of labour and economies of scale. The more people participating, the greater the volume and variety of goods and services that became available to participants. The institutions of money and open markets succeeded in expanding the possibilities for cooperation far beyond the wildest imaginings of those who helped bring them into service.

For centuries the system and the population it supported expanded with no evidence that we would ever come to natural limits. Thomas Malthuse was among the first to suggest that the human population needed to stay within bounds or we would overwhelm the Earth's ability to feed us. Malthuse was a long way ahead of his time. To this day, economists point to Malthuse and say that his predictions about limits were wrong. They go on to assert that predictions of absolute limits will always be wrong.

Concerns about limitations surfaced again in the early 1970s with the computer generated predictions of resource exhaustion and economic collapse published in the Club of Rome's book, *Limits to Growth*. These were followed, in 1987, by the "urgent notice" mentioned in Chapter 1, issued by the United Nations Commission on Environment and Development. In 1992, the U.S. National Academy of Science and Britain's Royal Society of London, two of the world's most prestigious groups of scientists, issued a joint statement warning of the need to accommodate biological limits.

That same year the Union of Concerned Scientists, a group that included 80% of all living Nobel Prize winners in science, issued a *Warning to Humanity* about overwhelming the ability of our planet to provide for us. In 1995, the International Panel on Climate Change joined the call for action to counteract our deteriorating situation. Scores of smaller organizations are regularly making calls of this nature.

To all these, economic decision-makers turn a deaf ear. Malthuse was wrong. The dates predicted by the Club of Rome were wrong. Using the "proof" that falling commodity prices demonstrate that we are moving farther away from material limits, we are encouraged to go forth and consume. If we were in trouble, the markets would tell us and make amends. Thus, all warnings are ignored.

In response, one skeptic of growth-everlasting, E. J. Mishan, pointed out:

> *A man who falls from a hundred-story building will survive the first 99 stories unscathed. Were he as sanguine as some of our technocrats, his confidence would grow with the number of stories he passed on his downward flight and would be at a maximum just before his free-fall abruptly halted.*

The elementary mathematics of continuous material expansion on a planet of constant size still warn of danger. Hazy skies at sunset, increasing rates of asthma and cancer, increasingly frequent weather extremes and melting ice caps call out for caution. Nevertheless, public policy throughout the industrialized world continues to promote and accommodate material expansion. The goal is not just to grow, but to grow at an exponentially increasing rate.

A number of reasons why the economic system as currently structured has to grow were discussed at the end of the previous chapter. They have to do with custom, perceived entitlement, insecurity and the lack of a plan for managing a mature civilization.

While whatever is normal appears natural, we are not destined to grow forever, any more than an individual is destined to be a child forever. When the economic system finally evolves into a form suitable to our mature state, we will come to see that as normal. Indeed, while the overall goal must change, many of the steps are little more than adjustments to existing patterns. If moneyed interests were to cooperate with the transition, it would take some time before the average person on the street would even notice. As for security, in the present order, the frustration of the increasing number of losers is only beginning to rise to the point where social upheaval will further complicate our challenge. The longer we wait, the more rapid and extreme the necessary changes will be. Security for all would best be served by an orderly transition.

There are many excellent steps awaiting implementation. Several are listed in the next few chapters. What is missing is the political will to acknowledge the need for change and to begin the process; in some quarters, decision-makers have yet to acknowledge the challenge. Acknowledging the goal would inspire millions of minds to address the details. Instead, the fate of humanity rests on faith in growth everlasting and the logic that, when faced with limits, we will overcome them because we have always done so. It does not make sense to test for absolute limits by pressing on in the same direction until something irrefutable knocks the wind out of our sails.

The Rules of the Game

There are lessons to be learned from the board game *Monopoly*. It was invented during the Great Depression and quickly became popular. It gave ordinary people an opportunity to play at capitalism when the real process was out of their reach. In the board game, as in the real world, those with quantities of money and, therefore, with the most property, are in a position to acquire far more than those without. As the game progresses, the gap between rich and poor grows ever wider until it becomes obvious who is winning, at which point, the poor usually acknowledge the victory of the rich and concede the game. An inexperienced player might carry on, in the hope that his/her fortunes would improve, but there is seldom such luck in the later stage of the game that would enable someone to come from behind and win.

According to the rules of *Monopoly,* the game is supposed to be played until any properties acquired by others earlier in the game, are mortgaged and eventually lost to the winner. Only when the winner has everything is the game officially over. In the real world, there is no "Chance" card for gaining the patent on a new technology with wide consumer appeal. If there was such a card, it would do for the lucky player what cars did for Henry Ford and personal computers did for Bill Gates. It would be a rare opportunity; one that would not change the outcome for most of those involved.

The normal play of the board game differs from the real life situation in two important ways. Losing everything hurts more in real life than in the board game and, the rich winners aren't interested in ending the game. While it makes sense to wrap up the game when the conclusion becomes obvious, the winners of the real-world Monopoly Game don't see it that way. Standard doctrine asserts that acquiring as much as possible is the purpose of life, and winning feels good. Coupled with the justification of the invisible hand, we can count on the winners manoeuvering to keep the game going for as long as possible.

Playing to Win

Money is a great servant, enabling millions to cooperate without ever seeing each other, but it can also be a ruthless master when it captures one's heart. How irresistibly sweet a tap into the money flow must be. The intoxication is sometimes sufficient for all traces of moral judgment to evaporate, save one: the value of turning money into more money. For many of those connected to large money flows, "good" and "bad" are clearly seen as "profit" and "loss." When personal wealth surpasses the level of any imaginable need, the addiction to gain becomes obvious. It matters not how vast the fortune has become, more is desired. Trouble emerges when the euphoria of copious abundance displaces thoughts about what one offers in return to the system of mutual provision.

In *Petrotyranny,* John Bacher documents how most nations that have gained windfall profits by exploiting oil reserves have fallen into militaristic patterns. From Gregory Baum's comments on the dust cover:

John Bacher s carefully researched book opens the reader s eyes to the evil role crude oil has come to play in the modern world, creating

dictatorial regimes, stirring up civil strife, generating wars among nations, and guiding empires in their policies of domination.

The morality of money has likely informed those with abundance ever since the first coin was struck. Money and its abuses were part of the Roman Empire and they returned with the ascension of money-based economies following the feudal age. Among those who found great opportunity, the Rothschild family is legendary. They rose to power as capitalism became established.

In 1743, Amschel Moses Bauer, a goldsmith, opened a counting house in Frankfürt, Germany. Amschel Moses was among those who saw the advantage of making loans in the form of receipts for gold in storage, and of multiplying that possibility by making loans in greater quantity than the amount of gold on hand. He was the father of Meyer Amschel Bauer whose practice became better known, by far. Over the entrance to his father's firm was a sign identifying the establishment. It depicted an eagle and a red shield — "roth schild" in German. Meyer Amschel changed his last name to Rothschild and proceeded, with the help of his five sons, to define the financial structure of the new Europe, and it seems, the world. "Let me issue and control a nation's money" the elder Rothschild is quoted as saying, "and I care not who writes the laws."

Early on, the Rothschild establishment learned that it was most profitable to loan to governments and kings as, not only were their needs large, they also had the power of taxation with which to guarantee their loans. When Meyer's sons came of age they spread out to manage branches of the family business. One remained in Frankfürt while the others moved to Vienna, London, Naples and Paris.

There is one particularly memorable story about Nathan, the son who had moved to London. Napoleon Bonaparte was a pain in the side of the European nobility. He was not of aristocratic background but, having reorganized France after the chaos of its revolution, he was very popular. Not only was he an impostor to power, he didn't want France to be in debt and beholden to money lenders. Napoleon remarked that: "One need only to consider what loans can lead to in order to realize their danger. Therefore, I would never have anything to do with them and have always striven against them." This did not encourage the money powers to overlook his lack of noble birth.

As the showdown with Napoleon at Waterloo was shaping up, the opposing forces were closely matched. Nathan had smuggled a large quantity of gold through France to finance the Duke of Wellington's army. With an extensive network of contacts, and favours to collect from past financial deals, Rothschild was able to transport the heavy cargo "right under the nose of Napoleon." Wellington was fortified, but the battle could yet go either way.

When the battle had played out in June of 1815, Nathan's communications system delivered the news to him a full day before Wellington's messenger arrived in London to tell of Napoleon's defeat. Nathan took up his accustomed place at the London Stock Exchange and, looking downcast, started selling British government bonds. Britain had sold a lot of bonds to raise money to fight Napoleon. If Napoleon had won, the country's finances would be on shaky ground. Others at the stock exchange knew that Nathan Rothschild had a good information network and, since he was selling British bonds, it was assumed that Wellington must have lost. Others started selling. Panic ensued and the price of the bonds plummeted. Nathan's agents then bought up most of the cheap paper and, thereby, took control of a large portion of Britain's debt at a small fraction of its value. When this story was published a hundred years later, in 1915, one of Nathan Rothschild's grandchildren sued to have the book repressed as untrue and libelous. He lost the case and was ordered to pay court costs.

Over 17 years of dealing in England, Nathan Rothschild reported that he had multiplied the money his father had given him 2,500 times. Brother James in Paris had, by 1869, an annual income of $40,000,000; at the time more money in a year than anyone in the New World had accumulated in a lifetime. Other brothers faired as well and, in addition, they formed partnerships and marriage bonds with other families of fortune. Governments and kings across Europe were beholden to the Rothschilds. As one French commentator in the 18th century, put it, "There is only one power in Europe and that is Rothschild."

Profiting from War

Once the morality of profit and loss replaces that of fairness and compassion, financing wars becomes totally rewarding. If a nation fails to win a war, it can lose everything. It will, therefore, do all that is possible to win. Nations at war are fertile ground for making large loans and, consequently, for expanding wealth. Sometimes the profit is made from the interest on loans, and sometimes the interest is moderate in exchange for access to resources, markets, safe passage or other business advantages that enable even more money to be made.

Quite apart from waging war to acquire resources from another country, war itself is a great opportunity for profit. To get a nation into a war, it is necessary for it to have an enemy that poses a real threat. If there is only a perceived enemy, it sometimes simply takes funds to equip it to the point that it is indeed threatening. If there is no enemy, financiers can fund a rebel movement and build it up to the point where its threat becomes real. If a country doesn't want to borrow money for war, there are ways around this for financiers: opposition parties can be funded, revolutions financed and, if necessary, leaders assassinated.

Manipulating the balance of power in ways that kept nations borrowing money to prepare for, and fight wars, was sufficiently evident in the 18th century that, in his book *The Creature from Jekyll Island,* economic historian Edward Griffin dubbed the process the "Rothschild Formula." It was not necessarily a consciously applied procedure. However, when informed by the spirit of financial gain, it is a rational way to go about the business of finding places to invest that will reap substantial returns.

The Bank of England was established in 1694 to create money for England's long conflict with France. Following that, Europe was at war from 1689-1697, 1702-1713, 1739-1742, 1744-1748, 1754-1763, 1793-1801 and 1803-1815. Griffin comments that:

> *The mark of the Rothschild Formula is unmistakable in these conflicts. Monetary scientists often were seen financing both sides. Whether ending in victory or defeat, the outcome merely preserved or restored the European "balance of power." And the most patent result of any of these wars was expanded government debt for all parties.*

The practice continues to this day. When George W. Bush declared his "War on Terrorism," he was promptly given $40 billion for the task. The money wasn't bank deposits, or even taxes. It was created out of nothing, and lent to the administration with the customary interest obligations. To get things started, the enemy had to be armed and trained — as the Afghanistan resistance had been in the 1980s, with U.S. money, in order to fight the Soviet forces there at the time.

* * * * *

One dramatic, yet relatively civil example of advantage taken for massive gain, is revealed by this memo circulated in 1891 by the American Bankers Association. It became public when it was read into the United States' Congressional Record 22 years after it was issued. It speaks of a time three years ahead:

On September 1, 1894, we will not renew our loans under any consideration. On September 1st we will demand our money. We will foreclose and become mortgagees in possession. We can take two-thirds of the farms west of the Mississippi, and thousands of them east of the Mississippi as well, at our own price... We may as well own three-fourths of the farms of the West and the money of the country. Then the farmers will become tenants as in England.

Although this was a remarkable multiple play in the "Monopoly Game" it was not unique in its inspiration. Such a move is viewed as shrewd business within the value system that holds the expansion of wealth to be the purpose of life. Aristotle would have frowned on the move as a *chrematistike* strategy. Coincidentally, or not, corporate-run agriculture began to emerge around that time.

There is abundant evidence that the winners have had the upper hand for a long time, yet it has taken until recently for the dangers of an overripe game to become critical across the board. The fundamental shift in the human condition has changed the nature of the game. As long as the Earth offered new frontiers, there were places where one might yet make a claim and prosper. As on the *Monopoly* board, before all the properties have been bought, opportunity remains. With the full Earth, opportunities are harder to come by and those behind in the global game find themselves increasingly pressed up against the limits.

While the nature of the game has changed, there are, more than ever, fortunes around the world invested and expecting the massive returns of compounded interest, demanding payment and prepared to foreclose if the payment is not forthcoming. The power that these expanding fortunes create is regularly used to the full to accommodate the further expansion of capital. Within corporations, through the media and in the halls of government, big economic interests press for greater advantages. They have to if they are to maintain their exponentially growing returns.

Oil Wealth and International Debt

Loans to the Third World were already causing problems when "petro dollars" started seeking exponential gain. In the early 1970s, Middle Eastern oil producers realized that they could apply standard doctrine and charge what the market would bear for their product. The price of oil quadrupled and huge amounts of money started to flow into those countries. Much of that money was deposited with Western banks where it could earn interest.

In search of places to invest all the new deposits, or the fractional reserve multiplier of same, the Western banks sent agents around the world in search of national leaders who were willing to commit their people to repaying loans. Large amounts of money were borrowed. Some was used for developing natural resources and industries, some for building up military forces, and some provided for the whims of the leaders. All were guaranteed by the nation states receiving them. Sometimes the loans jump-started business ventures that provided concrete benefits to the country involved and generated the funds to pay back the loans with interest. When the money was used to buy weapons or feather the nests of corrupt leaders, repaying the loans became problematic.

Even when the loans were invested in productive enterprises like agriculture, mining and manufacturing, which could earn foreign exchange, a problem emerged. Such loans were being made to many countries. With numerous enterprises subsequently coming on-stream and offering similar commodities to the world, markets became flooded and prices dropped to the point where many of the debtor nations were unable to earn enough to service their loans.

Now as then, once hooked with unpayable loans, the magic/curse of compound interest works its wonders. The problem becomes critical when a country is unable to make regular payments and more money has to be borrowed to avoid bankruptcy. This makes the loan total larger and the corresponding payments either larger, or spread out over a longer period of time. Instead of developing to meet the needs of their people, many developing nations found themselves obliged to focus, above all else, on production for export. It is colonialism all over again, except that exploited nations don't actually get invaded unless they actively challenge the legitimacy of their bondage.

Over time, the countries in the worst shape have been abandoned by commercial banks. The most indebted countries looked like they might go bankrupt, causing the loaned money to disappear. Many such loans have been sold to the World Bank and the International Monetary Fund (IMF), which are willing to provide emergency funds, under certain conditions.

In order to qualify for help from the World Bank and the IMF, countries have to agree to Structural Adjustment Programs (SAPs) based on the premise of economic theory. They are expected to adopt the culture of Western capitalism and foster conditions where private interests can maximize profits. Even the most basic expenditures on social services, health care and education are considered "luxuries" that should be cut back or removed from public control until their "economic house is in order." Applicant countries are required to privatize key national industries and essential services on the assumption that the private sector and its "invisible hand" will operate them more efficiently, and so that the country can turn the money from selling those assets over to the banks as loan payments. (Remember that the game is not over until the losers have mortgaged and lost the properties they held earlier in the game.) Finally, SAPs require debtors to open up their borders to foreign investment to encourage private capital to enter the country.

According to conventional market theory, these prescribed conditions will transform debtor countries into lean, mean, money-making communities. While the conditions do favour some money-making organizations within the country (and from outside the country as well), they are devastating to the poor. The market mechanism is an excellent way to organize the allocation of resources when the people involved have money. When people have no money, their broken lives are written off as collateral damage.

Structural Adjustment Programs are famous for sending large numbers of people into desperate poverty. With subsidies removed from basic foods, water, cooking fuels and housing, many can no longer afford the basics of life and are forced into desperate actions.

In his book, *The Globalization of Poverty,* Michael Chossudovsky documents how IMF Structural Adjustment Programs undermined the well-being of the peoples of Rwanda, the former Yugoslavia, Argentina and other troubled nations. "Entire countries," he wrote "have been destabilized as a consequence of the collapse of national currencies, often resulting in the outbreak of social strife, ethnic conflict and civil war."

A great deal has been reported about these consequences in the commercial press, but very little about the role played by the debt money system's drive for exponential returns on loans to those countries. A case in point: Large volumes of international speculative capital were enticed into the South Korean economy in the 1990s. In response to financial liberalization, prices of real estate and business stock soared as more and more capital sought to profit from the rapid growth. Eventually it became obvious that the assets being bid up were overvalued. In 1997, international capital started harvesting its gains. When investors were seen accepting lower prices, the trickle of disinvestment became a flood.

Following the pattern of such crashes, the negative feedback cycle eventually caused the value of Korean money and the goods it produced to fall drastically. When coupled with increasing interest rates aimed at keeping money in the country, the investment cycle drove large numbers of businesses into bankruptcy, threw millions out of work and depressed the entire economy. As a result, South Korea's productive assets could be purchased at "fire sale" prices, thereby enabling the financial giants in their endless quest to make their fortunes grow.

Much of the above can also be applied to Thailand, Malaysia and Indonesia. These "Asian Tigers" all voluntarily converted their economies to conform with the neo-classical ideal. They initially prospered and their success was held up as an example that all developing nations should follow.

> [Usury is] *any bargain, in which one party obviously gained more advantage than the other, and used his power to the full.*
> 16th century British parliamentary debate

Joseph Stiglitz was the chief economist and vice-president at the World Bank from 1996 to November 1999 and had an inside view of how the IMF dealt with the crisis that overwhelmed the Asian Tigers. Indeed, he was fired for criticizing how those crises were handled. According to Stiglitz, consolidation of economic control around the world appears to be a hidden agenda of the World Bank and the International Monetary Fund.

In an article published in the *London Observer,* following an interview with Stiglitz, Gregory Palast (author of *Armed Madhouse: Dispatches from the Front Lines of the Class War*) outlined the four-step program that the IMF imposed on every nation that came to it in distress:

1) The first step is, privatization. Stiglitz said:

> *Some politicians, using the World Bank s demands to silence local critics, happily flogged their electricity and water companies."You could see their eyes widen" at the possibility of commissions for shaving a few billion off the sale price.*

Stiglitz described the most prominent example of this in his letter of resignation.

> *The rapid privatization urged upon Moscow by the IMF and the [U.S.] Treasury Department had allowed a small group of oligarchs to gain control of state assets.* [The U.S. Treasury Department is 51% owner of the World Bank.] *While the government lacked the money to pay pensioners, the oligarchs were sending money obtained by stripping assets and selling the country s precious national resources into Cypriot and Swiss bank accounts.*
>
> *Output plummeted by half. While only two percent of the population lived in poverty even at the end of the dismal Soviet period, "reform" saw poverty rates soar to almost 50 percent...*

2) Step Two is capital market liberalization, i.e. allowing foreign investment. "In theory this allows investment capital to flow in and out. Unfortunately, as in Indonesia and Brazil, the money often simply flows out."

"Stiglitz calls this the 'hot money' cycle," says Palast. "Cash comes in for speculation in real estate and currency, then flees at the first sign of trouble. A nation's reserves can drain in days."

"And when that happens, to seduce speculators into returning a nation's own capital funds, the IMF demands these nations raise interest rates to 30%, 50% and 80%."

"'The result is predictable' said Stiglitz. Higher interest rates demolish property values, savage industrial production and drain national treasuries."

3) Step Three [is] market-based pricing — a fancy term for raising prices on food, water and cooking gas. This leads predictably, to Step-Three-and-a-Half: what Stiglitz calls 'the IMF riot'." (In World Bank documents, obtained by Palast from another source, were suggestions that the Structural Adjustment Programs "could be expected to spark 'social unrest'.")

4) Step Four is free trade. "This is free trade by the rules of the World Trade Organization and the World Bank, which Stiglitz likens to the Opium Wars. 'That too was about opening markets,' he said. "As in the nineteenth century, Europeans and Americans are kicking down barriers to sales in Asia, Latin America and Africa while barricading our own markets against the Third World's agriculture."

Stiglitz ended his own statement on the process by asking: "... did America — and the IMF — push policies because we, or they, believed the policies would help East Asia, or because we believed they would benefit financial interests in the United States and the advanced industrial world?"

The interests served are those in need of sustainable investment opportunities. This need arises from the insatiable goal of growth-addicted economies. It is managed according to the profit and loss morality that takes root firmly in the hearts of those who drink deeply from the money flows that are meant to nurture mutual provision.

Corporate Globalization

The four-step program of the IMF uses the advantage of the lender over the borrower to impose the agenda of "corporate globalization" and the World Trade Organization (WTO). Such globalization is based on faith in the mechanisms of international trade: faith that the effectiveness of markets and the tangible gains that have been realized in the past, and from division of labour, mass production and trade will bring huge additional benefits if universally applied. The vision is of a capitalist heaven where the entire world competes under the benevolent guidance of the invisible hand in open markets.

This grand vision no doubt informs those who populate departments of foreign affairs and international trade in nations around the world. These well-meaning people were all taught this faith in the management schools where they were trained, or on the job, by people of that faith. The evidence that global civilization is not responding as anticipated just muddies the brilliance of the vision. It has yet to be recognized as repudiation of that vision.

Industrial development in the Northern countries was accomplished by protecting their young industries and markets with effective trade barriers. The brazen contradiction of expecting newly industrializing nations to succeed by doing the opposite should awaken unbiased dreamers. How might fledgling economies really be expected to fare in competition with the world's most powerful

209

interests? Huge numbers of people have already become alienated by the scale of the nation state. It is no wonder that only those with global reach seem to appreciate the vision of operating on a planetary scale! The changes that have taken place in the nature of markets, self-interest, efficiency, and competition were outlined earlier. Add to this the challenges emerging from the full Earth situation and the imminent reduction in the availability of transportation fuel, and the vision of a one-world economy must be challenged.

The true believers will point to many developing countries and say that the GDP of those countries is growing. They either do not know, or choose to forget that GDP does not speak for the well-being of the people of individual countries. It speaks for the well-being of money. Before the word "globalization" made it into popular language, those promoting international trade changed the measuring stick. GNP, which measured the amount of money being made within a nation for use within that nation, was changed to GDP, which measures money made within a nation regardless of where that money goes after it is made. With GNP, the possibility at least existed that the benefits of that money would be spread around within the country. In money's imprecise way, it indicated how well the country was doing. The new measure indicates the potential a country offers as an investment opportunity. The money recorded as GDP includes profits and loan payments going to outside interests. In countries colonized through monetary globalization, these payments to outside interests can make up a large portion of GDP.

The contribution of such globalization to the "End Game" is never publicly explained. At this late stage, drawing developing nations into the game is like annexing additional *Monopoly* boards on to one where the identity of the winner has already been clearly established. It is not an invitation to join the game as equals. With winning interests having internal budgets greater than most Third World countries, the inexperienced newcomers are far more likely to be consumed to accommodate the growth of the giants than to find a level playing field upon which they might rise to affluence.

For nations to let go of their ability to feed their people, and abandon the provision of other essentials on the strength of economic theory, is extremely short-sighted. Especially when the theory is left over from the days of an "empty" world with seemingly unlimited energy. With cheap energy, it may appear more efficient economically, to focus on specialties and trade for food from other nations, but increasing energy costs and absolute shortages will drastically change the calculations. It takes generations for a population to develop a viable farming culture, yet those skills and customs can be lost in a single life time if they are not passed to the next generation.

Farmers, environmentalists, trade unionists and social justice, peace and other citizen activists, are protesting the agenda of the global trading regime. Enormous opposition has been expressed, and the message that something is wrong with the present globalization agenda is getting through to the public. Unfortunately, it has yet to be taken to heart by policy-makers.

In April, 2001 a G8 (the richest industrialized countries) meeting took place in Quebec City, Canada. The authorities had erected a 10-foot fence around the area where the trade negotiations were being held, making old Quebec City look like a fortified camp. Hundreds of thousands of protesters arrived and staged mostly peaceful demonstrations. They expressed their concerns about the world diving blindly into an economic system that ignores social and environmental considerations and operates beyond the control of democratically elected governments. So much tear gas was used on the demonstrators over the three days that local supplies were exhausted and more had to be rushed in to enforce the official policy of keeping the demonstrators away from the meeting area. When asked how the meetings had been seen by its Canadian hosts, an employee of the International Trade section of Foreign Affairs here in Canada, reported that the organizers felt the meetings had gone very well and that the process was on track.

I suspect that these public servants, each playing their part in the grand scheme of things, truly believe that applying the fundamentals of classical economics will benefit humanity. It is my hope that eventually, some of them will recognize how the scale and context of economic growth has changed since the benefits of market-based mutual provision emerged from feudalism.

Meanwhile, the spirit of "the game," is alive and well. Huge amounts of wealth are actively poised, seeking opportunities for gain. Satellites scan the Earth from space looking for schools of fish, forests and mineral deposits where capital can move in and turn them into money. The trade deals of corporate globalization open the doors of nations, enabling capital to move in and out, to secure the profits necessary to advance the game. When everything available is not enough, the abstract world of speculation provides a precarious, yet potentially unlimited field for investment. The material world offers many opportunities, but the mathematics of exponential growth exceeds Earthly bounds.

The Virtual Economy

Following the humanitarian disaster of the 1930s, steps were taken to prevent speculation from getting out of hand again. The warning sign of ballooning asset values had been noted in the 1920s, but no one took action. The 1929 Crash could have been minimized by raising reserve requirements or interest rates or otherwise curbing the expanding volumes of credit that were being created to inflate the bubble. Such action would have brought the speculative economy down before it reached the dizzying heights from which it eventually crashed. The economic managers of the day, however, chose to let the balloon continue to swell, to burst of its own accord. They feared that, if they were seen to be putting on the brakes, they would be blamed for the losses suffered.

After the 1929 Crash, there remained clear evidence of market manipulation, and the increasing volumes of money that had been created by banks to play the market. Well-financed speculators could be traced pooling their money and running up stock values to attract the attention of individuals looking to get involved in "the action." The stock market appeared to be pumping wealth into the hands of participants. With new investors eager to buy up the latest wonder stock, the big players sold it to them, leaving them with an empty bag.

In an effort to prevent future catastrophes like the 1929 Crash, the 1933 *Banking Act* was passed in the U.S. This was the same Act that established deposit insurance. Because of the catastrophe that came from allowing financial institutions both to create money and to speculate with the money they created, banks were required to choose between the business of taking deposits and making loans, and the business of dealing in stocks, bonds and other securities. The law forbade doing both.

A number of things have happened since that have eliminated this separation. In the original Act, overseas securities were not included. At that time, trade in national currencies and "derivatives," like the future production of commodities, and the potential for change in the value of stocks and currency, which are extensively traded today, were practically non-existent, and in some cases had not yet been imagined. Consequently, they were not mentioned in the Act and banks traded freely in these markets as they emerged. The limits imposed by the *Banking Act* were further eroded by court challenges around vagaries in its wording, and concerns that the emerging markets might be lost to overseas competitors. The result is that banks are, again, extensively involved in financial speculation. The deposit insurance part of the 1933 *Banking Act,* however, is still in effect.

Deposit insurance, as explained in Chapter 9, protects people with bank accounts from losing their money if their bank gets into trouble. The vicious circle of loss of confidence, deposit withdrawal, and confidence shaking bank line-ups and closures, is thus, largely avoided. This is good for individuals, and to an extent it stabilizes the financial system. At the same time, however, by guaranteeing that depositors won't have reason to hold them accountable, the big banks no longer have to be cautious. If their speculation goes bad, the government will bail them out. This opens a whole new mechanism for making money grow.

In 1984, the seventh largest bank in the U.S., Continental Illinois was caught in a credit crunch. Creative bookkeeping and inflated dividends aiming to assure shareholders that business was as usual, necessitated the sale of a profitable credit-card operation to provide for current expenses. The public did not see beyond the facade of normalcy, but large investors saw trouble and started to withdraw their funds. In four days, $3.6 billion was withdrawn. Within another week the total amounted to more than $6 billion.

The possibility of such a large bank failing stimulated rapid action at the Federal Reserve and the U.S. Federal Deposit Insurance Corporation (FDIC). Although only 4% of Continental's deposits were covered by deposit insurance, all depositors were repaid in full: even those with deposits greater than the maximum insurable amount. Between the FDIC's payout and the Federal Reserve's generous credit, over $9 billion was provided to Continental Illinois to maintain the appearance of normalcy. All that money was created out of thin air, and, attached to it all was the obligation to pay interest.

The bailout cycle works like this. When a large bank gets into trouble, the government creates money by borrowing from other banks to refund the troubled bank's depositors. Sometimes, the money borrowed from one bank is used to reimburse that same bank for the investments they had in the troubled bank. The lending bank then gets both its investment back from the troubled bank and starts receiving interest on the money they created to enable that repayment. It is a profitable arrangement courtesy of taxpayers.

The "creative bookkeeping" of the Continental Illinois bank was a harbinger of Enron, World Com, Global Crossing, Parmalat and other major economic players who have been unable to meet the expectation of exponentially expanding wealth. When expectations grow beyond realistic possibility, what is left besides trying to create the illusion of growth? After all, most of the money in the system is the illusion of credit. Banks create it out of nothing, why not corporations?

Another example with a private business, happened in the late 1990s. Long-term Capital Management (LTCM) was making money grow. John Meriweather and associates started their project by raising $2.2 billion from rich investors. They used that money as collateral for loans to buy $125 billion in securities. The securities in turn were used as collateral to borrow $1.25 trillion, with which they made a wide variety of investment bets in the financial markets. When a number of the bets soured in September 1998, the scheme collapsed. Sixteen U.S. banks, having created volumes of credit for LTCM, were in danger of default. The scale of the operation was big enough to threaten the stability of the entire financial system. *The New York Times* reported that, coordinated by the Federal Reserve Bank of New York, a "hastily assembled consortium of international banks and brokerage houses took possession of the faltering firm and pumped in $3.65 billion to prevent a disorderly collapse."

The financial world of today is similar in many ways to how it was the late 1920s. Speculation is rampant and huge amounts of debt are being created to fuel the process. The setbacks of Black Monday in 1987, and the "Asian Meltdown" in 1997, were taken in stride, as were the financial crises of Mexico's near default and Argentina's economic collapse. Huge numbers of people descend into hard times as their countries lose out, but internationally, growth is sustained and the game continues. The bubble continues to expand even as its material foundation diminishes.

Until we recreate our economic system we are in a precarious position. With each incremental advance in the growth progression it becomes increasingly more difficult to achieve the next increment. Whenever a major player succumbs to the impossibility of perpetual growth, the system is in danger. If it were not for the massive build up of military and security expenditures that commenced soon after the high-tech bubble burst in 2000, there would be no telling where the North American economy (and the world's economy) might be today.

The "War on Terror" has helped keep money circulating. It is an ultimate make-work program that provides huge growth opportunities in the manufacture of massively destructive weapons and then doubles those opportunities through contracts to reconstruct the things those weapons destroy. The international agreements that have been broken to accommodate that increment of growth, the assertion that if one has the power one has the right to take whatever one wants, and the atmosphere of fear and suspicion that the enterprise is causing, are disrupting international cooperation in ways that will have untold consequences as we try to deal with the challenges of our full Earth.

We are entering what John McMurtry calls "the cancer stage of capitalism." In his book by the same name, McMurtry explains how money has traditionally been used by people to enable them to better care for themselves and their offspring. With the transfer of power from people and their governments to institutions dedicated to the multiplication of wealth, money has begun to use people and the rest of the living world for the purpose of reproducing itself. By taking control of the money supply and demanding payment for its use, "the money game" has put civilization at risk.

The change, from life using money to beget more life, to money using life to beget more money, is where the problem becomes potentially terminal. Our bodies use the capabilities of individual cells to maintain the well-being of our whole selves. When cells begin to draw, without reserve, on the life energy of the body in which they are located, to serve their own exponential multiplication, the host is in trouble. These cancerous cells have no interest except to grow. They don't care that their extraordinary success as individuals will destroy the community they inhabit, and with it, themselves.

Does anyone actually believe that the Global Monopoly Game can be played until "everything" is owned by one group of people?

What would that look like?

What would we do next?

How long might we continue to play "The Game" before it collapses? There are better ways to manage mutual provision.

Economic Solutions

It is not easy to live in a way that does not degrade the environment or exploit other people and species. Most of us earn our pay working within the economic system and we buy what we need from it. If, by following the opportunities offered, we accelerate damage to ecosystems and human communities, the system's abstraction seldom reveals the connections. If we do see the connections, any relief that changing our individual behaviours might provide seems inconsequential compared to what it would take to solve the problems.

While a person might think from time to time about problems and the need to change, messages negating those concerns are everywhere. The message to consume ever more is delivered so constantly and through so many potent media that we seldom recognize the indoctrination we are subjected to.

The present system evolved by making the most of opportunities. In the early years, the side effects appeared minimal compared to the advantages gained, and so the basic pattern spread and flourished. Over the centuries it has become entrenched. It continues to expand, powerful in its narrowly defined efficiency, and insulated from signs of danger by denial, firmly rooted in habit, pride and vested interests.

Nevertheless, a small but growing number of people are making the effort to reform their lifestyles in order to minimize their negative impacts. While individual actions can seem inconsequential compared to the magnitude of the change required, they have an effect far greater than the actual reductions to social impacts and resource flows. Actions should not be avoided because the problem looks too big. Personal actions are testimonial to the larger vision. They help pioneer new patterns of behaviour that can inform and inspire others, as well as reinforce the will to press for change at the structural level. When actions are based on the realization that life offers more when one gets off the treadmill of accelerating earning and spending, personal rewards abound in terms of stress reduction, free time and increased opportunities to enjoy life.

People have begun new businesses that are benign by design. Some are motivated by conscience, others bet that society will grow up and that their venture will have a head start in the new game. Whatever their motives, the people involved are to be supported and strongly commended for pioneering the possibilities for others to witness. They provide a model, and hope for those facing the serious challenges posed by our huge and expanding civilization.

While individuals, by making the effort, can considerably reduce the negative impacts of their lifestyle, legitimacy is still bestowed upon the growth ideology and most people seem content to "go with the flow" — there is enough to do without trying to recreate the world. Anything else requires extra thought and effort and can carry with it a sense of rebellion that many are uncomfortable with.

The next few chapters are about adjustments that can be made to the structure of the economic system to incline the cumulative effect toward sustainability. After making such changes, everyone could continue to do what people have always done — try to get as much service and pleasure as possible from what is available. The difference would be that the rules of the game would take social and ecological factors into equal account along with financial ones. Products that cause problems in their production, use and disposal would be priced so as to provide the funds needed to correct those problems. Products that do not cause such problems would, consequently, be less expensive. Full-cost Accounting would result in a "level playing field" with all enterprises having the same rules. Advantage would go to those who find the most creative ways to avoid contributing to the problems, rather than those who leave the costs for others.

The dilemma we face is that, unless society acknowledges the looming problems as yet unacknowledged by present economics, it will be very difficult to institute the changes described here. And until the new goal is reflected in our legal structure, popular legitimacy may not be enough. Moving the growing acceptance into governing policy is the purpose of the "Question of Direction," which is discussed in Chapter 15.

Before this proposal for tipping the balance of legitimacy toward sustainability is presented, it will be helpful for the reader to picture the sort of changes that can advance the new goal. It is possible to reorganize our system of mutual provision in ways that will incline everyone's actions toward long-term well-being. We would still make our own decisions, but, in some important ways we would be playing a new game. When we can show how huge improvements in long-term security can be produced through such adaptations, it will become easier to gather the support needed to make the changes.

It is possible to reorganize our system of mutual provision in ways that will incline everyone's actions toward long-term well-being.

Change, whether positive or negative, however, tends to make people uneasy; we are uncertain of how a new situation will affect us.

The first step, therefore, does not involve change. The first step involves opening our eyes as a society and looking closely at how present circumstances are already affecting us.

11 First Steps

Measuring Well-being

The present measure of progress accounts only for economic transactions. By augmenting these with accounts of social and environmental considerations, we would get a much more accurate picture of how we are doing in the world today. Decisions informed by such a "Triple Bottom Line" — social, economic and environmental — would surely be more effective at achieving long-term well-being.

> *Indicators are powerful. What we count and measure reflects our values as a society and literally determines what makes it onto the policy agenda of governments. As we enter the new millennium, these indicators tell us whether we are making progress, whether we are leaving the world a better place for our children, and what we need to change.*
>
> Ron Colman, Director, *GPI Atlantic*

Measuring progress solely in terms of how much money is changing hands, as is presently the case with GDP, can be misleading. By that logic, when pollution makes people sick, the cost of their medical care is added to the GDP. The costs of replacing stolen property, purchasing security equipment, trying people in courts and putting them in jail all contribute to a higher GDP. If increasing GDP is our goal, sickness and crime are good, and policies that might significantly reduce them would be counterproductive.

A dramatic example of how GDP gives a distorted view was provided when two storms hit France just after Christmas, 1999.

Winds gusting to 200 kilometres per hour killed 91 people, cut electricity off from over 3 million people and left 360 million trees "ripped from their roots or snapped in half." Damage was estimated at $11.8 billion U.S., of which $7.2 billion was covered by insurance and government. The remaining $4.6 billion fell, by default, to unfortunate citizens. The vast amount of materials and labour needed to rebuild was seen as an economic stimulus as it moved money out of institutional accounts and into the hands of contractors. Denis Kessler, the vice-president of one of France's business think tanks noted that, "This disaster will be mostly positive in terms of Gross Domestic Product."

The collapse of Canada's East Coast cod fishery in 1992 illustrates the hazard of basing decisions solely on how much money something is making. Year after year that fishery had been reporting higher earnings — the ultimate sign of success in the GDP world-view. Decisions were made to continue with the policies that led to this success. Annual quotas were set as high as 230,000 tons and bigger fishing boats were subsidized to bring in more fish. The "success" continued year after year until, with no warning from the economic measure, the fish stocks collapsed and the industry was shut down. Thousands of people lost their livelihoods, and the communities they lived in became depressed and dependent on government support. In 1999, the cod fishery was reopened on a smaller scale with the quota set at nine thousand tons. By 2002, the quota was reduced to 5,600 tons, but fishermen were unable to find even that much cod. Canada's Northern (Atlantic) Cod — once so plentiful that they could be caught by lowering a bucket over the side of a boat — was officially listed as an endangered species in May of 2003.

These and countless other observations contradict the faith that more money flow means increased well-being. While this concern has been voiced numerous times over the last century, great strides have only recently been made toward establishing more accurate measures. Hazel Henderson had been writing about it for years. Herman Daly and John Cobb presented an "Index of Sustainable Economic Welfare" in their 1989 edition of *For the Common Good.* The Canadian National Film Board's production, *Who s Counting?; Sex, Lies and Global Economics* helped popularize Marilyn Waring's book about what would be considered important if women were asked how we might measure success. In October of 1995, a group called Redefining Progress had their watershed article, "If the GDP is Up, Why is

America Down?" published in the *Atlantic Monthly*. Since then, numerous organizations, including the Atkinson Charitable Foundation, with their Canadian Index of Well-being and the David Suzuki Foundation in their Sustainability in a Generation program, have taken up the task of developing and promoting better measures of well-being.

Genuine Progress Index

Making decisions primarily on the information provided by GDP is like driving a bus using only the speedometer. The GDP "speedometer" has its place, but it doesn't explain some matters of consequence.

With the Northern Cod fishery, for example, the industry's contribution to GDP was rising steadily until just before it disappeared. Another instrument on the dashboard — one that measured changes in fish stocks — could have provided information that would have cautioned those driving to steer clear of the "overshoot and collapse" disaster that followed.

Several "instruments" that should be on the dashboard of our proverbial bus, are described below. Their purposes would be to: end the confusion between constructive and regrettable expenditures; recognize unpaid work for the benefits it provides to families and communities; keep a closer eye on the adequacy of employment opportunities; provide a "balance sheet" type account of natural resource stocks; record, for comparison, the amounts of various pollutants released into the environment, their levels of accumulation and their effects; and monitor other factors that people feel might affect our well-being.

When the opportunity arose for me to work with a Member of Parliament promoting a Genuine Progress Index (GPI) for Canada, the people already involved in such work quickly offered me their wholehearted cooperation. These included Ron Colman of the GPI Atlantic, Mark Anielski of the Alberta GPI and Sandra Zagon with the Canadian Policy Research Networks to name a few of the most active in Canada. Perspectives were shared, understanding grew, techniques were proposed, and after numerous drafts and revisions we had a proposal for national legislation.

The result was the *Canada Well-Being Measurement Act,* which will be discussed here following an explanation about measuring genuine progress.

Separating Constructive and Regrettable Expenditures

The value to society represented by the amount of money spent producing food, shelter and tools, providing education and creating works of art, differs substantially from the value we receive from money spent on medical assistance for people with avoidable diseases, replacing stolen property, treating people for addictions, or cleaning up oil spills. The former, constructive expenditures up to the point of comfortable sufficiency, contribute directly and positively to human well-being. The later, called regrettable expenditures, are only necessary because we have failed to avoid problems. While remedial work is important when problems are identified, increasing regrettable expenditures should not be mistaken for progress.

Increasing activities that provide for human needs and enrich our lives has a generally positive effect, as long as the things produced get to those who need them. The negative repercussions of resource depletion and pollution from excessive consumption are accounted for in subsequent categories below.

Food consumption illustrates the line between constructive and regrettable expenditures. When people are truly hungry, more food is distinctly positive. However, when people are becoming obese from over-eating, additional consumption of food can contribute to costly medical problems that degrade their lives. The diabetes industry thrives on such over-consumption. Cases of Type 2 Diabetes have climbed in unison with the expansion of the fast food industry. Worldwide, approximately 30 million people had the disease in 1985. The number is in the range of 150 million today. The World Health Organization expects 300 million cases by 2025. While fast food outlets do offer salads and other non-problematic dishes, most of their customers hunger for sugar, salt and fat. Type 2 Diabetes is largely preventable, but the excessive consumption of fat and sugar, the major contributing factors, create complications that add substantially to GDP.

The direct health care costs for treating diabetes attributed to obesity is over $400 million annually in Canada. Eli Lilly and Company, manufacturers of the synthetic insulin needed by diabetics, sold $901 million worth of the drug internationally in 2001, a substantial contribution to GDP. The announcement that Lilly will be constructing over 80,000 square metres of new production space, at a cost of $1,383 million, has been presented as an economic boom. If it were not for the enormous amount of human suffering that makes it necessary, it might be so. However, with the disease in the U.S. contributing to the deaths of 200,000 people annually, news of the expanding industry is more accurately described as an unfolding disaster.

The costs of avoidable health problems, crime, family breakdown, traffic accidents, natural disasters and wars all contribute to increased GDP, but, to a large extent, are indications of trouble rather than progress. By separating such regrettable expenditures from positive ones, a Genuine Progress Index can provide policy-makers with much better information upon which to make decisions.

Accounting for the Value of Unpaid Work

Imagine the state of society if people didn't take out the garbage, do the dishes, or clean and repair their homes; if parents didn't care for their children and no one took the time to look after people who are sick or aging, unless they were paid for each hour. Chaos and discomfort would result very quickly. Civilization could grind to a halt within a generation. The work that people do for their families and for their communities provides enormous benefits to the well-being of society. Yet, because money is not exchanged for this essential work, it is considered worthless by the GDP measure.

Other voluntary work that goes unaccounted for by GDP includes Guides, Scouts, Big Brothers and Big Sisters, service clubs, soup kitchens, and a great deal of the activities that make community events, like amateur sports, theatre, fairs and festivals, possible. The absence of these would greatly diminish the quality of many lives.

Much of the work that is done for free is also done in other circumstances for pay. A GPI would establish the value of unpaid work by taking the average pay rates for the various activities and multiplying those rates by the approximate number of volunteer hours spent at each sort of task. The sum total would provide a measure of the contribution unpaid work makes to well-being in society. If circumstances arise, or decisions get made that reduce the amount of unpaid work taking place, GPI accounts would be able to compare the loss against the benefits those changes brought about. Such comparisons would make it possible to determine if progress was, in fact, being made.

A Balance Sheet for Natural Resources

Balance sheet accounting has been standard practice in business since the late 1700s. If a business is making clothing out of cotton cloth, for example, and 100 pairs of pants and 100 blouses are made, the new stock of finished goods will be accounted for as inventory worth a certain amount and available for sale. At the same time, the amount of raw cloth that was used up in the production process will be subtracted from the material stock inventory. The value of the clothing is worth more than the value of the cloth, so money is being made. But, if the company does not account for the reduction in the raw materials presently in stock, they may be caught without sufficient inventory to produce the next run of garments.

By the same reasoning, when natural resources are extracted from the Earth it is worthwhile to account, not only for the value of the materials brought into the human economy, but also for the reduction of those resources in the natural world.

Understandably, our economic system emerged without such balance sheet accounts. Just a few centuries ago, human numbers and the extent of our actions were relatively inconsequential. With vast, sparsely populated frontiers, the Earth seemed to offer a limitless supply of raw materials. It is no wonder that we did not bother to compare our consumption with overall supply; we had no concept that the Earth itself was finite.

This is no longer the case. We have extensively mapped available natural resources around the globe, and our level of consumption has grown exponentially to where mathematical projections predict serious supply problems for fresh water, forests, fish, fossil-fuel and soil fertility, among others. If we hope to make decisions that will not leave our offspring holding an empty bag, balance sheet accounts of natural resources use are critically important.

There are three types of accounts needed: renewable resources, non-renewable resources that can be recycled, and non-renewable resources that are destroyed when they are used.

Renewable Resources

The use of renewable resources would be accounted for in comparison to their rate of renewal. Fish, trees, crops and water flows are like money in the bank. They produce a certain amount of "interest" on a regular basis. As long as we need and consume only the annual production, we can do so forever. If we consume living resources at a rate faster than they can grow, we diminish the "capital stock," thereby reducing the amount that can grow from it in future years.

Over-exploitation can also depress the quality of capital stocks. Where forests are clear-cut, the soil, no longer protected from the elements by vegetation, can erode, leaving it unable to grow trees as well as before. All the commonly used renewable resources have been studied thoroughly enough that, given the political will to act responsibly, rates of renewal and safe maximum levels of extraction could be established. Balance sheet accounts could then keep track of the amount of the various resources "in stock" and the various rates at which we are extracting resources from those stocks.

Recyclable Non-renewable Resources

Two accounts would be required to monitor the use of non-renewable resources that can be recycled — metals and minerals. A balance sheet, would keep a record of how much of each resource is being extracted relative to known reserves. Another account would track the rate at which each resource was being recycled. Together these figures would tell us when rates of consumption approach the edge of what can be sustained. Much of the necessary information is already being collected.

Non-renewable Resources that are Lost when Used

The final type of balance sheet account would be for non-renewable resources destroyed when used. This refers primarily to fossil-fuels — coal, oil and natural gas. Since the rate at which fossil-fuels are formed is negligible compared to the rate of use, we have to consider the present resource as being all that will ever be available. Any use, with the exception of some recyclable plastics, decreases overall supply. Balance sheet accounts for these resources would compare consumption with increases in the efficiency with which we use the resources and the amounts of energy-generating capacity that are developing from renewable energy sources. This would provide critical information about how much energy we presently need, how much of that we can provide from renewable sources, and how much time we have to develop the renewable sources and energy efficiency that will be necessary as fossil-fuel produced energy is used up.

Pollution Inventories

The other side of resource consumption is waste. A great deal of waste is created in the process of making products and because very few products are kept around for long, almost all products become waste. With the exception of some art, furniture and architecture, everything we use is eventually considered waste and thrown away. Some of this "waste" is recycled, some is effectively isolated at landfill sites, and the rest escapes into groundwater flows or is released into the air and surface water. Natural processes can absorb some of these releases. But, while some of it is harmless, some of it is disruptive to ecological systems and poisonous to living things.

A GPI would account for pollution by volume and toxicity and compare the amounts produced to the capacity of the environment to absorb it. As a civilization, we should know how much pollution we create, whether that volume is increasing or decreasing, how much is persistent, how much is effectively absorbed, and how much has negative effects on people, other living things and ecological processes. As with recyclable, non-renewable resources, much of this information is already available for monitoring. A GPI would collect the information in one place and present it in a format that anyone could access to see how we are doing.

Two Perspectives of Health

Almost by definition, a focus on health determinants in our core measure of progress will shift attention from treatment to prevention. Since an ounce of prevention tends to be worth a pound of cure we might expect expanded measures in the health field to lead toward a healthier population at less cost.

Ron Colman, *GPI Atlantic*

The field of health provides an example of how different actions are taken in response to different sorts of measurements. Traditionally, the health of a population has been measured in terms of how many people have been afflicted by various diseases, how many have died and what the average life expectancy is. Another approach would be to measure the circumstances that influence people's health, known as "the determinants of health." These include food quality, community stability, income distribution, education, pollution levels, quality of employment, exercise, stress, participation in decision-making and other such things that make people more or less susceptible to disease. Rather than just providing money for treating people who are already sick, as we try to do in response to information about illness, measuring determinants of health would result in programs aimed at improving the circumstances that cause people to become ill.

Other Factors of Concern

Along with the above types of measurement, there are numerous other factors that affect our well-being and quality of life. These include the quality and quantity of employment and leisure time, durability of goods, dependency on foreign investment and on imported goods, levels of violence, quality of health care and education and the costs of crime. These and anything else arising that might be a threat to long-term well-being should be monitored.

If directing the affairs of society while considering only the GDP is like driving a bus using only the speedometer, each of the accounts described above is like an additional instrument on the bus's dashboard. With more instruments to keep track of relevant factors, a rear-view mirror to see how things have changed, and a clear windshield through which to look out for any new obstacles that might arise, we may yet steer our way to a sustainable future. The International Institute for Sustainable Development (IISD) has developed a measure based on the dashboard analogy. For more details, see their web site at: http://www.iisd.org/cgsdi/dashboard.asp

Aggregation

The individual indicators represented by the instruments on the bus's dashboard would themselves be determined by "aggregating" a number of related aspects of the issue in question. For example, an indicator representing the health of a community or country might take into account the following factors: the extent to which people are exposed to toxic substances; job satisfaction; income disparity; involvement in decision-making; levels of stress; and instances of disease and mortality. An indicator for the conservation of nature could look at forest cover, wetlands, habitat loss, threatened and endangered species, nutrients and toxins, alien species, and global environmental change. Economic prosperity, while still including GDP, might be more accurately viewed by working in measures of employment and underemployment, poverty, savings and investment rates, natural resources, and environmental conditions that effect productivity, security, and sustainability.

While each of these encompassing categories might be reported with a single figure, the various components from which they are aggregated should be accessible to anyone who wants to take a closer look.

GPI Sees the World Differently than GDP

In the mid 1990s when the organization Redefining Progress worked out GPI figures for the previous 30 years in the U.S., they discovered a serious trend. A great deal of the GDP growth, which Americans were told meant that all was well, could be accounted for as expenditures aimed at fixing mistakes from the past, borrowing resources from the future, and moving voluntary activities out of homes and communities and replacing them with paid work. The main categories for which they compiled comparative statistics were crime, family breakdown and other regrettable expenditures, household and voluntary work, income distribution, resource depletion, pollution, long-term environmental damage, changes in leisure time, lifespan of consumer durables and public infrastructure, and dependence on foreign assets. What they found was that GDP and GPI were almost the same in 1970. The GPI then began to drop below the GDP by 1% a year over the next 10 years. This increased to a 2% per year decline in the 1980s and 5% per year in the 1990s. This decline in social and environmental well-being answers the question asked in *Atlantic Monthly s* October, 1995 article, "If the GDP is Up, Why is America Down?" People sense well-being on a far deeper level than just how much money is being made and spent. When the things people value are being lost, they tend not to feel so good.

Developing measures of well-being along these lines bears a similarity to great advances in evolution. In the distant past, primitive organisms had little sensitivity to the world around them. They simply consumed what they could and grew. As time went by, the creatures able to sense light and motion had an advantage over those that could not. They could notice danger and act to avoid it, or sense food and move toward it. As sight, hearing, smell, taste and touch became more and more developed, the organisms that possessed them did better than those without. As a civilization, we are expanding our capacity for sensing the world around us. Most of the measurements discussed above are being made, but until they become a comprehensive sensory system with permanently established "nerves" making the information available to all who might use it, we are, as a society, still in the early stages of evolving the senses we need to succeed in our changing world.

Canada Well-Being Measurement Act

The opportunity arose in 1997 to propose a formal GPI for Canada. In the federal election of that year, during an all-candidates debate, Dr. Peter Bevan-Baker, the Green Party candidate for the Leeds-Grenville riding in Ontario, explained the Party's commitment to instituting a Genuine Progress Index. The idea caught the Liberal candidate's attention. Joe Jordan asked Peter questions about it at subsequent all candidates meetings and, after winning the election, he called Peter in and asked him if he would help draft a proposal for a Canadian GPI. Because Peter's time was filled with four young children and a very busy dental practice, he invited me along to help. For the next four years, most of my time went into coordinating the drafting of the *Canada Well-Being Measurement Act* and preparing materials encouraging people to consider the idea and to urge their Members of Parliament to support it.

The idea is a popular one. Lots of people contacted their representatives, talked with others in their communities and wrote articles expressing the importance of such well-being measurement. Early in 2003, the proposal, revised as Private Member's Motion M-385, was selected for discussion in the House of Commons. On June 2, a brief debate took place and the next day the resolution was passed 185 to 46. For details, see the following website:

http://www.SustainWellBeing.net/7GI/Hansard-June2-03.shtml

Motion M-385

That, in the opinion of this House, the government should develop and report annually on a set of social, environmental and economic indicators of the health and well-being of people, communities and ecosystems in Canada.

The content of Motion-385 is derived directly from the objective of the *Canada Well-Being Measurement Act*. Should government act on the motion and adopt the *Measurement Act,* it would instruct the House of Commons Standing Committee on Environment and Sustainable Development, to "receive input from the broad public through submissions and public hearings" to determine "the broad societal values on which the set of indicators should be based."

Public inquiries into what various communities feel is important consistently reveal interest in the factors described above. There is little doubt that, if asked, members of the public will identify the full spectrum of social and environmental issues encompassed by the sustainability outline inside the front cover of this book. It is essentially the same question that led to the recognition, back in 1974, that the goal of sustainability was the common thread amongst most voluntary citizens' organizations.

Once the topics of concern are identified, the Act goes on to identify the Office of the Auditor General of Canada as the institution to coordinate development of the indicators, the collection of data and, eventually, the reporting. Statistics Canada, other government departments, social institutions and citizens' groups could all provide relevant information and make arrangements to collect information about new issues as they arise. The point of the Act is to bring it all together into regularly updated images of how we are doing as a country, and to make that information available to everyone. To provide, in essence, a "nervous system" connecting the sense organs developed by concerned sectors of society to the society as a whole.

The Auditor General's office and, in particular, the Commissioner for the Environment and Sustainable Development in that office, would report on the indicators directly to Parliament and, consequently, to the Canadian people. It is particularly important that the reporting of these indicators be independent of political interests. If the information uncovered by measuring the various factors of well-being were under the control of politicians, that pesky denial psychology would likely, on occasion, tempt them to withhold details that might cast an unfavourable light on their policies. Better to develop our senses outside of the political process where such temptation would be minimal. The ability to sense danger is every bit as important to a mature society as it is to each of us individually. Who among us would want to be blindfolded by someone else because they felt our awareness of danger did not suit their interests? The purpose of a Genuine Progress Index is to get information about trends in matters related to well-being, without bias, to where it can provide the stimulus for individuals, businesses and governments, to make informed decisions.

As this book is being prepared for publication, the Atkinson Charitable Foundation is moving forward to produce a GPI for Canada. Many of the key people who worked on the *Canada Well-Being Measurement Act* have joined in that process. It may be that the way to get clear reports on the state of our social, environmental and economic well-being is to develop such senses within the realm of the non-profit sector. We can look forward to the Canadian Index of Well-Being. (More about Well-Being Measurement is available at: http://www.SustainWellBeing.net/well-being.shtml)

A Cooperative Synergy

One of the most promising realizations arising from this work has been that such a monitoring process blurs the ideologies that separate people. Everyone across the political spectrum, and elsewhere, would be invited to identify what they feel requires attention. The indicators set would then take all substantial concerns into account. Later, when the indicators are reported, it would not be clear which indicators originated from which interest groups. They would all be seen as matters of concern and the statistics would show where problems are being solved and where effort is needed to prevent damage. The message would be uncluttered by preconceived notions about the sort of people who brought each concern forward.

Establishing a system to track matters of concern does not require change. It is a much more comfortable and less controversial step than some of those that follow. Putting it in place would acknowledge the concerns, however, and if some of the indicators were to show decline, taking action to deal with them would follow a natural logic.

The UN System of National Accounts Provides a Target for Change

There is a scene in Marilyn Waring's, National Film Board video, *Who s Counting,* in which she goes to the library at the United Nations to locate the official version of *The System of National Accounts.* Nations are required to use this system if they wish to participate in international financial programs. It implies sound management. Ms. Waring takes the book off the shelf and opens it up. The camera focuses in on a sentence that says, "Subsistence production and the consumption of their own produce by non-primary producers is of little or no importance." While few in the affluent world subsist from the land, such food-production is critical to the health and survival of billions of people in the developing world. As for work in our homes, without it, chaos would quickly unfold. Bearing and raising children, caring for our elders, preparing and serving food for one's family, maintaining our homes, transporting family members, and all manner of volunteer work in our communities are all marginalized and devalued by this form of accounting. To say these things are of no value is to say that money is the only measure of value.

Because the *System of National Accounts* prescribes an international standard for measuring progress, it would be a good target for change. If it were to include the full spectrum of social, environmental and economic factors that affect the well-being of nations it would provide invaluable guidance for the entire international community.

The principles of well-being measurement can, and should, be applied at any level. *The Canada Well-Being Measurement Act* is intended for use at the national level, as are *The Calvert-Henderson Quality of Life Indicators,* http://www.Calvert-Henderson.com and the Happy Planet Index, http://www.happyplanetindex.org; GPI Atlantic: http://www.gpiatlantic.org, encompasses the four Maritime Provinces; the Alberta GPI, http://www.anielski.com/Publications.htm, reports on a single province; and The Federation of Canadian Municipalities, http://www.fcm.ca, has developed a program that is currently being used by 20 cities and towns and can enable any community to develop quality of life indicators at the municipal level. At each level where decisions are made, indicator sets can give feed-back on how those decisions affect well-being.

Ecological Footprint

One of the most potent devices for illuminating our relationship with the Earth is the idea of the "ecological footprint." This brings measurement to a personal level.

When someone takes a step, his or her foot makes an impression in the ground. The extent of the impression depends on the size of the foot, the weight of the person and what kind of footwear they are wearing. Similarly, the life of a person leaves an impression on the land and life of the planet. The nature of that impression depends on how one leads one's life.

Dr. Mathias Wackernagel and Prof. William Rees identified the impact of a person's life as their "ecological footprint" and developed several techniques for calculating this "footprint." They tally various factors such as the type and size of one's dwelling, the amount of water used, diet and other consumption habits, type of transportation used and the frequency and distance of travel, participation in conservation and recycling activities, and other things.

When Wackernagel and others calculated the average ecological footprint for a variety of nations, they found that each Canadian, on average, used 7.8 hectares of the Earth's surface — about 15 football fields. We were surpassed only by Australians at 9.0 hectares, and

Americans at 10.3. People in the United Kingdom and Germany, by comparison, averaged 5.2 and 5.3 hectares, respectively. These and other details, including an opportunity to calculate your personal footprint are available at: http://www.footprintnetwork.org

If everyone on Earth had a "footprint" similar to Canadians, we would need four more planets the size of Earth to support us. While this is a serious problem, it need not continue this way.

A possibility for resolving this problem is revealed in the answers given by an elementary school class in Newfoundland. Their teacher, Jean Harding, first asked her pupils to list the things that they wanted in life. They mentioned houses, cars, travel, and all manner of things, most of which would increase the size of their ecological footprint. Then she asked them to list the things that they valued most. They wrote things like a special relative, their friends, playing games, pets, favourite foods, and warm summer days. For the most part, the second lists were composed of experiences that caused little or no negative impacts. Jean's final question was to ask why they had not included the things they valued most in their lists of what they wanted? As a riddle, this suggests a possible future.

If the voice of advertising fell silent; what would people want?

The World Game

Humans are not short of creative ability. What we need is the political will to apply our creativity toward the challenges of our times. The challenge is no longer to create enough capital to build an industrial society. That game has been "won" many times over. The new game might be identified as "The World Game," to use a phrase coined by Buckminster Fuller during the World Design Science Decade of the 1960s. The objective of the World Game is "to make the world work for one hundred percent of humanity for all time to come." Since human well-being depends on healthy ecosystems, it is technically redundant to say "for 100% of humanity and planetary ecosystems." However, since there is little in our cultural heritage to assure that this extension is included, it is worth making it clear. The objective of the "New World Game" then, is to make the world work for 100% of humans, other species and for all living systems, for all time to come.

With a team of design students at the University of Illinois in Carbondale, Fuller researched and produced a set of documents titled *World Resources Inventory; Human Trends and Needs*. Fuller felt that systems could be established that would fulfill human need for all time through comprehensive, anticipatory design. He knew the critical importance of solving the world's problems and he knew that we have the intelligence to do so; points which he made clearly in his book *Utopia or Oblivion*. In another book, *Operating Manual for Spaceship Earth,* he clarified the obvious; this planet and the energy incoming from the local star, is all we have to work with. Like on a spaceship all the needs of the passengers, the life support, and the operating systems, must be provided for on board, for the duration of the journey. Our planet is finite and has to be treated with attention, respect and competence.

When individual people find that they have grown up and realize that they will need an income, shelter and companionship for many decades to come, they look for long-term solutions. As a species we have matured and are similarly faced with the prospect of being here for a very long time. As Fuller's *Design Science Challenge* illustrated, it is time to look for long-term solutions to the needs we will have to meet over the tens of thousands of years ahead of us.

When establishing the rules of the New World Game, it is important to emphasize the "100% of humanity" part of the broad design criteria. At first glance, this is seen as a directive not to forget the world's destitute, but it is also important to assure the presently privileged that a sustainable order does not wish hard times on them — 100% means everybody.

With the vast amounts of knowledge available today, we have the opportunity to define the rules of the new game through logic and goodwill. There is much of value in traditional social patterns, but there should be no deterrent to a fresh look. Beware of any models that discourage questioning. If the reasons behind any custom are justified, an open inquiry will see their value. However, if a custom is maintained to preserve an unjustified advantage, we must weigh the costs and benefits of the practice. The challenge is not to give advantage to any new group. We all have similar stakes in the New World Game. While disproportionately large winnings from the present competitive game, may seem capable of insulating some from overshoot and collapse disasters, a crippled planet would come to haunt us all. It will be, as Fuller foresaw, utopia or oblivion. Our best chances will come from seeking solutions that will serve all.

There are three essential criteria for a renovated system of mutual provision:

1) Everyone needs opportunities to participate.
2) The role that community plays in well-being must be recognized.
3) Environmental limitations must be respected.

Everyone Needs Opportunities To Participate

Food, clothing, shelter, education and health care are essential to well-being. People must have these things; to acquire them, everyone needs opportunities to work at some aspect of the economy so that they can trade for what they need. In addition, for personal well-being, most of us need to create, develop skills and feel useful. The match between these needs and our need for income is far from coincidental. Personal well-being and the well-being of communities has always depended on the ability of individuals to contribute.

If everything necessary for well-being can be produced without everyone's involvement, what are the others expected to do? It is one thing to be supported if one is unable to work; it is very different to be able to work, yet have no opportunities to do so. Even if the budget is available to support those with no access to work, and the money provided without stigma or the fear of being cut off, people feel better and lead healthier lives when they are partners in mutual provision, rather than being dependent on others.

Reframing Efficiency

A system is not efficient unless it has room for everyone to do meaningful work. The commonly understood meaning of efficiency is to produce more product with less spending on materials, energy and labour. This is still true for material and energy, assuming quality can be maintained, but it is no longer true for labour. Gone are the days when there was far more practical work to do than there were people available to do it.

Before mechanization, productivity depended on muscle power and most people made do with basic provisions; surpluses were gathered up by the land-owning nobility. With the advent of machines, much more could be produced with the same amount of labour. Productivity was growing quickly to match basic needs, but there were also factories to be built, and machines to make, as well as roads, railways and urban housing to accommodate the new productive order. Labour remained a limiting factor.

By the beginning of the last century, the physical structure for the industrial order was in place in Europe and North America. Work weeks dropped from 70 hours to 40 hours and, as described in Chapter 8, increasing consumption and waste were chosen over further decreasing work time as the means to keep the system in balance. Unemployment became, and remains, a problem, as productivity continues to increase.

Efforts to further increase wasteful consumption are running into a variety of obstacles. Increasing disparity in income leaves us with more rich people who already consume as much as they can and more poor people who cannot afford to expand their consumption. A growing sector is choosing to enrich their lives through living, rather than through acquisition. Others are limiting their consumption in response to warnings and expanding awareness about pollution and resource depletion. As the negative consequences of materialism, corporate globalization and environmental stress become increasingly personal, these trends can be expected to continue. A rational response to resource limitations and waste problems will eventually mean fewer jobs and a greater need to spread the available work around.

While there is a huge amount of work to be done restoring damaged ecosystems and social structures, and reorganizing things to accommodate the next new productive order, we have yet to muster the political will to apply ourselves to the task. Under circumstances where work is in short supply, it is inefficient to continue to install machines that replace workers.

A truly efficient system involves everyone in meaningful work. If there is not enough work to keep everyone busy 40 hours a week, it would be a sign of success to reduce the work week. After all, the purpose of work is to produce what people need. If our level of productivity is such that need is satiated with 30 or even 20 hours of work from everyone each week, it should be cause for celebration, not hard times. If those 30 or 20 hours from everyone are sufficient to provide what everyone needs, it should be possible for everyone to earn enough to meet their needs. For people to experience hardship in the midst of so much abundance speaks of bad management.

Responsible Production

It bears repeating — the New Game must involve everyone. Efforts to perpetually expand production are shortsighted and we can expect nothing but trouble from a system that thinks that people who are excluded can just let their children starve. Desperation leads to desperate measures. Whether those measures are theft and insurrection, or attempts to grow food on marginal soil or in other ways to try to draw more resources from the Earth than can be sustained, the results are bad news for everyone. Better to acknowledge our success at productive efficiency and shift our focus to the efficient involvement of all people.

If all the goods and services needed by the human family are taken into consideration and a large enterprise produces 2% of that total, yet provides only 1% of the population's need for work, its operation would be dangerously inefficient. In such a situation, that enterprise is responsible for the fear and deprivation experienced by the portion of the population that is squeezed out of the system by its inefficiency.

Communities are Important

The New Game will recognize the extent to which individual well-being depends on the well-being of our communities.

Humans are social creatures. We are almost totally dependent on cooperation, even when that cooperation is masked by economic relations that provide no connections between people other than the money they exchange. We have been mutually dependent for so long that our emotional selves — our sense of who we are and our appreciation of life itself — are extensively tied to the people we know and love, those we depend on and those who depend on us.

In his 1969 publication, *The Frontiers of Being,* Duncan Blewett identified the "Law of Feeling." It is based on the observation that when someone does something positive for someone else, the person making the kind gesture tends to feel good about themselves and, by extension, about the world. Since then, biochemists have identified a parallel change in the amount of serotonin present in the individuals involved. Levels of the mood-altering hormone have been seen to increase in the person doing the good deed, as well as in the one receiving it. Those who witness such acts of kindness, even though they are not directly involved, also experience a measurable increase in serotonin.

While those with serotonin active in their nervous systems tend to feel good, those without are prone to depression. Lack of personal bonds can set a person adrift in despair as much as a lack of food and shelter. While loneliness, or negative personal encounters, are less likely to kill a person outright, they can warp and scar one's character in ways that seriously affect the quality of one's life, work and, often, the lives of those around one. The damaged personalities that result can set into motion vicious circles where acting out their pain can similarly damage the emotional balance of others, sending disruptive waves of dysfunction through communities for generations.

On the other side of the picture are the effects of respectful, caring relationships. Children raised in an atmosphere of love, acceptance and encouragement are much more likely to be healthy and able to make positive contributions to society later in life. They are less likely to get sick and more likely to heal quickly when injured.

For tens of thousands of years before industrial-scale economies, mutual provision was maintained almost entirely within local communities. The services people provided as individuals in the form of food, shelter, clothing, emotional support, entertainment, defence, knowledge, care for those who could not care for themselves, and more, were known to their peers. Individuals knew others were important to their well-being and others knew how those individuals were important to them. Appreciation, acceptance and belonging were natural outcomes of mutual provision at the community level.

In today's mass society, there is little opportunity, outside of household tasks and volunteer work, to gain the satisfaction of providing directly for someone else's needs. We often do not know what the people around us contribute to mutual provision, just as they are frequently unaware of the contributions we make. It is little wonder that the work lives people lead often fail to provide for social needs.

Communities seem unimportant to today's economic system since goods and services flow regardless. However, personal contact remains critical to individual well-being. Unfortunately, people separated from their traditional foundation in mutual provision find their emotional necessities of life have become relatively insecure. More than ever, we are dependent on a spouse, our neighbours, or others in our personal community, for the appreciation, acceptance and belonging that had been the natural compliment of mutual provision. Too often, personal networks of support atrophy to only a connection with one other person and any children that might result. It can be an impossible burden for one person to fill all of another person's social needs. If there is a subjective change in the perspective of either of the partners, much can be lost.

With my woodworking, I have the good fortune of getting to know the people for whom I make things. I can walk around the village and sense a connection with each of them. The same goes for borrowing a neighbour's lawnmower or lending my circular saw, helping set up the seating for the local theater, attending a bake sale for the school's extracurricular activities, or just getting into a conversation at the local grocery check out. Every positive interaction within a community adds to its cohesion. Even without clear economic connections, cohesive communities provide a foundation for personal security, well-being and, thereby, better health.

When large-scale economic developments disregard the role of communities in our individual well-being, they can be very destructive. Building large, dangerous motorways through communities blocks the casual communication that people share. Diverting commerce from main streets to "Big Box" stores at the edge of town reduces opportunities for encountering people with whom one might have the sort of subsequent encounters from which communities grow.

Standard Doctrine says always to pay the lowest possible wages. This is the antithesis of care and can rip through the bonds of community. Full-time work that pays a wage insufficient for covering basic expenses, work related injuries that receive no compensation, or the massive disruption that takes place when a company moves its operation elsewhere, can spread hardship and disillusionment.

Material insecurity is a huge stress that often manifests as anger and resentment rippling out from people in crisis. The connections of poverty, alcoholism, violence and family breakdown are well-known. Far too often it takes a huge toll. The depressed state that often results, also has economic consequences through absenteeism, dispirited work, theft and even sabotage.

Another problem of an economic system where the well-to-do use their advantage to gain further benefits is that it increases the gap between rich and poor. Studies have been conducted by the *British Commission on Wealth Creation and Social Cohesion* and the *Canadian Centre for Policy Alternatives* among others, showing that, provided that basic needs are met, the differences in wealth within a community affect the well-being of individual members more than do absolute levels of wealth. If there is a large difference between the richest and the poorest in one community, the distorted sense of worthiness, and the consequent health problems are greater. This is true even where the poor in the community with the greater discrepancy have more wealth than most of the people in the more equal society.

This is not to say we should be striving for absolute equality. Daly and Cobb put it clearly:

The goal of an economics of community is not equality, but limited inequality. Complete equality is the collectivist s denial of the true differences in community. Unlimited inequality is the individualist s denial of interdependence, and true solidarity in community.

Recognizing our interdependence and accommodating the communities that serve those needs are essential.

Local Scale Business

The sense of powerlessness that arises when employees have no say in the circumstances of their work is more likely in the anonymity of large institutions whose overriding goal is expanding profits. On a smaller scale, at least, people are personally known and, hence, gain respect where it is due.

We can take direct action to create and support community-scale enterprises. Working with the sense of purpose that E. F. Schumacher alluded to in his comments about doing a really good job, enjoying oneself, producing real quality with one's own hands and brains, in one's own time, at one's own pace, we could live effectively through local systems of mutual provision where each person contributes. With local enterprises, the connection between one's activities and the well-being in the community is more obvious. What may not be available in affluence is made up for by the relevance of one's work, sense of belonging and the strong ties that develop when people deal personally, trading in the necessities of life.

Democracy

Personal and community considerations stand a better chance of being respected if there is an underlying commitment to a democratic process. By this I am not referring to the practice of voting every four years to choose who the rulers will be. Democracy implies the involvement of people in decisions affecting their lives. When people have clear channels for being heard by accountable representatives, they will speak up for themselves and they will band together to insure that the needs of their communities are not being trampled.

The process of consultation described in the Appendix, aims to draw out the inherent power of any group of people willing to work together toward common ends. The respect involved inspires cooperation and a virtuous circle is initiated that serves a wide range of human needs.

Proportional Representation

A large step that can be taken toward participatory democracy at the parliamentary levels is to elect governments through proportional representation (PR). Among the developed countries, Canada, Britain and the United States are the most significant holdouts from such systems. Germany, New Zealand, Austria, Switzerland, Denmark, Greece, Iceland, the Netherlands, Portugal, Sweden, Norway, and Spain, among others, have legislative assemblies that allocate seats to the different parties in proportion to the number of votes cast for each party. The holdouts are still using the "first past the post" system, where each position in the assembly is won by the candidate with the largest number of votes. In an election with more than two parties participating, the winner's total can easily be less than half of the votes. This means that the decision-making body does not represent what the electorate wants.

With "first past the post," a government can gain majority power with a minority of votes, enabling it to impose its views even when more than half the voters see the world differently and do not support the perspective of the winner. In Canada, since 1921, there have been 15 majority governments, but only 4 were elected by a majority of the votes cast — 1940, 1949, 1958 and 1984. In the 1984 election, the majority government was delivered on the strength of 50.03% of the popular vote. In the 1988 election, the Conservative Party of the day won a majority with 43% of the vote and signed the first "Free Trade" agreement with the U.S. In that election, 52% of the votes were cast for parties that opposed that agreement and campaigned against it.

Different political parties represent different ways of viewing and dealing with different issues. With a PR system, the people who make up governments represent the views of the electorate in a balance similar to that of the people represented. Because there is seldom a clear majority, it is necessary for issues to be discussed and the legislation adapted until a consensus, or near consensus, among representatives can be achieved. This regard for the interests of others is a first step toward the cooperative model where decisions are made to serve everyone.

In addition to leading legislators toward solutions that serve the common good, PR systems rekindle citizens' interest in voting. A person's vote becomes a wish rather than a weapon. Rather than the adversarial nature of voting against what one wants least, having one's vote count toward what one believes in generates enthusiasm in

243

the hope that minority views will be heard. With the present order voters stay home in droves. The truth about what they want from government does not have a chance of emerging. With PR, because every vote counts toward representation, voters tend to be more interested in participating.

The cooperation necessary to make a PR government work can break up the log jam of competitive counterforces and dissolve the accumulating resentment about imposed dictates. It could open the way for looking at the problems at hand as if we want to solve them for everyone. As decisions become the product of mutual education and discussion rather than ideological stances, trust can grow. With trust comes a more open sharing, better understanding and greater potential for the synergies of co-intelligence to emerge.

There are a variety of ways that PR can be implemented to balance the various considerations of geographic representation and ideological representations. There are too many varieties to describe here. Suffice to say that variations have proved effective in countries large and small, and in places with populations sharing a common heritage, as well as those where the people come from a wide variety of backgrounds. For more information see: www.fairvotecanada.org

Environmental balance has to be maintained

Much has already been said about the rise in importance of the two-fifths of ecology that were of little importance to economic practices when the Earth was relatively empty of humans. Now that people are everywhere, resource supplies and waste are significant factors. We have clever ways of stretching these limitations, but in the end we cannot escape them. They need to be accounted for and accommodated for our world to work into the future.

Including everyone, respecting community and preserving environmental health are not typically accommodated by the present market economy. Unfortunately, the opposite seems to be the case. If these features are to be secured, there has to be another means.

Law

The "governor" on early steam engines was so named because of the role it played analogous to government. Its purpose was to keep the engine from running too fast. It consisted of weights attached to arms hanging from a shaft that rotated as the engine turned. As long as the engine was running within safe limits, the arms hung down

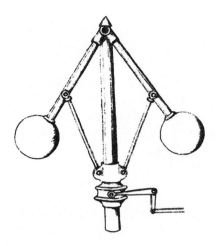

and did nothing. If the engine started accelerating toward an unsafe speed, centrifugal force propelled the weights outward and the motion was relayed to a mechanism that reduced the amount of power going to the engine.

In the same way that the governor was active only when the operation it governed became unsafe, many laws and governance are only necessary when limits are being over-reached. As long as people treat each other fairly, there is no need for intervention. If some people try to take advantage of others through cunning or violence, laws define the limits, and the governing process can intervene to prevent damage that could make the system dysfunctional.

Legitimacy and legislation come from the same root. Legitimacy emerges from a sense of what is right for a people. Legislation codifies legitimacy; it clarifies boundaries and feeds back a message that has a strong influence on what people feel is legitimate.

Legal codes are the rules of the game, defining what is fair (acceptable) and what is not fair. In the age of small communities, the moral equivalent of laws were the ethics of fair play, supported by respect, concern for people one knew and peer pressure. These elements enabled individuals to know where they stood and what was permissible. Around the world, as societies expanded, religious guidelines emerged to help maintain order between people. As populations expanded further, legal codes were produced, taking "government" further by prescribing more specific guidelines for a broader range of activities and identifying punishments for transgressions. By defining fair play, a majority who may be disposed to ethical behaviour, have clear boundaries to work within and they are protected from the few who might take advantage of opportunities at the expense of others.

Along with the complexity of our activities, our legal structures have expanded. With urbanization, for example, sanitation became an issue. To avoid epidemics of contagious disease, governments had to take responsibility for providing water and sewers. Another outcome of urban life is that it does not provide the opportunities for self-sustenance that rural life does and thus, people unable to find paying jobs find themselves in desperate situations. This forced governments to take elementary responsibility for social security. As societies have evolved, governments have picked up responsibilities for minimum wages, employment insurance, health care, education, transportation, communications and a host of regulations to define fair play between individuals and between businesses and individuals.

Some government skeptics note that a large part of governance — legal enforcement in particular — has focussed on protecting the wealth of those who have it from those who do not. The lines get fuzzy for some philosophers trying to distinguish the legitimate protection of the things people have worked hard for, from gains made by wealthy interests, which have increased their advantage by, among other means, influencing legislation.

As the rich/poor divide grows ever wider, the question arises as to whether or not governance is still in the interest of fair play. This suspicion, in turn, is being nurtured to encourage people to reject elected government in favour of letting the economic process govern. Governments, some say, interfere with the way that the market system takes care of us. Ironically, it is the discontent of economic losers that is being rallied to support the removal of government influence over the Global Monopoly Game, which, by its nature, must render everyone losers except the advantaged few. The cheerleaders of minimizing government involvement are the same interests whose power to dictate prices is a conspicuous reason why markets are failing to maximize public benefits.

There is a place for law and governance as the scope of today's economic cooperation encircles the planet and new areas of concern emerge. We have experience governing the interactions involving individuals and/or businesses of moderate scale. Considerable progress had been made toward orderly relations between nations, but as some corporations become more powerful than most nations, we are entering new territory. Furthermore, the changes taking place in humanity's relationship with the living processes of the planet are enormous and highly significant. If we are to avoid social disruption and environmental overshoot and collapse, we have to legitimize the goal of sustainability and adapt the rules of the game so that the social structure will accommodate that end.

Few of us like to be told what to do, so reactions can be expected when rules are changed. Most of us will choose consistency over change and will defend what we are familiar with until it becomes clear why changes are necessary.

Even when an individual initially resists change, there is a chance that he or she will see the validity of that change, if the case for the change is made clearly, in terms they understand. When the same reaction takes place at the level of corporate entities possessed of great wealth, the resistance can be huge and openness to understanding can be lost in the abstraction of their magnitude and corporate structure. Lawyers and public relations experts are often given large budgets with instructions to stop a proposed change. For professionals, obstructing a legislative initiative is a job with an objective. Coming to understand why the change might be a good thing is not in their job description.

Remember the auto industry's resistance to mandatory seat belts, improved mileage and exhaust emissions controls? In each case they said it would cost fortunes to comply. Large numbers of jobs would be lost. It might even bankrupt the industry! Similar arguments were made around legislation to reduce acid rain, and are expressed each time raising the minimum wage comes up for review. In the end, however, when such changes have been pressed into law, few, if any, of the industries involved disappeared. In some cases, where resource efficiency or waste reduction were required, profits actually increased.

Governance and laws are meant to avoid excesses that might cause serious problems. We have no problem agreeing that murder should be discouraged. None of us wants to be killed, so it is in everyone's interest that murder be outlawed. Business interests understand that it is inappropriate to gain competitive advantage by killing the management of competing firms. It is not a huge step from there to agreeing that we should not kill or maim the ecosystems upon which we depend, and from there to acknowledge that not killing or injuring whole communities or nations has a legitimate logic.

Legitimacy is the fulcrum upon which this understanding can be levered into place. Legitimacy is embodied in the legal structure and the legal structure is shaped by political processes. Ultimately, however, legitimacy is the product of the public will.

When we have acknowledged the need to involve everyone, preserve communities and maintain ecological health, there are numerous steps that can be taken to redirect our economic process away from destructive practices and toward more sustainable ways of living. By adjusting the system's structure, all economic activity would begin to contribute to these goals. It would not be necessary to inspire a generation of saints, yet we could regain hope for the future our children will inhabit. What follows are practices that could be instituted to help bring about a sustainable world order

12 Practical Changes

A Just Transition

Nobody wants trouble and almost everyone will oppose changes that will disrupt their lives. Fairness is in order. The objective of change is to improve everyone's world. The costs and inconvenience of the transition should not fall disproportionately to the people involved in the sectors most affected.

To preserve the integrity of society, viable transition strategies are needed to help affected individuals and businesses realign their activities so that they contribute toward the new goal. A "just transition" implies that inconvenience will be shared. Policies acknowledging the right to fair compensation, retraining and the development of new opportunities, address common concerns. In the words of the New York Labour Institute, "This allows communities to shift from the divisive question of 'Why make any changes?' to 'What would it take for each member of the community to embrace change?'"

The Canadian Labour Congress acknowledges that the restructuring ahead of us is comparable only to the Industrial Revolution. The rules of the New Game require that the system must include everyone. "Just transition" policies provide a compassionate safety net, signalling that we are all in this together and that, together, we can jump into the future, expecting to land on our feet.

One way to provide security in the presence of substantial change would be to guarantee a basic livable income. The idea is to provide enough support for all members of society so that no one lacks sufficient food and shelter. Some studies suggest that if we count all the expenses of welfare, health care, emergency shelters, soup kitchens, policing, courts and corrections that it would be considerably less expensive to ensure that no one ever reaches a state of desperation.

In addition to easing the fear of change as we shift to a sustainable order, such a basic income would eliminate the fear that underlies population growth - that of poverty in old age. It would also remove the fear of doing one's job so well as to be self-eliminating. People could forget about building in obsolescence and, instead, follow their conscience and make quality, durable goods. Services could be provided, where possible, in a way that clients would have no need to return for more. If fear were no longer motivating us, the desire to be useful and needed would emerge from the shadows and people could develop their unique talents, follow their inspirations and respond to the needs of their communities. Furthermore, the good will that could be expected in a society that cared enough to secure all its people, without stigma, would nurture co-intelligence. So prepared, we could proceed to take steps necessary for the transformation.

Full-Cost Pricing

It is not in society s interest to charge only for the direct costs of putting goods on the market. If the production and disposal of goods creates problems it is unjust to expect taxpayers to pay for correction, and it is immoral to leave the problems for future generations.

Joe Jordan, M.P. 1997 – 2004
Leeds-Grenville, Ontario, Canada

Among the first structural changes we can make to accommodate a sustainable world order are those that lead to full-cost pricing. If prices can be made to reflect all the costs that arise with products, the market will take us a long way toward long-term well-being.

In recent years, so much disruptive change has been inflicted in the name of "market forces" that many are wary of the words. It is true that key aspects of the market process are distorted by powerful participants who can dictate prices and wages, thereby distorting the common good that markets would otherwise advance. That said, there is still a functionality to the mechanism that can help protect the long-term interests of people, communities and ecosystems if we choose to adapt it for the task.

To review, conventional accounting determines the price of a product by adding up all the expenditures made in its production and distribution. These include the costs of raw materials, labour, tools, transportation, and capital, with an additional mark-up for profit. These do not add up to the full-cost, however. Recall from Chapter 7 that conventional economics is only three-fifths of ecology. The impacts of production on resource supplies and waste are the other two-fifths. Along with the negative impacts that sometimes result from insensitive treatment of people and communities, these are referred to as externalities. They are called external because they don't have to be paid by those managing the process and are, therefore, external to accounts. Mother Nature does not issue invoices for the work of absorbing waste released into the air and water, yet, communities can be left with the expenses of treating the illness that results from such waste. Future generations cannot bill the present for what is forever lost to them and there is no line item to pay for disruptions caused in communities when major facilities relocate in search of cheaper labour or lax environmental standards. The problems, and the expenses incurred, result from the production, use and disposal of goods, but those external costs are not automatically included in the price.

Determining prices by adding up all the costs associated with products, both internal and external, would provide an enormous boost to the cause of long-term well-being. Market prices calculated to tell the social and ecological truth, in addition to the economic truth, serve the common good in a number of ways, including:

1) Products causing a lot of external problems will be more expensive, and fewer people will buy them. Reducing the amount of production reduces the unfortunate side effects.

2) When the full-costs are included in prices, the portion attributed to what had been externalities can be directed toward paying those costs. This could fund remediation efforts to directly improve deteriorating situations.

3) Full-cost pricing would encourage companies to develop production techniques and management policies that cause as few negative consequences as possible. Creative problem-solving would bring down the cost of products making them more competitive.

4) The overall effect would be that responsible enterprises, those businesses that: treat their employees fairly; make the extra effort to avoid polluting; utilize recycled and recyclable material; and/or use minimal energy or renewable energy sources would become more competitive. Consequently, their products would claim a larger market share and the world would become a better place to live.

The problem of black lung disease can illustrate various ways of internalizing an externality. Black lung disease is a debilitating and sometimes fatal illness that afflicts those who frequently breathe in coal dust (mostly coal miners). The costs of this disease are paid one way or another. The first question is, should the costs be paid entirely by the miners and their families, or should the external costs be internalized and shared? Any sense of fair play speaks to sharing the costs. Miners are not paid enough, nor is their role glorious enough to warrant giving their lives to the cause.

If the miners and their families are not to pay the costs of black lung disease, the next question is what is the best source from which to pay them?

A public health care system that cares for the miners would spread the medical costs throughout the entire population. It would, however, not help miners avoid the disease or encourage safer practices by the mining company.

In some countries, employers pay into worker's compensation programs that take care of workers injured on the job. Higher fees are paid by more dangerous enterprises and the cost finds its way into the price of products to be paid by all consumers. While this is fairer, a company can simply pay the compensation insurance fee and let the institution managing the fund take care of the miners who get sick.

Greater benefits result when the external costs are paid closer to the source of the problem. If coal mining companies are required to make direct payments for the medical, rehabilitation or mortality costs of the miners, a similar, or perhaps greater expense will find its way into the cost of coal. In addition to the associated reduction in mining and the consequent black lung disease, another influence comes into play.

Because the expense is responsive to either improvements in or deterioration of mining conditions, the perennial urge to keep costs down is triggered. Efforts would be made to develop mining techniques with less exposure to coal dust. The consequent reduction in health problems is good for miners, and would lower the company's expenses, thereby increasing their competitiveness. The financial feedback would encourage further clean-up efforts.

While the companies that voluntarily take responsibility for external costs can be at a competitive disadvantage, this is not always the case. Inspired by the expenses they assume, the urge to innovate can lead to rewarding results. By reducing waste and increasing energy efficiency, they can reduce their expenses. By treating employees well, they receive dedicated service and quality workmanship. Add to this, growing public appreciation for any attempts to address the problems of our times, and there are good chances for success, even while the system still allows the abuse of leaving external costs for others to absorb. When society as a whole finally demands corporate responsibility, the companies that have voluntarily pioneered such adaptations will be way out in front.

Pressing Externalities on to Accounts

Unpaid external costs are accumulating as harm done and opportunities lost. We are no longer a young innocent civilization. Our impacts are obvious when we choose to look. It is time to become accountable for those impacts and to assign responsibility.

For years, enormous suffering and expense have been absorbed by tobacco smokers and public health services. The tobacco industry denied that its product caused harm and it obscured evidence suggesting otherwise. Finally, in 1998, the link between tobacco, illness and death became sufficiently clear that a lawsuit filed against the tobacco companies by state governments in the U.S. was successful. The tobacco industry was fined $251 billion to reimburse the medical costs of people affected by its product. The money to pay this enormous fine is being raised through substantial increases in the price of cigarettes and other tobacco products. The increased cost due to the fine essentially internalizes the health costs of the product. In addition to helping pay for the harm the product causes, increased cost discourages smokers and would-be smokers and sends the message that tobacco is not safe.

It is interesting to note that an earlier attempt in Canada to discourage smoking and raise revenue by taxing tobacco products was unsuccessful. Consumers protested the government-induced price increase, and smuggling tax-free cigarettes from the U.S. became a big business. As a result the tobacco tax law was repealed. The fine from the law suit, in contrast, cannot be avoided and the companies were forced to raise the price of their own products. The prices are at a similar level to when the taxes were applied, yet consumer protests are conspicuously absent and smuggling is no longer profitable. (The U.S. case is still before the courts. In 2005, lawyers for the tobacco industry won an appeal, a ruling that itself is being appealed.)

Tobacco is not the only industry being forced to assume external costs through legal actions. In Japan, thousands of citizens banded together in 2002 and successfully sued the government for "failing to protect them against the respiratory and other harms of auto pollution pervading the public roads, and for failing to regulate the mass production of fossil-fuel-burning cars by government-licensed car manufacturers." In North America, medical accountants are now tallying the costs associated with the rapidly increasing consumption of "junk food." And worldwide, insurance companies are recording claims associated with climatic disasters that have been growing ever more serious as carbon dioxide levels in the atmosphere rise.

Tracking down external costs associated with products and their production, and suing for compensation is a labourious, though effective, way to internalize externalities. Another way is through a new approach to taxation.

Tax Shifting

> *Today's fiscal system, a combination of subsidies and taxes, reflects the goals of another era — a time when it was in the interest of countries to exploit their natural resources as rapidly and competitively as possible. That age has ended. Now natural capital is the scarce resource. The goal is to restructure the fiscal system so that the process reflects the truth, protecting the economy's natural supports.*
>
> Lester Brown, *Eco-Economy*

> *Get taxes off our backs and on our side.*
>
> Alan Durning and Yoram Bauman,
> Northwest Environment Watch, *Tax Shift*

Once we agree that prices should carry the full-costs of products, one of the most reliable ways to get externalities on to the books is to tax their creation.

Taxes added to represent externalities are sometimes referred to as "Pigouvian Taxes" after Arthur Cecil Pigou who suggested in the 1920s that, for the market to act effectively it would be necessary to adjust prices to include the costs of externalities. By adding external costs to internal costs, prices would represent the full-cost and the effectiveness of markets for serving the common good would be restored.

It is important to clarify that the service offered by smart taxation can be provided without any increase in the amount of taxes paid overall. The objective of tax shifting is to remove taxes from things we want, like employment and local investment and, in their place, gather the revenue needed by governments from things we do not want, and wish to discourage, like pollution, resource depletion and urban sprawl. When things are taxed they become more expensive, and when something becomes more expensive, we tend to get less of it. Similarly, by removing taxes from labour, and local development, they become less expensive and we can afford more of them.

As things now stand, the costs of resource depletion, pollution and urban sprawl are not clearly identified. Similarly, the social costs arising from careless and self-serving activities are hard to pin down. Fortunately, we do not have to know exactly what the costs are. We need only decide what we want — either to eliminate the problems, or to have the problems paid for by the people who enjoy the products or services that generate them. There are a number of ways to move external costs to where they belong, through strategic taxation.

When the extraction of natural resources is taxed, it gives a strong signal that those resources are important. It encourages everyone to conserve and recycle. Each time a purchase is made, these considerations are remembered in the price. The same is true when waste and pollution are taxed.

Ideally, the rate of taxation would be equal to the costs of the damage that products cause in their lifecycle from production to disposal. To the extent possible, the taxes paid would reflect the damage the purchases cause. The Market's failure to include the external costs would thereby be corrected. Even if exact costs cannot be calculated, taxing undesirable side effects will provide some compensation and lead to a reduction in the occurrence of those effects.

Encouraging Tax Avoidance

Few things inspire creativity and ingenuity like avoiding taxes. When taxes are shifted to things society doesn't want, people could be legitimately encouraged to find ways of doing things so that they didn't have to pay the taxes. If one wants to pay less tax — pollute less, waste less — go right ahead! If the challenge of sustainability is being seriously addressed, a portion of the tax money collected would be available for programs to train individuals and businesses to recognize how best to do things in ways that incur less taxes. Short-term self-interest could thus be tapped to reduce our negative impacts.

Carbon Tax

In this era of climate change, one of the most talked about tax shifts is to reduce employment taxes and instead gather necessary revenue from a tax on carbon emissions. In their book *Tax Shift*, Northwest Environment Watch did some calculations on carbon taxes. With a tax on carbon equivalent to 8¢ per gallon of gas in the U.S. and 3¢ a litre in Canada, they figured the wholesale cost of natural gas would go up by 15% and coal by 49%. The difference is because the amount of CO_2 released per unit of energy is greater with coal than with natural gas. Along with proportional rates on other greenhouse gasses, this tax would allow payroll taxes to be decreased by 25%. Most households in the Cascadia Watershed, where the study was done, would gain more from reduced income taxes than they would pay out toward the increased fuel prices. (Cascadia represents an ecological geographical area that includes the lands from British Columbia to Northern California, including the parts of Idaho and Montana that drain into the Pacific Ocean.)

A number of pollution taxes have already been legislated in Europe with promising results. Back in the mid-1970s, the Netherlands initiated taxes to discourage the release of heavy metals into the environment. By the mid-1990s releases of lead, mercury, cadmium, copper and zinc fell between 86% and 97%. In his book *Eco-Economy*, Lester Brown, the president of the Earth Policy Institute, lists numerous tax shifts that have been instituted in European countries. Sweden, Denmark, Spain, the Netherlands, the United Kingdom, Finland, Germany, Italy and France have all taken steps to shift tax revenue off personal income and wages and, in Denmark's case, agricultural property, and on to energy, carbon fuels, and waste. The amounts of tax shifted range from 0.1% to 3% of total revenues. In Germany, their 2.1% shift of taxes from wages to energy sales amounts to personal income tax reductions totalling $20 billion U.S.

Polls show that on both sides of the Atlantic 70% of voters favour tax shifting to deal with pollutants. In his May 24, 1999 *Fortune Magazine* article, *Gas Tax Now*, Harvard economist, Gregory Mankiw, argues for lowering income tax in the U.S. by 10% and putting a 50¢ per gallon tax on gasoline. This move, he says, "would lead to more rapid economic growth, less traffic congestion, safer roads and reduced risk of global warming — all without jeopardizing long-term fiscal solvency. This may be the closest thing to a free lunch that economics has to offer."

Taxes on commodities have an advantage in that they are relatively easy to collect. There are only so many well-heads and mine-mouths yielding non-renewable resources. While renewable resources present many more places where tax would have to be collected — farm gates, fish docks and forest roads — these are far fewer than the multitudes of sales outlets presently engaged in collecting sales tax. Given political will, taxes could easily be shifted off employment and on to resources and pollution. In a very short time, this would lead to more people working at jobs that respect ecological limitations.

Resource tax skeptics might think that such a system would be subject to disruption, because if we got good at avoiding pollution, for example, government revenues would fall. This is a logical expectation and, where tax shifts have been implemented, a certain drop of the offending activity is anticipated and factored into setting the initial rate of taxation. If revenues fall below the required level, the rate of taxation can be raised to encourage further improvements, thereby continuing to reduce offending activities. In cases where problematic situations are practically eliminated, other, lesser problems could be addressed, in turn, in a similar fashion.

Running out of problems to tax would be a wonderful outcome. It may be possible to get to that place. Certainly, the limitations of our planet seemed, at one time, inconceivably beyond our reach, yet, we have come well within sight of them. Similarly, although it appears that we have limitless problems, if we choose to make their solution a priority, we might well bring them under control. If any species is able to do this, we are.

In the event that identifiable problems did become scarce, it is likely that the reduction of revenue would be more than matched by reductions in health care and disaster relief expenditures. International tensions would also ease, reducing the amount of public resources diverted to military activities. In combination with measures to moderate extremes in wealth distribution, social and environmental problems would be drastically reduced. Other expenses that remained for education, health care, administration, etc. could be provided for by taxing the resources that, by the nature of human activity, would be cycling through the population in the processes of living.

Concerns that tax shifting might make a country less competitive internationally are not well founded. In fact there are many competative advantages to be found with such a tax policy. With resource and pollution taxes matched by reduced taxes on labour and property development, the overall price levels would remain constant. Reduced taxes on labour, however, would increase competitiveness and the ingenuity set in motion by increasing taxes on resources and waste, would stimulate additional efficiencies. As the problems of resource supplies and pollution further unfold, the countries who are first to implement tax shifts will find that they have suitable products and technologies to offer that others have yet to develop.

Georgian Taxes

Another area where tax shifting can be advantageous is property tax. Here the "Georgian" perspective can be helpful. Henry George was a Philadelphia-born economist, who took his ideas into the realm of politics in the late 1800s. His proposed taxes would shift the burden of public revenue from buildings and put it on to the land where buildings stand. City properties that are well serviced, and where there are lots of people, would be taxed more than peripheral areas. While a landowner contributes to his or her land's value when he or she improves the property, the improvements are only one among many contributors to that land's value. Most of the increase in the value of a piece of land results from things that are done on other properties surrounding it. If the community builds a subway, for example, the land that the subway makes more accessible becomes more valuable because it is easier for people to live, work or do business there. Proximity to sewers, water, electrical services, residential population, schools, hospitals and local businesses all make land more valuable.

Henry George thought that the value acquired by land because of improvements provided by the surrounding community should be taxed to raise the money needed to accommodate that community. It seemed then, as now, unfair for people to reap personal gain from changes in land value brought about by local improvements made through the efforts of others.

On the other hand, buildings are the product of their owner's ingenuity and effort. Presently, when someone spends their time and money improving a building they own, their taxes go up. This is hardly a just reward for industriousness, and often a disincentive. If, instead, public revenues were collected from taxes on site/location value, any benefits arising from building new buildings or improving existing ones would belong to the people who make the efforts and the investments.

If a person is using the land's potential, they would be able to earn enough to pay the tax. If they were ambitious, they could further improve the facilities on the land, increasing their earning power without increasing their taxes. Their taxes would only go up if the efforts of people in the vicinity were to make the entire area more valuable. Should this occur, that area would also offer increased commercial potential and the active owner could easily keep ahead of the taxes. Where rising taxes do become a problem for inactive owners, discretion would be in order to distinguish between those who seek to gain from the efforts of others and those who have lived and grown old in a neighbourhood.

While recognizing the benefits of green spaces by exempting publicly accessible natural areas, the only situation where taxing non-agricultural land would be more onerous than the present situation would be speculation, where land is purchased and held, inactive, waiting for its value to rise. If the taxes make speculating unprofitable, idle properties can be sold for purposes that are more useful to the common good.

The inspiration of Henry George continues long after his death. The present generation of tax shift enthusiasts often note the commonality between taxes on resources and taxes on site or location value. Forests, fish, fuels, minerals and water, like land, are all blessings from the natural world. That these things are not created by human beings makes suspect any claims to exclusive control over them. The natural resource base is what all of us, human and otherwise, depend on to sustain our lives. It is appropriate that public revenue be based on the shared heritage of natural resources. On the other hand, our labour, and the products, buildings and equipment that we create with our labour arise from individual effort. Assuming that the value of what they disrupt in the process is accounted for, it makes sense to leave much of the value of what individuals create to be enjoyed by those who make the effort to create it.

Most natural resources are within the public domain. Why should the common good not receive a substantial portion of their market value when such resources are extracted by a business enterprise? The business is entitled only to the value they create from working with the natural resource. If a large corporation says they cannot operate if the resource isn't provided for free, or next to it, a more local and responsible enterprise would likely welcome the legitimate profits to be made working with nature's bounty. Taxing the use of the natural resource base would encourage its conservation, and not taxing labour and the things we create with labour, would encourage more of both.

Applying the Georgian perspective to open land is more complex. To start with, respect is due to other living things. Land is essential for all life forms and, since humans already dominate the larger portion of productive territories, measures have to be taken to assure that space remains for non-humans. Once ecosystem integrity is fortified by dedicating natural spaces, we can consider the integrity of the land needed by humans.

Depending on how the land is used, the original fertility can be diminished or it can be preserved and enhanced. The difference has a huge impact on long-term well-being and should be treated accordingly in land use and tax policy.

Our dependency on land for food is absolute. Regardless of the potential for profits or taxes that urban uses of arable land present, it is a serious loss whenever it is built upon or paved over. Taxes, subsidies and regulations need to reflect the essential value of food land and natural spaces, and serve to preserve it.

Taxing urban site/location values would encourage more efficient use of urban land, thus reducing the pressure to sprawl outward. Lowering site values on portions of lots that are dedicated as reserves for forests, wetlands and other habitat would encourage their preservation. Other tax incentives could encourage best practices for preserving fertility.

Like oil or copper, the existence of natural fertility is not a product of human efforts. Following the Georgian tax model, the tax rate on land should be proportional to its productive potential and access to markets. Understanding that agricultural land cannot be sold for urban development, the more fertile the land, the higher the tax rate. That said, the potential is not available until someone has cleared it and prepared it for growing crops. Georgian reasoning would allow those who prepared the land to keep the benefits of their efforts. While lifetime benefit may be due to individuals who clear land, corporations, which have no natural life span, should be subject to limitations. As a result of human over-encroachment on natural areas, entitlement for clearing additional land might well be a thing of the past.

Garbage Tax

Some external costs can be easily quantified. The cost of garbage disposal resulting from excess packaging and of goods designed for disposal after a single use being clear examples. By taxing a company's productive output that is destined soon to be garbage, the costs of disposal can be properly assigned, and an incentive created for the production of more durable and recyclable products with minimized packaging.

Advantages of Taxing Resources, Rather than Income.

A certain amount of money is necessary to run a country, but where the money is taken from is a matter of choice. Decisions about what is taxed and what is not taxed play a significant role in how a country develops. Much would change if taxes were drawn on the use of resources rather than on personal income.

1) Resource intensive goods would become more expensive and labour intensive ones would become less expensive.
2) Individuals would have more money to spend, thereby stimulating the economy.
3) There would be more jobs because the labour component of production would cost less.
4) Restoration and repair for reuse would also be encouraged, resulting in more work and less garbage.
5) More care and artistry could be afforded, thereby producing better quality and more esthetic goods.
6) Goods that last would have even greater appeal.
7) The use of recycled materials could be encouraged by taxing them less than newly extracted resources.
8) Respect would be cultivated for the limitation of natural resources and for the impact of their removal.

Tradable Pollution and Resource Extraction Permits

Permit systems fix the amount of environmental harm and then let the market set the price. Taxes set the price and let the market decide the amount.

David Roodman, *The Natural Wealth of Nations*

Like environmental taxes, tradable permits internalize external costs. With taxes, the cost of polluting or extracting natural resources is added to accounts when the tax rate is set. The market then determines how much of the associated activity people are willing to engage in at the increased price. With tradable permits, the level of extraction or pollution is established by the volume of permits issued, and the market determines how much participants are prepared to pay for the limited permits.

For example, in 1986, Australia was concerned about exhausting its lobster fishery. The amount of lobster that could be regularly harvested was determined and permits sold allowing that much harvest to take place and no more. Fishers bid against each other for the permits, thereby setting the price of the permits. The cost of the permits then made their way into the price of lobster, thus representing the scarcity of the lobsters and reducing consumption. The fishery is reported to have stabilized and appears to be continuing at a sustainable level.

In another example — the biggest to date — the problem of sulfur dioxide pollution and the resulting acid rain was addressed in the U.S. with a permit trading scheme. The objective of the program, started in 1990, was to cut SO_2 emissions in half by the year 2000. Permits were assigned to the biggest producers of SO_2 in proportion to their 1980 emission levels. (The retroactive date was used to avoid penalizing producers who had already voluntarily reduced their emissions.) Any company that could reduce their emissions for less than the cost of the permits could make money selling their extra permits to those who found it cheaper to buy permits than to reduce emissions. The trading process inclined those who could make reductions for the least cost to do so first, advancing the goal, while those for whom it was a more costly process could buy time to make changes. Over time, permissible amounts were constricted, increasing the incentive to reduce emissions and continuing the pressure for change.

When the scheme was getting under way, the industry spokespeople estimated that the permits would end up costing $1,650 U.S. per ton. The U.S. Environmental Protection Agency figured the cost would be closer to $660 U.S. per ton, while the environmental community promoting the system, said it was more likely to be only $330 U.S. per ton. As it turned out, the goals set for the year 2000 were achieved by 1995, and the price of permits only reached $100 U.S. per ton because techniques for reducing SO_2

became so effective that it wasn't worth it to continue polluting within the confines of the goal.

While some are repelled by the idea of selling permission to pollute, it is, nevertheless, a significant step forward from polluting at no cost. While taxing pollution raises greater amounts of money as the amount of pollution increases, permit systems define a maximum level for a pollutant and the price of the related activities does whatever it has to do to bring popular demand in line. The mechanism has produced some positive results and deserves a place amongst the policy tools available to integrate human activity with the environment.

With either environmental taxes or permit trading regimes, it is advisable not to upset the apple cart by starting out too aggressively. Too large a tax, or too tight a restriction on permissible emissions might disrupt industries that, whatever their faults, are employers and suppliers of goods. By starting out gently, the legislation sends a clear message that change is in order with respect to the over-consumption of resources and pollution. This gives the industries involved time to direct their creative ingenuity toward adjustment. With the stated intent to progressively tighten the system within a defined schedule, raising the taxes, or reducing the volume of permits available, creates a growing economic incentive to follow through with improvements. Where changes are not made, the costs of inaction would grow, causing holdouts to become increasingly less competitive.

The European Organization for Packaging and the Environment includes such multinational enterprises as Dupont and Philip Morris. In a document on a *European Solid Waste Tax,* they expressed their approval,

> *... provided it is first introduced at a relatively low level but with a clear commitment to a steady increase in the tax rate. This will give industry time to adjust and an economic incentive to ensure that companies do adjust.*

Resource Depletion

In *For the Common Good,* Daly and Cobb suggest a system for aiding the market in the difficult task of managing the depletion of non-renewable resources. They suggest that permits be required for the extraction of resources for which limitations are in sight, and that extraction be limited to 2% of proven reserves. The permits to extract that 2% would be auctioned off and the price of the permits would eventually be included in the price for which the materials are sold. If a resource is plentiful, 2% would be more than anyone had need of and the permits to extract would be inexpensive. If the resource became scarce, however, the extraction permits would become more expensive and the price of the resource would increase, discouraging inefficient use and encouraging the development of alternatives.

After the first year, if there are no substantial additions to the supply, the second year's 2% extraction allocation would be somewhat smaller. It would be calculated from the 98% remaining after the first year's extraction. With each year offering a little bit less of the resource to be consumed, the incentive for efficient usage and for developing alternatives would increase.

At present, the market will signal the need to conserve and seek alternatives, but not until that resource ceases to be available in the quantities that people need. One of the most significant failures of the market as presently managed, is that it has given us few indications that a major crisis is near. Once oil wells are drilled and hooked up to pipelines and refineries, their flow can be technically enhanced to continue fairly consistently until the wells start to produce salt water. The last barrel of oil will power cars and heat homes as well as any before it, but when there isn't more, when absolute shortages occur, our entire oil-fueled system of mutual provision could descend into chaos. By limiting extraction to 2% per year, signals of shortages would start to be felt while we still had a decade or more for action, and a quantity of the resource in question with which to make the massive adaptation.

Subsidies

There is something unbelievable about the world spending hundreds of billions of dollars annually to subsidize its own destruction.
Lester Brown, Earth Policy Institute

Worldwide, governments spend $1.5 trillion ($1,500,000,000,000) U.S. dollars each year to subsidize various activities. Of this, $700 billion contributes directly to environmental destruction.

Having a population that knows how to read and write enables a broad range of possibilities that are not available to illiterate people. It is well worth pooling resources through taxation to make sure that everyone has, at minimum, a basic education. Public schools are subsidized because they provide something of value to all of society.

While there will always be young people needing basic skills, ongoing justification is not as readily available for subsidies granted to other activities. There are many subsidized activities that were considered important in the past, but which no longer warrant public support. Some date back to the 18th century when colonial powers gave grants and concessions to encourage the exploitation of distant resources to feed the industrial revolution unfolding in Europe.

Fisheries are a prime example. According to a report from the U.S. National Marine Fisheries Service in 1998, worldwide subsidies to fishing industries totalled between $14 and $20.5 billion, roughly 20% of overall industry revenue. Fishing has provided food and livelihoods since before recorded history. By investing in more boats, nets, and fish-processing facilities, it has been possible to employ more people, increase food supplies and generate additional wealth. That is, up until we touched the limits of fish stocks.

The global catch of ocean fish peaked in 1988, and has been declining ever since. Despite a global fishing fleet capable of catching almost twice as many fish as the oceans produce annually, money continues to be pumped into the industry to build more boats and fishing equipment. It's not difficult to see that the public money involved could be put to better use.

Another example is the $400 million spent annually by the U.S. Forest Service building roads into forests to enable logging companies easy access to trees given to them at a fraction of their value. While creating jobs, forests disappear, taking with them wildlife habitat, recreational opportunities, economic spin-offs from tourism, climate control and the ability to absorb run-off and prevent erosion. Clearly, these are not the outcomes intended from this use of public funds.

Similar difficulties can arise from some agricultural subsidies. Irrigation subsidies can lead to overuse of water, salinisation of soils and the depletion of groundwater reserves. Fertilizer and pesticide subsidies can lead to overuse, the disruption of nutrient cycles and food chains, and the poisoning of people, wildlife and groundwater.

Once subsidies are flowing, however, people can become dependent on the jobs they create. Sometimes, individuals and organizations playing key roles in subsidized sectors prosper immensely, even to the point of gaining political power. While the need to encourage an activity may change, or even disappear, other interests served by money flows can keep subsidies in place long after they stop serving the common good.

While there is plenty of opposition to eliminating subsidies that have outlived their usefulness, the results of such changes can be beneficial. In Bangladesh, subsidies for fertilizer accounted for 4% of the national budget. When this provision was dropped, small-scale farmers became competitive and the cost of food actually decreased. Pesticides in Indonesia were heavily subsidized and used in great quantities with serious side effects. When the government phased the subsidy out between 1986 and 1989, the use of the poisons dropped to a small fraction of the previous volumes, and by 1990, thanks to a recovering ecosystem, rice production increased by 11%.

Perhaps the biggest subsidy dilemmas of the present day are those providing for energy. The dynamics became quite clear here in Ontario, Canada, when the government moved to deregulate the production of electricity. Soon after, the price of electricity began to rise, reaching twice its previous cost. Many Hydro customers were upset, complaining about the expense and talking about how they might reduce their usage.

Redirection of subsidies to upgrade owned and rented facilities to energy-efficient standards, so that all sectors of society would reduce their energy use, could have prevented the public outcry about rates. Instead, the political waves caused the government to reverse its plans and peg the cost of power at the earlier level of 4.3¢ per kilowatt hour. Just a few months into the new policy, they had already spent hundreds of millions of taxpayers dollars to pay for energy costs that the reduced rate did not cover.

As a power consumer, I can't say that I was disappointed when my Hydro bill was reduced, or when I received my $75 rebate cheque just weeks before Christmas (and the election expected to follow). For many years, I have minimized my electricity use, but this turn-around provided a new appreciation of how cheap the product can be to buy. From the perspective of what it costs me directly, there was little point in further reducing my usage. That same impulse, multiplied by the 12 million people in Ontario, is likely resulting in enormous waste that would have been avoided had the prices remained at the higher level.

The other tragedy of this reversal was that it put renewable energy projects back on the shelf. While the full-cost of electricity was being charged, wind generation was competitive — business plans for wind power were being developed. But as soon as the electricity price was pushed down again, the economic math no longer worked and the projects were abandoned. (Please note that privatization of such a utility is not necessary. Full-costs can be charged without having to add the additional cost of private profits or running the risks of service being compromised to increase the bottom line.)

In contrast, both Denmark and Germany have power subsidies that favour wind. As a result, the installed capacity to generate power from this renewable source is growing faster than any other form of electricity generation. There are now hundreds of "wind co-ops" where a cluster of families can pool resources and build wind powered generators. With the power distribution network required to purchase wind power, loans for such projects are essentially guaranteed. When the wind co-ops retire their debts, they have free power for themselves along with some income from selling the excess. Replacing dirty power generation with clean is a bonus shared by all.

The shape of human settlements is affected by subsidies favouring individual gasoline powered transport. Incentives provided to oil producers during WW I to encourage energy self-sufficiency continue to be paid, making some of the most prosperous businesses on Earth also among the biggest recipients of public welfare. In the U.S., in addition to direct subsidies, over $100 billion is spent annually by governments to construct, maintain and patrol highways above and beyond all the revenues collected from license fees and taxes on gasoline and vehicles. This massive figure more than doubles if military preparations and wars fought to maintain oil supplies and supply lines in foreign countries are included.

Subsidies for automobile transport, along with tax structures that favour car-dependent suburbs, have led to vast residential areas sprawling out over good agricultural land and natural habitat. The resulting energy and automobile-dependent lifestyle is literally cemented into place by the architecture. In the U.S., 87% of all trips are taken by car and only 3% by public transit. By contrast, in Europe, where the shape of human settlements were established before the car and where subsidies do not favour auto culture to the same extent, 40 - 50% of trips are taken by walking or bicycle and 10% by public transit. In light of the massive subsidies to private automobile transportation, protest is suspect when it rises up against subsidizing public transport.

Supply and demand provide a good starting point for determining prices. If pollution, resource supplies and community stability are not recognized by the market, remedial taxes and marketable permits can bring them into the accounts. Where particular goals are recognized as important, like CO_2 reduction or local employment, related activities can be stimulated by directed subsidies. While taxes and subsidies can be powerful factors shaping the evolution of society, they need to be reviewed regularly to make sure they do not create more problems than they solve.

After decades of having public services reduced to accommodate the demands of exponential capital growth, people are understandably concerned that legislated change will further reduce their well-being. As the Monopoly End Game becomes more widely identified with its destructive nature, and as it becomes popular knowledge that the common good is not always best served by the invisible hand of unattended markets, the governments we create will, hopefully, focus more directly on serving public interests. It will take some time before governments are again trusted, making it all the more important that a strong social safety net not only be in place, but be seen to be in place, ready to cushion the transition. People must be assured that no one will be made to suffer disproportionally during the changes that are necessary for everyone to do better. When concerns about fair treatment and personal well-being are satisfied, we can expect cooperation from the vast majority and the rekindling of hope in the future.

Other Programs

While taxes and subsidies can stimulate markets to serve desired goals, there are other ways for businesses to become more benign. The Green Dot , Extended Producer Responsibility and The Natural Step are programs that can direct our creative mutual provision toward the goal of sustainability.

Green Dot

In Germany, producers of goods have to pay to put a green dot on their products. The fee is to pay for the disposal of their packaging. The more packaging, the higher the Green Dot fee. In addition to providing funds to dispose of packaging garbage, this program has inspired all manner of innovations to reduce the amount of packaging sold with products. The reduction of wasted glass, metal and plastic amounts to a million tons a year: down from the 30 million tons of waste that were being produced annually when the program began.

Extended Producer Responsibility

Product stewardship places responsibility for the disposal of products with the manufacturer. When a consumer is finished with something he or she has paid for, the manufacturer has to take it back to make sure that it is disposed of properly. Such a requirement encourages producers to consider the repair and/or recycling of their product while they are still in the process of designing it. In this way, the eventual waste problem can be minimized by design before the product is made.

In parts of Europe, Asia, and Canada, "take back" legislation, covers a range of products including automobiles, computers and hazardous household products that are being taken care of responsibly, by design. Xerox has saved $2 billion, while keeping a billion pounds of electronic parts out of landfills. Such product stewardship is also practised by Hewlett-Packard, Bayer, BSEF and Mercedes-Benz. Mercedes-Benz now designs its cars so that the components can be reprocessed and reused. Dashboards, arm rests and other parts can be easily removed during disassembly, and the number of different types of plastics being used has been reduced to enable their easy separation when the worn out cars are recycled.

The Natural Step

One of Sweden's leading cancer researchers, Dr. Karl-Henrik Robert, spent years working to identify conditions within which productive activity could be truly safe. The cells of human beings, he noted are so similar to the cells of other animals that they have to be examined at the molecular level to find differences. For eons, all cellular animal life has been composed of the same naturally occurring materials. Nothing alive is prepared for changes in the chemical make-up of the environment from which we draw the substance of our physical forms. New chemicals, reacting within living things, can cause problems for which there are no biological solutions.

Dr. Robert developed a list of conditions that, if applied, would end human induced environmental disruptions. He presented his findings to other scientists, redrafted the criteria taking their comments into account, and again presented them to his peers. After numerous drafts, all agreed on the basic tenets. By applying the criteria to our productive activities, industry can become as benign as the productivity of plants and other animals.

The Natural Step's System Conditions:
1) Substances from the Earth's crust must not systematically increase in the biosphere.
2) Substances produced by society must not systematically increase in the biosphere.
3) The physical basis for the productivity and diversity of nature must not systematically be diminished.
4) We must be fair and efficient in meeting basic human need.
(More details can be found at www.naturalstep.org)

These are essentially the elements of the sustainability outline that relate to material production. They imply:

1) Cyclic material use to keep the substances we take from the Earth's crust from being dispersed into the environment;
2) Using renewable energy sources to avoid accumulating CO_2;
3) Respecting the regenerative capacity of living things and the integrity of life forms and
4) Justice.

Since its introduction in 1989, the Natural Step has been adopted as design criteria by numerous corporations. One such company is Interface Flooring based in Atlanta, Georgia, U.S.A. Inspired at a presentation given by Dr. Robert, then Interface Chairman, Ray Anderson, decided to apply the system criteria to his international commercial carpeting business. Over the company's years in business, five billion pounds of its product had ended up in landfill sites after its useful life was over. During that period, each pound of the petroleum based material took two pounds of fossil energy to process and more to deliver to customers and then to the landfill. As described in *Natural Capitalism,* Mr. Anderson "... realized that not throwing more energy and money into holes in the ground represents a major business opportunity." Interface Flooring has since designed a system where carpeting is leased as a service, and their product is now installed as tiles. When the portions that experience the heaviest traffic get worn, only those worn tiles need be replaced, reducing the amount removed by 80 – 90%. In this newly developed process, even the 10 – 20% that is removed is no longer thrown away. Instead, the worn tiles are separated into fibre and backing, each of which is completely reprocessed and combined again into new carpet tiles.

By training employees to think about the system's conditions and to look for ways of applying those conditions to the various processes they are familiar with, great strides have been made toward an environmentally rational carpet business. Today, waste carpet from the business approaches zero. The company is also developing natural fiber materials to replace the petroleum feed stock and, at their branch plant in Belleville, Ontario, they have contracted to buy wind-generated electricity for use in their operation.

The "new" Interface Flooring is a great success. Its consumption and waste, particularly of petroleum products, have dropped substantially. As it turns out, thanks to the resulting cost savings, they have also increased their profits — all before any structural steps have been taken by government to encourage full-cost accounting. When those changes are instituted, Interface will already be way out in front of the pack.

International Action

We live in a global community and, while many issues of mutual provision are matters to be dealt with entirely within individual nations, there is much that requires cooperation between nations and will require solutions applied at the global level. In addition to the work of the United Nations, there are efforts being made to introduce sustainability enhancing policy simultaneously in various nations. Information about Simultaneous Policy can be found at: http://www.simpol.org

Taxing Speculation: The Tobin Tax

Self-enrichment is encouraged in our economic system because becoming wealthy has traditionally involved providing goods and services of value to others. As I have shown in these pages, this is no longer always true. Today, fortunes can be made speculating in financial markets without increasing the common good, or worse.

Since money changed from gold into cyber-stuff in 1971, financial speculation has skyrocketed. While the real economy has little more than doubled, the volume of speculative trading has increased 15 fold. Over a trillion dollars a day is presently exchanged, tax free, through international currency deals. This is a hundred times more than the amount spent on all goods and services combined. At the same time, we have been forced to cut back on education, health care, employment insurance and other benefits. A tax on speculation would bring much needed money back into the civil economy.

Income from speculation can be taxed, when it can be traced within a single country, but there is no sales tax on the transactions themselves. Taxpayers might well wonder why buying or selling financial products is not taxed the same as the buying of food and clothing or the selling of goods and services? Why does financial trading receive preferential treatment when it comes to tax collection?

Until looking into it, I thought that financial markets existed to raise funds in order to establish large-scale production facilities. Certainly this was their origin, and for new ventures it is still the case. However, as the co-founder and editor for 15 years of Business Ethics magazine, Marjorie Kelly, points out in *The Divine Right of Capital,*

> *There is only the smallest bit of direct investment in companies going on. What is at work is speculation, the trading of shares from one speculator to another. Another word for it is gambling... since these words have a less noble cast to them, we prefer the word investment, for it keeps us from confronting the stark reality.*

Kelly goes on to compare the value of new common stock to the total value of shares traded on the New York Stock Exchange. Productive investment only amounts to 1%. In another calculation, more complimentary to investors, Kelly compares the new investment to the increase in the total value of stocks, rather than to the sum total of stock traded. For the 1998 – 1999 time period, the productive portion represented 7% of the total. While not much, 7% suggests some benefit to society.

When factoring in the figures for net extraction of capital from companies through stock buy-backs and dividend payouts, however, Kelly points out that, "the stock market, in reality, is not 1% or 7% productive, it is less than 0 percent productive."

Not only is there no justification for such a tax exemption, there are good reasons to put a small tax on financial speculation in general, and currency speculation in particular. Hundreds of billions of dollars wait poised in computer memories, looking for the slightest fluctuations in currency and stock values from which a profit can be wrung. When such an opportunity arises, vast fortunes swoop in at the speed of light to buy and sell the currencies that are the blood of nations. For fear of triggering an "attack" on its money, the financial policy of most governments is crafted to appease currency speculators, rather than to serve the needs of their citizens.

The Asian Tigers were mentioned earlier. With deregulated economies and borders open to foreign investment, speculative money poured into those countries, inflating the value of assets and public expectations, and then flooded out in the familiar cycle. With depressed economies, unemployment, high interest rates and subsequent bankruptcies, distress became widespread. Capital returned through the open borders to pick up productive assets at bargain prices. The experience is not unique to the "Tigers." It is a familiar pattern in this late stage of the "Game."

The damage caused by short-term speculation could be minimized with a Tobin Tax, named after James Tobin, the Nobel Prize winning economist from Yale who proposed it in 1978. The small tax, suggested to be one-quarter of one percent or less, would increase the amount by which a currency or other asset would have to change in value before it offered any possibility for speculative profit. The tax would affect mostly those who gamble in financial assets solely for monetary gain. It would have little or no impact on the majority of citizens, except that the financial system would be more stable.

Originally conceived for currency speculation, the application of such a tax to other speculative dealings is now also proposed. At one-quarter of one percent, the tax would not discourage investment in enterprises making real goods or providing real services. It often takes years to launch such enterprises. Investors would pay the speculation tax only once, when they made their investment. After that, such "real" investment would go on earning income for years. The same tax, however, would act as a wet blanket on speculators seeking quick profit by buying one day and selling the next.

In Good Taxes: The Case for Taxing Foreign Currency Exchange and Other Financial Transactions, Alex Michalos explains that 80% of all speculative transactions are purchases resold within seven days or less; 40% are resold in two days or less. At two-tenths of one percent, this tax would amount to 48% in one year if the speculative capital was turned over every business day, 10% if the turnover was once every week, 2.4 % monthly and so on. It becomes clear how such a small tax favours long-term investments over dealings in financial markets for short-term gain. By making short-term speculation less profitable, currencies and stock markets would become more stable and the world would likely find an increased supply of capital for productive investment.

Productive investment would also be served in another way. Presently, when major developments are planned in another country, developers will purchase funds in advance from the country where the development is scheduled to take place. Such "hedge" funds protect against possible changes in the value of that currency. Buying francs or pesos at a good rate now may prevent having to buy them at a more expensive rate when the time comes to build. If currency values could be trusted to stay the same, hedge funds would be unnecessary and the money tied up in them could be invested in productive enterprises.

The other side of a speculation tax is that the money raised could be used to address some of the major problems facing the world. In its 1994 Human Development Report, the United Nations Development Program estimated that the cost of wiping out the worst forms of poverty worldwide, by providing basic energy, water and sanitation for the most needy, would be between $30 and $40 billion annually. Estimated revenue from a Tobin Tax suggest that it would raise double this amount or more. Rather than being lost, this money, trimmed from speculative activity, could flow into poor communities giving them opportunities to accommodate mutual provision at the local level.

Opponents of the tax say it would be impossible to collect since many of the transactions involved are between nations. The transactions are, however, thoroughly accounted for by the various Securities Exchange Commissions. If the world decided to collect the tax, cooperation could be made a condition of access to the financial and other services of the international community. The arguments for enacting such a tax were clear enough for the Canadian House of Commons to pass Motion 239, in February of 1999, by a two-thirds majority. The motion recommended: "That, in the opinion of the House, the government should show leadership and enact a tax on financial transactions in concert with the international community."

For more detail on the Tobin Tax, including arguments raised against it and responses to those arguments, see Alex Michalos's 1997 publication *Good Taxes,* or visit: http://www.currencytax.org

13 Monetary Reform

The money system is so pervasive that it is easy to think that it is a consistent part of human affairs. Something has to serve the role of blood in society, enabling the movement of goods and services between people. In one form or another, by enabling vast numbers of people to cooperate, money is a key element of civilization. Nevertheless, monetary systems come in different styles and they incline their civilizations toward different ends.

Money has evolved through many forms since the days predominated by barter. For all its forms, the only essential things money has to do are:

1) to provide a standard measure through which the relative value of different things can be compared; and

2) to serve as a medium of exchange to enable trade between people.

Depending on the type of monetary system in use, there are additional functions that money can fulfill. Not only are they not necessary for the primary functions to work, they can interfere more than they assist. The first of these was mentioned earlier:

3) to serve as a medium for storing value.

There are two additional functions that sometimes arise:

4) to function as a tool for speculative profit and

5) to function as a tool for building empire.

Our present monetary system is used for all five functions.

Using Money to Store Value

One way of measuring "intelligence" is to find out how many cause and effect repercussions a person can anticipate in advance of an action. Thinking ahead and being prepared for economic troubles, illness or old age is a sign of intelligence. Although it is a good thing to be prepared for the future, using money to store value can actually make that future less secure than it needs to be.

Anyone familiar with the Great Depression of the 1930s, or even the recessions of the early 1980s and early 1990s has a sense of the disruption and hard times brought on by the boom/bust cycle. Using money to store value isn't necessarily responsible for the cycle, but it can amplify it substantially. Look again at the cycle with an eye on how storing value in money plays a role. When times are good, there is less concern about the future and people are more likely to spend their money rather than save it. Most people are working, money is flowing and it appears likely that earnings will continue to replace what is spent. This attitude is self-fulfilling since the more people spend, the more work there is producing goods and paying out money that can, in turn, be spent. When this confidence inspires people to spend their savings, (money they had taken out of circulation to store value) and particularly when they extend that saved money with loans to buy a bigger house, a new car, a holiday or whatever, the upswing of money in circulation can cause inflation. Good times and confidence can thus sow the seeds of their opposite. Inflation or some unexpected event can sour public confidence, inclining people once again to store their wealth, rather than spend it. Storing value in money, however, takes it out of circulation, goods are not bought, there is less work and consequently the downturn is self-amplified.

Using Money for Making Speculative Profit

Problems arising from using money as a tool for speculative profit were discussed earlier. The volumes of money caught up in the speculative sphere now dwarf the amounts used for trading goods and services in mutual provision — the "real economy." This makes the real economy irrelevant to the stability of the monetary system. Policy can no longer be made to address concerns of full employment, sufficient housing or adequate nutrition, health care and education. Money decisions must be made to address the concerns of those who dominate the speculative sphere. Widespread bankruptcy, unemployment and associated hard times were precipitated in

Thailand, Indonesia, Singapore, South Korea, Malaysia, Russia, Brazil and Mexico during the 1990s, as a result of speculative activity. These experiences are more than enough to keep most countries obedient to speculative markets, even while the immediate needs of their populations call for other priorities.

Using Money as a Tool for Building Empire

The final function money can serve, though unnecessary to its essential functions, is as a tool for empire building. The Soviet example is a safe one, now that it is history. The countries in the Soviet Union's sphere of influence were united monetarily with what were called "Comecon" currencies. These currencies were convertible only into Soviet rubles and, while that provided some advantages for trading with the USSR, it made it difficult to trade outside the Soviet sphere, if such trade did not fit with the empire's ambitions.

Today, we have a global system without a global currency. To trade internationally the money of the most developed countries are used as "reserve currencies." U.S. dollars are used for almost two-thirds of all international trade. To a lesser extent, British pounds, Swiss francs, the Japanese yen and recently, the euro are also used. Any other countries that want to trade internationally have to collect enough of these reserve currencies to do their business. This means that the originators of the currencies can help themselves to whatever the world produces, pay in U.S. dollars and not have to worry about many of those dollars coming home asking for U.S. made products in return. This is an immense benefit for the countries producing the reserve currencies, but it a disadvantage for those who most need a break.

Local Currencies

With the present monetary system heavily engaged in all five functions described above, it is not surprising that some communities are left behind by the Global Monopoly Game. National and global money is, for them, in short supply. Local Economic Trading Systems (LETS) like those described in Chapter 9, are one way in which communities can lift themselves out of a slump by refreshing the opportunities for the people involved to trade with each other.

Creating Community Currencies Should be a Human Right.

A fair-minded reflection will see the validity of people creating currencies so they can provide for each other's needs. Who could object if a hungry person were to repair a broken chair in trade for a bushel of potatoes. When whole communities are lacking in national currencies, it makes sense for them to create their own so that they can measure the value of each other's efforts and accommodate exchange. An accessible currency is essential in all but the smallest of communities.

Money and Interest

Whether backed by gold, cattle, grain or public confidence, there are only three types of money: money bearing interest charges, currency bearing no interest and currency with a demurrage fee.

Interest-Bearing Monetary System

Considerable space has been filled above discussing the creation of money through interest bearing debt. Debt-based money is a powerful growth stimulant. The pressure of accumulating enough scarce money to pay back loans with interest, and the necessity for new loans to be made to make that repayment possible, keep people hustling. Allowing interest charges encourages money out of storage and into use, providing many benefits. As the foundation of our economic system, however, it has some serious problems.

For a start, debt-based money increases in value over time, making it an effective medium for storing value. We've already looked at how holding on to money when things look uncertain intensifies the boom/bust cycle. Another problem is that it tends to accumulate in the hands of fewer people as the rich-get-richer and the-poor-get-poorer Monopoly process churns away. Concentrating wealth concentrates political power, which tends to make decisions to serve its own interests. Growing disparities lead to health problems, resentment, and, if left unchecked, desperation and violence.

Sewer and water systems were among the first public works following the industrial revolution. The health consequences of the new high-density living conditions of factory towns were immense and by providing water and sewers to keep things clean, contagious diseases were brought under control. Centuries later, we take these systems for granted. Cities like Kingston, Ontario, are faced with the expensive task of rebuilding their aging sewer and water systems. The cost of the job is estimated at over $200 million. If the city has to raise that money from private banks, the final cost, when principal is paid back and interest fees gathered and delivered, will be between $400 and $600 million.

When a nation's money is created by private institutions, the costs of interest payments can impoverish governments. In the 2003 Canadian Federal Budget, $37 billion was earmarked for interest payments. When federal, provincial and municipal government debts were added up that year, the annual interest charges totalled close to $65 billion, more or less, depending on interest rates. Billions of dollars had to be cut from education, social services and other programs, largely to enable interest payments. While the cost effectiveness of some government programs can and should be questioned, the advantages of education and available health care are obvious. The questions not asked are:

1) What value do we get in return for these huge payments of interest?
2) Are these payments an effective use of public money?

These questions are all the more relevant in Canada, because the Bank of Canada charter clearly states in *Article 18* that it can lend money to the Government of Canada or to other jurisdictions at nominal interest rates. Creating money through this legal channel would enable support for the nation's infrastructure and health care without massive interest charges.

Over the years, the economically faithful have written a lot about how the government cannot be trusted to create the money supply. They write that governments spend carelessly and that deficit spending is inflationary. Similar concerns, however, also apply to privately created money. With no public control over private money creation, except the disruptive mechanism of raising interest rates, private lenders have almost unlimited scope for creating money. While it might be difficult to get $10,000 for a small business, tens of million are frequently created to be lent (or used directly) for speculation. At least government has open accounts. The private lenders who presently create the money supply have no mandate nor intent to use the billions of taxpayers dollars they receive for the common good.

Why do we not protest when banks create money for speculation, yet become uneasy when governments do the same thing to pay for education and health care? There is a familiarity to the lack of protest over the inflationary and self-serving applications to which banks put the interest payments they receive from the public treasury. It is the same pattern as that described earlier in connection with full-cost accounting. When rising cigarette prices resulted from taxes, there was widespread public protest. When the manufacturers were fined and, to pay the fine, had to raise the price to the same high level, the smoking public was remarkably accepting.

As long as the money supply continues to be created through debt, anxiety will thrive. Debtors mortgage their homes and businesses as collateral for bets that they can win the rat race competition for scarce money and make their monthly interest payments. With debtors on side, striving to avoid bankruptcy, this system, powered by fear, remains an effective stimulus for expanding the economy. Unfortunately, the pie must grow continuously and at an accelerating rate, for such a system to keep "working." While the human family is stretching the Earth's limits to maintain growth, the vast fortunes accumulating in private hands are luring poor nations into debt slavery, and through speculative gambling, destabilizing the economic structures upon which mutual provision depends.

A significant amount of the anxiety resulting from debt-based money could be alleviated by creating money in amounts equivalent to the interest required by outstanding loans. The money could be spent into circulation by the nation for health care, education and other programs of public benefit. This injection of debt-free money would at least make it possible for everyone with loans to earn enough money to repay their loans without having to bankrupt others or require additional loans to be made.

Money System Requiring no Interest

The Bank of Canada was established to maintain the national money supply. As mentioned above, *Article 18* of its charter relates specifically to situations such as Kingston's sewer and water works, and other municipal, provincial and federal infrastructure projects. The Bank of Canada can manage such accounts as effectively as a private bank. Instead of setting the interest rate to maximize profit, however, such friendly loans can charge an interest rate sufficient to match inflation, plus enough extra to maintain the municipality's interest in repaying the loan. If all payments are made in an orderly fashion, when the loan is finally retired, the interest payments, minus inflation and management costs, could be returned to the municipality for the continued maintenance of the city's infrastructure.

For 35 years after the Bank of Canada was established, it lent money to Canada at nominal interest rates. Since the interest was paid back into the general revenue of the Canadian government, the portion of the nation's spending that was financed by the Bank of

Canada (around a quarter of the budget) was interest-free. This arrangement financed much of Canada's participation in World War II, and afterwards, built houses, roads, schools, universities and hospitals, started Medicare and initiated the Canada Pension Plan.

These things were the products of Canadian ingenuity and labour. The interest-free money simply enabled Canadians to participate in creating the quality of life of which they were capable.

They were good times: unemployment was low, inflation was low, interest rates were low, and public debt was low.

Whether through the workings of a central bank established to nurture well-being in a country, or through local communities creating currencies to accommodate trade among the residents, when money is put into circulation without an onerous interest fee, there is a far greater potential for creativity, trust and cooperation.

Demurrage Currency

Trust and cooperation get another boost when people use a monetary system with a demurrage charge.

Demurrage is a small fee regularly subtracted from the value of money. The rationale behind a demurrage charge is that money is a public service, like a postal system or public transportation, and that a small user fee should be levied on its use.

The difference between a demurrage charge and an interest charge is that interest is a demand for money in addition to the principal, while demurrage is a charge subtracted from the currency itself. While both are fees for having money, the difference in the impact the fees cause is immense.

Demurrage can be applied in a number of ways, but, in essence, it means that if you are paid $100 today, and use it right away, you have a hundred dollars of purchasing power. If you hold on to it for a month, you would have to pay a "parking fee" of $1, and if you hold on to it for another month the fee would rise to $2 and so on. Obviously, this is an incentive for you to spend your money sooner rather than later.

Demurrage changes the nature of the monetary system in a number of significant and beneficial ways. Primarily, that currency would no longer be suitable for storing value. In long-term storage, the "parking fee" would reduce your holding to nothing. To receive the full value from one's income, it would have to be spent within a short while. When it is spent, the people receiving it would also want to spend or invest it as soon as they could. Over and over, the currency would be spent at the first practical opportunity, employing people at each step along the way.

As the saying goes, "Money is like manure. It's not good unless it's spread about." Demurrage currency is structurally suited for circulation rather than for collecting in piles. The tendency for such a monetary system to stimulate employment, is, in itself, a good reason to consider adopting it.

Investing in a Better World

The point is not to discourage saving. Once we have taken care of our immediate needs, it is natural to save for retirement, education, a new business or other interests. Demurrage currency would assure that an inclination to save doesn't have the side effect of taking money out of circulation. Instead, for our future needs, we would look for tangible things to invest in that would maintain value or even grow in value over time. Insulating the house and other energy efficiency measures would reduce future costs; maintaining buildings and equipment would preserve and enhance their value; buying tools can reduce our expenses by enabling us to do things for ourselves or to increase our income by doing things for others; investing in local energy production and local food-production creates additional value with time.

When long-term well-being is thoroughly integrated into economic policy, investment institutions would be focussed exclusively on maintaining the world within sustainable bounds.

If one wanted to save for the grandchildrens' education, for example, one could invest in such institutions and they would organize truly beneficial productive work. There are countless things we can do to improve the world around us so that, over time, our security and the opportunities available will be as good or better than at present. Even small amounts of savings could preserve their value through such arrangements.

Discounting Goes into Reverse

With the present system of interest-bearing money, the value of anything in the future is discounted. The return expected from planting a forest or insulating a home would be weighed, unfavourably, against the potential earnings of that money if invested in an exponential growth scheme. The further into the future one looks, the less "rational" it seems to use money for anything besides financial investment. Planning for the seventh generation becomes a joke.

With demurrage currency, such discounting no longer applies. Faced with the choice of purchasing something that will last or a cheaper item that will leave us with some of the depreciating money left over, the inclination will be to buy more durable items. By storing value in the maintenance of buildings and equipment, the creation of things and nurturing things that grow, our world would be actively upgraded. The currency spent on this upgrading would go back into circulation, maintaining employment and, in turn, giving more people opportunities to decide how they think their savings can make the world more valuable in the future. Over time, we could expect a great deal of improvement in the human condition and our consequent security.

Decentralized Decision-making

It is notable that with a demurrage currency system, decisions about what to invest in to improve the future would be made by every person earning money. It is much more likely that as individuals we would invest in food, shelter, durable goods, healthy forests and fields, education and art to upgrade our world directly, rather than war planes and bombs to force economic advantages from others. Demurrage would reprogram the invisible hand by shifting the medium for storing value away from money and into the restoration, maintenance and upgrading of the world around us. There would be no need for moral persuasion; the basic economic structure would divert people's self-interest toward more sustainable practices. Multiplied by the economically active population, the changes in outcomes would be massive.

Demurrage Currency Systems have Worked Before

Monetary systems based on demurrage have existed for a long time. Economic historian, Bernard Lietaer, uncovered several examples. The earliest of these was in Egypt. The biblical story of Joseph's interpretation of the Pharaoh's dream about seven years of abundance followed by seven lean years is well-known. Much grain was stored during the time of plenty and, consequently, starvation was avoided during the lean years. Our world might be very different today had that story included an explanation of the grain storage system — the basis of Egypt's economy for over a thousand years.

Most people in those day were farmers. After harvest, they would put their grain into storage and receive in exchange, pieces of pottery called "ostraca" upon which was inscribed the volume of grain they had deposited and the date of delivery. The farmer could trade the ostraca for other goods or services, and anyone could go back to the storage depot and return the ostraca for the amount of grain it indicated, less a fee to cover the cost of storage and loss to rodents. The ostraca, which have been uncovered in Egypt by the thousands, were, in effect, a commodity-based currency that was traded throughout the population. The grain storage fee was a demurrage charge.

Because the storage fee increased with time, those who received ostraca were inclined to invest, rather than hold on to it. Monuments that last forever were one expression and, for the common folk, irrigation systems and other land improvements were another. The productivity so inspired, gained Egypt a reputation as the "bread basket" of the ancient world; a status it enjoyed until the Romans forced it to adopt the Roman monetary system, complete with interest charges. Since then, Egypt has been a "third world" country.

European Middle Ages

From about 1050 to 1300 AD, several demurrage-type currency systems existed throughout Europe. In Germany it took the form of "brakteaten" currency. This currency consisted of silver plaques that were issued by the local lords, recalled from time to time and reissued in a somewhat thinner form, effectively creating a demurrage charge.

Rather than hoarding this literally shrinking currency, people invested in durable things. Notable among these were the grand cathedrals, almost all of which were constructed during that time. In addition to being places for worship, community gathering and festivities, these cathedrals were destinations for pilgrims. A city or town with a grand cathedral attracted pilgrims and, like tourists today, pilgrims would stay in local accommodations and buy local produce. In France, the city of Chartres still earns substantial revenues from people coming to see its cathedral, 800 years after it was completed.

Lietaer points out that not only were most of the great cathedrals built during this time, but records show that mills and other assets were maintained at high levels of upkeep, and the quality of life of common labourers was also very good. Perhaps, relative to their times, better than today.

Demurrage in the Twentieth Century

Not all examples of demurrage currencies are from pre-capitalist times. In 1930, the owner of a bankrupt coal mine in Germany maintained operations by paying miners with "wara," a local "stamp scrip" backed by coal. The scrip, as monetary notes are sometimes called, had squares on the back where the current month was stamped to keep the money valid. A small fee was charged with each stamp to cover the associated storage costs of the stored commodity.

Miners were able to buy their food and other necessities with wara, and the idea spread rapidly throughout the depressed country. By the latter part of 1931, wara were in use throughout Germany. Over two thousands corporations were cooperating by accepting and paying out wara, and a variety of additional commodities were added to coal to back up the currency. Unfortunately, the German Central Bank asserted it's monopoly on money creation and had the experiment prohibited.

The word was out, however. Bernard Lietaer describes the following experiment (reprinted here with permission) that took place soon after, just to the southwest of Germany.

The 1930s in Austria

In 1932, Herr Unterguggenberger, mayor of the Austrian town of Worgl, decided to do something about the 35 percent unemployment of his constituency (typical for most of Europe at the time). He convinced the town hall to issue 14,000 Austrian shillings worth of "stamp scrip," which were covered by exactly the same amount of ordinary shillings deposited in a local bank.

After two years, Worgl became the first Austrian city to achieve full employment. Water distribution was generalized throughout, all of the town was repaved, most houses were repaired and repainted, taxes were being paid early, and forests around the city were replanted.

It is important to recognize that the major impact of this approach did not derive from the initial project launched by the city, but instead had its origin in the numerous individual initiatives taken in the process of recirculating the local currency instead of hoarding it. On the average, the velocity of circulation of the Worgl money was about fourteen times higher than the normal Austrian shillings. In other words, on the average, the same amount of money created fourteen times more jobs.

More than 200 other Austrian communities decided to copy this example, but here again the Central Bank blocked the process. A legal appeal was made all the way to the Supreme Court, where it was lost.

Lietaer speculates, "We will never know for sure whether Hitler would have been propelled to power if the people of Germany had been allowed to continue to solve their problems from the ground up and find employment and dignity in their own communities." He wonders, "Would it not have been worth letting them try?"

Lietaer and co-author Belgin reveal much more about the institution of money in their book: *Of Human Wealth: New Currencies for a New World.* For more information see:

www.ofhumanwealth.com and www.complementarycurrency.net

Experiments with locally issued, emergency currencies took place in the U.S., as well. In the 1930s, 400 cities and thousands of communities and organizations were issuing emergency currencies to enable citizens to trade while the federal currency regime was stagnant. Many of these were stamp scrip and worked so successfully that in February of 1933, bills were presented in the U.S. Senate and the House of Representatives to issue a stamp scrip nationwide. Concerns were raised about how demurrage currency encourages decentralized decision-making. The issue was brought to the attention of President Roosevelt who soon after prohibited "emergency currencies" and announced the New Deal, with its large-scale centrally directed projects, as a means of getting federal currency back into circulation.

Despite objections from central banks, there is merit to separating the measurement of value and trade functions of money from the storage of value function. Lietaer, who is clearly enthusiastic about such evolution in our trading medium proposes,

> ...that we choose to develop money systems that will enable us to attain sustainability and community healing on a local and global scale. These objectives are in our grasp within less than one generations time. Whether we materialize them or not will depend on our capacity to cooperate with each other to consciously reinvent our money.

With all the options available for the creation of money, one can imagine an order whereby the fundamentals of civilization — sewer, water, education, health care and environmental protection — could be secured with interest-free money, where mushrooming fortunes could be kept in check with demurrage currency, and where individuals could provide capital to someone else's enterprise and draw a reasonable interest from the success of that enterprise.

A New System of Exchange

In this age of abundant transportation, trade between nations is far easier than it has ever been. Consequently, the financial exchanges between nations are more complex. The detachment of money from its material foundation in 1971 in some ways eased this complexity by creating a medium that can flow easily and quickly through computer communications. At the same time, this flexibility has enticed vast fortunes into speculative markets seeking to profit by quickly moving to buy and sell anything that changes in value. Huge quantities of money rush at the speed of light, into and out of nations, inflating the value of their money and then draining that value out again, often leaving a trail of bankruptcies and unemployment in its wake.

For most of the first centuries of international trade, monetary exchange between nations was moderated by the weight of gold. The currencies of most trading nations were backed by gold and could be exchanged with each other through their relative values in that common medium. When a nation imported a greater value of goods than it exported, it would make up the difference in value by transferring an amount of gold equivalent to the difference.

Following the disruptions of the two World Wars and the 1930s depression, the world's economic order needed redefinition. In 1944, forty-four nations were represented in the Mount Washington Hotel at Bretton Woods, New Hampshire, U.S.A.m where the details for a new monetary order were discussed. The British delegation, led by John Maynard Keynes, and the U.S. delegation, led by Harry Dexter-White, presented different proposals.

Keynes felt it was important to avoid the large imbalances of trade that had left disadvantaged countries seriously in debt previous to the World Wars. It was a vicious circle where nations with trade deficits found their economies depressed and at a further disadvantage, while creditor nations were stimulated by their positions and gained further advantage. The result was a structural disparity.

Keynes had worked out a proposal that would have instituted an international trading currency to be called the "Bancor." This would be accompanied by an International Clearing Union (ICU) through which trade accounts would be balanced. All currencies would be linked to the Bancor at a fixed, but adjustable rate. All nations would be expected to aim for a zero balance with the ICU since both credits and deficits are destabilizing to the world community. Both deficit and surplus accounts would be charged a small interest rate: the former, to encourage producing for export, and the latter, to encourage the spending of surpluses on goods from nations with deficits. In addition, if further stimulus was needed to encourage others to buy their products, nations could adjust the value of their currencies. The ICU system would have been a helping hand of considerable strength for underdeveloped countries working to build themselves into modern nations. In essence, it would have guaranteed markets for what developing nations can produce and given them a stable foundation upon which to develop. It would have been a New Game.

Both the international currency and the mechanism for equalizing accounts through trade, rather than debt, were rejected by the United States. The U.S. forced its preference using the leverage of the British war debt that it held. *The Bretton Woods Agreement* settled on reaffirming the gold standard and stabilizing exchange rates by committing governments to maintain a consistent value for their currency in terms of gold. Where there was pressure on a currency, the nation's central bank was obliged to maintain its value by buying their own currency on the open market with gold or other stable currencies. In the event that enough "hard currency" was not available to support the nation's money at the agreed value, the International Monetary Fund was created to provide loans to do the job. This measure gave the government involved time to entice foreign investment by raising interest rates, and to cut government spending to make more domestic money available to balance accounts. With investment flowing in and expenses reduced, the value of the currency would rise to its prescribed level and the country could pay back the IMF loan. While national currencies were still backed by gold and, therefore, exchangeable at reliable rates, this credit arrangement enabled more flexibility by reducing the amount of gold that had to be shipped from place to place.

The *Bretton Woods* arrangement lasted until 1971, when President Nixon removed the U.S. from the gold standard, leaving the rest of the world with little choice but to do the same.

Freed from the material constraints of backing money up with gold, money creation went into high gear. Debt expanded massively, intensifying the rat race of nations and businesses everywhere competing with each other to gather interest payments. Without debt obligation, farmers, fishermen, foresters, industries and governments would all have more liberty to act on concerns about natural resources, pollution, and the well-being of people and communities.

Unfortunately, as hostages to speculators and lending agencies, such concerns take a back seat to feeding the run-away monetary system. Poverty is spreading throughout the world while unimaginable wealth accumulates to the credit of a few. Health care, education and other social services are increasingly undermined to make way for accelerating money creation. All this dysfunction is occurring at a time when our ability to provide for human needs has never been higher. Surely we can do better.

These last few chapters have described a number of ways to incline the economic system toward more promising ends. Around the globe, a great deal of thought has taken place to work out details. In December of 2000, a conference was convened at Noordwijk aan Zee in the Netherlands to consider how the global economic structure might be recreated. Its aim was to develop a new "Bretton Woods Agreement" for the 21st century. The participants were not empowered to change the economic structure, but the gathering signalled that the time has arrived for reorganizing how the world manages mutual provision.

At this convention, the Foundation for the Economics of Sustainability (FEASTA) prepared a proposal that has come to be called the *Feasta Noordwijk Treaty*. It provides an informative look at how an economic system designed for sustainability, stability and equity can direct us toward those goals. Details can be viewed at www.feasta.org. The 11 clauses of the proposed treaty, with accompanying explanations, provide a fascinating overview of the economic principles that affect our world. How much brighter the future would be if the economic order were set up to encourage sustainability rather than to accommodate an ultimate win in the Global Monopoly Game.

In brief, the key elements from the *Feasta Noordwijk Treaty* are a call for the creation of parallel currencies at local, national and international levels.

The international currency would be backed by carbon dioxide emission permits. These would be issued annually in quantities compatible with a gradual reduction of those emissions toward a harmless volume, and would be distributed to countries proportional to their populations. Poor countries that don't produce their share of CO_2 could sell permits to countries that have become rich using more than their share. This source of income would enable many of the indebted countries to pay off their debts and encourage everyone to minimize the production of greenhouse gases. As customs and technologies evolve, enabling more satisfaction with less carbon emissions, greater amounts of activities would be possible within the limiting influence of the CO_2-based currency and more of that currency could be circulated.

As well, each nation would maintain two national currencies, one for trade between the people and one for storing value. Because the former could not be attacked speculatively, nations could stimulate employment, manage environmental resources for long-term viability and maintain quality health care and education through the skills and cooperation of their people.

Individual regions and communities would also have the right to create local currencies thereby enabling employment stimulation on a local basis without disrupting the balance of the national economy.

When desired, one currency could be traded for another through exchange mechanisms established for the purpose. These "money markets" would balance supply and demand and establish an exchange rate for conversion that results in no net changes in the overall supply of each currency. People could save and invest by buying "store of value" currency with what they have earned in the exchange currency or they could trade their "store of value" currency for exchange currency to make purchases. Another exchange mechanism would enable one to make substantial investments in another country, or repatriate such investments, but the process of converting different currencies would be too cumbersome for moving large volumes of speculative cash on short notice. The proposed treaty with detailed explanations can be found at:

http://www.feasta.org/documents/feastareview/meyer.htm

It may be hard to imagine a civilization where the needs of all are met without depreciating the environment, where speculative capital has little choice but to serve real need and where nations and regions have the ability to make decisions in the interest of their people and the environment that supports them. However, such a system is possible!

Remember, we are a tremendously gifted species. The sorry state of our present affairs is a result of inertia from very different times, perpetuated by misdirected self-interest. Our challenge is not whether or not it is possible to live secure healthy lives for countless generations, our challenge is to identify the direction in which we need to move to accomplish that end, and to exercise our democratic power so that we can proceed to do so.

Transformation

14 Cultural Foundations: Working Together as Societies

While there are many ways to adjust our economic system to better serve the times, change does not come easily to such a basic structure. Societies are held together by assumptions and agreements that, to a large extent, are learned at an early age and maintained at the subconscious level. If a new perspective were introduced at this level, civilization could move as one into a new era. In search of how we might introduce new values, what follows looks at the common ground underlying cooperation and at some of the ways it has evolved.

Ants and bees are famous for their ability to cooperate within their respective colonies. So complete is their cooperation that some argue that beehives and anthills are more like single organisms than colonies of separate creatures.

The extent of human cooperation is no less remarkable. Imagine how we would appear to observers who are as much larger than us as we are larger than ants. Such observers would see vast numbers of people growing enormous quantities of food, harvesting timber and mining minerals, while others transform these things into useful forms and, still others, distribute them around the planet. The large observers' conclusions about how we manage to achieve the impressive level of cooperation might be similar to how we imagine the cooperative impulse of ants or bees. Human societies are in many ways a fractal of ant colonies. From that perspective, this chapter is about parallels between the human phenomena and the instinct that we presume directs the cooperation of social insects.

In the event that our enormous observers also had the capability to observe the social insects, they would note many similarities with humans. It is less likely that they would note the primary difference — the far less common actions of those who choose to apply their free wills in ways that diverge from accepted norms.

As humans, we are capable of far more complexity than social insects. In particular, the capacity for individuals to independently conceive of, and take action, makes human communities interesting. Amidst the multitude of motivating and restraining influences we receive from our biological selves, the natural world and our society, the way we act is still, in some measure, up to each of us as individuals.

We like to think of ourselves as self-directed, but how much of what we do is actually directed by our individual wills, free from outside influences?

Some aspects of our lives function almost completely independently of our wills. Our hearts beat, our food is digested, cells are repaired and replaced. It is perhaps fortunate that our wills do not function in these areas. On the borderline of self-control are the ways in which we deal with fear, hunger, fatigue and reproductive desire. These inclinations emerge from our instinctual beings; yet, the way we respond is subject to individual will as we weigh the possibilities and circumstances of our lives.

Beyond that point, what we think and do, and with whom we share the products of our toil, are matters of personal choice. At least, they can be. Although few of us are beyond manipulation, we are usually able to exercise our wills and choose our actions. Even under a totally despotic regime, where many are enslaved, there have been plenty of instances where individuals have defied those who care nothing for their interests. Consider the Taino people, who once lived on the Caribbean Islands. They had a culture that so favoured freedom that when Columbus tried to enslave them, they chose death over working for masters. As a result, their culture was extinct within seventy years of Columbus' arrival.

The example of the Taino is not meant as a comment on the love of freedom versus the will to survive. It is an introduction to the notion of culture. How is it that some populations could be forced to work as captives while the Taino could not?

The answer lies in the elements of culture that form the underlying perspective through which we see the world. They seem to be learned rather than received as genetic inheritance. As such, they are theoretically subject to our wills, but, because they are received at an early age and underpin fundamental aspects of our world-views, we tend to accept them as how the world is, rather than as perspectives that we can adapt at will.

The elders of any society remember when things have gone well and when they have gone badly. Stories based on such observations have been passed down from generation to generation. Prior to mass-media, this cultural inheritance was the bulk of what each person experienced beyond their day to day perceptions. After many generations a world-view becomes established to provide the background understanding that helps a people succeed. It guides them with information about what actions are most likely to have positive or negative results. Individual wills are still free, but they are informed by the extensive experience embodied in their heritage.

In every society caregivers start communicating the culture even before the young begin thinking. Indeed, the different languages passed on to children lead to different ways of thinking and contribute substantially to the nature of one's enculturation. The information we receive in our earliest years is internalized and the source forgotten. A large portion of the choices we think we freely make are strongly influenced by underlying cultural directives learned in childhood. When faced with circumstances upon which actions must be taken people seldom feel the need to review the whole situation. There is so much in the world that reconsidering each and every experience, with our free will, would take lifetimes. So we tend to accept the views collected and passed on to us.

Belonging is important to most people. Throughout time, personal survival was dependent on being accepted by our group. Knowing the boundaries of acceptable behaviour, therefore, has a deep-rooted importance. With adherence to the social order comes the promise of material security, psychological balance, good sleep and a clear idea of how to use one's time and creativity. Well-employed creativity, shared through a society, becomes material security. Being accepted by and belonging to such a social order brings peace of mind. Accepting the content of one's culture is the price of admittance.

After tens of thousands of generations during which our survival was clearly a result of working together, an inherent respect for social order is present in almost all of us. Our loyalty to all manner of orderly conduct remains long after necessities are safely taken care of. Indeed, we can thank our orderly cooperation for keeping so many of us far removed from any immediate issues of basic survival. Unfortunately, as this book outlines, there are new threats to well-being that have yet to penetrate our inherent cultural order. While respect for established order runs very deep, the snail's pace at which that order is grasping the serious nature of present threats is spawning frustration and rebellion in some people. Nevertheless, the underlying element in human culture, which can be viewed as parallel to the cooperative instinct of ants, remains a crucial part of our condition. It is a key to securing the future.

While I will be using the word "religion" to identify any such bodies of accumulated experience, I am not referring specifically to formal organized religions. Although they originate from the same source, Christianity, Islam, Judaism, Hinduism, Buddhism, Baha'i and the rest have been codified into clearly defined systems. The formalization of religions makes them both easier to communicate and harder to change.

Because the formal religions evolved in different cultures, they came to be explained in different ways. Differences make people suspicious. If an individual ant or bee were to act in a manner outside the norm, it would be identified as "other" and expelled from the colony. The same is true for humans who step too far outside local norms. Now that people from different cultures live together, troubles can arise both from different perspectives and from the sense of otherness that people of different backgrounds get from each other. The conflict that can arise has made the word "religion" a loaded term. Nevertheless, the tendency to accumulate experience to enable successive generations to be effective remains a consistent human trait.

Ant colonies are likely very similar today to the way they were the first time a human wondered in fascination at the business of the little creatures. The cultural/religious undercurrents of human communities, on the other hand, have undergone enormous transformations as circumstances and understandings have changed over the ages. The numerous "sub-sects" that most formal religions have developed testify that they do evolve over time.

Today, in many places, people from different cultures peacefully coexist and cultural differences are increasingly taken in stride. This lends hope to the project of evolving the conventional wisdom. Indeed, the widespread adoption of the tenets of market economics has provided some of the common ground that is making inter-cultural cooperation easier.

The intent of this chapter is to look at the evolution of religion in the Western world and how that relates to the current economic system. It is my hope that by tracing part of the evolution of this element of culture, in the context of the Western experience, we will be able to grasp its nature and collectively apply our wills to consciously reshape it to serve our current needs. Regardless of how you feel about organized religions, please join me in viewing the phenomena of religion as a set of values, principles, understandings and ways of acting that, when shared, enable large numbers of people to act effectively together.

Religious Evolution

The return of daylight, warmth, and fresh food have always been cause for celebration in parts of the world that experience Winter. Spring has been celebrated since ancient times. Changes in the celebrations of Spring provide evidence of religious evolution.

Even with central heating and year-round access to fresh food, the outdoor warmth and longer days of Spring are still greatly appreciated when they arrive. Imagine how much greater the relief would have been when the only food people had was what they had saved from the previous Fall. Fresh vegetables might be a cabbage or some carrots from the root cellar. Depending on the previous harvest, there might be some grain remaining — or not. If the surplus was used up, one faced the difficult choice between feeding seed grain to hungry children or saving it to grow the next year's food. Perhaps a rabbit, or some other creature could be caught in a snare set out in the cold.

The melting snow, warm air and fresh green growth to eat would be cause for much thanksgiving: thanks given to the mystery of the seasons; thanks that the promise of past experience is again fulfilled; thanks that the darkness is again pushed away by the Sun and that the world is filled again with life. The wonder of fertility is preserved in the celebration's name. Easter and estrogen, the female hormone, both come from the same Latin root *oestrus*.

In the Christian tradition, this period of transition is observed as Lent. The period begins on Ash Wednesday with the giving up of various foods, eggs in particular, and perhaps a habit or two. It continues for 47 days, until Easter Sunday when the resurrection of Christ is celebrated with a great feast. While observing Spring in this way has been the Western tradition for nearly two thousand years, few know of the earlier traditions from which it evolved.

After the long Winter, whatever food was stored from the previous harvest would be getting low. This, in itself, would be cause for some fasting — getting by with less, until things began to grow again. The seasonal abstinence, however, pre-dates agriculture. When life was based on hunting and gathering, young animals were easy game for experienced hunters. By letting the younger animals escape in the Spring, it helped assure that enough of them would grow up to maintain the supply of game in the years ahead. The same goes for eggs. Without central heating, electric lights and the long history of selective breeding, chickens didn't lay eggs in all seasons. Their evolution had taught them to lay in the Spring so that the chicks that hatch would have all summer to grow strong enough to live through the next Winter. Although eggs were a tremendous source of nutrition, people knew that if they wanted more birds for the years to come, it was best to abstain from eating eggs when they first appeared. Pancake Tuesday, the day before Lent begins, continues as an opportunity to use up any eggs on hand before giving them up until Spring, as the ancient tradition prescribes.

As had been the custom of European cultures since before the time of Christ, the arrival of Spring is determined by observations of the Sun. Pre-Christian Europeans observed the quarters of the year: the Summer and Winter solstices — the longest and shortest days that commence those seasons — and the Spring and Fall equinoxes when those seasons begin with days and nights of equal length. The eagerly anticipated return of life and the warmth of the growing season had long been known to follow the Spring equinox. The crucifixion and resurrection of Christ is recorded as following a full moon. Accordingly, these are joined each year to find the date for Easter. The resurrection of "the hope of the world" is celebrated on the first Sunday after the first full moon following the Spring equinox.

Another clear example of this overlapping of religious festivals is where the Christian celebration of Christ's birth is laid over the older celebration of Winter solstice. December 21 is the longest night of the year and the beginning of Winter. As the days of Fall get shorter and shorter there is a tendency for people to become agitated. In the ancient past, the alarm was likely greater as there would be little, besides faith, to assure people that the shrinking of the days would not proceed until all was dark and frozen. After years of observation, the elders knew that this would turn around at Winter solstice, when the days begin getting longer again.

The ability of pre-technical people to identify the subtle changes in the length of days is testimonial to the excellence of human perception. The point I want to make is that our ability to sense the world around us and to make sense of what we observe have been human characteristics for a very long time. There is no reason to believe that these capabilities were any less acute five thousand or a hundred thousand years ago. In some ways, our plethora of technical equipment gets in the way of observing the natural world. There is a tendency today for us to employ most of our observational abilities looking at things people have created. One study found that a large proportion of the population can identify hundreds of corporate logos, but less than a dozen local plant species. During the countless generations spent without mass produced distractions, entire lifetimes were spent observing the land and life. Multitudes of observations would have been layered generation upon generation, revealing fine details about the things and processes that made up the world around. With respect to the seasons, without telescopes, or even clocks, the ancients accurately identified the timing of the solstices and equinox.

To this day, the loss of daylight in the Fall is cause for distress and depression for many in temperate regions. The return of the light begins so subtly that it takes a few days before most people notice. Four days after solstice, Christmas is celebrated. With the return of the Sun, the "Son" is born, bringing hope into the world. To the traditional hope for returning light and warmth, the new faith added hope that people could forgive old disputes and treat each other as they themselves like to be treated. The hope for peace and good will between people mixed well with the hope for a new growing season. The union of these two traditions continues to this day.

Many people today are aware of the approximately 22 degree tilt of the Earth's axis and how that brings about the seasons. Few are aware of the smaller secondary tilt, which also effects the lengths of the days and nights. Identifying the effects of this secondary tilt without equipment is further testimony to the acuity of our "primitive" ancestors. While it is sufficiently impressive that they could identify the exact timing of the seasons, this further detail is remarkable.

As we approach the Winter solstice, from around December 11, the evenings start getting longer even though the mornings are still getting shorter. Until solstice, the mornings get shorter in greater measure than the evenings get longer, so the days, overall, continue to shrink. After solstice, the mornings continue to get shorter, but the evenings are adding more daylight than mornings lose, so the amount of total daylight increases. It is not until January 6, "the twelfth day of Christmas" that the mornings also start to get longer. This subtle point in the seasonal cycle must have been known at the time the Christian traditions emerged. The evidence is the observation of "Little Christmas" on that date. As tradition holds, Christ was born just long enough after Solstice that a casual observer could feel the days getting longer. The Magi, three Kings from the East who came with gifts, followed the star and arrived on "Little Christmas," just when the seasonal change toward longer days was complete. To say that the star they followed was the Sun would be controversial, but the alignment of beliefs with astronomical events is cause to celebrate the human senses.

Whatever tradition one follows, the festivities of late Fall and early Winter serve an important social purpose. Preparation for the celebration, and the feast itself, distract people from the depressing circumstances of diminishing light and deepening cold. By the time all the fuss is over, the days are obviously getting longer, directly providing the hope needed to get through to Spring.

The layers of successive religious observations are most distinct at Winter's beginning because, wherever Winter is experienced, the need for mutual distraction prior to that turning point is great. Not only is it a clear example of the Christian traditions evolving from their earlier counterparts, it also provides evidence of the new religion that now overlaps Christianity.

What was the celebration of Winter solstice became the celebration of Christmas, adding a new morality of peace and good will, to the hope of returning light. In our present age, this critical time has become a time of increased spending into the economic process. Whole sectors of the economy have come to depend on the spend-fest, which might now be called "Giftsmas."

It is with complete sincerity that I suggest that the economic process, Capitalism, has ascended as the religion of our era. As with the Christian overlay of Pagan traditions, there are still many residual elements of Christian values and festivities, but, increasingly, it is the values of profit and loss, investment, return and trade that provide the common understandings that are the underlying foundation upon which cooperation within our society is maintained.

The adoption of the "Market Faith," and of the more extreme fundamentalist sect, the "Faith of the Bottom Line," did not take place overnight. The process evolved out of the Christian tradition over a period of many centuries. Before describing that evolutionary progression, however, an outline of an unrelated approach to economics as practised in traditionally Buddhist communities, will provide some contrast. This different perspective will, hopefully, help us to note details in our own situation that might otherwise be passed over because our own culture is so familiar.

Buddhist Economics

> *Do no harm.*
>
> Underlying Buddhist principle

In that it is evolving separately, the approach to economics that comes from the Buddhist philosophy appears unrelated to the West. As it affects mutual provision, which is the business of all people, it is, of course, closely related. People need each other to survive. The role of economics is always to help numbers of people to provide effectively for each other's needs. This is done in a variety of ways.

In the Buddhist world-view, writes one of its philosophers, J. C. Kumarappa, "The essence of civilization is not the multiplication of wants, but the purification of human character." Towards this end is the Eightfold Path that, among other things, includes the quest to understand how good and ill arise, and aspiration toward kindness, non-violence and right livelihood. Livelihood is what one does to participate in society. It involves more than the production of goods and services; it enables one to develop skills, find fulfillment and overcome self-centeredness. Mutual provision is, therefore, seen as more than a process of work and trade between people; it provides a means for people to clarify the meaning of their lives and to refine their characters.

This difference in perspective results in significant differences in how decisions are made. In the Western model, labour is often viewed as something to be avoided. Business sees labour as an expense to be eliminated if possible and workers dream of how they might have an income without having to work.

In the Buddhist perspective, to organize an economy so as to minimize work would seem odd. If there were already not enough work to go around, reducing it further would be considered distinctly antisocial. Even if those without work were given enough money to live comfortably, the provision of material needs is only a part of work's purpose. A. W. Phillips' revelation, explained in Chapter 7, that the cost of goods can be kept at a lower level if a certain amount of unemployment is maintained, would be viewed as a sad disregard for people in favour of material things.

The Buddhist perspective is not antagonistic to material goods; they are necessary for life and can provide enjoyable experiences. What is regarded as undesirable is craving and attachment; situations where a person's life is dominated by material things and where, when something is lacking, even if it is not necessary for life, the quality of that person's life experience is depreciated.

In the West, the primary emphasis is on expanding consumption to increase the GDP. The Buddhist approach is focused more on providing what people need with a minimum of intervention. Since the extraction of resources always causes some disruption to the land and life, ways of organizing mutual provision that require unnecessary extraction are seen as a form of violence — the antithesis of the value of kindness. If a way of life cannot provide for itself from the local area, the people must bring in resources from further away. This would be looked on leniently, but a trend toward escalating dependency on far-away resources, as evidenced by increasing transportation, would signal failure and a deterioration of security. Dependency on distant resources holds the danger of stimulating organized violence, which tends to result when different people make competing claims on resources. Non-violence means living without wars, or other coercive measures used to gain control of resources, markets or sources of cheap labour. When people can nurture their personal satisfaction on fewer resources rather than more, both the people and the natural world are better off.

Respect for all living things and, in particular, trees is a part of the Buddhist world-view. Adherents are encouraged to plant a tree every year or so and to nurture it until it is well established. The ecological and economic benefits of such a practice when followed by whole communities are great.

Work helps people feel useful. We are appreciated for what we do for others and feel personally fulfilled when we are appreciated. When work is broken down into tiny segments in the interest of maximizing productive efficiency, on an assembly line for example, much of the personal benefit of feeling creative, providing a service, and having our contribution recognized are lost. Compensation in money provides only a fraction of work's possible benefits.

If the purpose of an economic system were to provide effectively for people's social as well as material needs, there would be far less stress than when a system is striving to perpetually expand. Less stress leaves people in a better position to develop their human potentials. And, if one advances in mastery of one's self, one is likely to be able to handle much more stress.

Buddhism does not want its adherents to worship the Buddha. The life of the Buddha is just an example of how, if one seeks mastery of one's self, one can become free from the cravings, attachments and other mental traps that cause so much suffering. Buddhist practices include a variety of techniques for being internally calm, preferably in a calm environment, and finding the "clutch" that disengages the mind. To be present with the all and everything, without inner comment or reaction, even for a few moments, can liberate a person.

A mind is a tool for doing tasks. It is an amazing tool, which gives us extraordinary capabilities, but like our hands, which are also worthy tools at our command, the mind does not always have to be in motion. Without the ability to disengage the mind, our capacity to remember the past and project into the future can be as great a burden as it is a blessing. Meditation is a practice for calming the mind so that we develop the capacity to disengage from self-generated mental chatter and debilitating mental traps. When one's mind is quiet, one can more easily perceive what else is going on. Subtleties of our own inner process can come into focus, be acknowledged, and released, sometimes providing long-lasting relief from conflicting emotions.

By practicing acknowledgment and release of subtle inner expression, an experience of observation can be entered that is free from self-generated content. From this attitude, other people and the world around can be seen more clearly for who and what they are. The purpose is not to stop thinking altogether, but simply to strengthen the capacity to disengage thought when it is not serving our purpose and to let other forms of awareness surface.

There is a saying in Buddhism that "kneeling at the Buddha's feet when in distress is like digging for water when one is thirsty. It is too late." The ability to detach from our mental activity can provide immense relief when one is stressed, but it would be very difficult to develop that capacity when stress has already become debilitating. The same might be said for adopting an economic system that puts human well-being at its centre, rather than the perpetual expansion of material consumption. It will take some time, goodwill, and a different allocation of resources to accomplish such a shift. We would best not wait until natural resources and good will are in scarce supply before we make the choice to travel a different path.

Capitalism as a Present Day Religion

From the perspective of religion, as defined previously, modern Western societies and others presently following the neo-classical economic model, are not secular societies operating from a basis of reason. As with all societies before, we operate from a religious foundation that enables cooperation on a broad scale. Capitalism is the dominant modern religion. The tenets of this sect are formalized through the writings of neo-classical economics and enforced by powerful institutions such as the International Monetary Fund (IMF), the World Bank and the World Trade Organization (WTO). Although lacking in compassion toward the disadvantaged and the environment, industrial capitalism is well established. The way in which it is introduced to countries that do not presently practice it resembles the vigour, certainty, and lack of regard for other perspectives, which have characterized the forced spread of other fundamentalist religions in the past.

People who do not organize their lives according to the tenets of conventional economics are said to be irrational. If whole countries operate according to other principles, they can be "excommunicated" from the credit needed to participate in the present order's global trading system.

Evolution of the Capitalist Faith

The impetus to reform or revolution springs in every age from the realization of the contrast between the external order of society and the moral standards recognized as valid by the conscience or reason of the individual.

R. H. Tawney

When the Roman Empire crumbled, people with the means for local provision endured by trading with each other. By means of strength and opportunity, those with local advantages claimed the right of dominion over various lands. Forming alliances to maintain their advantages, the kings and lords of the time let peasants use pieces of land in exchange for portions of what they could grow. Most people worked the land, while a smaller number produced the clothing, tools and other items people needed. Mutual provision was accommodated mostly by trading one type of good for another. Several hundred years passed in the low-key stability of the Middle Ages.

Inquiries about how civilization moved from this local trading culture to the international money culture, led me to three historical texts: *The Protestant Ethic and the Spirit of Capitalism,* by Max Weber, 1917, *Religion and the Rise of Capitalism,* by R. H. Tawney 1922 and *Catholicism, Protestantism and Capitalism,* by the Italian historian Amintore Fanfani, published in 1935. These books provide a detailed picture of how Capitalism evolved from the Western heritage. An abbreviated version follows.

A central stimulus for the evolution was the expansion of the territories over which economic activity was coming to be shared, and the subsequent increase in the use of money as a means to conduct trade between the diverse peoples across those territories.

The Renaissance emerged as the scope of trade expanded. With trade and travel increasing, ideas spread, and with them, improved techniques for producing goods. With improving agricultural efficiencies and other productive techniques, more people became involved in producing goods for sale. As trade expanded, the convenience of dealing in money became more obvious. Eventually it became essential.

In particular, the dealings of the Catholic Church and of governments required considerable amounts of money. It was recognized that their work could not be carried on without credit. Money borrowing arrangements for large-scale transactions by kings, feudal magnates, bishops and abbots frequently involved the payment of interest, yet were seldom challenged as usury. Indeed, as early as Pope Nicholas III (1277-1280), a record shows that Archbishop Peckham was threatened with excommunication if he did not pay the interest on his loan to Italian money lenders.

While loaning money at interest was still considered a sin, the problems it caused the rich were seldom as soul shattering as they were for the poor. The objective of prohibiting usury was, in Tawney's words "simple and direct — to prevent the well-to-do money-lender from exploiting the necessities of the peasant or the craftsman... it was a part of Christian charity." The dangers of usury on the institutional scale were not so obvious as was the power of those institutions and the benefits that accumulated capital provided.

The double standard by which the prohibition of usury was enforced and the abuse of consequent financial opportunities eventually spawned Martin Luther's Protestant Church. It is ironic that while Church dealings in interest helped motivate the Reformation, the Reformation itself came to provide a foundation for the device it protested.

Interest did not rise from deadly sin to the foundation of civilization in a single step. It moved forward in waves, fell back and moved forward again over a period of several hundred years.

Money is far more flexible than produce. Below, Tawney quotes from an early account that was presented to justify the use of money and loaning it out for interest.

> *The parson of Kingham bequeaths a cow to the poor of Burford, which is "set to hire for a year or two for four shillings a year," the money used for their assistance. Cows are mortal, and this communal cow is "very likely to have perished through casualty and ill-keeping." Will not the poor be surer of their money if the cow is disposed of for cash down? So it is sold to the man who previously hired it, and the interest spent on the poor instead. Is this usury? Is it usury to invest money in business in order to provide an income for those, like widows and orphans, who cannot trade with it themselves?*

The argument stood to reason, yet it provided the thin edge of a wedge, which has since brought us the debt money system of today.

The size of the institution of the Church was itself a catalyst for change. While local parishes might be supported with produce and labour contributed by the faithful, the tithes sent to Rome were transported as money. These donations to the faith were used to operate the institution and perform its charitable tasks. This use of money in quantity, over broad territories, provided a "nursery for the money culture."

With large amounts of money arriving in Rome, management of money became an important part of Church business. In addition, the laymen employed to collect tithes for the Pope enjoyed a new perspective. As these people travelled, they saw that in some areas certain goods were abundant and inexpensive, yet in others, the same goods were scarce and valuable. Having money "on hand" for periods of time, before it was to be delivered to Rome, provided an opportunity that was not always resisted. After all, carrying goods from producers who wanted to sell them to people who wanted to buy them was a service to those people, as well as a source of personal profits.

It was also the case that these budding entrepreneurs were not known in the territories where they traveled. They did not have the same relationship to local laws that they had to laws in their home territories. Actions that, if taken in their communities would have tarnished their reputations, were far less likely to give them grief when taken far away from home. Add the protection of the Church, which they enjoyed as a result of their primary duty, and the lessons learned about money, time, trade and opportunity led to a new profession — a merchant class arose.

Over time, banking began to flourish in the trading centres on the Mediterranean and, although prosecution for usury was not uncommon, the financial dealings of ecclesiastical elites prevented comprehensive application of the law.

As towns and cities emerged and grew, their governments were peopled by the rising merchant class who created rules more favourable to the expanding business culture. At the same time, grievances abounded about unscrupulous advantage being taken of many who had little to fall back on. The inherited morality was out of step with the emerging world of commerce.

In 1517, as the 16th century dawned, Martin Luther nailed his proclamation to the door of the Castle Church at Wittenberg. Luther denounced the paying of interest to compensate for possible loss and the practice of investing in rent-charges, both of which were by then allowed by the law of the Roman Church. Luther's Church would refuse usurers the sacrament, absolution and Christian burial.

Not long after the Reformation began, John Calvin, the Puritan visionary, established rigorous rules for commerce. Because Calvin emerged from a society based on commerce, financial dealings and trade were understood as a practical part of living. Tawney explains that Calvin's vision,

> *... no longer suspects the whole world of economic motives as alien to the life of the spirit, or distrusts the capitalist as one who has necessarily grown rich on the misfortunes of his neighbor... It is perhaps the first systematic body of religious teaching which can be said to recognize and applaud the economic virtues. Its enemy is not the accumulation of riches, but their misuse for purposes of self-indulgence or ostentation.*

For Calvin, the problem was not with money; it was with the actions of people. "The triumph of Puritanism," Tawney explains, "swept away all traces of any restriction or guidance in the employment of money." This referred to restrictions on usury. The moral code that accompanied that step was very strict. The faithful were to conduct their business for public betterment. They were to work hard and not take advantage of others. If they were dealing with the poor they were to give advantage to them. It was okay to make money — the public was served by such activity — but those making the money were advised not to use it frivolously for personal aggrandizement or entertainment.

Working hard, yet spending little is a formula for saving money, but what benefit are savings if they sit unused. Better to expand business and provide abundance for the community. If one cannot further expand one's own activities, someone else should use the savings and do so. Calvin, as a prophet from the emerging money culture was not fond of money lenders but saw the advantages of loans and interest. His doctrine compensated for possible problems by reiterating the guidelines for morally appropriate business. Charging interest was acceptable, provided it did not exceed an official maximum, and loans to the poor were to be made without interest. The exchange must be as much in the interest of the borrower as to the lender and excessive collateral must not be demanded in case of default. Making loans might be appropriate in particular circumstances, but it was considered reprehensible as a regular occupation. It was unjust for a person to take economic gain for themselves in a way that injured another.

Personal morality, as opposed to Church laws, was expected to govern people's actions. The faithful were encouraged to follow their calling, to work hard for the glory of God and to prosper. Emerging state laws accommodated the "work hard and prosper" part and many followed the prescribed morality of frugality and fair play. There were others, however, who focussed mainly on "prospering" and came to overlook the part about treating others well.

Adherence to the mundane values of the marketplace brought many a call for the new Church to rule on what was legitimate. The merchant class was growing in size and power and pressure was increasing for letting business be run by its own laws. The will to enforce the laws against usury diminished. By the end of the 16th century the relaxing standards led to so much advantage being taken that peasant rebellions became frequent and conflicting demands from the two sides inspired municipal authorities to ask the Church for guidance about usury. Moral authorities became bogged down in deliberations while business flourished.

In 1571, the shift that had been brewing for centuries was expressed in legal statute. The British House of Commons repealed a law dating from 1552, which had asserted the prohibition of all interest as a *vyce moste odyous and detestable, as in dyverse places of the hollie Scripture is evydent to be seen*. This abandonment of the old law was seen as a victory for the common businessman over the dictates of theorists who 20 years previously had imposed a utopian morality on business.

The unifying principles of the day said it was one's duty to work hard. Working hard is a road to material wealth. If one's duty was so profitable, it followed for some that profit-making was their duty. The morality of the invisible hand emerged and by the early 1700s, "Men were generally all for themselves."

The culture of money, with all the advantages it had to offer, had become acceptable. The religious foundation of society had evolved to allow the growing number of people who lived by commerce to feel okay about their lives. Thus the new order of money was integrated into the traditional order.

In most communities, the impulse to profit was balanced by the social concerns of the earlier faith. In others, the draw of the Market Faith grew ever more prominent and allegiance to the other concerns has faded with the generations.

Holy Growth: The Market Faith of the Bottom Line

The guiding principles of the "Market Faith" are the processes of open markets, supply and demand, trade, economies of scale, division of labour, salaries, consumption, investment and interest. This is a religious philosophy in the sense that it constitutes a common understanding, which accommodates widespread cooperation.

To the foundation of guiding principles, add the mystery of the "invisible hand," by which self-interest and even greed are seen to serve the common good, and the market faith is complete. Capitalism interprets becoming rich as the Market's blessing on worthy souls. Increasing money is the guiding light. All a person need do for salvation is maximize the amount of money they make. A society need only continue to increase the amount of money being traded (GDP) and all that is good will follow.

One can see how faith in the market process has emerged from its massive success. However, as Chapters 6 through 10 have shown, over time, with the mushrooming volume of economic activity and, particularly, with the ascension to the sect focused solely on the bottom line, things have changed. A number of considerations that were scarcely noticeable as the capitalist revelation became established, have become problems. These are the externalities described earlier: the destruction of the natural world, the finiteness of the natural resource base, the needs of other life forms and people, present and future, that do not participate in markets; all these are simply not accounted for. Capitalism, and its global aspirations, are being pursued with "blind faith." The enormity of the dangers still largely overlooked by the present order calls into question the continued legitimacy of its underlying values.

As with the Reformation (when the Church of Rome splintered into various Protestant sects), there has been some turmoil in the Market Faith as interpretations have varied.

Propelled by the material strength emerging from the faith, and with the coincident emergence of fossil-fuel to energize mass production, the power of the British Empire grew to an unprecedented size. The dislocation and suffering that lay in the wake of the conversion was only obvious to those it affected and to those who later came to read the works of Charles Dickens and others writing at the time. What the world saw was military might and a wealth of material goods. Other European nations were adopting the faith and a long series of wars began as the various nations, feeling the surge in material power provided by industrial production, sought to acquire the natural resources, labour and markets of the rest of the world. With each conflict between nations, the financiers, who had first mastered the Capitalist creed, saw their wealth and power grow.

As the 20th century dawned, the amount of power experienced by industrial Capitalist nations as they accelerated their draw on abundant reserves of fossil energy was orders of magnitude greater than anything ever before experienced. It was with a sense of omnipotence that different industrial powers clashed in the two World Wars. Among the stakes in these conflicts were the colonial empires established by the first industrialized nations. Industrial might clashed with industrial might. When the dust had settled, tens of millions of people were dead, and industrial might had won control of the world. With so much of Europe in rubble, the United States, which had enjoyed the stimulus of wartime production without the losses of being attacked, became the center of the Faith.

It's only significant rival was the divergent sect of state-run Capitalism, led by the Soviet Union.

This other Capitalist sect shared the same tenets of industrial expansion through investment, development and trade, but they differed on one point — who was to be recipient of the consequent wealth? The West, led by the U.S. and England supported the amassing of private fortunes. The Soviet Union believed that the fortune should belong to the state. They also believed that, instead of having producers battling with each other to determine what and how much should be produced, that production quotas should be set by committees of producers negotiating in coordination with the state. Both camps had long since lost sight of the original principle of small firms competing in local markets.

The sect believing in private fortunes found the state focused sect to be blasphemous beyond bearing and began to undermine it at every opportunity. In particular, those who had become super-rich following the "Bottom Line Faith" wanted this alternative interpretation of the faith exterminated because it was challenging their control. The resultant "Cold War" lasted from the end of the Second World War, (when the U.S. hired the German experts who had worked to undermine the Soviet regime during the 1940s war), until the Soviet Union collapsed in 1990.

The "Faith of the Bottom Line" has since become the fundamental state religion of most of the world's nations. Growth is the goal that bonds people together in common purpose. Those in the lead are using all their persuasive power, and all the advantages that their wealth provides, to convert all who follow other faiths. Holy war has been carried on around the world with all manner of propaganda, blackmail and atrocities being committed so that the "one true religion" of Growth for private enrichment might reign supreme. Underlying all transactions of this sect, almost unnoticed behind the scenes, is the institution of debt-based money and the power of the immense fortunes acquired thereby. Since the victory of Private Capitalism over State Capitalism, there has been a steady string of structural changes made to the global economic order, which make it almost essential for other nations to adopt the particular sect of Capitalism practiced by the U.S. and other Western countries. Woe befalls the nation that does not accept the "Market" as the foundation of all that is civilized. What the Vatican and Crusades are to Christianity and Mecca and Intifada are to Islam, Washington and the Pentagon are to Capitalism.

Continuing Religious Evolution

In the Market Faith, the people of the greatest value to society are the rich; those with the greatest ability to move money through the market. This includes wealthy people and the extremely valuable super-people — corporations. The huge corporations are not gods, but they are, perhaps, on a par with archangels. Corporations have been canonized with the legal rights of living people, yet they can be in two places at one time, or a thousand places — there is no natural size at which they stop enlarging — and they can live forever. Furthermore, thanks to limited liability, no one can be held responsible for the full extent of damages that a corporation might cause. By law, these super-entities may serve no goals before the central tenet of the Faith — to make as much money as possible.

Where making money is seen as the greatest good, these super entities are saintly. But with no morality beyond profit and loss there is danger in their power. From a broader perspective, these entities, far from being the most respectable and beneficial of "people," are responsible for enormous social and environmental problems. Writing back in the early 1970s, social philosopher, Stephen Gaskin, pointed out that demons are immortal beings with enormous power on the physical plane but no sense of morality. To call corporations demons would be extreme, but so too, in centuries past, would have been the thought that usury might shift from deadly sin to prime social good. So much depends on the perspective from which something is viewed.

Any extreme carries with it the essence of its opposite. It is a mistake to suggest that corporations have no sense of morality. They have a strong sense of morality — that of Capitalism. Their faith is in the bottom line. From the perspective of the invisible hand, "profit" and "loss" are "good" and "bad" respectively. There is no doubt that corporations aim to do good. Following their faith, they have come to provide the majority of manufactured goods and a vast portion of the food upon which we depend. If giant corporations all suddenly disappeared, we would quickly face a new spectrum of immediately serious problems. Any thoughts about significantly changing the world order have to acknowledge this level of dependency and proceed with due respect and compassion for all involved.

Faith in "Markets" is not entirely out of order. There was room enough when the themes of hope, peace and good will were added to the religious festivities that marked the seasons and paid respect to the regenerative power of nature. So too there is a place for honouring economic exchange in our future world. We produce different things that must be traded to get what we need. Markets can maintain a remarkably effective balance within the guidelines set by a conscious civilization.

Those of the Bottom Line Faith realize that guidelines helping those with money to make more money help to increase GDP. While legislative interventions made to increase personal advantage and wealth can lead to increased monetary activity, they are ultimately counter-productive. Such interventions break the spell by which the "invisible hand" serves the common good. No longer do supply and demand provide the best goods and services at the lowest price. By contrast, were interventions made to include the needs of the poor, of other species, ecosystems, future generations and the long-term supply of natural resources, positive effects would result. Such interventions have much in common with the way prescription lenses intervene in the vision of the near-sighted.

The need to sharpen our focus, and attend to deteriorating situations is obvious to anyone who looks at the evidence. The contrast between the moral dictates of Market Capitalism and the criterion necessary for long-term well-being are increasingly obvious. They create the sort of contrast that, as Tawney said, "is the impetus which has always motivated reform." Our challenge today is to add the morality of sustainability to our evolving belief system. If we can accomplish this, the seventh generation might yet have an opportunity to flourish.

15

How to Get There from Here: A Question of Direction

Legitimacy

Legitimacy is a key ingredient of civilization; perhaps it is *the* key ingredient.

A biological analogy can help illustrate the role legitimacy plays in cultural evolution. If, in a society, the shared patterns of understanding and belief, as described in the last chapter, fulfill the role of DNA, legitimacy is the life force. DNA molecules are chains of atoms arranged in a specific order. Each life form has a unique DNA that contains within it (or resonates with it) all the information that is necessary for a single fertile cell to grow into a mature organism, providing that the cell is alive. Without life force, biological DNA is only a complex assembly of chemicals prone to decomposition. When life is present, the DNA serves as a template, guiding the growth and maintenance of the life form it encodes. Whether it is a plant, animal, fungus or bacterium as cells divide, the DNA for that particular life form is reproduced so that each new cell has a copy. Depending on the position that various cells find themselves in, they will grow into an arm or an eye, a root or a flower. Using the foundation "understanding" embodied in their DNA, different cells and clusters of cells follow the basic code and, together, grow and maintain a complete, mature organism.

A society grows in ways that are informed by the philosophy of the people. Until a system of understanding and beliefs is animated by legitimacy, it is only a philosophy. When people subscribe to such a system, their life energy works through that system. How they live their lives, the views they express, what they work at, how they invest, and how they vote, create the structure and form of the society embodied in the philosophy. Each person and organization follows the basic premise of their culture, varying depending on whether they find themselves as builders, caregivers, miners, managers or retailers. Together they produce and trade the complex array of goods and services that enable the civilization to proceed.

When accepted and acted upon, different world-views produce different worlds. Legitimacy is the animating power and it is the product of our many individual wills. That said, we have looked at how our choices are extensively influenced by what others think, the religion of our times and the legal structure. While legitimacy is affected by all these things, the form into which society evolves is ultimately a product of individual wills: yours, your friends, your family, your colleagues, your neighbours. If we want to resolve the mounting tension between the perpetual expansion model and the requirements of long-term well-being on our finite planet, it is the freedom of our wills that can define the new direction.

In the mental cosmology identified by Freud, the tendency to adhere to social order has a permanent position in our subconscious psychic makeup. Within each individual, there is an instinctual, impulsive "id," which seeks only personal satisfaction. The id is moderated by the "ego." While one's id may want to cross a street, the ego seeks to protect the individual by looking into reality for circumstances, such as oncoming cars that might threaten well-being. To avoid danger, the ego restricts the rudimentary urges of the id. Similarly, the "super-ego" exerts an influence on individual behaviour to have us maintain personal well-being by heeding the factors of well-being, as perceived by the larger society. Parents, teachers, religious spokespeople, politicians, legal codes, advertising and media imagery all contribute to forming the super-ego's version of what it is to be good and secure.

The super-ego's influence on individual behaviour may be for the good of all, or for the good of some elite, which has used its advantage to influence conventional wisdom to serve its own ends. Nevertheless, once the conventional wisdom is established, it guides most individual action and requires a long evolution or willful effort to change. Moving one's individual "vote" of legitimacy from economic expansion and placing it with long-term well-being is the basic move. When enough people make this move, legitimacy will shift to reflect new realities and priorities.

We do not lack the ability to transform our world. The problems we face are understood and most of their solutions known. Transformation will proceed with remarkable speed once the balance of legitimacy tips toward long-term well-being. This chapter proposes a technique for tipping that balance focusing on one point. It is the point of contrast between the dangers of continuing to expand the existing order and the possibilities for long-term stability should we choose to apply our creative potential to that end. By focusing attention on this contrast, the balance of legitimacy can be tipped.

Those who apply their will to extending the old order have the advantages of inertia and wealth. Those promoting sustainability have the advantage of growing necessity. The increasing contrast between the two views will inevitably require reconciliation. Our inclination is always toward self-preservation and it is becoming increasingly clear that change is essential. How many opportunities will be lost before the shift takes place depends on how long it takes to rally enough individual wills to counteract the persuasive influences employed to promote the illusion of Growth Everlasting?

Fluctuations in the Super-Ego: Getting Even

Tensions between old and new perspectives have existed throughout the ages. Looking at how legitimacy has fluctuated in the past can help us understand the present. The issue of retribution is a case in point. It has been an issue for thousands of years and the tension continues today.

An "eye for an eye and a tooth for a tooth" was the accepted ethic 20 centuries ago. If someone did harm to another, inflicting equivalent harm on the perpetrator was seen as just settlement of the score. It relieved resentment and served as a deterrent for others who might cause harm. At the same time, however, it could cultivate enduring rivalries perpetuated by cycles of revenge so complex that the origins are lost and offense and retaliation become indistinguishable. This dangerous custom was countered by potent imagery spread through the stories of Christ and other prophets. A new vision challenged the convention. It promoted forgiving the trespasses of others and thereby, offered a resolution to violent cycles of revenge. With this ethical shift, "we-versus-them" identities of independent small communities could more easily fade away, expanding the possibilities for cooperation over broader territories.

This progressive step toward better cooperation has been set back in recent decades. Note how often people on television and in movies shout condemnation at, and otherwise aggressively confront, those who cross their interests. As individuals, when resentment and rage are directed at us, turmoil erupts inside as adrenaline enters our blood and we prepare to fight or flee. When such scenes are portrayed in moving pictures our moods are stimulated in resonance. The stimulus catches our attention, time passes and we are entertained; eventually, we are trained.

The prevalence of such violence may be attributed to the relative ease with which such scenes can be produced. The circumstance need only be acted out with appropriate music and sound effects and moods are affected. We are naturally curious about and stimulated by danger. We want to recognize it so we can avoid it ourselves. By contrast, portraying situations that trigger feelings of wonder, gratitude, honour, love or respect require far more talent to conceive and enact, and more discernment to appreciate.

Entertainment value aside, the role model of people "getting even" seems to cripple many in their social interactions. Nothing causes us to become defensive quicker than an attack. One may defend with a quick counterattack, or just leave the scene physically or emotionally. None of these responses gets those involved any closer to understanding their differences or finding common ground for cooperation. Time and again, I see people in social movements taking issue with their colleagues in the style portrayed so frequently by the mass media. Such gestures almost guarantee misunderstanding. How much more effective could we be if we had more models for the cooperative resolution of differences?

So frequently have I seen such confrontations between allies, that I imagine a conspiracy on the part of those who control the media. What better way to render their opponents impotent than to implant futile means for settling differences in the public's subconscious? In any case, ineffective styles of communication deflect a large amount of positive effort that would otherwise help make the world a better place.

Some wise advice I heard years ago said that any action taken to "get even" was a mistake. I have remembered this frequently when responding to situations that disturb me. Often I have edited out caustic comments from my writing only to find that, although mellowed considerably, I still have the tone of putting the other person down. Several edits are sometimes needed to identify and remove ever more subtle attempts to "get even." On a good day, I can render the writing to the point that it simply calls attention to the offending action and asks for clarification in the interest of common concerns and better solutions. In the cases where I could not bring myself to mellow the reproach completely, more often than not, I found that I had stimulated obstructions that would not have arisen had I succeeded in removing the retributive tone.

Within the movements working for justice, environmental health, community development, peace and self-realization, there is so much common ground that differences need not be destructive. Even between real adversaries, those wishing to do things others consider harmful and the communities trying to stop them, there is often enough common interest for progress to be made, providing acrimony is not stirred up with insults and personal accusations. On occasion, a "poison pen" letter of condemnation will stimulate a sense of urgency and purpose, attracting allies in order to right a wrong, but it is as likely to inspire those who had created the "wrong" to build defenses, or even to mount a counter attack.

We would do well to identify and eliminate retribution as a legitimate way of responding to difficulties. Mahatma Gandhi showed the way with his non-violence movement. If we want to increase well-being into the future, I believe his tactics of clear, principled, respectful, non-violent confrontation of mistaken attitudes and actions to be the appropriate approach. Though Gandhi was not a Christian, his inspiration re-energizes the same shift in values that Christ promoted two thousand years ago.

The Golden Rule or the Rule of Gold

Among the elements to be honoured from the distant past is the well-known imperative, to treat others as we would like to be treated ourselves. This is the essence of self-regulation in a society. Present in practically all cultures, it is perhaps the tap root of civilization. Through this ethic, the collective organism comes into existence. Treating another as one treats oneself provides a foundation for trust and cooperation. When this value is shared by a population, its ability to co-create understanding and to act as one, resembles the mutual support of the cells, organs and limbs of a single organism cooperating to be something greater than it could possibly be as many parts. With this ethic, the collective human organism comes into being with the superhuman capability that enables us to thrive as societies.

In some ways, the ethic of serving society by pursuing individual self-interest is a corollary of this "golden rule." When people improve their individual lots by producing goods and services for trade, their individual efforts merge into a social entity. One person subscribing to this ethic would treat others as potential customers and, in turn, wish to be treated the same. That is, he or she would want to be offered the goods and services of others in trade.

While this invisible hand version of the golden rule has enabled huge economic advances, it has also produced the growing gap between rich and poor. The philosophy of self-interest has inspired and excused manipulation of the system in ways that provide further advantage for a few over the many. With time, the system has become lopsided.

Ultimately living only for personal self-interest has to end in tragedy. Individual lives end with death. When people grasp that their own well-being depends on the well-being of those around them and begin to identify with their community, death is no longer as terminal as it is in isolation. An individual will inevitably pass from the scene. A community can aspire toward everlasting life.

The Choice Before Us

With several hundred years of re-enforcement, the perspective that material expansion is the ultimate good is well entrenched at the subconscious level. Its inertia is immense and efforts to perpetuate it are well funded. In some situations, expanding economic activity may still be a means to necessary ends, but the time has passed for expansion to be an end in itself. The present and future well-being of individuals, communities and ecosystems must be clearly seen as legitimate goals. Concentrating less on consuming and focusing more on living, designing for durability, recycling basic resources and eliminating toxic releases must find permanent legitimacy. The means have to be developed to share the rewards of increased efficiency, minimal material throughput and the consequent reduction in the amount of work necessary to maintain humankind.

The present tensions between the steady state and the material expansion models has been growing for many decades, but the first substantial response in the conventional wisdom wasn't until the glimpse of hope that surfaced in the late 1980s, with the Brundtland Commission Report. For the brief period before the economic downturn legitimacy shifted to the ethic of sustainability. That episode ended because the solution of reducing human impacts on the environment fundamentally contradicted the conventional goal of exponential economic expansion. Steps were quickly taken by the cheerleaders of growth everlasting, to reclaim the focus of legitimacy.

Along with the problems of resource depletion, pollution and ecosystem disruption, the Brundtland Commission recognized the problems of poverty and underdevelopment. For those with insufficient food, clean water, shelter, education, health care and livelihoods, development is critical. Enabling people to work within their own territories to provide necessities for each other, shared the new legitimacy with reducing the destructive impacts of the highly industrialized world. It was on this development hook that the deposed orthodoxy staged its comeback.

After the Commission's report, *Our Common Future,* was tabled, the countries of the world were to experiment with ways of providing for the needs of the present without reducing the ability of future generations to meet their own needs. The global community was to meet in five years to share related experiences. That UN Conference on Environment and Development took place in Rio de Janeiro in 1992. By the time the conference was convened, the recession of the early 1990s had turned a lot of attention toward getting the economy growing again. At the conference, "development" (confused totally with growth) shared center stage with the need to find environmental stability. From there, the old legitimacy reasserted itself using the rhetoric of aiding underdeveloped nations, and then catapulted the money-serving mechanisms of corporate globalization on to the well-meaning aspirations of a concerned world.

Sufficiency in basic necessities is an important requisite of long-term well-being; meeting the mathematical expectation of exponential money growth is not. The legitimacy held by sustainability for a short time in the late 1980s was subverted. When it again rises as our legitimate goal, we will want to secure it there. Individually, by will, we can each establish our "vote" for a sustainable order. For that order to regain and hold on to legitimacy, it will take a large number of people applying their wills, and reinforcing each other by letting it be known where they stand.

Sifting Through Traditions

Having individual impulses moderated by the super-ego has two sides. It is both a tremendous asset that has guided us through the ages, and a shackle that now binds us to ways of doing things that are leading toward disaster. Those who seek to transform society have the critical task of assessing the composition of our super-ego and separating those elements that threaten us from those that can help secure the future.

A distinction has to be made between the elements that have been relayed over generations because they improve our common lot, and those that have followed a similar path, but are no longer relevant in our full world. In particular, we need to identify and moderate the inflated values that have been given to greed and self-interest in the name of the invisible hand. In order for the internal, super-ego moderator to serve a positive role in today's world, the exploitation of disadvantaged people and the degradation of the environment have to be widely recognized as antisocial.

As the present model of progress delivers us deeper into environmental disaster and social disruption, individual dissonance will increase. If the Monopoly winners insist on continuing "the game" to its bitter end, the urge to rebellion will grow. We need to offer an understanding of how legitimacy is assigned by the will of individuals, and to initiate open debate about what is and what is not acceptable. Such a process to sort through the "right" and "wrong" of the present value set could avert the chaos that might easily arise as people see their future being destroyed by a power structure that does not see the problems it is causing and seems unwilling to look. We need a "Reformation." We cannot afford the huge setback that would come from pursuing the present system until it either breaks of its own negligence or is disrupted by violent rebellion.

Human Purpose in a Changing World

The super-ego's subconscious role in supporting the human purpose, hasn't changed. It promotes behaviours understood to enhance the common good. When that purpose is usurped by elite power groups, they must, nonetheless, profess the common good, if not in terms of overall well-being, at least, in that of security. Without effective propaganda, it would become obvious that the end result did not serve a viable and inclusive mutual provision. If they cannot convince the people that we are all served by serving their goals, active repression through violence and fear becomes the only way for them to maintain control.

As circumstances and opportunities change, understanding about what best serves the common good also changes. Attitudes about retribution, lending money at interest, slavery, the role of women in society, democracy, sexuality, and many other issues have shifted over the centuries. Always we evolve. Problems inspire visions of change and those so inspired share their thoughts. As a growing number of people come to see well-being in the new way, the paradigm begins to shift. At first the new ideas are opposed, sometimes violently. But gradually, if the vision is true to the human condition and how the world appears, the number of people who understand it grows. Finally, as the new perspective becomes established, the attitude and consequent ways of being become second nature. As surely as we have come to know that the Earth revolves around the Sun, we will come to understand that our well-being depends on integrating human culture within the flows and limitations of ecological reality.

How long will it take for the subconscious shift to take place? This is a question of huge relevance. Each one of us influences the answer by how we apply our will. If we act with the resolve of one who sees a car speeding ever closer on a collision course, we may yet preserve well-being for our childrens' children.

The change process is well under way in terms of public awareness of the problems at hand. Unfortunately, the fundamental belief in growth everlasting looms ominously. The belief is a roadblock propped up and defended autocratically by people with enormous means, and more than enough interests vested to trigger deep denial about the problems and solutions of our time. Until the need for change is seen to be widely understood, most people will not resist the pressures to conform. As long as economic growth is recognized as the goal of society, "good" citizens will seek satisfaction through consumption. Most people do not have the conviction to resist what appears legitimate. As long as our governing institutions proceed to adjust the law to accommodate expansion, we will have work to do to convince people that legitimacy should be assigned elsewhere.

> *Capitalism is the extraordinary belief that the nastiest of men, for the nastiest of reasons, will somehow work for the benefit of us all.*
> Economist, John Maynard Keynes

The idea of letting society self-organize through competition between unrestrained, self-interested, ambitious people is a recent addition to the conventional wisdom. At most, it is a few hundred years old — practically newborn compared to the hundreds of thousands of years that people have cooperated in mutual provision. As a lifestyle, self-interest tends to create lonely people and competition creates losers. Nevertheless, the ideology asserts that the common good is best served by these potent motivators. Even if it were once true, it is no longer so. Only in terms of its self-selected measure of expanding gross wealth does it continue to produce results, and that only in some quarters.

By other measures, the present order is failing. Many of those who have benefited in recent decades have cause for anxiety. Without warning, distant shifts in the globalized economy can undermine their livelihoods. Even for those with "secured" wealth — everything paid for and money in the bank — the underlying processes upon which their lives depend are in danger. Fuel for the machines that drive our world is in precarious supply. Chemical pollutants contaminate the air we breath, the water we drink and the food we eat. Many types of cancer stalk rich and poor alike; families and communities are disintegrating and resentment spreads. Amidst mountains of material goods, we cannot assure our children a secure and healthy future.

We live in a parody of the joke about the surgeons who, upon emerging from a very complex medical procedure, announce that the operation was a success, but the patient died. It speaks of misplaced priorities. People need things, and it is the purpose of business and industry to produce those things. However, if the productive process undermines well-being, it is not successful. It is a misplaced priority to say that activities are successful simply because they make money.

A Three Fold Social Order

> *Fascism should rightly be called Corporatism as it is a merge of state and corporate power.*
>
> Benito Mussolini

Writing in Germany in 1919, Rudolf Steiner recognized the danger of wealth concentrating under the control of one sector of society. He saw problems brewing in the power that business was exercising over government, and he saw further problems arising for social well-being as a result of the control that the business/government combination was exercising over the cultural life of society.

Steiner understood why the business sector had access to the material and financial resources of the community; producing material goods was what they did. It was not in the interest of society, however, for the business sector to have control over all aspects of human activity. In his book *The Three Fold Social Order,* reprinted as *Toward Social Renewal,* Steiner makes a case for recognizing that society is made up of economic, political and cultural sectors. These three, Steiner saw respectively as the cultural manifestations of willing, thinking, and feeling. Each sector has particular areas of concern and in each area, the people involved are the ones best informed for making decisions in those areas.

As Steiner saw it, the economic or business sector would manage the production and distribution of goods and services. The business community understands what has to be done to meet people's needs and the necessary work. They are also accustomed to applying the will to getting it done. At the same time their natural assertiveness needs to be tempered by the "rights" or political sector.

The political sector would be responsible for justice in the relationships between people. By thinking through the implications of various sorts of advantage, and assisted by the democratic process, this sector would work to maintain balance between different groups of people and between the rights and responsibilities of individuals, communities and institutions. This sector might, for example, determine that everyone needs opportunities to work, and that view would be weighed against the advantage of allowing unemployment as a means to keep the cost of labour down and profits up.

The final sector is that which encompasses the potentials of people as feeling individuals: education, religion, the arts and other cultural activities. It is not in the long-term interest of society for its children to be raised as fodder for production and consumption, nor to fit into the master plan of some political vision. The cultural sector would see to it that children were nurtured with the best of opportunities to grow into strong, capable and confidently independent individuals able to give meaning to their lives from within themselves. Training for particular vocations would come after nurturing the greatness of individual humanness and would be directed by personal observation of the needs of their communities. The ongoing education of adults and the support of theater, art, literature, music, dance and other expressions of culture would be accommodated with resources from the sector where wealth is produced.

With the wealth of society distributed among the various sectors to be managed and worked with by the people most familiar with and affected by the functions of each sector, each area of society could flourish, adding its potential to the health of the whole.

In his day, Steiner's *Three Fold Social Order* could have prevented the calamity of the fascist power that sought to impose its political ideology on civilization. It could serve us as well today.

Steps in Transition

The shift in priorities that our civilization needs to undergo to accomplish long-term well-being will not take place in a single bound. Grasping the nature of a sustainable economic order will come in stages. Industries adopting the Natural Step, Extended Producer Responsibility or programs, as described in Chapter 12, can move us toward sustainability by reducing fossil-fuel use and the waste they produce, while at the same time conforming to the principles of the economic expansion model. Renewable energy provides a further bridge. With its foundation in the material production of equipment, its positive effects can be multiplied by the application of intent through conservation. Health care and education are of unquestionable importance. They will have a presence in any social structure and they provide an exemplary way to move the focus of society away from the limited realm of material processing and toward the unlimited realm of life-based potentials.

By stepping away from accumulation and consumption as the purpose of life, security would become the product of working respectfully with natural cycles. By extending respect to other people, adversarial competitiveness would give way to caring cooperation and the possibility would expand for creating a truly elegant culture through co-intelligence and participatory democracy.

Renewable Energy

Renewable energy provides a toehold for the new legitimacy. Unlike petroleum, where long ago the energy was captured and rendered almost ready for use, renewable energy and storage systems require sophisticated, manufactured equipment making them expensive. A cost benefit analysis would show that more comfort and service can be derived from investing in conservation measures than in building additional equipment. Understanding that conservation can accommodate human need better than expanding production is crucial.

Energy conservation combines elements from both paradigms. From one perspective, it is a full participant in the "investment-production-compete-for-market-share" world of the growth economy. energy-efficient light bulbs, motors, appliances and vehicles are all products of profit motivated businesses. From the other perspective, conservation involves recognizing limits and taking steps to live within them. While this impulse can still lead to product purchases, it gives legitimacy to considering one's life style and choosing less consumptive activities. Through this window, the focus shifts toward the sustainability perspective.

The conventional wisdom around energy supply has oscillated notably since the early 1970s. Up until then, energy was strictly a growth industry. Following the 1973 Oil Crisis, concern for energy conservation reached a high point. Programs were instituted to encourage the insulation of homes and businesses, speed limits were reduced to boost fuel efficiency and subsidy programs were initiated to advance the development of wind, solar and small-scale hydro electric generation. Pioneering low consumption lifestyles was not part of the official response to the energy crunch but it was a natural inclination for conscientious people. The vision has been growing ever since.

Between the high price of fossil energy and encouragement to conserve, consumption levels did drop, and the energy producers were not pleased. Among the first things that Ronald Reagan did after his election in 1980 was to cancel the funding for alternative energy programs, slowing progress in those fields to a crawl. Speed limits were increased and a blind eye was turned to the promotion of sport utility vehicles and 4X4 trucks for personal transportation. Exempt from the fuel efficiency requirements of personal transport, yet sold by the millions, these heavyweight vehicles ended energy conservation in transportation. Claims of increased safety have since unraveled, leaving the public with inefficient transport and increased danger of pollution, fuel depletion and large volumes of steel traveling at high speeds. A review of the Ford Motor Company's 2003 vehicle line-up, showed that only one of those models gets better mileage than the 35 miles per gallon with which their 1912 Model T cruised the highways.

Such was the first oscillation of legitimacy between producing energy to maximize monetary returns and extending the utility of a resource through conservation and the development of alternative energy sources: one was driven by monetary growth and the other, carried within it, the seeds of the "life perspective."

As anxiety mounts again over petroleum reserves, another oscillation is presently taking place. With well over 500 billion barrels of oil consumed since 1973, most oil fields outside the Middle East are past their peak of production and in decline. Those who still believe in perpetual expansion continue to muster vast military forces to secure remaining supplies so that they can continue with business as usual. Those who view the world from the sustainability perspective are moving slowly forward, developing energy-efficient and renewable energy producing equipment. These new businesses fit inconspicuously into the old legitimacy as ambitious growth industries preparing to fill a growing need. At the same time, they are important components of a sustainable economy and are increasing the legitimacy of their compliment — conservation.

Health Care and Education

The scope for shifting paradigms expands further in the fields of education and health care. Critical to any society, the way these sectors are developed changes significantly depending on which values a society holds. Despite the seemingly self-evident truth that a population is far more productive when it is healthy and well-educated, the money paradigm considers health care and education expendable when accounts get tight: the returns are less concrete and often longer-term than suits conventional monetary expedience. Loan payments are due monthly, economic performance is measured quarterly, and governments are reviewed on their performance every four years or so. A basic education, on the other hand, can take a decade or more, and, like health care, is most effective as a life-long process. Unfortunately, from a monetary perspective, which legitimizes only profit, the gains from industry and speculation are more tangible than the returns from good health and education.

Unlike material production where technical innovation can increase the amount of work each person can do, the work of teachers, doctors and nurses requires dealing one-on-one with students and patients. Efforts to increase "productivity" end up lowering the quality of the service. When the measure of all things is money, working directly with people suffers. Technological innovations in manufacturing and some services enable higher pay through increased productivity per person, without disrupting the customary balances between wages, profit and prices. For the wages of teachers and health care personnel to keep up with that of their peers in manufacturing, however, additional revenue must be found or other services cut. The money paradigm says the additional costs should be carried by those receiving the services. Such policy in health care and education, however, creates serious divisions. In health care, those who would receive treatment for a serious illness contrast with those who might die for lack of care. In education, those who must study long years to take on challenging jobs are contrasted with those who must live by menial labour. Such harshly divided classes frequently lead to deep resentment and social instability.

Education in the money paradigm aims to train people for jobs. Raising the price of education limits the number of people who might seek jobs in professional fields, virtually assuring that only the children of those already well off will fill those jobs. Education for life aims instead to produce emotionally stable, confident citizens, with a variety of knowledge. While skills by which individuals can contribute to mutual provision are important, so too are history, philosophy and the arts. These subjects help people understand the world, make informed choices about democratic options and increase the quality of human experience. The sciences are learned, not simply to expand production, but to assure that such production can coexist harmlessly within the social and natural environments. Furthermore, education is a bountiful component of the life paradigm. By pursuing education for the wonder of knowledge itself, satisfaction can be gained for entire lifetimes with almost no additional material throughput.

Except for the cost of living for the teachers, from the sustainability perspective, education costs almost nothing to deliver compared to a transportation system or consumer products. Once developed, knowledge is free. A teacher can explain a topic to many people. While all will know more than they did before, the teacher loses nothing for passing the knowledge along. It is possible for poor countries to have a very well-educated population. Once basic support for those who enjoy learning is provided, they will be able to absorb and share the bounty of information that humankind has produced. Unfortunately in the Money End Game, developing countries are told to reduce investments in education when lending agencies pressure them to gather money for interest payments.

In the realm of health care, the economic growth model finds opportunity in sickness. Diabetes was mentioned earlier, and drug prices are another infamous example. The extension of patent protection for drugs was a concrete action to accommodate economic growth. Patented drugs are often sold for hundreds and, in some cases, thousands of times as much as it costs to produce them. This makes drug companies among the most profitable investments around and assures that their sales will continue to inflate the GDP for years to come. While the resulting increases in GDP, with minimal increase in material throughput, is promoted as a win-win solution for growth and sustainability, the moral repercussions of charging inflated prices for badly needed medication are compromising.

Cancer is a growth industry. Tens of billions of dollars are spent annually treating the poor souls whom it afflicts, and many millions more are spent studying the disease and looking for a cure. In all the research, however, the obvious connections between increasing concentrations of cancer-causing chemicals in the environment and the increasing incidence of cancer is largely ignored. Making money doing practically anything is so revered that it is considered almost anti-social to try to solve the problem at the prevention level. It does not bode well for preventative solutions as long as we are entrenched in the value structure of growth everlasting.

Nevertheless, the new paradigm is making appearances here and there. The successful legal suit against the tobacco industry mentioned in connection with full-cost accounting is a landmark example. The legitimacy gained for prevention in that one case will make it easier for future cases where money-making activities threaten well-being.

The expensive equipment and complex procedures that drive medical costs up are the tools necessary for curing illness after it has taken hold. Maintaining good health is not an expensive undertaking when it is approached from the angle of prevention. Mostly what good health requires is knowledge about the factors that contribute to individual well-being, and the will to encourage each other to lead healthy lives, rather than promoting the consumption of products and lifestyles that undermine our health. Knowledge, as discussed above is the product of attention, thought, communication and goodwill. Research to determine the causes of problems can be expensive, but once it has been conducted, the understanding can be reproduced indefinitely at little or no additional cost. Nourishing food, exercise, a community of friends, and the opportunity to participate in mutual provision and the decisions that affect one's life will keep most people in good health.

Cuba provides an excellent example here. The island has been under an economic blockade since 1962. Without the benefits of unrestricted trade and finance, the most abundant resource available has been the life-based capabilities of the people. Even so, in 1988,

Cuba was awarded the Health for All medal by the World Health Organization (WHO). The medal recognized it as the only developing country to attain the health goals that the WHO hoped all third world countries would achieve by 2000. Cuba received the medal again 10 years later for having more doctors serving in other countries than the WHO itself, and for having lowered its infant mortality rate from 60 per thousand births in 1959 to 6.5 presently. By comparison, the U.S. has an infant mortality rate of 6.9 per thousand births.

A recent edition of the *New England Journal of Medicine* said of the Latin American School of Medicine in Havana: "[It is] sponsored by the Cuban government and dedicated to training doctors to treat the poor of the Western hemisphere and Africa. Twenty-seven countries and 60 ethnic groups are represented among [the school's] eight thousand students." Of these, 88 are from disadvantaged parts of the U.S. In exchange for free education, students are required to commit to practicing medicine back in the poor communities from which they came.

Another example is China's "barefoot doctors." China's present medical system was started during their revolution in 1935, by a Canadian, Dr. Norman Bethune. Bethune had already achieved notoriety for a variety of things. These included the procedure — which he first performed on himself — for curing tuberculosis by collapsing a lung, and the creation of the first mobile medical unit upon which Mobile Army Surgical Hospitals (MASH) are now modeled. Before going to China Bethune had been a professor at McGill University in Montreal. To this day, in his honour, each year two professors are chosen from the McGill Faculty of Medicine to tour China and lecture at medical schools there.

My father, Dr. Mark Nickerson, was head of the Department of Pharmacology at McGill when he was chosen in 1975, to be one of the "Bethune Professors." One of my dad's specialties was post traumatic shock — the sort of complication that sets in after a severe injury, such as a very bad burn. In China, he was expecting to deliver a talk on the methods he had been developing, but before the lecture he was given a tour through a large hospital. To his surprise, the post traumatic shock complications he was accustomed to dealing with here in Canada were almost nonexistent there. In North America, 20% of serious burn victims might develop such complications. In China, the figure was around one-half of one percent. The "barefoot doctors" were responsible for the difference.

Because the new order arising in 1935 had almost no medical services available, Bethune trained people to train others in medical procedures. A kind of voluntary pyramid scheme of medical information sharing developed. By the time of my father's visit, if someone in China didn't have a job, he or she received first aid training. If there was still no work, they received more sophisticated training. Over time, a great many Chinese have been trained in all manner of medical procedures. One in every 80 people there is a health care provider. What this means to accident victims is that sophisticated first aid is available anywhere in the country soon after an accident. The shock complications don't develop because of the speed with which accident victims are treated. My father's specialty was irrelevant and it was necessary for him to quickly come up with another topic for his lecture.

Even today, China is not yet rich by Western standards, but 30 years ago it was far less so. The difference in this health care system, at that time at least, was that medical procedures did not have to respond to the structural scarcity of a debt-based money system. Human ingenuity could be directed toward other ends.

We have some of the advantages of the life-based approach with Canada's Medicare system. Although it is heavily influenced by a profit seeking drug manufacturing industry, and tight restrictions on who can provide medical care, the services are primarily in the interest of a healthy population. Even as powerful lobbies campaign to allow "for-profit" medical facilities, there is a trend to shift Medicare's focus from treating illness to promoting wellness. While we aren't training welfare recipients to give their neighbours first aid yet, there is a growing effort to keep people out of the "medical treatment market."

Many communities in Ontario are fortunate to have community health centers. The doctors on staff are paid a salary rather than per visit and, as a result, have nothing to gain from people getting, or staying, sick. The primary focus of these centers is to encourage healthy living. By helping people to understand how health is affected by stress, pollution, quality of employment, income distribution, exercise, nutrition, participation in decision-making and the like, communities are prompted to work toward improving the quality of life for everyone.

Health care straddles the line between the material focus, which can be lucratively harnessed for monetary expansion, and the life focus, which can provide significant increases in well-being with almost no material requirements beyond the sustenance of those providing the services. The economic growth approach might be seen, from the life-based perspective, as taking undue advantage of people's weaknesses, while the life-based approach would be considered worthless, distracting or counterproductive where monetary expansion is the measure of success.

Life-based Activity

Renewable energy systems support the sustainability perspective by introducing conservation. Education and health care can take this a step further by showing some advantages of focusing on well-being, rather than profit. Both of these can, and presently are, managed in ways that also serve monetary expansion. Shifting one's focus from consumption to life-based activities takes one completely out of the money perspective and into the life model. When we make this move, we can expect opposition as it challenges the present order's deepest illusion — that material things are the essence of wealth, well-being and satisfaction.

Once basic nutrition and shelter are secured, the illusion that life depends on material things is a trap. Until we realize how, we too, are caught by the materialist illusion, there will be a tendency to dismiss life-based solutions as lacking legitimate content.

Material goods have built-in tollgates. Those who possess the material can demand money from anyone who wants what they have. Satisfaction derived from life, and from developing the capabilities of aliveness, offer few such tollgates. One might, for example, be able to charge for giving music lessons, but once a student catches on, he or she could well derive pleasure from music for the rest of his or her life without ever paying again. The case is even more pronounced when it comes to gaining satisfaction from a good friendship, or the appreciation of the things we can see, hear, taste, feel, smell and understand. Even when lessons introducing such things are purchased, the return business can be minimal.

Because of our material focus, modern education often neglects the basics of how to be a good friend, what makes relationships work, and how to raise children to be creative, self-motivated, responsible citizens. We are not taught how to eliminate the undue influence that past traumas can have on present circumstances. Such lessons would produce huge benefits in terms of long-term well-being, but they could also cause a serious setback for GDP. Psychiatrists, lawyers, prison guards and physicians would lose a lot of business and, if people had fulfilling lives with less residual trauma, far less gratification would be sought through consuming material goods and other addictive behaviours. The economic expansion model could be in serious trouble. Investing in such education would only pay off if we measured progress in terms of well-being.

I think again of my friend John's comment about the "poor" Asians he visited in the early 1970s. When things got tough, they "just huddled closer together in the great love they had for each other and it was okay." One wonders whether or not such people are actually poor? With access to traditional lands, they could support each other forever, cycling their nutritional needs through natural processes and working together to maintain their shelters and other necessities. In the closeness of community, the gratification that comes from helping those one knows can transform work into passing time with friends. There are few in our money culture who enjoy such security.

> *One who is content with little, has much.*
> Lao Tsu

Financial security always seems to be an issue. The debt-based money contrivance keeps everyone on the edge. After generations of pursuing self-interest, and with television claiming our time and teaching us to want so many things, community bonds are all-too-often absent and the sense of needing something never far away. The material dream requires a lifetime of hard work or exploitation, yet seldom does it provide the sense of having arrived. If our purpose was mutual provision without having to compete over a monetary supply kept scarce by design, a whole new world of possibilities could open up. By recognizing security as having enough to get by in the material realm, it is possible to become still inside and breathe in the wonders of life. Time to live and to help those close by is available to anyone — no gate, no ticket. All that is required is to appreciate sufficiency and open up to what life offers. There is a security bonus in that civilization based on enjoying life has a far greater chance of enduring than one seeking perpetual material growth.

Voluntary Simplicity

One of the growing trends in North America today is the movement of people to simplify their lives. Working long hours can be stressful on individuals and alienating for their families. By avoiding the trap of materialism and, instead, enjoying what life offers, one can have far more time for living and do less harm to the Earth in the process.

A trip to your local garbage dump can provide a firm grasp of this concept. The tradition of "dumping" garbage lost some of its legitimacy in the 1980s, so the facility is now called a "landfill site." Now, there is likely an associated recycling program and the garbage will be carefully covered so that rain water runs off and away, rather than percolating through the often toxic contents. Whatever the improvements, however, your experience will be the same; you will still find huge volumes of used goods and truckload after truckload of things upon which people spent good money, days, weeks or months earlier, coming to be buried. Imagine how much was paid for the contents of each of those truckloads. People worked hard for that money; by spending it, they willed the conversion of the natural world into products that they possessed for a time and then threw away. While doing their bit for an obsolete economy, the futility of their efforts is obvious as one watches the trucks unload.

Material security, in the form of excellent nutrition, comfortable, energy-efficient homes, sufficient clothing, excellent tools, close families and communities, and lots of time to be creative and enjoy the wonders all around, can be achieved for all, if we so choose. Even the basic physical gear of education, health care, sports and the arts is within our grasp. What cannot be maintained is the steady and increasing flow of goods that are produced with the intent of being used up and discarded to make way for more of the same.

"Voluntary simplicity" costs far less than a life pursuing material goods; it is more satisfying because the enjoyment is real in the way our lives are real. It is a vision that we can realistically offer our children and grandchildren. A sense of knowing that we are passing a world of fulfilling possibilities on to our children would be priceless, in and of itself.

A Step in Good Faith

Both feminine and masculine are found in each of us, in varying proportions. Nevertheless, the underlying dichotomy exists and provides a useful reference. While the statements in this paragraph and those following are broad, with many exceptions, "feminine" attributes are most frequently found in women and "masculine" attributes most frequently found in men. Most of the present order is run by men; we are strong, stable and motivated. We are also full of personal ambitions; just the thing for a system that promotes self-interest and competition as the best way to serve the common good.

As the collective human condition shifts from adolescence toward maturity, the qualities of cooperation and inclusiveness become more appropriate. These qualities are more commonly found in women. When making decisions there is a tendency for women to think, "What will work for the children?" rather than "How can I win." Considerations of pride, power or conquest are less likely to distract their focus from the common good. Feminine attitudes are the essence of the Seven Generations perspective. We need more of them.

There are women in positions of power today who got there by competing with and winning over men. With women, as with men, there is a full spectrum of qualities. Within the current structures, it takes masculine qualities to get to "the top." Think back to Prime Ministers Margaret Thatcher of Britain and Golda Mier of Israel, both of whom demonstrated that they had "the balls" to wage war. This is not the conciliatory attitude I'm suggesting would surface if women filled more positions of power. Gro Brundtland provides a different example. As the Prime Minster of Norway, she chaired the World Commission on Environment and Development that produced *Our Common Future* described in Chapter 1. That statement of concerns led to the great hope that humankind might rise to the challenges of our times.

George Mully became a friend and mentor as we worked together in the late 1980s on the video in the Guideposts for a Sustainable Future discussion kit. Earlier in his career he did projects for native communities where he learned how leaders were chosen within the Six Nations Confederacy. He explained that while the leaders were men, they were chosen by the women. If someone was ambitious and wanted to lead, he was disqualified. Leadership wasn't about personal ambition, it was about service to the community. How was it known which men harbored personal ambitions and which did not? The women knew, because they had known them since they were babies.

It will take a strong sense of trust, fair play and the will to survive to raise the feminine influence on decision-making up to par with the masculine. A healthy balance is needed.

There must be ways for the masculine and the feminine perspectives to coexist. Among mature, responsible adults, it is unnecessary for the boisterous to submerge the accommodating. If a commitment to democratic process exists, opportunities to speak should be possible for those who prefer to let a moment pass after one person has finished talking, before adding another perspective. The technique of consultation (see the Appendix) provides suggestions.

Marilyn Waring is the godmother of the well-being measurement movement. She served three terms in the New Zealand Government — the first, as the only woman Member of Parliament. In her second term she chaired the Public Expenditures Committee. There she learned how disconnected the GDP measure was from much of what is valuable in society. Most of what women traditionally do is ignored in GDP tallies. Raising and educating young children, keeping peace in the home and community and the care of aging parents, to name a few critical activities, are not counted. Because they do not contribute to the GDP, those essential services are officially invisible and few public resources are made available to assist those providing such services. The lack of compensation, or even social recognition, causes some to feel it is not legitimate work. With people seeking to contribute in ways that are recognized, these critical roles in society are increasingly neglected.

Proponents of economic expansion argue that people express their will through how they spend money. Marilyn Waring believes that our will is more accurately expressed by how we spend our time. If public resources were distributed relative to where helpful time is spent, rather than where money is made, our world would evolve differently.

In the southwestern Indian state of Kerala, in part because of the traditional custom where women were responsible for family wealth and men married into families, but not into control, the women have had a definite say in how that society's resources are allocated. This has resulted in European standards of literacy and health, along with population stability, all on an average income of $330 per year. This, and other examples of what happens when women are empowered, led to the 1994 United Nations Conference on Population making the education of young women a central part of the global population stabilization strategy.

The attitudes of cooperation, and of caring for those who cannot fully care for themselves, are important elements of what we must accomplish. Whether through genetic propensity, cultural training or from the long and loving work of raising children, these are qualities most consistently found in women. The more women are empowered

337

to make decisions in society, and the more comfortable that men become with their own capacity for nurturing, the more influence these qualities will have on the world our children will inherit.

Managing Public Opinion

The twentieth century has been characterized by three developments of great political importance: the growth of democracy; the growth of corporate power; and the growth of propaganda as a means of protecting corporate power against democracy.

Alex Carey

Understanding the world is a product of thought, which is a product of experience. Experience comes from two sources; the world as we see it and, what other people tell of their experiences. This latter source includes the experience embodied in the conventional wisdom as delivered through our language and culture, topics from our education, the experiences of our peers, and presentations by the media. Most people relay experiences as accurately as they are able, subtly participating in the collective mind by which an open, trusting society makes its way through time. Sometimes, however, people feed information into our experience that is selected or contrived so that we think what they want us to think.

The promotion of material acquisition in the conventional wisdom poses a major obstacle. To rise effectively to the sustainability challenge, as many people as possible must have a clear understanding of what the problems and opportunities are. While much information is being distributed, vested interests employ a great deal of creative effort to divert attention from the challenges and proposed solutions, and to reinforce the goal of perpetual expansion.

Manipulation of public opinion is not a new situation. It was well established in 1915 when the major financial houses of the U.S. were afraid that $1.5 billion in "Rothschild Formula" type war loans to Britain and France were in danger of going bad. German U-boats had successfully cut off shipping to Britain and food supplies for the civilian population were estimated to be sufficient for only six to eight weeks. In *The Creature from Jekyll Island* Edward Griffin gives extensive details about news media control and how, with some cooperation from Britain, the U.S. was ushered into World War I.

Early in the 1900s, financial interests were buying up newspapers to gain control of editorial policy. In 1905, a cooperative

Congressional Representative from Pennsylvania, Joseph Sibley, wrote about the need for media control: "An efficient literary bureau is needed, not for a day or a crisis but a permanent healthy control of the Associated Press and kindred avenues." On February 9, 1917, another Representative, Oscar Callaway, from Texas, reported to the U.S. Congress. The J. P. Morgan interests had taken steps:

> ... to control generally the policy of the daily press. ... They found it was only necessary to purchase the control of 25 of the greatest papers. ... An agreement was reached; the policy of the papers was bought, to be paid for by the month; an editor was furnished for each paper to properly supervise and edit information "regarding the questions of preparedness, militarism, financial policies, and other things of national and international nature considered vital to the interests of the purchasers."

Through the network of public information so acquired, considerable editorial space was invested to inspire the U.S. participation in the war. Even so, the public didn't buy it. Ten to one, they opposed entering "Europe's war." Additional tactics were then added to the effort.

The Lusitania was a British passenger ship that had been retrofitted so that the lower decks could carry military cargo. For its May 1915 voyage from New York to Britain, in addition to its passengers, it was loaded with a large amount of military supplies for the British war effort. The German Embassy in Washington protested the breach of international neutrality treaties and sent prepaid ads to 50 newspapers in the U.S., for their travel sections, warning potential travelers that they were at war and that British ships traveling in British waters were targeted for destruction. Of the 50 papers to whom it was sent, only the *Des Moines Register* printed the notice. Under the pretense of saving fuel, the Lusitania was ordered to travel at three-quarter speed. When it entered the war zone, its rendezvous for escort with the British Destroyer Juno was canceled and the captain was left to sail, unprotected, right into waters known to be occupied by German U-Boats. Not surprisingly, the slow moving target was sunk, killing the 195 American passengers aboard. Then, predictably, the newspapers took up the cry. Americans had been killed; the nation must enter the war. And they did.

Quoting Lundberg from his book, *America s Sixty Families:* "The declaration of war by the United States, in addition to extricating the wealthiest American families from a dangerous [financial] situation, also opened new vistas of profits." Some $35 billion were created and spent by the U.S. as the war progressed, nearly doubling the money supply and consequently lowering the purchasing power of the dollar by nearly 50%. With net profits of nearly $38 billion, wartime industries were the winners, while the whole population shared in the hidden tax through inflation.

> *Of course the people don t want war. But after all, it s the leaders of the country who determine the policy, and it s always a simple matter to drag the people along whether it s a democracy, a fascist dictatorship, or a parliament, or a communist dictatorship. Voice or no voice, the people can always be brought to the bidding of the leaders. All you have to do is tell them they are being attacked, and denounce the pacifists for lack of patriotism, and for exposing the country to greater danger.*
> Nazi Reich Marshal Herman Goering, at the Nuremberg trials

News reporting, or withholding, and its ability to mold public opinion aside, the media — television in particular — is dedicated to cultivating consumer demand. In *The Last Hours of Ancient Sunshine,* Thom Hartmann describes many aspects of our culture that keep us ignorant about how we live on Earth today. His main theme is that over the last few generations we've developed an almost total dependency on fossil-fuel — oil in particular. Ancient sunshine is a lyrical description of fossil-fuels; literally, the energy in petroleum is sunshine that was absorbed by plants hundreds of millions of years ago. The information media has only begun to acknowledge that this resource will be practically exhausted within the lifetime of today's children. It would seem a message of importance, as this one detail renders all decisions about increasing dependency on long-distance trade and travel mistaken, yet it is not an issue considered suitable for media attention.

What the commercial media does consider important is for people to buy things; commercialism thrives on short-term thinking. Using the analogy between individual stages of maturity and the behaviour of society, Hartmann points out that young children have not the slightest awareness or concern about the future; "Gimme now" encapsulates their attitude. "The primary immature cultural concept that - 'you are the most important person in the world' – is shouted at us daily through TV, the primary spokesvehicle of our culture,"

Hartmann continues. The constant reinforcement of this message keeps us immature. The reason he gives for, "the persistence and intensity of these messages is simple: when people behave like children, wanting immediate gratification for their every desire, they are ideal consumers."

Premonitions in the late 1940s about control of public opinion led George Orwell to write his famous novel, *Nineteen Eighty Four.* In the world he described, every aspect of life was centrally controlled. Fiction was broadcast as truth and history was re-written to maintain control of the public mind and serve the political aspirations of the rulers.

After reading that book in the 1960s, I remember counting down the years as 1984 approached. The year arrived, and with it, in Canada, the election of a government that gave us the first of the "Free Trade" agreements. Ninteen-eighty-four is now two decades past. In 2003, 50 million people assembled on a single day, for common purpose, in dozens of countries around the world. Never had an event taken place of such size and geographical diversity. It was an event of globally historic proportions. However, since its purpose was to protest against the American establishment's war plans for Iraq, it received only passing mention in mainstream news. With very few exceptions, that media has been purchased by wealthy interests and it is diligent in presenting views of the world that support its owners. It is no coincidence that these people are from the same small community that is intent on winning the Global Monopoly Game.

It is timely that, for many of us, the Internet has arrived, providing a source of information that is not controlled by commercial interests. It has already breached monopoly control of the news. The stark differences between what is reported by individuals on the spot and what the commercial media says, has stimulated the critical faculties of many. The ranks of those who would change the focus of our culture are swelling as the self-serving motives of the Monopoly winners come to light. The goal of "shopping-until-we-drop" is giving way to sustaining the land and life.

The Internet was designed by the U.S. military to provide dependable communications, even if large portions of the infrastructure were destroyed. The robust design makes it safe from disruption, at least, so far. However, as we attempt to prevent blind commercialism from driving civilization to overshoot and collapse, we are well advised not to put all our communications eggs in the

Internet, or any other basket. As that medium proves effective, we can count on steps being taken to limit its usefulness for opposing the Global Monopoly Game. For good measure, keep an eye out for other means of communicating. In particular, look for opportunities for personal encounters. Person to person communication remains the most secure, direct and trusted means of sharing experiences.

Reframing Legitimacy

Across many cultures and through many centuries, ostentatious displays of wealth by those at the top have helped cement the social hierarchy and stabilize power. While in the past these affluent displays have been too small to damage ecosystems, their expansion through the middle class dream have grown into a highly destructive custom.

> *Every step of economic expansion comes at the expense of wildlife habitat and the health of ecosystems.*
> Dr. Brian Czech, *Shoveling Fuel for a Runaway Train*

Brian Czech is a Ph.D. wildlife biologist working in the U.S. He also serves as an adjunct professor at Virginia Tech. After years of documenting environmental degradation and thinking about the social order causing it, he wrote a book titled, *Shoveling Fuel for a Runaway Train*. Czech explains "that every step of economic growth comes at the expense of wildlife habitat and the health of ecosystems," and that after a good standard of living is provided for, further economic growth is actually uneconomic. "To say the economy is growing sounds like something good," he explains. When children or crops grow it is a good thing. When an economy is already more than big enough to provide for all its people's needs, further growth is not a good thing. Were it reported that the economy is "bloating" rather than growing, we would be more inclined to recognize the problem and do something about it.

Dr. Czech suggests that such a reframing of our language could help direct our culture away from self-destruction. Using language, like "the bloating economy" to more closely reflect reality is a start. So frequently in the media conspicuous consumption is presented as admirable, encouraging viewers to wish it for themselves. In fact, Czech asserts that consuming beyond what is needed for a secure and healthy life is "a narcissistic disregard for posterity," and recommends social pressure as a means to discourage such dangerous behaviour.

He suggests identifying the wealthiest 1% of the population — those who consume the most resources — as "the liquidating class," and says they ought to be "castigated" for "the wanton destruction of the grandkids' natural environment."

Czech is sensitive to the danger of alienating those who might be allies in reframing public opinion. Hence, the 1% focus. At the time he wrote his book, (published in 2000) the top 1% in the United States were gathering to themselves 62% of all the new wealth being created. Their net worth was equivalent to that of the bottom 90%. Conspicuous indeed.

On the other side of the "public opinion revolution" are those who act with respect and restraint. Whether their restraint be out of choice or necessity, if they feel good about what they are doing, they won't strive to join those who needlessly destroy the natural world. They can take pride in their frugality and enthusiastically pioneer the wonders of seeking satisfaction from their lives rather than from stuff. Those who are capable and wise enough to live with minimal disruption of our living planet could be called the "steady state class." Those who excel at living lightly on the Earth will be the new heroes and our young will look up to the best of them, seeking to emulate and surpass their feats.

It could happen, but it will take considerable creativity on the part of those who presently grasp the challenges we face. Of special importance to the success of this "Steady State Revolution" is how the act of castigation is borne out. "Acts of violence," says Czech, "will only backfire, especially in the post 9/11 world."

Resistance to Change

If material acquisition were truly the dominant value of the human species, then surely capitalism would find it unnecessary to spend $450 billion a year to propagate it throughout the world.
David Korten, *The Post-Corporate World*

The notion of living with minimal material demand and gaining fulfillment from life is irreconcilable with the established order. If we start to get anywhere, we can expect some serious opposition.

Already, over four hundred thousand million dollars are spent worldwide each year promoting the consumptive way of life. Imagine the persuasive creativity that can be bought with such a budget. Imagine further, how budgets for public persuasion would swell, and what additional tactics might be employed if the legitimacy of letting private interests create the money supply and charge interest on it, were challenged. Lenders are presently making over $60 billion a year on interest from Canadian governments alone. The figure in the U.S. is in the hundreds of billions of dollars. If you were on the receiving end of such an annual appropriation, what portion would you consider investing to cultivate the conventional wisdom so that people felt it was acceptable to continue moving such volumes of public money into your hands?

Those best served by the present culture are wealthy beyond imagining. They are unlikely to give up their advantage without resistance. It is unclear whether such resistance would be from a consciously organized class, or a natural synergy of people and processes that resonate with the established order.

In some ways our prospects would be brighter were it the former and all we had to do was convince a few thousand people at the top that the survival of their children depends on developing a new perspective about living on the Earth. Elite clubs of the very wealthy, such as Bilderberg, the Trilateral Commission and the Bank for International Settlements meet together and plan strategies for perpetuating the Global Monopoly Game. If these are indeed where decisions are made, the clubs could be addressed and perhaps convinced to join in a new game.

Far more likely is the existence of a synergetic whole, greater than the sum of all the actions taken by many millions of people acting on the premises of the perpetual monetary expansion model. Adam Smith described such people as being informed by the capitalist spirit. Rudolf Steiner called the underlying inspiration of industrialization a "time spirit." When multitudes of actions are informed by a common philosophy, their effects reinforce and build upon each other, producing coherent results. So well do such complimentary actions mesh together that they can be seen as the work of a super-human entity. This is the Collective Human Organism. Informed by the invisible hand and its values of self-interest, consumption and growth, the acts of millions of individuals and thousands of corporations become a cohesive force producing common ends.

The advertising agency hired to promote one product or another is not, through its work alone, responsible for shepherding our collective consciousness toward insatiable consumption, but it gives energy to that end. The road-builder driving his bulldozer over an endangered plant is unlikely even to see it, much less understand the significance of his actions. Lawyers hired to resist forward-thinking legislation and lobbyists making campaign contributions, in the interest of particular advantages, by themselves, make only small differences. While living from the cash flowing through the system, the people involved are likely no more aware of the cataclysmic impacts they contribute to than the cells of your fingers are aware of their contribution to your work. The clubs of the rich and powerful may make decisions and initiate programs with widespread impacts, but I suspect, within their perspective of the world, most of them believe they are doing good.

Whether we are dealing with individuals or a collective consciousness doesn't really matter. Individuals respond when the conventional wisdom changes. With a new perspective, individuals would make their choices differently. More opportunities would open up in some areas, and in other areas prospects would be less appealing. Overall, a different synergy would cause different effects to emerge. As we apply ourselves to helping individuals understand the new perspective, it becomes increasingly clear that this is the new legitimacy. When our role within the planetary ecosystems is confirmed by conventional wisdom, we will recreate civilization in a mature form that can enjoy this planet, the energy of the Sun and the many wonders of living here, for seven generations and beyond.

A Question of Direction
Goals are the seeds from which the future grows.

Hold for a few minutes in your imagination the thought that people of similar beliefs form a collective presence. Imagine that the sum of all the concern, thought and inspiration responding to the limits of our planet and the challenges of community well-being constitute a new Time Spirit. This inspiration of our times is gradually ascending in the conventional wisdom while the earlier inspiration, focused on expanding material wealth, loses its relevance. The new Time Spirit grows in strength and capability with each person who grasps the problems at hand or pictures any aspect of their solution.

The "Question of Direction" strategy aims to advance this evolution by focusing attention directly on the choice that exists between the two perspectives — material expansion or sustainability. Which of these goals is the most appropriate at this time?

345

When we hear questions, it is human nature to think about answers. To grasp a choice, one must know what the options are. If we can put the "Question of Direction" on the public agenda, every thinking person will consider the options. When the choice is recognized, most people will see the need for establishing a

sustainable balance between people and the Earth. With each additional person who recognizes the choice, and pictures himself or herself on the side of sustainability, the conventional wisdom shifts to speak more clearly for change.

The alarm has long been sounding and the gathering evidence has already inspired legions of individuals and organizations to join the call. Most people know we need to do something. But we have yet to grasp that there are enough of us to shift the perceived legitimacy. Through our circles of families and friends, our organizations, clubs and religious communities, we have the means to put the Question of Direction in front of practically everyone. If we can communicate the meaning of the basic choice, a democratic opportunity would emerge that could establish a huge mandate for basing policy and action on the goal of sustainability. Democracy has evolved to make this choice.

Why then do so many of us feel that we cannot redirect the inertia that drives our world to grow until we drop?

In part it is because, with broadcasting and mass distribution publication, the views of a few are amplified, enabling them to influence the conventional wisdom far in excess of their proportion in the population. Living in a world saturated by media images that subtly (and not so subtly) support the present order, makes it very easy to imagine that the need to redirect toward sustainability is a minority view. For this reason, it is critically important to raise the alternative option directly with others. First hand evidence that others recognize the new goal is necessary to break free from the illusion that perpetual material expansion continues to be seen by many as a valid goal.

When that illusion evaporates, we will see the goal of sustainability become the popular legitimacy.

Concentrating our Power

> *If we don t change direction, we ll end up where we re going.*
> Anon

Knowing what we are trying to accomplish makes a big difference when it comes to making decisions. A clear answer to the Question of Direction would affect decisions made about where tax money is raised, how that money is used, what is done with public lands and even the nature of the monetary system. All this on top of giving the population a green light for basing its own decisions on the new goal.

To establish the new goal, there are advantages to condensing the emerging world-view down to a word or a phrase. Because this book has been about the two perspectives, I can present the Question of Direction as the choice between "growth" and "sustainability." Both words refer to entire world-views. As words, standing alone, however, both can be spun into meaninglessness. While the words themselves are used in many ways, the Question of Direction is not about the words. It is about the world-views that the words can represent. That said, one cannot describe a whole world-view while asking a question about it. In order to question the underlying goal of society, we have first to clearly identify the vision and establish labels with which we can easily refer to it. Establishing such a frame of reference will require a lot of communication.

While the mainstream media will occasionally produce stories that advance understanding of citizens' issues, they are unlikely to help question the underlying goal of society. Reaching the population through citizens' networks will take more imagination than passing $10 million to an advertising firm and telling them to sell the issue; it will take personal involvement. Fortunately, personal contact and information flowing through peer groups enjoys far greater credibility than any other means of communications. The Seventh Generation Initiative exists to collect and pass along suggestions and materials for raising the Question of Direction through personal contacts and citizens' networks. Together we can press the question forward for public reckoning.

Enormous progress has been made in understanding the issues affecting long-term well-being. People, organizations and networks abound who, together, can explain the full spectrum of social and environmental problems and how we might solve them. If we can concentrate this wisdom into a sound bite, we can offer it as a clear and appealing choice.

By linking the word, "sustainability," or the phrase, "long-term well-being," to the outline inside the front cover of this book, we can anchor the word or phrase for our purpose. Recall that this outline emerged from a study of the inspirations and concerns of citizens. The outline provides criteria by which the world-view can be clearly identified, and by which plans and actions can be assessed for compatibility with the goal.

Where the reference is distributed, we can ask: "Is this where we want to head as a society?" While "this" doesn't mean anything by itself, with the reference in hand, that one small word can bring to mind the entire world-view. We can then ask the Question of Direction in a sound bite. Where circumstances make it impractical to relate the outline above and ask a question about it, providing the reference in advance is a necessary step.

Noam Chomsky describes the problems that distributing the reference overcomes. "Concision" is the word he uses to explain how the media can avoid new ideas without appearing exclusive. Chomsky is most widely known, not so much for his expertise in linguistics and how language is used, but for his outspoken views about peace, justice and the environment. (He's for them.) In the 1992 National Film Board's production, *Manufacturing Consent,* Chomsky describes concision as a format in which he can be invited to present his ideas on talk shows without the sponsors having to worry that he might convert people to his way of thinking. Typically, a guest is given three or four minutes to comment on some matter of public interest. As long as what a person has to say supports the perspective that the media has been broadcasting, three or four minutes is enough time to add a detail or two. However, if what one has to say contradicts the established view, the time limit makes sure that one cannot provide enough background information to back up an alternate perspective. Without the relevant background, divergent views look foolish, or don't make sense to an audience steeped in the perspective of the status quo. So too, the Question of Direction makes little sense without an explanation of the alternative goal — sustainability. With the reference for sustainability in the hands of an audience, however, the Question of Direction can be asked concisely.

We will have to be creative to move the Question of Direction forward. The potential of the approach is in its ability to maneuver around concision when the sustainability reference has been distributed. Delivering the sustainability reference to the public, in advance, is a means to the end of reviewing the underlying goal of society and choosing the new direction.

A Better Way to Live

Well-being can be sustained when activities:
1) use materials in continuous cycles.
2) use continuously reliable sources of energy.
3) come mainly from the qualities of being human (i.e. creativity, communication, movement, appreciation, and spiritual and intellectual development).

Long term well-being is diminished when activities:
4) require continual inputs of non-renewable resources.
5) use renewable resources faster than their rate of renewal.
6) cause cumulative degradation of the environment.
7) require resources in quantities that undermine other people's well-being.
8) lead to the extinction of other life forms.

http://www.SustainWellBeing.net

The opportunity has presented itself at a number of gatherings to distribute business size cards bearing the above outline of sustainability on one side. The other side, as shown below, can advance the issue in different ways.

One such gathering was a government sponsored event with the word "sustainability" in the conference name. There were close to 400 people present. At an early plenary, I stood up and mentioned that the word sustainability was being used frequently and questioned whether the meaning outlined on the cards was the same meaning understood by the organizers or, if their understanding differed, in what way was it different? A copy of the card (shown below) with the reference facing up was present at every place at each table in the auditorium. While my question was evaded by those in control, I'm sure that most

---

To move effectively toward
Sustainability
the goal must be clear.

The reference on back can focus discussion:

- **Is this what we mean by sustainability?**
- **If it is not, upon what point(s) do we disagree?**
- **For what reasons?**
- **Is there anything missing?**

7th Generation Initiative
RR #3 Lanark, Ontario, Canada, K0G 1K0
e-mail: sustain5@web.ca   (613) 259-9988

---

of the 400 people present were considering their own position and listening for answers that were conspicuous by their absence. Well over half the cards left the room with participants. I collected the rest for future use.

The Fine Line Between the Goals

An understanding of where conventional practices become unsustainable is necessary so that we avoid having our efforts buried under the illusion that the present order can continue through non-material growth.

A Question of Direction

Is it proper, now that our biggest problems result from our size, to hold growth as a goal? Would the guidelines on the back of this card make a better goal?

7th Generation Initiative
RR #3 Lanark, Ontario, Canada, K0G 1K0
e-mail: sustain5@web.ca   (613) 259-9988

In the Question of Direction, "growth" refers to material expansion, that is, increasing the throughput of material and/or energy flowing through the economy. This differs from increasing the amount of service derived from a consistent, or reduced, amount of materials and energy. In some cases, non-material activity can make the GDP "grow." Educational activities can generate revenue without requiring much material throughput. Cultural events, music, sports, theatre and the like can make a lot of money without increasing material consumption. Patent drug sales and other enterprises that are able to charge substantial prices, thanks to intellectual property rights, can also add to the GDP with minimal resource consumption. Why then, can we not maintain the economic growth system by concentrating on non-material commerce?

While there is a huge amount of value that people can get from non-material activities, such activities do not lend themselves well to making the huge volumes of money needed by an advanced growth-based system. It is hard to charge for "things" that have no material form. In addition, because little or no material is required, such "things" can be reproduced often with little or no expense — a recipe for abundance, low price or even free exchange. While such abundance is good for people and for sustainability, low prices don't help much with economic expansion, and free exchange is the content of nightmares for those dedicated to GDP growth.

There has been some progress over the years in that the amount of value derived from a given volume of materials and energy has increased. Such developments are generally in the right direction and ought to be applauded and encouraged. Unfortunately, the movement toward more wealth generation from reduced material consumption peaked following the oil crisis in the early 1970s and has diminished since then. While the trend looked promising, it only slowed the rate at which material throughput increased. There is little reason to believe that such increased efficiency could bring material expansion to a halt while perpetuating economic expansion. In the meantime, the argument is effectively used to deflect scrutiny away from the growth ideology and the need for a new goal. Wishful thinking and applied denial are necessary to imagine an economy growing for seven generations without increasing material consumption and waste.

When the smokescreen of growth without material expansion is presented, the fine line of validity can be identified by asking about planned obsolescence. For much of the last century, to meet the expectations of expanding production, many producers have depended on designing products to be thrown away and on promoting the accompanying values that enable people to feel okay about such waste. Disposable products are produced because durable goods would stifle growth. From the sustainability perspective planning obsolescence is a dangerously wasteful practice that has to be phased out to secure the future.

Whenever someone argues that we can have perpetual economic expansion and sustainability, point to planned obsolescence and ask them where they stand. To make the world work over the long-term, we not only have to stop planning waste, we have to find appropriate ways to serve the needs that are presently met by such waste. While every person needs the ingredients for healthy life, and opportunities to contribute to mutual provision, making garbage in exchange for a wage is not appropriate. A sustainable civilization shares the goal of maximizing resource efficiency, but is fundamentally different when it comes to designing for and promoting durability.

Advantages of Asking the Question of Direction

While the Question of Direction ultimately aims to redefine the goal of society, there are numerous benefits that make asking it an end in itself. By empowering the word "sustainability" with our hopes and dreams for the future, we can forge a useful tool, a wedge, which, through that single word, can introduce a new world-view dislodging outdated beliefs. That single word has entered a public dialogue; the reference clarifies its meaning. The reference to sustainability unfolds into a broad spectrum of concerns. Each area of interest has a constituency of citizens' organizations that can offer details for understanding and solving the problems on which they concentrate.

One might look at the multitude of volunteers and non-profit workers as a "government in waiting" — a shadow cabinet. Governments divide the work that has to be done into departments. The existing citizens' networks of concern might be viewed as the departments of natural resources, waste management, renewable energy and energy conservation, agriculture, development, health, justice and self-actualization. "Constituent Issues," on page 354, provides an index pointing to many of the concerns we are looking to address by choosing sustainability over perpetual economic expansion. By linking each topic to the people and organizations that are working in that area, we could create a directory to the various "departments" that are prepared to lead us out of the present crisis.

Finding Our Way With a Map of Words

Words provide a map. Having clearly defined terms or phrases by which to refer to the elements of a big-picture vision, any words such as sustainability make it much easier to communicate the option.

The first European explorations of the Americas provide an analogy. The explorers knew nothing about the continents. An expedition could spend an entire season exploring the coast. If, late in the season, they discovered a large river pouring into the ocean, they could take a reading on the stars, record where the mouth of the river was and name it for the records. The next year they could return directly to that place and spend the entire season exploring the river. With points along the river similarly located and named, any navigator with the charts could set out and travel directly to a chosen place.

So it is with words. When objects, phenomena and ideas are identified, we mark them with words. When someone else wants to learn about the same things, he or she starts by learning the words that identify the subject matter and go on from there.

"Sustainability" is one of these words. It's definition marks the territory, so that anyone who learns the term can recognize the basic considerations. Having the territory symbolized by a single word makes it easier to draw attention to related matters.

In Bakavi; Change the World I Want to Stay On (1977), I tried to introduce a word from a relatively unknown language to represent the goal defined by the eight-point outline. The traditional story, from which the word "Bakavi" was taken, resonated nicely with our challenges, but we found persistent resistance to, and suspicion about, the unfamiliar term. "Sustainability" and the term, "long-term well-being" are at least from the present language. When accompanied by the outline, it is sufficiently clear for asking the Question of Direction. What sounds we use to represent the vision do not matter. As long as people come to know what the vision is, we can ask together, "Is this what we want to accomplish?"

One of the defining qualities of humans is our ability to create symbols that enable us to refer to things we've come to recognize. Propaganda masters have done an amazing job of discrediting words and phrases that represent views contrary to those of their employers. Nevertheless, I can't imagine them being able to subvert our symbol-making ability enough to eliminate the vision of a sustainable world, no matter what it is ultimately called.

Frame of Reference

I first grasped what a frame of reference was at a roller derby in 1968. I had never heard of the sport until someone handed me a ticket one day, as I walked down Bloor St. in Toronto. I had some time, so I went into Varsity Stadium, sat down and watched. As I watched, I was mystified. Two teams roller-skated around a heavily banked track as fast as they could. Every now and then they would all stop skating and a score was recorded. I couldn't figure out how the points were being made. During intermission I asked a cameraman what was happening. He explained the rules of the game. When the action started again, the formation made sense; I could identify the strategies, see when a point was coming and for whom it would be recorded. The rules of the game provided a frame of reference with which to assess what I was seeing.

Today's social and environmental circumstances are a good deal more complex than a roller derby, but the basic patterns are not

beyond the comprehension of people with moderate interest. The eight point outline of sustainability provides a frame of reference. For most people today, the issues of our times provide, at least, moderate interest. The same process of recognition is dramatically illustrated with the following pictures. Take a good look. What do you see?

These pictures have been rendered by eliminating detail from specific drawings until they are no longer easily recognized by most people. Can you make out what either of these are? When you think you know what the original pictures were, or when you give up, turn the page. Now look back at the first drawings. Once you have seen the originals it is easy to make out the less detailed renderings. The second set of pictures provide a frame of reference with which to assess what you are looking at.

I am grateful to Rupert Sheldrake for permission to use his illustrations. The experiments he conducted with these pictures point to hopeful signs about how collective understanding evolves.

Sheldrake's team had been studying DNA molecules trying to find how they might carry enough information to guide all the complex steps of growth that an organism goes through from the first fertilized cell to maturity. They could not find enough opportunities for storing information amongst the atoms in the DNA, so they began testing for a field of information, which resonates with the growing organism. They called it a "morphogenetic field" or "morphic field." The morphic field of mice would be different than that of oak trees or humans. Through their respective fields, mice, oak trees or people would have a subtle connection to the earlier experiences of their kind.

After Sheldrake and his team produced these pictures, they showed one from the first set to several million viewers over the

British Broadcasting System and then showed them the reference picture so the viewers would recognize the pattern. Then they took the pictures to mainland Europe and showed both sets. What they found was that more people recognized the picture that had been revealed in Britain than the one that had gone unseen. While not conclusive, these results add support to the notion that as more people come to recognize a pattern, it becomes easier, consciously and unconsciously, for others to recognize it. In *The Presence of the Past,* Sheldrake describes other experiments that have produced similar results. If the theory is correct, human beings have a morphic field, which, as more and more people have similar thoughts or experiences, becomes increasingly charged in a way that makes it more likely that others will think and experience things that way.

Delivering the sustainability frame of reference to people is a side effect of the Question of Direction program. Such delivery gives rise to effects that are promising in themselves. They:

1) Nurture Understanding

With a frame of reference for considering news items, personal experience and concerns, people can more easily see the pattern of human ecology. As the pattern becomes more familiar it is easier to recognize and appreciate which choices contribute to sustainability and which create problems. The concern people experience when they hear of problems often fades soon after recieving the news. If they grasp the pattern into which the issue fits, they are more likely to see the evidence for themselves and not forget. They may even begin recognizing problems without being prompted.

2) Stimulate Vision

It is much more productive to work toward something positive than to expend effort resisting negative things. As pattern recognition develops around this composite issue, so does the ability to project the pattern into plans for action. Each person who starts projecting sustainability into his or her future plans, inclines the whole of society a little more in that direction.

3) Outline Areas for Debate and Investigation

The sustainability outline is subject to scrutiny. People are encouraged to look at it critically and to call attention to errors or omissions. The eight points provide a framework for locating the fine lines between activities that increase problems and those that help solve them. When activities are found to be part of the problem, the same criteria can be used to look for safer ways to accomplish similar ends.

4) Clarify Values

As more and more people and organizations acknowledge the need, sustainability will be increasingly recognized as a value to be encouraged. Similarly, non-sustainable activities will be recognized as detrimental and will be discouraged.

5) Build the Political Will to Tackle the Crisis

There is enormous strength in our institutions. As more and more people recognize the goal of sustainability, the more practical it will appear to support the goal politically. When the critical mass is reached, society will become committed to reaching for that goal. The crisis at hand is enormous. To address it with anything less than full social commitment is a gamble with the lives of all of our children.

6) Manifest Courage

When people observe world events in the context of sustainability the vision will look all the more promising. Through the frame of reference, people concerned about the different areas will come to recognize more clearly that they share a common goal. Morale will improve as we recognize how widely our concerns are shared. Knowing we are not alone can make the difference between frustration and action. Mutual support generates strength. People are willing to take greater risks when they know that others are supporting them, and that their efforts will not be in vain.

Constituent Issues: The Work of Society's Natural Immune System

The collective understanding of those who care about people, communities and ecosystems constitutes a single vision. By reiterating the outline of sustainability as an index with sub-indexes linking to the websites of the multitudes of people, groups and institutions presently working on better ways to live, that vision could be revealed in all its detail. Such an index could start with:

Solutions
1) Cyclic Material Use
   Natural cycles such as those that are harnessed through organic agriculture and cycles that are maintained through active recycling programs;
2) Safe Reliable Energy
   Renewable energy, conservation, substitution, interim measures;
3) Life-Based Activities
   Community, health, democratic decision making, creativity, communication, coordination (sport, dance, etc.) appreciation, learning, spiritual development, voluntary simplicity.

Problems
4) Depletion of Finite Resources
   Fuels, minerals, species, cultures;
5) Overuse of Renewable Resources
   Forests, fish, soil fertility, public money;
6) Pollution
   Atmosphere, water, soils, nuclear power, propaganda;
7) Inequity
   Domination and exploitation of the poor, women, aboriginal people, other groups, degradation through desperation, lack or failure of democracy, failure to consider future generations;
8) Species Loss
   Endangered species, endangered spaces (habitat).

In addition to issues that link directly to the eight specific areas of the sustainability reference, there are other concerns that overlap various aspects of the reference to the extent that they are best accessed in their own fields. These include:

Encompassing Issues
   Peace, militarism, work, economics, health, population.

As with the clear windshield on the proverbial bus of well-being measurement, such a setup for viewing visions and concerns should always have space to accept new issues that might arise.

Details about all of these issues and sub-issues are already available on the Internet. Assembling an index tying them together would demonstrate that, rather than being a multitude of special interests, there is a coherent, encompassing vision available for recreating civilization.

The Task at Hand

A vision without a task is but a dream.
A task without a vision is drudgery.
A vision with a task is the hope of the world.
        Carved in the wall of an 18th century church in England

As pointed out in Chapter 1, there is only one power available to citizens that does not require violence or great wealth. It is the power of collective persuasion. Each of us can contribute subtly to advancing the new goal through our thoughts and prayers. We can advance it substantially by reaching out in conversation and writing, and further, by sending the ideas out through our various networks of family, friends and associates. When the issue has come to be recognized in our communities, we can multiply our efforts and give legitimacy to the goal through the democratic process.

To effectively ask the Question of Direction we have to demonstrate to ourselves and to others that, collectively, our many approaches to improving well-being provide a coherent vision about which we can ask: "Is this how we want to recreate the world?"

It remains important for each community to continue refining the understanding of its particular issue area, and how best to deal with it. The overall goal is advanced with each development in each sector as we continue with our research, education and organizational efforts. If, in the process of our work, we can point out that our particular insights and solutions are part of the new legitimacy offered through the Question of Direction, our collective persuasive impact will multiply.

The work already underway to create a better world is, by simple addition, impressive. Furthermore, citizens' concerns enjoy far more credibility in the eyes of the public than the concerns of either governments or businesses. Each community of interest in the spectrum has its own reasons for bringing the overall issue forward. The Question of Direction can be asked from each perspective. By pointing out how individual issues fit within the big picture vision of long-term well-being, we can cultivate recognition of that common cause and offer it as a distinct choice. As a movement of movements we can project the question into the public forum where making a choice will be in order.

A Handy Communications Aid

For years I have been printing cards with the sustainability reference on the back and distributing them wherever opportunities arise. They have proved very effective for introducing the issue. Some versions, such as the two shown previously, introduce the topic of sustainability and the Question of Direction. Others have served as business cards for individuals, small businesses, organizations and networks willing to present the sustainability reference along with their particular interests. The front of the cards can say anything; they can provide contact information, serve as membership cards, invitations, tickets or as handouts. The eight-point frame of reference and URL, http://www.SustainWellBeing.net, on the backs follow, wherever the cards go, as food for thought.

The card format is simple, familiar and inexpensive. Many individuals have a shoe box or a drawer where they keep cards, in case they want to make contact with a plumber, retailer, organization, or the possibility for a sustainable future. Provided at a meeting, a whole room full of people can receive the reference. Nothing need be said that might distract from the primary purpose of a meeting or of handing out one's business card. On the other hand, if an exchange seems appropriate, the card can be presented, reference side up with an invitation to discussion. Every person and group has channels of communication: chance encounters, canvassing, newsletters, meetings, websites, etc. If we choose to raise the question of what we want to accomplish as a society, we have the means to do so.

Once the cards are read, individuals receiving them know what we are talking about when we ask, "Should we pursue the goal of sustainability?" I've come across the cards on refrigerator doors and bathroom mirrors, and have heard dozens of accounts of people pulling them out of a purse or wallet, sometimes dog-eared and worn, to provide an explanation of sustainability during a conversation. They are often distributed at meetings where sustainability is on the agenda — or where it should be on the agenda.

* * * * *

Given the state of the world today, the choice described in this book is a critical topic for public discussion. Nevertheless, the question has yet to come up as a clear public issue, and we can count on the currently powerful going to considerable lengths to avoid having it do so. It is much easier to control the public agenda than to control the outcome of a public reckoning, if it were to occur. If we are successful at getting the question in front of the population for a decision, the minority, presently winning the Global Monopoly Game, would likely make a huge investment to discredit the initiative. We could expect stories about the disasters that would arise from such a popular decision to be spun from every possible angle and likely, as has been done before, reinforced by a constriction of the money supply so that the warnings could be matched by measurable deterioration.

Life, money and illusion — all three would be present, perching the human project at the edge of fate. We would want to be clear about what is inevitable and what is within human control. If a substantial portion of people understand the options, opportunities and consequences of the choice, we could stare down the desperate attempts of the passing Time Spirit and launch a new era of cultural evolution. In this new era, people would value the opportunities for a long-term human presence on the Earth and would enthusiastically accept the responsibilities. This would include a recognition of the responsibility to respect the needs of each other, other living things and the next seven generations.

Then, we will indeed have matured as a civilization.

16 A Crack in the Road: Motor Culture

I Took My Car to the Corner Store

I took my car to the corner store,
*   to get a loaf of bread;*
It turned out to be quite a trip,
*   when all was done and said.*

First I took the doors along,
*   as they were first at hand;*
A trip with each, my heart did pound,
*   the exercise was grand.*

Next I took the hood and trunk,
*   they easily came undone;*
The body posed a bigger task,
*   it could not be moved as one.*

I'll not tell all, about the chore,
*   with torch and saw to render;*
Suffice to say, when it was done,
*   I could carry every member.*

But for the engine, I had to cheat,
*   its weight too much for me;*
I brought a wagon to the task,
*   man powered, though, you see.*

With fenders, gears and manifolds,
bumpers, clutch and brakes;
My heart and lungs were racing now,
a little rest I d take.

Oh how I love my motor car,
its chrome and paint do shine;
The neighbours stare as we go by,
I m so glad that it is mine.

The tires I choose to roll along,
a wonder is the wheel;
After axles, tranny and padded seats,
I was ready for my meal.

Alone, one man, but for his car,
the corner store s so handy;
I got the bread that I came for,
some cheese and also candy.

The joys of transport are so grand,
the world is there to roam;
I took my car to the corner store,
now I have to take it home.

Motor Culture

This topic is difficult. It contains elements that challenge one's comfort zone. Fearing that all I've said about mutual provision might be dismissed when I question this (apparently) essential aspect of contemporary life, I've debated with myself for months about whether or not to include it. Yet, I feel it must be examined.

From the start, I want to assure you; I love my car. It is a source of frequent delight as it moves me from circumstance to circumstance, connecting me with people and places of interest and beauty.

One of my earliest memories as a child is of visiting a mall with my mother. I would have been seven or eight years old. Someone was selling raffle tickets for a little red car. I remember thinking in awe about how, if it were mine, I could move around effortlessly. I could go anywhere, quickly.

People have always envied birds; without a moment's notice, they can take off to places near or far. With ease, they rise above buildings and trees and off they go, their will to move unchallenged. We don't need planes to experience this freedom. The depths of Canadian Winter aside, is it not a thrill to open the car door, sit down, buckle up, start the ignition, and be off and away? In less than a minute, the destination of my choice is a foregone conclusion. It takes time, alas, but I experience a kind of meditative trance in which I sit, mindful of the road and traffic, yet otherwise lost in thought. The next thing I know, presto, I'm where I want to be. It's magic — the power to imagine and it becomes so.

The birds probably do exert themselves when they fly above the trees. Just like we feel exertion when we walk or run. A walk to the next town, 20 kilometres away, would have me looking for a place to rest. But in my car, I sit and relax on the way and can step out on arrival, fresh and ready for whatever action inspired my journey. It costs me almost no personal life energy to make the trip.

The power behind this magic is, of course, fossil-fuel: solar power captured by plant life millions of years ago and deposited irregularly about the Earth.

Sitting on top of a small mountain in the desert outside of Los Angeles, an old friend and I felt the heat radiating from rocks that had spent all day under the intense Sun. Night had fallen and we were watching the lights of a car on the road far below. It struck us that the light we were seeing coming from the headlights of that car had something in common with the heat coming from the rocks upon which we sat. They were both delayed sunshine; the difference was the length of the delay. Our backsides were being warmed by the previous day's Sun. The light coming from the car below had shone to Earth many millions of years ago. The rock would be cool by morning. How long will the ancient sunshine last?

It is remarkable how fast mental defences rise when the unreliability of fossil energy reserves is mentioned. Of the difficult truths we must acknowledge, this one is perhaps the most absolute. It is hard to look directly at it. Yet if we do not act upon the information, we cannot hope to meet the future prepared.

A New Form of Human

Notable among the things that early explorers brought back to Europe from the Americas were the crops people grew in the distant lands; corn, tobacco and potatoes are the best known. The potato soon became very popular with peasant farmers and created a revolution in lifestyle. Easily grown in many types of soil and producing three times the yield of wheat, potatoes increased the food supply. Peasants growing potatoes could feed all their children, and have most of them live to raise children of their own. The population exploded.

A similar upswing of population has taken place on a much broader scale with the introduction of fossil-fuels to our diet. Not that, as individuals, we eat coal, oil and gas, but as a civilization they have become the primary energy food powering our collective metabolism. An oil well is like a drinking straw in the mouth of the Collective Human Organism. The power of ancient sunshine feeds us as surely as the energy from a potato enables a person to dig the soil, plant, cultivate, harvest and chew cooked potatoes to power the cycle. Fossil energy feeds us by powering tractors to sow, cultivate and harvest plants, producing fertilizers, irrigating and processing crops, and delivering all these to market, and finally to where they are used.

Our population has exploded in the fossil-fuel age. Part of the increase is directly due to the abundance of food that mechanized agriculture enables. Another significant portion is due to the things we have been able to learn, thanks to the time freed up by machines. The combination of increased food supplies, improved education and expanded knowledge of health care have made it possible to support far more people than the Earth had ever seen before.

Although coal had been used for heating since ancient times, our relationship with fossil-fuels did not get serious until 1727 when the first steam engine began pumping water out of a mine. In 1765, when James Watt invented a steam engine that could power a rotating shaft, the Industrial Revolution began. Attaching motors to machines for combing wool, spinning it into thread and weaving it into cloth were among the first advances. Motors, "metabolizing" fossil energy, have been expanding the size and material abundance of civilization ever since.

This transformation of society resembles the great cellular revolution of two and a half billion years earlier. That was when large, sluggish cells learned to cooperate with mitochondria. The mitochondria were efficient at releasing sunshine stored in bits of organic matter, and would share that energy with host cells. That alliance, between different types of cells, set the stage for the biological evolution that has brought us practically all the plants and animals alive today, ourselves included. In our new symbiosis, we have formed an alliance, not with another life form, but with mechanical tools that can make huge quantities of stored Sun energy available for our uses. This new alliance has set the stage for massive changes in the nature of our collective form.

As fast as motors could be built, they were attached to machines freeing up more and more labour for doing other things. It is no coincidence that the abolition of slavery corresponded with the availability of inanimate energy to do heavy work. Seven years after James Watt's steam engine, Lord Chief Justice Mansfield ruled that English law did not support slavery. In 1807, Great Britain prohibited the slave trade and, in 1820, started to enforce that prohibition with its naval supremacy. States in the U.S. began outlawing slavery in 1827 and, in 1865, the 13th Amendment to the U.S. Constitution abolished slavery throughout the Union. It was far easier to keep machines running, by oiling bearings and shovelling coal, than to maintain a community of captive humans. With a viable alternative source of physical effort, the long-felt dissonance and denial about treating other humans as cattle was finally relieved.

The first practical steam-powered locomotive was built in 1803, initiating the transportation age and, in 1859, the first production oil well was drilled in Titusville, Pennsylvania. Oil paved the way for the emergence of "Homo automobilis." Portable and fluid, gasoline and diesel fuels made small vehicles practical; 1885 saw the first internal combustion engine powering an automobile. Auto-mobility — this was the essence of my childhood fantasy — the ability to move individually and effortlessly over distances.

With mechanization, humankind became hugely more powerful than ever before, but the distribution of that power was far from equitable. "Just transition" was not a part of early industrial thinking. Instead of thousands of rural, cottage-based, craftspeople producing thousands of blankets, the woolen mills were producing tens of thousands of blankets. Instead of the earnings from the blankets being spread across the countryside, they were concentrated in the hands of the industrialists who owned the factories with a minimal portion going to the relatively few people operating machines. Blankets became abundant.

The revolution was underway and one thing after another was mechanized. Those who controlled the productive facilities prospered fantastically. Since they had the wealth, they made the decisions.

Their mechanized factories were producing much of value and they were making it available at a lower direct cost. This, they felt to be service enough. Their active interests were focussed on producing more. And produce more they did, and more, and more. Presently, we bring hundreds of thousands of new electric and gasoline motors to our service every year, each one linked into our energy systems, drawing inanimate power.

Where the culture of industrialization went, so too went mechanized transport. Railways were built across continents enabling the transport of raw materials, people and processed goods. Transit systems were set up in cities to enable people to get to and from work, to stores, and wherever else they wanted to go.

The location of industrial facilities in cities and the availability of mechanized transport has led to cities of unprecedented size. In his book, *The City in History,* Lewis Mumford described how cities have always been limited in size by the speed at which people have been able to travel across them to import fresh food and perform other essential tasks. When people walked everywhere, a city of 25,000 was very big. With horses, chariots and the appropriate roadways, as with Rome at the time of its empire, the population could rise as high as a half million or more. Enter the internal combustion engine, which powers trolleys, buses and automobiles, and cities with millions of inhabitants become commonplace; some now number twenty million souls, and more.

The logistics of providing for millions of people are massive. Mechanized transport made big cities possible and it continues to meet their needs, but not without costs. Air quality, traffic congestion, sprawling suburban territories and subservience to distant fuel supplies are increasingly drawing down the quality of life. Motor vehicles are responsible for the consumption of two-thirds of all the oil consumed in the U.S. Of the energy used by a car over a 10 year life span, 40% is used to manufacture it.

Power Corrupts

There are more and less efficient ways to get around. What is better and what is worse depends on how the options are measured. If rail were relied on for transport it would take less energy to operate and would cause less pollution than do buses or cars. Its operation can be quieter and less hectic. On the other hand, the independent manoeuverability of buses and cars offers more flexibility (assuming provision of a comprehensive road system), and the consumption of gasoline, tires and the vehicles themselves generates a great deal of economic activity and associated return on investments. The one is efficient from the sustainability perspective, the other from the economic expansion perspective.

It also seems to make a difference for whom money is being made and whether they have sufficient power to adjust things to serve their own interest. A public transit system just moves people around; a population dependent on cars delivers serious profits.

On numerous occasions I've heard complaints about inconvenient public transit schedules. One example is Vancouver Island Rail running from Victoria, BC, at the south end of the island up to the north, through the communities on the eastern coast. The trains could take a person from up-island into the city in the morning and bring them back in the evening. Instead, they are scheduled to go to Victoria in the afternoon and leave Victoria first thing in the morning. To see a doctor or to access city stores, passengers from up-island have to plan for two nights in Victoria. Perhaps the train is aiming to service city passengers visiting and vacationing in rural areas. Whatever the reason, people aren't using the line much and the owners would like to close it down. Some of those living up-island could be forgiven for suspecting that the schedule aims to encourage the use of cars.

The motives behind the Vancouver Island train schedule are not clear, but manipulating transportation systems to convert people to car use is not unknown. During the last century, owners of auto related industries destroyed numerous public transit systems in order to expand the purchase and use of cars.

In New Day Films' *Taken for a Ride,* Jim Holzer, a worker on Los Angeles' now defunct commuter railway, says,

> *They don t take the service out, they just cut it back. They ll take and cut it from 10 minutes to 12 minutes, from 12 to 15, from 15 to 20, from 20 to 30. So they reduce the service... every time you reduce the service you make it less attractive. And the less attractive the fewer riders. And then they say, "Well see, we can t make any money." So they abandon it.*

Holzer's account is in regard to an enormous operation that took place in the U.S. to increase automobile use. In 1922, only one in ten Americans owned an automobile. Everyone else got around by trains and electric trolleys. The then president of General Motors, Alfred P.

367

Sloan, considered this to be a great business opportunity. What unfolded in GM's efforts to capitalize on that opportunity holds a place as either one of the best business moves of the century, or one of the most infamous, depending on one's point of view.

Sloan and his company wanted the other 90% of the population to drive cars, or at least, ride in buses with gasoline motors built by GM. They bought the Yellow Coach bus manufacturing operation and founded Greyhound and National City Lines as front organizations through which to work. Then they bought up rail transit systems throughout the United States and replaced the service with buses. Compared to the relatively quiet, quick and odourless transport of rail travel, buses were loud, smelly and cumbersome. However, by slowly reducing the rail and bus services offered, most people eventually gave up on transit altogether and bought cars.

GM was eventually joined by Standard Oil of California, Mack Truck, Phillips Petroleum and Firestone Tire in what turned into a tremendously lucrative project. Working through Yellow Coach and Greyhound, their manoeuvering went undetected for years. By 1946, they controlled the transit systems in 83 cities.

Eventually they were discovered and antitrust suits were filed. Found guilty, the companies were fined $5,000 each for dismantling transit systems that would cost around $300 billion to replace today.

Whether or not the private automobile, with its appeal of flexible, personally-directed, transport, would have become as common as it has without such interference, will never be known. The "playing field" is far from level. Roadways are built and maintained with tax dollars, fuel supply companies receive hundreds of millions of dollars in subsidies every year and the costs of air pollution are not included when people buy or fuel their cars. How might we determine which form of transport is most cost effective?

The established fact is that roads and fuel distribution networks are spread across whole countries, car maintenance and repair people can be found in every town and many places in between. As many as one out every six workers in North America is employed producing and repairing cars, building, maintaining and policing roads, managing insurance and licensing programs, and producing and distributing fuel for the automobile system.

It is easy to own a car in the industrialized world. While industry aims to build as many new vehicles as they can sell, the old ones keep on running long after their upholstery is smudged and the frames start to rust. Today, for a few hundred dollars, one can buy a car that will travel faster than any human had ever moved up to a hundred years ago. The cost, as vehicles get passed from first to second to third owners and on, can drop to less than what it would cost to melt the iron.

Not only can we travel faster than any creature on Earth, we can carry large quantities of material on our way. Auto-mobility is not restricted to small vehicles of a ton or two. For different purposes we can form metals into trucks, tractors, backhoes, bulldozers, boats and planes. Powered with mobile fuel, these products of our ingenuity can move vast numbers of people about the Earth, and rearrange fields, forests and mountains to suit the will of those with the money to control them.

With car ownership in many developed nations approaching one per person, we might consider ourselves a new species: Homo automobilis. The impact of large populations of these creatures is immense. Figuring an average of 100 horsepower per car, the planet's present auto fleet would represent seventy billion horses. A horse eats about a ton of hay per year and a good hay field will produce three tons of hay per acre. This means to feed just the auto fleet we would have to dedicate 21,000,000,000 acres — ten times the land mass of Canada. In terms of arable land, this is almost double the area presently used worldwide for crops, pasture and forest products. With auto-mobility accounting for less than half our mobile mechanical needs, agriculture and commercial transport would take at least as much more, just to feed our mobile power habit.

Comparing the auto fleet to using horses is imprecise in a number of ways. Cars don't have to be fed when they are not used. Horsepower ratings are calculated to flatter engines or be kind to horses, and if we were, in fact, dependent on hay fuelled transport, we would surely trim excess power use where possible. Nevertheless, with North American vehicles ranging from 105-340 horsepower and being used by the millions almost every day, the point remains that our auto-mobility consumes a lot of energy.

As individual creatures in a symbiotic relationship with autos, we have developed appetites and expectations. I call the relationship symbiotic because even though the people are the only living partner, we are not the only partner served by the relationship. On average, owning an automobile costs seven or eight thousand dollars a year. And that's before adding up the hundreds of millions of dollars that we pay directly and indirectly through taxes for building and maintaining roads, health care, resulting from accidents and pollution and other car related services. According to David Roodman's research in *The Natural Wealth of Nations,* Canada subsidizes oil and gas concerns to the tune of $5.9 billion a year and, in the U.S., it is estimated that $111 billion is spent by government each year on roads and road maintenance. Military operations cost more still. So, yes, we get a lot from our cars, but the system also demands a lot from us.

In less than a lifetime we have taken auto transportation for granted, totally recreating our world to suit its use. Because the automobile has been assumed, much of the developed world would be practically useless without cars. Among the most car dependent structures are suburban settlements. They provide row upon row of spaces for people to settle and raise their families, but they often lack stores and employment opportunities that would enable people to live their lives without regular travel. The low population density and long distances make bus servicing expensive and, because almost all suburbanites already have cars, they seldom use the limited bus service in those areas.

With millions of people depending on cars, the road systems can be overwhelmed. Estimates of the amount of time that people spend stuck in traffic run as high as 56 hours per year in Los Angeles and average 36 hours throughout the United States. With Europe's rail lines being bought up by private interests and service being reduced to maximize short-term monetary gain, people are increasingly turning to cars. Time lost in traffic is also on the rise in that part of the world.

On occasions when I have to drive into Ottawa for a morning appointment, a delay is almost inevitable at one intersection where the Hunt Club bridge connects the city across the Rideau River. Waiting for three or four cycles of the traffic lights before passing is not unusual at rush hour. Sitting there one morning, watching the cars and trucks go by, it struck me how transport-intensive the lifestyle of *Homo automobilis* is. How many tons of steel do we move just to get to work in the morning?

Ottawa is a small city, close to a million people. Approximately 25% of them drive to work, and their cars weigh, on average, a ton. (This is definitely a low estimate, as my car weighs that much and is among the smallest available.) This means that over 200,000 tons of iron are transported each morning of every working day. That's just to get started in one small city. With four hundred million people in

North America, the total transport of iron in the morning ritual on this continent alone is well over one hundred million tons.

We have created a situation where getting to work on a single day requires moving more material than was moved during any single year in the eighteenth century, and probably more than throughout entire centuries before that. That's just to get started. The work we do and the goods we move in our transport-intensive economy are additional. And everyone has to get home again at night.

That is not very efficient, yet we pride ourselves on the sophistication of our technology. We are very clever, for sure, but so much of what we do with our cleverness at this time in history would come to little if it were not for the ancient sunshine upon which we feed.

Many of us expect to live this way forever. Millions of people take for granted an hour-long drive to and from work. It seems reasonable to drive four hours on a weekend to visit friends or to board a jet plane and circle half the globe for holiday amusement.

Easy transport has scattered our families and friends far and wide. Like building homes far from work, we create situations where we would lose our roots if we didn't continue consuming large quantities of transportation. We seldom realize that before the car, most people went through their entire lives without travelling 100 miles from where they lived. Now, it is almost unthinkable not to cross an entire continent for a friend's wedding or to attend the funeral of a family member.

Transport has become so common in the overdeveloped world and we have become so dependent, some people assert that it should be a human right. The only problem is that it is impossible to sustain. Without even considering the health impacts of car exhaust or the environmental disruption of climate change, we will soon not be able to pump as much oil out of the ground as we have become dependent on burning. Since we started burning petroleum, we have always had more, yet, the time is not far off when we will have less.

"This cannot be!" cries our collective denial. "Things will always be as they are. We cannot live without motor culture, therefore this news is false, not true. It has been, and should remain, banished from thought."

Recall the extraordinary capabilities of human beings. Our kind is destined to live on Earth for a very long time to come. We can deal with this. As individuals and collectively, we have to deal with this.

Ten thousand generations of our forebearers did not raise us to abandon our children to impossible dreams.

The Hubbert Peak

When M. K. Hubbert made the comment about our ignorance not being as vast as our failure to use what we know, he was referring to the peak in resource consumption that now bears his name. The flows and ebbs of resource exploitation have been thoroughly studied and found again and again to follow a similar pattern.

As a practising geophysicist focussing on non-renewable resource exploitation from 1937-1989, Dr. Hubbert became a leading authority in his field. In 1956, he identified the pattern in resource exploitation now known as the Hubbert Curve. The curve begins when uses are discovered for a natural resource and production begins to supply the small initial demand. With a commercial supply on hand, use expands and new uses are found. Demand grows and production increases to provide for it. Eventually, the most easily exploited reserves of the resource are exhausted. Due to the increasing difficulty of producing from more remote or lower quality reserves, supply begins to level off and then decline. The high point is called the Hubbert Peak. For any resource, when the peak of production is passed, supply no longer follows demand as it had since the resource first came into use. From that point on, demand must be adjusted to match supply. Unless rationing is implemented, the price of the resource must go up until demand drops to a level that can be met. Production of the resource continues to decline until it is practically gone. The shift, from where demand determines how much of something is produced, to where the supply determines how much can be used, is the essence of the fundamental change that has taken place in the relationship between people and the Earth.

In the late 1950s, Dr. Hubbert calculated that U.S. production of oil would peak in 1970. The record now shows that his prediction was only four years early. The peak of production is not the end of supply; it generally arrives when about half of the total reserves have been extracted. The peak does, however, signal that supply can no longer keep up with demand. Present advances in production methods can increase the rate at which we extract oil from existing reserves. While they do not extend the volume of a reserve, they can maintain production near peak rates when decline would previously have begun. As a result, such methods can push back the time when we will experience the first limits, thereby making the decline steeper when it does arrive, leaving us less time to adapt before the shortfall becomes serious.

We are within a decade of the worldwide Hubbert Peak in oil production. Some say we passed it in 2001 — others had predicted 2005. Few serious analysts expect it to be later than 2010. When the peak is passed, it is estimated that the rate of decline will begin with shortfalls in production of around 600,000 barrels a day. The shortfall would grow from there until conventional oil reserves are practically exhausted in 40 years. (By comparison, production of oil from Alberta's abundant tar sands, after 20 years of development and tens of billions of dollars invested, is around a million barrels a day. Tar sands oil is not included in the conventional supply curve because it takes a substantial portion of the energy produced to extract it.) Financial analysts with Bloomberg, calculate that we would need to invest $105 billion, in exploration, development and production, every year, to maintain present rates of supply. (This estimate assumes that there are quantities of petroleum yet to be discovered.)

In its May 5, 2006 press release, *The Coming Decline of Oil* the Earth Policy Institute stated:

> *... Matt Simmons, head of the oil investment bank Simmons and Company International and an industry leader, says in reference to new oil fields: "We've run out of good projects. This is not a money issue, if these oil companies had fantastic projects, they'd be out there [developing new fields]."*

We can thank the slowdown in the world economy around the turn of the century for slowing the increase in demand that has thus far kept our oil appetite within the range of production capacity. However, with China and India maturing as industrial economies, demand is again growing. At the time of publication, production has been stretched to 84 million barrels each day. Saudi Arabia says it can supply more, but in the form of heavy, low grade crude for which there is presently insufficient refining capacity. The hurricane seasons of 2004 and 2005, particularly hurricanes Katrina and Rita, disrupted the Gulf of Mexico oil and gas production. Due to the fragility of energy supplies this caused extensive fluctuations in the world price of fuel. Supply is close enough to demand that we can continue to expect the price of oil and gas to rise and fall in relation to weather forecasts.

Climate change might ease the use of heating oil in Winter, but the increasing use of air-conditioning in the summer will eliminate any energy-savings.

With the peak of oil production upon us, one country's output can make a substantial difference. Because Iraq has been forbidden throughout the 1990s from exporting more than a minimal amount of oil, overall production has been less than it might have been. With the production peak clearly in sight, and not trusting Iraqi President, Saddam Hussein, with oil revenues, one can imagine the incentive the U.S. had, with its 60% dependency on imported oil, to replace Saddam with someone who would sell them Iraqi oil, or better yet, provide direct control.

When I first wrote this section, the Iraq invasion was underway and already, huge contracts had been announced for U.S. and British companies to rebuild Iraq after its water and electrical systems, roads and other infrastructure, had been destroyed. It would be a convenient loop for the money pouring in from renewed oil sales to then flow directly back to the countries that dropped the bombs. It is a stimulus for economic growth that worries me a great deal.

The whole affair would be a grand business venture if it were not for the widespread death and trauma involved and for the enormous amount of ill-will created internationally. When the invasion took place in 2003, control of Iraq's oil production might have enabled a continuation of the low oil prices upon which the American way of life depends. Whatever becomes of Iraqi oil, the price will, at best, fall and rise once again when the global ability to pump the critical resource passes peak potential.

Colin Campbell is an authority on modern petroleum exploration and production technology. He clearly states the inevitable:

> *Oil has to be found before it can be produced, meaning that there is an obvious relationship between discovery and production. It follows that the peak of discovery in the 1960s, which is now an historical fact, has to be followed by a corresponding peak of production.*
>
> *The general situation seems so obvious. Surely everyone can see it staring them in the face. How can any thinking person not be aware of it? How can governments be oblivious of the realities of discovery and their implications? How is it possible, given the critical importance of oil to our entire economy.*

Campbell says the popular notion that proven reserves are increasing, as the big oil companies search around the globe, are mostly due to reporting practices — "... for good regulatory and commercial reasons," reserves were not all reported when first discovered. At present, "the world consumes four barrels of conventional oil for every one it finds." A half-dozen separate analyses of petroleum reserves are available at: www.hubbertpeak.com.

The Spirit of Motor Culture

As hundreds of millions of us enjoy the ease and convenience of personal transport, we regularly put our money into the systems that produce fuel, cars and roads. Our money is our power; it embodies our skills and efforts. Collectively we grant enormous power to the spirit of motor culture. It has become an economic and political power unto itself. Unfortunately, power will do things to sustain itself that decent people would not do.

Every minute as we drive, thousands of explosions take place in the motor a few feet from our hearts. Push the gas pedal to the floor. Feel the power. Imagine the power of a transport truck or a locomotive. An Abrams tank burns three gallons per mile or 252 gallons an hour. A B52 bomber turns 3,612 gallons of fuel into CO_2 and water each hour that it flies. If the cells of our bodies together create ourselves, and the sum of all the people in a society make up a collective human presence, what is the synergetic character of motor culture?

In *Petrotyranny*, John Bacher documents case after case where oil wealth has financed aggression and oppression. Any person or country controlling petroleum revenues can collect enough money to purchase masses of weapons and pay people to use them.

When the age of direct colonial rule was ending and previous colonies were gaining independence, it was the countries with oil that found themselves embroiled in civil wars and dictatorial rule. Angola, Equatorial Guinea, Gabon, Indonesia and the major oil producers in the Middle East, have all had their democratic options thwarted by the wealth that accompanies the oil under their feet. Even within oil-producing countries with democratic governments, political and economic power plays, inspired and financed by oil wealth play large roles in the way those countries are run.

The nations with the world's biggest weapons industries are also the most dependent on oil. They are always willing to sell guns, bombs and other equipment to any regime that will assure access to their oil. Even when trade with such countries is discouraged, ways are found to do so by trading through third parties or simple stealth and deceit. Recall the Iran-Contra scandal where weapons were covertly sold to Iran by U.S. officials to fund the destabilisation of Nicaragua's elected government. Although both the sale of weapons to Iran and supporting the Contra insurgency in Nicaragua were forbidden by law, those committing the crimes, when tried and found guilty, were let off the hook with near hero status.

"Oil interests dominate dictatorships and have considerable influence in the democratic world," contends Bacher. "Democratic power is best enhanced by cutting the biggest form of tribute from democracies to dictatorships — payment for oil." Bacher proposes reducing the wealth we turn over to oil interests by wholeheartedly developing alternate, renewable forms of energy. This tactic temporarily found favour during the 1973 oil crisis, following the Brundtland Report in the late 1980s, and during the Clinton Administration. These efforts and other movements to reduce oil dependency and/or greenhouse gas emissions have been countered with well-funded and largely successful lobbying. Petroleum remains the Emperor of time spirits.

And a callous Emperor it is. When *Planning for Seven Generations* was published in 1993, I suggested that the "recent shoot-out in Kuwait against Iraq was largely a cooperative venture among industrial powers" [to maintain control over Kuwait's oil reserves]. "Such assertions of control might proceed differently if the spoils were seen as too limited to go around." ... "If Armageddon is to be fought, it may well be between large non-sustainable economies trying desperately to control disappearing oil supplies."

Since that time, there have been various applications of military might that made strategic natural resources available for consumption by the powers that dominate global markets. The massive lead mines of Kosovo (which Hitler had taken at the beginning of the Second World War to make batteries for his U-boats) mysteriously escaped bombing when NATO went to war there. No longer under socialist control, that lead is available to produce electrical storage equipment for the New World Order. A further advantage of the Kosovo war was the opportunity for the U.S. to build what will be its largest military base in Europe, on the edge of Macedonia. The base will overlook the pipeline route from Burgas (Bulgaria) on the Black Sea to Vlore

(Albania) on the Mediterranean, a critical link for exporting oil from the western part of the Caspian Basin.

Suggestions that B52 bombers did the initial groundbreaking for the oil pipeline through Afghanistan are undoubtedly black humour. The truth seems as dark, but not as funny. The region around the Caspian Sea is one of the last substantial, untapped reserves of oil on Earth. The pipeline route through Russia and the Balkans can service the western side of the Caspian Basin. For the eastern side, the most direct route to oil tankers would be from Iran, but Iran has been out of Western control since its revolution. As a second option, the U.S. energy giant UNICOL had been negotiating with the Taliban to build the Trans-Afghanistan pipeline. When the Taliban awarded the pipeline contract to an Argentinean company, force came into play. After the U.S.-lead attack to oust the Taliban, the new leader of Afghanistan, Hamid Karzai, was conveniently familiar with the pipeline proposal, because of his position negotiating with UNICOL before the Taliban fell out of favour. Only six months after the invasion, Afghanistan's newly selected "leader," and the presidents of Turkmenistan and Pakistan, signed a memorandum of understanding to begin construction of the pipeline from Turkmenistan's gas fields through Afghanistan to the Pakistani port city of Gwadar. (At the time of publication, no company has been willing to brave the continuing hostilities to commence work on the pipeline.)

Huge moral compromises have been made to keep the oil flowing in the volumes we have become dependent on, but nowhere on Earth is there enough oil to continue for a single lifetime, let alone for seven generations. Until, and unless, we develop lifestyles that are not dependent on oil, we are at risk. As long as we seek to extend our oil habit at the expense of less developed countries, we may win. Besides individual acts of desperation, they have had little capability to fight back. While some might think that some factions in Iraq have put up a fight over the oil fields there, oil wars with larger powers, such as China, Russia or Europe could be Earth shattering. Even if we make it through, winning the final contests between fully industrialized nations, we will still have to play a new game when the oil fields are practically drained. How long might Canada hold the U.S. at bay if we wanted to preserve our oil resources for our own use?

Those who take the new game seriously, and leave the old game to those with less imagination, will find themselves way out in front in the years to come. We would all be further ahead if we dedicated present fuel reserves toward setting up the new game, rather than wasting them on tanks and rockets to destroy other nations, only to delay the inevitable for a few more years.

Are the cells in a person's leg responsible when that person punches a neighbour in the face? Are we responsible for the crimes committed to fuel our cars? It is glorious, the freedom to move around like birds. We are offered all manner of justifications for the fighting that makes it possible. Eagerness to accept these stories is testimony to the power of denial. We would have liked to believe that the U.S. troops were greeted with cheers when they entered Iraq, yet, we would be very skeptical if we saw reports of Canadians or Americans cheering the bombardment of their own cities. The underlying dissonance in each of us should rise with each population bombed into destitution, until we find sustainable ways to live so that we no longer have to fight to survive. Then, as when motors made slavery unnecessary, we will be able to relax within ourselves and pursue the wonders of living.

From the Pot to the Fire

As 2006 progresses, the price of oil is on the rise, and with it, new possibilities. Two articles caught my attention while this manuscript was being edited. One was about a U.S. Army report stating that they could manufacture all U.S. military liquid fuel requirements from coal. The other was from Venezuela, where President Chavez says that, if the price of oil remains above $50 a barrel, Venezuela can claim larger reserves than Saudi Arabia. At that price enough energy could be afforded to manufacture gasoline out of the thick petroleum that remains abundant.

The implication of these reports is that we could see additional decades of careless oil consumption before supply limitations force change. Believing that the fuel crisis is postponed will be a relief for many, at least for those who can afford the increased price.

Moving from thoughts that an unresolvable energy crisis is upon us, to thinking that we have many years to go before the problem becomes catastrophic, can cause one's mood to swing. It is a mood swing not unlike that which would accompany a close brush with the law. Picture yourself in court with evidence piled up against you, threatening prison time and steep fines, and then being found not guilty. Such an experience would increase one's respect for the law, particularly if one had strayed close to the line of infraction. As a species, we are brushing close to the law that governs minimum resource supplies. Most of the world is still being spared the punishment that comes from breaking that law.

Lest we become complacent, however, the potential for expanding oil reserves comes by way of a considerable increase in the amount of energy needed to bring each of those barrels to market. As such, continuing with our careless energy use would compound the critical problems of climate change — a problem governed by the Law of Tolerance. It is imperative that we become familiar with both the Law of Tolerance, and the Law of the Minimum (both introduced on page 55). It will serve us to develop a solid respect for these laws of nature before we cross one line or another in our pursuit of perpetual economic expansion.

What Can We Do?

Think of all the people you know and love, and all the people they know and love. There is strength in our relationships and there is great potential in our creative abilities. Drawing on the security of all our relations, we can look directly at the challenge at hand. It will not go away until we accept that it exists and until we begin making decisions to solve it. Expanding our dependency will not help.

Turning Highway 16, which heads south from Ottawa, into a four-lane highway (416) was heavily promoted during the 1990s. Proponents argued that it would increase economic activity in all the small communities along its route from Ottawa at one end, to Prescott on the Saint Lawrence River at the other. The expansion cost was $323 million.

Even before that road was completed in 1998, there was a boom in housing construction in Kemptville — at the time, a forty-five minute drive from Ottawa. Now, whole new communities exist, consisting largely of people who sleep in towns along the highway and drive to Ottawa for work. With the new highway came expanded maintenance costs, increased daily consumption of gasoline, increased wear and tear on a fleet of cars, and many thousands of hours spent driving. Most of these things have monetary costs that are added to the GDP. And, new residents in these communities do spend some of their money locally, thereby enhancing local jobs. By the GDP measure, the 416 has been a successful development project.

From the sustainability perspective, however, the building of the 416 has created ongoing liabilities. There are now new fixed expenses that draw down natural resources, add to the CO_2 problem and send local money out of the area to maintain the flow of fuel and cars. If, by contrast, that third of a billion dollars had been spent on local businesses, focused on energy conservation, renewable energy and on developing family-run farms to grow food for local consumption, the accounts would be very different. Beside avoiding the increased costs of an extended auto system, energy dependency could have been reduced, thousands of jobs created and food security increased. The local economy would have been enriched by circulating its money locally, rather than sending it out of the country to buy food and fuel from distant places.

The logic of GDP measured economics hinges on cheap transportation. How long can we avoid paying the costs? With the road-building lobby now focusing on making Highway 7 west from Ottawa into four lanes, I wonder how much further out on the limb we will go before we start to base decisions on what we know about the long-term viability of motor culture.

Energy Efficiency

Given our present dependency on mechanized transport, there are interim solutions to be found in making such transport more efficient. Hunter and Amory Lovins of the Rocky Mountain Institute (RMI) have been promoting "Hypercars" for a decade. (See their book, *Natural Capitalism*) It is possible, they say, with existing technology, to build cars that weigh one-third to one-half what current models weigh. With a hybrid-electric drive, fuel efficiency can be further increased by transforming the forward momentum into electrical energy when brakes are applied. That energy can then be used to help propel the car forward again when needed. Such cars, streamlined for minimum air resistance, would travel 80 to 200 miles per gallon (about 35 - 85 kilometers per litre). Thanks to RMI's persistent encouragement, major auto makers are beginning to produce such cars. They will surely help, but are they a solution, or will they just encourage us to overlook the challenge?

Other technical solutions propose converting the transportation fleet over to ethanol or hydrogen. As with Hypercars, these technologies are thought to offer some relief as we face the early challenges associated with the peak and decline of conventional oil. Ethanol is basically alcohol made from grain, which is, in theory, renewable. In reality, however, the corn that presently feeds ethanol plants is produced using large amounts of fertilizer and fossil-fueled equipment. Research compiled by the National Farmers Union (NFU) in Canada indicates that it takes as much energy to produce ethanol as the ethanol provides. Along with providing no additional energy, twice as much CO_2 is released; one amount when conventional fuel is burned to produce the ethanol and, another when the product itself is burned. On top of that is the diversion of soil productivity away from feeding people in favour of feeding machines. Darrin Qualman, the Executive Secretary of the NFU says; "Ethanol production takes food from the poor and transforms it into transportation or recreation for the rich."

Hydrogen and fuel cells, which can turn hydrogen directly into electricity, offer some potential for meeting energy needs. However, because it takes more energy to produce than it can return, hydrogen is not a source of power. Chemically produced from diminishing supplies of natural gas, hydrogen can also be produced with electrical energy from any source. By storing energy from solar and wind generators in the form of hydrogen, the power becomes portable, making it a good battery system. An enormous number of windmills and solar panels would, however, be needed to provide even a half of the energy we get from oil. If we were able to produce even that much, questions would arise about whether to use the power for cars or for heating, for industry or for operating food-production machinery.

Some say that we could get far more transport for the energy invested if we were to use trains more. Iron wheels, rolling on iron tracks, take considerably less energy than do rubber tires rolling on asphalt. Further, it is possible to transport as many passengers on a single pair of tracks as it is on a four-lane highway. The amount of land and money required to provide service is, consequently, lower for rail. For the same amount of energy, trains can move two to four times more tonnage miles of freight than can trucks. Although trains used to have a similar advantage over cars for passenger transport, following the 1970s energy crisis, improvements in automobile efficiency rendered the two modes almost equal. Both operate considerably short of their seating capacity, leaving their relative efficiency subject to assumptions about the average number of seats filled. If the effort were made to make passenger rail service more efficient, it would in all likelihood, regain its more energy-efficient status.

As it is, the issue is one of convenience; one still has to get to and from train stations. While this can be done effectively with public transport, such transport has to be available and convenient. In many places, this is not the case. With subsidies for car travel running as high as thirty-to-one over those for train travel, it is difficult to compare how convenient public transport will become when we get serious about making energy reserves last.

Regardless of how efficient the various systems are, the greatest energy-savings are available in reducing the distances traveled. My inclination is to look toward conservation for solutions. For many of our present energy uses, there are substantially more efficient ways to get the same amount of service. There was a time when it was common for the front, ground floor of buildings to contain businesses and for the owners and workers to live in the back and in upstairs apartments. Huge amounts of travel could be eliminated by again mixing retail and residential structures within neighbourhoods, encouraging home businesses and providing opportunities to work from home.

Early work from the Rocky Mountain Institute (RMI) focused on generating "nega-watts" of energy. The RMI had been asked what could be done about the pollution and fuel consumption problems arising from a new electrical generating station. Its solution was to invest in nega-watts. A nega-watt is a watt of energy saved. For example, a 20 watt compact flourescent light bulb produces the same amount of light as a 100 watt incandescent bulb. By using the energy-efficient bulb, 80 watt-hours are saved for each hour of use. Or, as they say to clarify the point, 80 nega-watt hours are "generated." Such nega-watts add up, especially when the millions of dollars that would be needed to build and fuel a new generating station are made available to invest in energy-efficient light bulbs, motors, appliances, insulation and the like. By the time a hundred megawatts worth of nega-watts are "generated," for example, it becomes unnecessary to build the new 100 megawatt generating station. Since the cost of saving energy is frequently far less than the cost of producing more, conservation makes local economic sense even if it reduces potential increases in GDP.

An extension of this approach exists in energy-saving companies (ESCOs). ESCOs manage a fund of investment capital that they make available for energy conservation projects. Trained energy efficiency experts come into a building, usually large commercial operations, but in some cases residential housing, and analyse the structure, services and equipment for ways to save energy. Recommendations are made for improving energy efficiency and, if the owners agree, a crew is employed to make the changes. The money required for upgrading the building is provided from the investment fund and is repaid from the value of the energy saved. The clients continue to pay their energy bills at the previous level, with the ESCO receiving the amount in excess of the lower actual expense. When the loan is paid off with reasonable interest, the ESCO goes on to retrofit other buildings and the clients are left with substantially reduced energy expenses. The payback time is typically two to four years. The same sort of service is offered by WASCOs— water saving companies.

There is no question that we could live the same way we do today using much less power. Increased energy efficiency is a critical first step. It will reduce the rate at which we are depleting energy reserves, and it will add legitimacy to the goal of minimizing energy use. The problem, unfortunately, is more profound than most of us imagine, assuming that we let ourselves imagine it at all. We are, after all, talking about maintaining a lifestyle that will have, over a three hundred-year period, consumed a "bank account" of stored energy that took 300 million years to accumulate. Even if we develop ways to capture Sun energy many thousands of times more efficiently than did the ancient carboniferous vegetation, we will still have much less capacity for moving loads than we exercise today. It will be necessary to find ways of getting started in the morning that don't require moving millions of tons of steel.

Yet, there is much cause for hope. For most of the five thousand years of recorded history, humans have managed to maintain their mutual provision with almost no need for inanimate energy. The popular view of ancient life is that it was "nasty, brutish and short." There is, however, reason to believe that earlier humans actually led more satisfying lives than most of us do today. The evidence available from studying the few tribes that survived colonization with their lands intact, is that they enjoyed nutritious diets, cradle-to-grave security within their communities, and rich cultural lives, and did so on an average of four hours of work a day.

We can do even better. Through the passing fossil-fuel era, we have learned an enormous amount about the world in general and about health care in particular. Much of this knowledge is not resource intensive and can benefit us for as long as good will is maintained. Detailed understanding of nutrition, psychological health and the rewards of learning, love and laughter can improve our physical well-being and quality of life forever. Such a knowledge-based civilization could exist well within the guidelines of sustainability, given a rational approach to population. The newly unfolding wonders of global communications through telecommunications and the Internet are well within a renewable energy budget and could be available for seven generations and beyond. It is an illusion of material expansion economics that we need large quantities of natural resources and energy to lead satisfying lives. There are huge enduring potentials for enjoying life while maintaining cyclic material use within a renewable energy budget. I would consider myself wealthy indeed if I were able to leave such a legacy to my children and grandchildren. What are the long-term potentials of material- and energy-intensive lifestyles?

In his book, *Hope, Human and Wild*, Bill McKibbon tells of how the main street in the Brazilian city of Curitiba was reclaimed. The new mayor, Jamie Lerner, sought to bring human activity back into the car-choked core of his city by turning the central road into a park. He challenged the city engineers to tear up the pavement, return the soil and plant trees and grass to create an environment for people rather than cars.

When the plan was complete, the reclamation was made over a weekend. People were soon flooding to the area and shopkeepers further up the road were asking for the pedestrian friendly area to be extended. Motorists, however, were not amused and organized to drive over the park land to reclaim it for their cars. After hearing word of the brewing protest, the mayor, rather than assembling police for legal enforcement, had drawing paper rolled down the length of the park. When the motorists arrived they found the area filled with families picnicking and children painting pictures out in the open air. "Motor Culture" made way for people on that day.

Already today, worldwide, most people manage without cars; 700 million was the last estimate I saw of the auto population. With the human population presently at 6.3 billion, it means that eight out of every nine people don't have a car. What do they know that we don't? How do they manage? It's not that they have more money than us and are thereby empowered to a greater extent. The concept that those without cars are the poorer for it, changes in the context of sustainability. The majority of people are able to provide for their material needs within their local territory and, on the occasions that they need something from further away, there are buses and trains to provide transport. What if we are mistaken in our assumption that having more material things somehow makes us better off? In terms of the future we might offer our descendants, there are good reasons to believe that those who have learned, or preserved, ways of living that require minimal material substance will have more to offer their offspring than will the materially entangled.

From the long-term perspective, when comparing how many material things a person has, sympathy may well be due to those who are so insecure in their being that they feel the need to pile material goods around themselves in ever greater quantities. Being accustomed to material affluence is a liability. We are taught that "the one who dies with the most toys wins," but it is misleading. The joke is only funny because of the clarity with which it exposes the style of life that the perpetual economic expansion model promotes.

One might argue that the world's poor are destitute and offer no models worthy of consideration. Here we must distinguish between those who have maintained the structure of their culture, and those who suffer the exploitation of the "toy makers." The poor whose lands have been taken over to grow cash crops to pay interest on foreign debts, are destitute in the service of bloating economies elsewhere. The debt traps, which they did not choose to enter, leave them unable even to afford the education and elder care that would stabilize their populations within the carrying capacity of their lands. This is not where the inspiration lies. If we were to remove the drag of financial colonialism, and the bottomless expectations stimulated by materialistic promotions, we would find countless examples of people who are able to live well within the means of their own territories.

Have I gone too far to suggest that concentrating on living can solve the problems of material overshoot? Life-based activities are, after all, the antithesis of material consumption. If you feel instead that human life requires a vast throughput of materials and energy, and think that the life-based pursuits I hang my hopes upon are airy-fairy dreaming, then the hope I offer will not ease your mind. How do you imagine looking at the "problematique"? What solutions do you see? I collect ideas and am eager to gather different perspectives. Hold tight to any other ways you can see for dealing with the problems. Please let me know what I have missed. Securing the future will take the best of what each of us has to offer.

Otherwise, remember that a key quality of being human is the tremendous fulfillment that living offers. If we can dispense with our adolescent economic structure and adopt one more suitable to a mature species, we can assure the basics of healthy life and make it our purpose to enjoy living.

Driving our cars is a thrill, and a great privilege. That power has enabled us to develop many of the things that make our future options much more diverse than they were two centuries ago. I intend to use mine to share this message and to work on building a community with its sights set on sustainability.

17 What Will Become of Us?

There are two directions in which our world might evolve in the years ahead. On the one hand, is the present track, where success requires increasing the amounts of monetary business conducted every year. On the other hand, is the order that would emerge if sustainability were the goal of decision-making.

Economic expansion has been the Western World's conscious goal since R. A. Butler proposed it as a goal for the British economy in 1954. Its seeds can be traced back to the Reformation, with roots that have been well established since the Industrial Revolution. The growth ethic has guided industrialization.

Thousands of millions of engines and motors churn away, processing natural resources and providing services for an expanding population. The people, in turn, tend to the machines, feeding into them rivers of oil and mountains of coal. Vast quantities of animals, vegetables and minerals are processed, while people continue to install ever greater capacity to process ever more. At each step along the way, money changes hands, supporting the goal of increasing the GDP.

The second option — sustainability — requires a change in priorities such as civilization has never before seen. The Agricultural and Industrial Revolutions were similar in scope, but took centuries to accomplish. The shift to sustainability will have to take place within a single lifetime. Of far more significance is that, while the moves into agriculture and industry followed the path of expanding human activity, sustainability aims for something fundamentally different. Sustainability aims for a steady, yet dynamic, balance between ourselves and the capacities of the planet we have grown to fill.

Steady, in that it must remain within the Earth's ability to provide resources and absorb waste. Dynamic, in that the substances from which we build our bodies and our economies must always remain in motion, flowing through regenerative cycles to supply our needs over the years, centuries and millennia through which our kind should expect to prosper on this gracious planet.

Between these contrasting goals, and their resulting impacts, there is a spectrum of possibilities wherein our future lies. Depending on popular awareness and personal effort, and the possibility that leaders might emerge who recognize our changed circumstances, we will incline more one way than the other. This chapter sketches circumstances at the opposite ends of the spectrum. Where we end up depends, in large part, on your will and on the will of others with whom we share the future.

As in the story from Chapter 2, where the man was looking for his lost car keys under the street light — because the light was better there — the "street light" of convention shines brightly on the path we have followed for so long; it is easy to imagine that we will find solutions continuing as we have. To continue exponentially expanding economic activity, however, domestic legislation and international institutions will have to be further adapted to enable ever greater quantities of the natural world, and of our social capital, to be converted into financial capital. How long it would take for this pattern to lead to chaos depends on where we look. Already there are people in many places whose worlds are becoming unlivable as a result of the present path. Such circumstances will overwhelm more and more people until the winners of the growth game recognize that something has gone terribly wrong. The world cannot afford to stand patiently by until these people see past the social and emotional filters that isolate them from the problems their "success" is causing.

More suiting to the human family would be for us to wake up, en-masse, to the challenge brought on by the fundamental change in our relationship with the Earth. If, in good faith, we were to use our present capacity for moving materials around and fashioning them into useful forms, we could meet the challenge at hand and adapt within a decade or two.

Foretelling the future is an uncertain task. It is also true that we do it frequently with impressive accuracy.

Throw a ball to a friend, and that person will see it flying through the air, sense its speed, and how high it is rising, and will, frequently, be able to put his or her hand, in advance, at exactly the point where the ball arrives. If there is a big gust of wind, the place toward which the ball flies will change. Your friend might sense the change and still catch the ball, or the change could come too quickly or be of an unfamiliar nature, in which case, his or her prediction of where to catch it could prove insufficient.

Projecting the expansion of human impacts is like preparing to catch a ball. The gusts that might arise include unexpected thresholds in ecosystems and changes in perceived legitimacy.

Two sets of images follow, one for each end of the spectrum of possible futures. I am not a fortune teller and cannot paint a picture of how life will be. Nevertheless, there are various situations that, it seems to me, will unfold as we pursue one or the other of these options. The images assembled below provide tastes of those possibilities. As I would like to leave you on a hopeful note, I will begin with the less pleasant option. From what I have gathered, if we continue on the present path, the dangers that we face are immense.

"Growth Everlasting:" Growing Until We Drop

The problems unfolding as we pursue economic expansion are of two sorts. There are environmental problems arising from accumulating pollution, diminishing resources and undermining the web of life. The other problems are social. They arise from growing inequity and in particular, from the desperation that arises when individuals and communities are faced with a loss in the Global Game that will leave them unable to provide for basic needs.

In the days of ancient Rome, those who could afford indoor plumbing had lead pipes installed to bring them water. Medical historians have assessed that lead pipes can result in lead poisoning, which dulls the mind, and that this symbol of affluence may have degraded the abilities of the ruling class and played a part in the Empire's collapse. Much later, London became the centre of wealth and power. Horses provided adequate transportation in the early days of that great city. As the British empire swelled, however, human activity in London mushroomed and the gutters of the main streets would occasionally clog up with horse manure and the sidewalks would run over with urine.

In neither of these cases, was success expected to cause problems. In both instances, the areas affected were small, yet they serve to illustrate that success can have unfortunate side effects. It has taken until the last century for our success to grow to the point where we are able to degrade entire regions and in some ways the planet as a whole.

While some progress has been made at reducing pollution in specific cases, like ozone depleting CFC's and some components of automobile exhausts, each year more toxic releases are added to the volumes already released in the preceding years. Much of the progress made in reducing pollution in the Northern countries has been accomplished by moving polluting industries to Third World countries where environmental standards are weak and where, as Lawrence Summers said in 1992 when he was chief economist at the World Bank, they are "under polluted."

Pollution is generally frowned upon, but judging from the actions taken, it is not considered serious. If more demand can be stimulated for a product, production is increased. If there are fines for exceeding pollution limits, they are simply tallied along with other costs of meeting that demand. *The National Pollution Release Inventory in Canada* and the *Toxics Release Inventory* in the U.S. document hundreds of thousands of tons of toxic materials that are released into the environment each year. With expansion of the economic process deemed essential, the toxic side effects are largely ignored.

The case of MMT, the manganese-based gasoline additive that was featured in a challenge under the *North American Free Trade Agreement*, makes the point. MMT was banned in the U.S. prior to being introduced in Canada. Nevertheless, when the Canadian government passed a law to ban its import into Canada, that law was brought to the NAFTA "court" as an illegal barrier to trade. The manufacturer, Ethyl Corp., claimed over two hundred million U.S. dollars for the loss of production profits and for damage to its "good reputation." The trade rules are such that Canada chose to remove its law, let MMT continue to be burned in gasoline and to pay Ethyl twenty million dollars for its trouble, rather than lose even more money trying to fight the claim. Since the advent of "Free Trade" agreements, there has been little in the way of new environmental regulations for fear that they would be challenged and rendered inoperable by the Trade Courts.

The trade rules aim to enhance growth, but they do so without acknowledging the dangers. Parallel to the accumulation of toxic by-products in the environment are increasing rates of asthma, cancer and other health problems. These occurrences, along with the disruption of communities, climate and other life systems, are simply not seen as problems. Quite the opposite. The costs of medicines, treatments and insurance claims are added to the GDP and displayed as proof of progress.

The problem of rising levels of atmospheric CO_2 has been widely known for decades. Through the Kyoto protocol, an international agreement was made to reduce CO_2 emissions relative to the amount produced in 1990. While some individuals and some communities have reduced the amount of CO_2 they produce, with the exception of countries whose economies have crashed since 1990, almost every nation has increased emissions; almost all conventional economic growth requires applying energy to natural resources.

When the Kyoto discussions were getting underway, the United States proposed waiting ten years before beginning reductions. This would have conveniently corresponded with the peak of conventional oil. Reduction would then be aided by the reduced ability to produce oil. Even the natural decline in the availability of oil, however, would have little effect on emissions as long as the ultimate legitimacy is given to capital expansion. Already there is substantial investment in facilities to mine tar sands, make oil from coal and to liquefy natural gas. Most of these methods release CO_2 during production in addition to that released when the product is burned. Without a willful shifting away from the growth ideology, demand will be met through profit-making investments in anything that will burn. CO_2 will continue to accumulate and the climate will continue to change.

For the ten thousand people living on the low-lying Pacific islands of Tuvalu and Kiribati, the melting of glaciers and polar ice caps, along with the expansion of warming sea water, heralds the end of their world. As the sea-level rises they are preparing to abandon their homelands. The small islet of Tebua Tarawa, which for generations had served as a navigational aid, has already disappeared.

In Peru, there are communities that depend on meltwater from the Quelccaya Glacier in the Andes Mountains. As the climate warms, their glacier is shrinking, and it is expected to have disappeared completely by the middle of the 21st century. The same is true closer to home for the people of Saskatoon, Saskatchewan, where, in the dry Summer season, they depend on meltwater from the Bow Glacier. The danger of losing their water supply as glaciers disappear threatens communities around the globe. Three hundred million people in western China face this same fate.

The vision of increasing wealth is the "promised land" of the capitalist faith and the undercurrent of desire stimulated by advertising. China, in particular, has become proficient at industrial growth. After more than a decade of economic growth at rates of 8-10%, China has reached a stage where many of its 1.2 billion citizens want and can afford to eat meat and drive cars. If that one country continues to raise its level of consumption to the point that currently bloats First World economies, global demand for auto fuels and grain for livestock would double. There is nothing in the growth equation to stop this from happening. The Chinese are capable of building and operating the machinery, distributing the products and reinvesting the profits. If they choose to maintain that course, only insurmountable resource limitations, or unspeakable aggression by competing nations, could stop them. Yet China is only one of many nations successfully following our lead and adopting the mechanisms of economic growth. India, whose rate of economic growth is only a little lower than China's, has a higher birth rate, and will soon be home to a greater overall population.

With most of the world tied into global markets, the repercussions of China's conventional economic rise will affect us all. I've spelled out enough details about the oil situation for you to do the math of doubling demand. It takes two to ten kilograms of grain to produce one kilogram of animal protein. With over one-third of all grain produced being fed to animals, global harvests are having trouble keeping up with demand. In 1990, grain reserves were 30% of one year's overall consumption. Over the four years from 2000 to 2003, people and our animals consumed 220 million tons more grain than was grown. This brought the reserves down to just over sixteen percent. We were fortunate that good harvests in 2004 saw international grain reserves recover by 26 million tons. Meanwhile, groundwater reserves used to irrigate several major grain-growing regions are being depleted and growing conditions are increasingly unpredictable because of climate change.

At an all candidates meeting during a recent Canadian federal election, I asked the local hopefuls how their parties intended to rise to the responsibility of leading us out of these critical resource problems. The answers from the representatives of both the major parties suggested that the problems were China's fault, implying that it was, somehow, okay for the government they wished to form to ignore the situation. With the exception of the newly emerging Green Parties, our politicians are unanimous in their goal of accelerating growth.

On the energy front, those dedicated to perpetual economic expansion propose nuclear power generation as a solution to diminishing conventional energy reserves. Back in the early 1970s, when nuclear generating stations were still being built across North America, opponents drew attention to the dangers of radiation that can emerge from the production, use and disposal of nuclear fuels. Dangerous to live by when locked in rock underground, uranium becomes far more dangerous when it is disturbed. Blasting, crushing, refining and transporting uranium releases radioactivity at every stage. Routine emissions in cooling water and air from within nuclear plants, increase background radiation, and spent fuel remains dangerous and must be isolated from living things for a period of time longer than civilization has existed. More dramatic are the dangers of catastrophic accidents within reactors and of nuclear weapons being made from the materials flowing through the commercial process. These dangers increase with each reactor built and with each year of operation.

While arguments about the dangers of nuclear technology gained many allies, they had little impact on the multi-billion dollar investment plans at that time. The catastrophic accidents at Three Mile Island and Chernobyl gave legitimacy to the worries of the nuclear critics, but it was the economics that brought construction of new plants to a crawl. Huge cost overruns on construction and the all too frequent repairs, costing hundreds of million of dollars, turned the tide. Nuclear energy was not profitable enough. As the cost of energy rises, however, the economics will again point to its profit-making potential. Already there is considerable promotion of nuclear energy as the solution to global warming and climate change. Power without carbon emissions! A solution to the problem of diminishing oil reserves! An expanding economy needs an expanding energy supply! The markets would be there, profits assured. In the present system, such development is only logical. It is not reassuring to hear suggestions that we should expect a reactor accident every now and then as the cost of being civilized.

When the Chernobyl nuclear reactor exploded, debris from the failed reactor was scattered across the roof of the building it was in. Robotic equipment failed in the effort to push the highly radioactive material back into the building. In order to finish the job, prior to casting a huge concrete block around the mess, young Soviet soldiers were employed. I viewed the video footage taken by an official in charge of the operation. The young men, as instructed, ran out on to the roof of the reactor with a shovel, picked up one scoop of debris, threw it into the hole and ran back behind the lead protection. Active duty in the danger zone was 60-90 seconds. Five thousand of those brave men died of radiation poisoning within a year, according to that documentary.

Such extremely high concentrations of radiation are typically found only inside nuclear reactors. Less concentrated is the contamination that comes from the use of depleted uranium (DU) in war. Because DU is twice as dense as lead and therefore has a greater impact when it hits a target, the U.S. has been using its nuclear waste to make ammunition. DU projectiles are capable of breaking through armoured vehicles and tanks. The enormous force propelling these shells causes them to shatter and burn when they hit a solid target, turning 10-70% of the DU into dust and fumes. The particles then drift in the fire storms and weather. Ten tons of DU were used in Kosovo; over 300 tons were used in the 1991 Gulf war, and it is estimated that to date, between one thousand and two thousand tons have been fired at targets in Iraq since 2003. The U.S. Army advises soldiers to wear respiratory and skin protection if they come within 25 metres of DU-contaminated equipment or terrain. The Uranium Medical Research Centre (UMRC), based in Toronto and Washington, found that within 10 years of serving in the first Gulf War, almost ten thousand U.S. troops had died. According to Arthur N. Bernklau, executive director of Veterans for Constitutional Law in New York, 56% of the soldiers who fought in the first Gulf War (325,000 out of 580,400), have "Gulf War Syndrome" or some other form of permanent medical problems. Canadian scientists from UMRC, working in Afghanistan, found extensive evidence that non-depleted uranium was also being used. Such ammunition is even more radioactive than DU. For generations after hostilities "end," these "nuclear wars" will be inflicting radiation-related illness and birth defects on the local population.

For now, unless you have the misfortune of facing the wrath of the United States, it is the peaceful use of radioactive materials that is most likely to increase the amount of radiation in our environment. It would take thousands of nuclear reactors to replace the energy we get from oil and an ever expanding number of additional facilities after that to maintain the exponential expansion of economic activity. Like petroleum, the uranium fuel for nuclear reactors is a limited resource that would be exhausted by massive dependency. In the meantime, nuclear fuel would have to be mined, processed and transported for all the reactors, and the spent fuel securely stored for tens of thousands of years. Spills, minor accidents and routine emissions from anywhere along the fuel cycle increase the radioactive background. Add to this the occasional meltdown of an old or carelessly maintained reactor and perhaps an occasional nuclear bomb, and we will need to prepare for a more radioactive environment.

The chance of being affected by radiation goes up with the intensity of the radiation and with the length of time that one lives. Micro-organisms and insects have short life cycles. The chance of radiation killing them, or disrupting their reproductive abilities, before they die of natural causes, is small. Humans live a long time, and in particular, it takes a long time before our young are able to produce young themselves. Were we to go the nuclear route and discover that we are unable to contain the radiation we extract from the Earth's crust, to adapt, we might find it necessary to reshuffle the customs of the family. For example, the younger children are when they make babies, the less likely it would be for their children to be damaged by radiation. Consequently, a custom would be in order to encourage reproduction at the earliest opportunity. With parents too young to raise their own children, grandparents would have to fill that role. These early breeders, upon reaching their late 20s and early 30s would get their turn at nurturing when they become grandparents themselves.

* * * * *

The problem of shrinking biodiversity increases with the amount of territory claimed by human activity. Nothing deserves oblivion at our hands. Who would want to see the death of the last elephant or panda, songbird or whale? Our world becomes sadder and lonelier as other creatures disappear.

For those who do not care for other living things, potential disaster might first register another way. Personal well-being depends on healthy ecosystems. The stability of ecosystems in turn increases with the number of species living within them. When the birds that eat insects disappear, our food crops become endangered as some pests swell in numbers. Abuse of the microscopic life-forms in farm soils reduces the soil's ability to maintain its fertility naturally and increases our dependency on energy-intensive, manufactured fertilizers. When the hole in the ozone layer expanded, allowing greater amounts of ultraviolet radiation to reach the oceans, plankton in the south seas dropped considerably in abundance. As major agents for taking CO_2 out of the atmosphere, their loss aggravates the climate problem.

With everything connected to everything else, there are countless interdependencies, known and unknown. It is folly to claim ever increasing portions of the Earth in the mistaken notion that the more we consume, the better off we are. Soaring prices, resource depletion, cancer, respiratory disease, climate change, and much more, all are emerging from our growing economy and all offer opportunities for more money to be made. The system has become self-defeating, yet, the conventional wisdom calls for accelerated expansion.

Social Repercussions of Growth Everlasting

While pollution can cause life-degrading illnesses, such problems usually come on slowly and are masked by traditional illnesses and the decline of old age. As for depleted resources, we are not strangers to increasing prices. Hyperinflation would be another thing. It is not being able to afford what one needs that makes resource problems onerous. Some people will be able to pay steeply higher prices for necessities, others will not. In the competitive atmosphere of the growth paradigm, the losers will become desperate and, while their plight may be linked to resource depletion, it will manifest as social problems. If we all face the challenges together, the burden would be shared and finding solutions would be a common goal. With the present set-up, those managing the system would not be affected until long after it became intolerable for the majority. Life threatening inequity results in resentment rising to disruptive levels and beyond.

Without moderating influences, the rich get richer and the poor get poorer. As the winners use their advantage to increase that advantage, moderating influences are eroded further. On the local level, poverty undermines public health and inspires acts of desperation. On the global level, efforts to extend markets, control natural resources and eliminate competing nations, lead to treacherous trade manoeuvering and offensive military campaigns. While local unrest resulting from inequity can be disruptive enough, nations whose well-being is subtly undermined, or overtly destroyed, by winning nations hungry for more, can rise up in vicious armed resistance.

If you recognize the need for people to find a balance with ecological reality, and to do so in a way that does not drive others into desperation, you likely recognize that we have an enormous task ahead of us. It will take widespread cooperation to accomplish. Limited opportunity, unmet needs and exploitation do not encourage individuals to give their best efforts to a world that appears not to care.

While the tradition of economic competition may keep those still in the game scrambling to produce more, those who are left behind are not contributing as they might. Even among active participants, large amounts of ingenuity and resources can go into an enterprise only to have it end in bankruptcy. Such competitive loss might result from a better product replacing a lesser one, yielding some public benefit amidst the lost effort. Too often though, it is aggressively marketed products that are mass produced, with as much of the cost externalized as possible, that squeeze out products of higher merit. When it is the advantages of size and wealth that determine who wins, the market's positive influence is defeated.

The bulk of the new wealth created since the "Free Trade" era began has gone to a very small portion of the population, most of whom live in a small group of nations.

Wealth begets wealth. When expanding wealth is considered the ultimate goal, giving those with money increasing liberty to expand their fortunes becomes a policy goal. Reducing taxes on large incomes gives wealthy people more to invest. When that money is invested, it probably does make more money, but does the process serve the common good? If the result of lower taxes is the depreciation of the education system, fewer people will develop their potentials and will have less to offer society as a whole. The poor will have fewer skills with which to work themselves to a better life, while the children of the well-to-do will have superior opportunities, thereby fortifying the divide between classes.

Although the rich are a very small proportion of the population, they get away with adjusting the system to serve personal ends because so many others have bought into the dream of getting rich themselves. With extensive folklore of rags to riches and the broad distribution of stories about the few who have broken into the upper class, a great many people foster the fantasy that their stock holdings, or their lottery ticket, will move them upward to where the advantages of the rich will be their advantages. Perhaps the greatest buy-in is through pension plans. Millions of us have small pension plans that benefit from the same growth prospects as multi-billion dollar investments. Because of our personal stakes, tiny though they may be by comparison, most of us condone the advantages arranged for the growth of the large money collections.

In days long past, allowing one small group to have substantial advantages over others had some justification. An elite who could draw on all the resources of a community would assure that, at least some individuals would grow up with adequate nutrition and enough education to be able to understand and look after the broader structure of society. The temptation to maintain circumstances of scarcity for others so as to justify the maintenance of elite privilege has wasted much potential. Today, maintaining an elite so that at least a few people can develop their full capacities is not a necessary precaution. If we choose, we are capable of assuring excellent nutrition, shelter, education and health care for everyone.

Media

While toxic materials accumulate, and social structures are undermined, the mass media tells us repeatedly that the GDP is up and that we have never had it so good. From a material perspective, and in the short-term, there is some truth to this. As long as the economic machinery is attached to adequate fuel supplies, it churns out material wealth. However, as more and more of our collective wealth is dedicated to paying interest charges and for fuel itself, there is less and less available for use by those who don't fit as cogs in the machine.

In another era, people might have discussed the economic structure, and other issues, to fill in the time between work and sleep. As in Roman times, however, where the circuses entertained the masses and kept their minds off the excesses of their leaders, television and other electronic devices keep people preoccupied. At least, in ancient Roman coliseums, people sat next to each other and conversations were inevitable. Today, one can walk down empty suburban streets at night and, in almost every home, see the flickering light of televisions, endlessly feeding people synthetic realities. While images of happy families in spacious homes, bringing in bags of purchased goods to set down on the kitchen counter reinforce the materialistic ideal, the tension, drama, hostility, deceit and horror that spice up viewing hours, numb viewers to the signs of real danger arising in the world around them.

Violence will be available in abundance as the Global Monopoly Game plays out. Over 2400 years ago, Aristotle observed that the tyrant declares war "to deny his subjects leisure and to impose on them the constant need of a leader." Today's news sings the virtues of restructuring the world to enable further growth, while sorry scenes of local tragedy distract viewers from the devastation of entire societies and ecosystems that are being perpetrated to support that growth.

In today's world, dictators are installed and propped up, and if they get out of hand, discredited and removed, all to maintain the flows of natural resources and to assure markets for mass produced goods. Chilean copper, lead from Kosovo, tropical fruit and sugar from Central America and oil, oil, oil – transportation supply lines and military bases to defend them — all in support of the growth illusion.

"War is the rich man's terror while terror is the poor man's war." said Sir Peter Ustinov. Has the Global Monopoly Game reached the point where endless war is necessary to hold losers at bay while bloated economic systems suck up resources everywhere and turn them into waste?

The individuals in each country who can deliver the goods are well paid for their collusion. If they have to oppress people in their country to deliver, the oppression is overlooked, and very seldom reported through the mass media. Perhaps we never have "had it so good." Perhaps we need all the interventions to maintain our accustomed levels of comfort. A key decision ahead of us is whether we will continue marginalizing whomever we must to gather resources for continuing growth, or whether we will acknowledge that long-term well-being requires a cooperative approach that recognizes and shares the constraints and bounty of our planet.

Some people are already over the edge. Their livelihoods have been usurped by huge companies determined to achieve their next increment of growth. Wells go dry as a nearby factory draws down the water table to manufacture its product and raise the GDP. Mass produced food floods local markets at prices that can't be matched by farming families. Faced by competition with billions of dollars in backing and no individual face to address, frustration can mount to suicidal proportions. Where overwhelming force is used to impose authority from far away, some choose to strap explosives to their bodies and detonate in front of symbols of their oppression. "The terrorists are cowards," pontificate the illusion spinners as commands are issued from a safe, comfortable office, thousands of miles away. Million dollar bombs, paid for by faraway taxpayers, are launched to blow up positions of resistance.

The Patriot Act in the U.S., *Bill C-36* in Canada, and similar legislation in other rich countries, move to restrict individual rights in ways that will be helpful in warding off the inevitable rebellions. As the game gets tighter and the losers within the rich world edge closer to desperation, such laws seem designed to help the winners maintain control. Political parties take turns paving the way for international money growth and then take the public's wrath for the damage done. At that point the other major party takes over again and continues with the process. They have no choice they say, "the deficit makes us do it," or "it is necessary to remain competitive." Who decided that nations should rely exclusively on private fortunes to maintain a debt-based money system?

Money is essential for individuals to trade their skills in a complex society. Why should one class own the medium of exchange? Why are they permitted to siphon off our tax money just so that we can have currency for trading with each other? Who makes the decision to keep the present arrangement out of public view and not bother to return money creation to the public domain? Imagine an individual whose body was not allowed to make its own blood, but was instead required to rent blood from a profit-making institution!

How long can people be fooled into thinking that the abuse of social and environmental resources is good for the economy/mutual provision? Are we like the frog who does not notice that the water in which it sits is getting hotter by the minute?

There are many bright minds among the elite and they are able to hire many more. They may have a plan. When the Roman Empire crumbled, the winners, at that time, had huge estates where they retreated with enough needy people to assure the labour necessary to till the fields and serve their various other needs. Many of these estates endured, evolving into the fiefdoms, principalities and kingdoms of the feudal era. Today, with government revenue diminished by tax cuts and dedicated to ongoing interest payments, education may once again become a privilege of the wealthy, putting lower classes at a disadvantage. How convenient it would be, in a world of declining energy resources, to have masses of lightly educated people to perform menial labour. For those with the wealth to pay for rising food prices and heating fuel, there would be plenty of losers to replace the motors that have done our work since the slaves were freed. Whether our labour would be to pay off unpayable debt or whether we would trade our freedom in return for food, the playing field could become so uneven that norms of indenture and slavery would return.

Times have changed since the Roman Empire, however. The battles of those days were fought with spears, swords and arrows. Today, if it comes down to seeing who will be the greatest of them all, the fireworks could change life on Earth forever. The U.S. may be the only "super power," but the title is only comparative. Almost any industrial nation has the capacity to put up an enormous fight at an equally enormous price. When the prize being fought over is enough fuel to bring in the harvest or to keep the people from freezing, the ferocity of a cornered animal would manifest through industrial might. Conventional war could be debilitating enough to bring civilization to an end. Nevertheless, if we just bombed each other back to the stone age with conventional weapons, some isolated communities would survive and probably thrive, as our present civilization became a topic of legends and fairy tales.

Far worse would be the fate if some huge hereditary wealth were to spawn simple-minded offspring who didn't understand the limits to material power nor the meaning of mutually-assured destruction. Yet, thanks to papa, such an offspring might hold the levers of power in a nuclear state. Their reaction to such a high stakes conflict could bring on years of nuclear Winter. When Spring finally returned to our abused planet, many forms of life would emerge from the soils and watery depths. In such a future, however, there may be no person left to receive or to applaud the ultimate Monopoly prize.

One Summer day, from the corner of my eye, I sensed struggle. The cat had a pigeon. The pigeon got away and flew to a perch far above the cat. Safe, or so I thought. The bird sat there for a minute and then, flew directly back to the cat.

Was it hurt to the point that its inner sense figured the cat might as well have dinner? I don't know. Could these creatures follow an urge to accommodate fate? What came to my mind was the widespread mythologies of hunting people, which hold that the prey gives itself to the hunter.

I've recalled the pigeon and the cat on many occasions. Recently it has come to mind in connection with the Punk/Goth style of some teenagers today — pierced body parts, chains, rough language and hard music accompanied by the poetry of anger, pain, death, violence and revulsion. It's quite a fashion statement. Are these young people sensing the pollution, exploitation, and strife that mark today's world, and preparing to give themselves, like the pigeon, to fighting the wars and enduring the desolation of the End Game? If it were not that we could be as comfortable, healthier, less frightened and more hopeful for the future, if we chose another route, we might well continue with business as usual. There is another option.

If Sense Prevails; Realizing our Potentials

There may be a pot of gold waiting at the end of the rainbows we chase, but chasing gold will not lead us to the rainbows.

While there is cause for despair in these times, there is no advantage in pessimism. We need not play the Global Monopoly Game to its bitter end. The prospects remain high for humans to have a very long and successful tenure on Earth. Our long-term success hinges on acknowledging that humankind's extended period of youthful growth is practically complete, and that it is time to accept the responsibility that comes with maturity. It is time to recognize our interdependence with the web of life and to stabilize our presence within that web.

The life force, upon which we will always depend, remains strong. Try for a Summer to stop life on a patch of moist, fertile soil that is exposed to sunlight. Without powerful poisons, it is a constant task. Our success is linked to cooperating with this resilient force.

To create a vision of something that does not presently exist, it makes sense to start with the closest parallel situation and work from there. For many hundreds of millions of years, life has sustained itself and evolved into more versatile and, it seems, more self-satisfying forms. Until very recently, the entire process was maintained in perpetual cycles. Water cycles endlessly throughout the biosphere; the elements of carbon, oxygen and nitrogen are abundant in the air; phosphorus and potassium can be found in most soils and sunshine bathes the Earth daily. Add to this small quantities of numerous other elements found in soils and we have the building blocks for practically everything life has ever done on this planet, up to a couple of hundred years ago.

All life is constructed from these elements. No matter how they are utilized, when a life is finished, the material components disperse harmlessly back into the ground, water and air, from which they can again be drawn into other forms of life. Ecosystems have become very efficient at capturing and recycling nearly all of the substances used.

Indeed, with new supplies slowly entering ecosystems from the underlying rocks, life has tended to increase the abundance of substances available for its use. Human beings emerged within this heritage and we have spent 99% of our time totally within these same cycles. For humans to live does not require diminishing this foundation of life.

Let us assume that the political will shifts our goal to sustainability before the present system exhausts conventional oil, or pollutes to the point of catastrophic climate disruption and/or health epidemics.

Lifestyles have always evolved with circumstances. The physical structures, so long as they include adequate nutrition, shelter and tools, do not matter as much as the attitude of the population. The problem of limited energy requires ways to eliminate unnecessary use. The long distances over which practically all our necessities are presently transported could be removed, making way for local employment to provide for local needs. In turn, the smaller firms that local provision supports tend to be more sensitive to the community and the environment where they work.

This positive scenario presupposes that the population has come to realize that its well-being is based on the well-being of the world around them. If the soil is healthy, there will be healthy food. If the community is healthy, the people will do their best to produce quality goods and services for trade to meet each others' needs.

Primitive people didn't have the same sort of accumulated knowledge that we do, but they would have had the same sharp senses, intelligence and creativity to apply to their world. Observations of the land and life, layered generation upon generation, would have resulted in a sensitivity comparable to that of a brain surgeon or a fine artist. While we are as capable as they were, our senses are often preoccupied by objects of our own creation, leaving many of us short of insight into the land and life. If we were to reclaim that intimate knowledge of the natural world and merge it with our present expertise, we could re-align our culture with the life process.

Food

Practically all of our real needs can still be met within the time-tested cycles of nutrient elements. Because of the extent to which our huge population has stretched the ability of natural systems to provide the nutrients we need, special care has to be taken to maintain sufficient supply within agricultural cycles. The basic principle is not complex. Wherever nutrients pass out of the food stream, whether during production, processing, preparation, meals or defecation, they need to be returned, uncontaminated, to biological processes that can render them ready for re-absorption by new plant life.

Recall your "long body," that cumulative total of nutrients that pass into and out of one's body from the moment of conception until one's last breath. Recognition of one's long body can inspire respect, through self-interest, for the nutrient cycles that make our lives possible. Respect and self-interest, coupled with appropriate infrastructure could lead to widespread participation. Burying the nutrient elements from food and "humanure" in landfill sites, or flushing them out to sea where they might be lost as sediment on the ocean floor is stealing from the future. Nutrients lost to the cycles could be the substance needed by our children and grandchildren to build their bodies. Full cycle nutrient management is a crucial concern that will have to become second nature for a mature society the size of ours. If concern for the common good is not sufficient to close the nutrient cycle loop, legislative back-up may be necessary.

Food is our most basic requirement, and the number one candidate for the use of available energy as limitations develop. The shorter the distance between productive soil and dining tables, the greater food security will be, both for delivery of food and for the return of nutrients to the cycle. Such nutrient cycles have a two billion year history and are as accessible to humans as they are to any other creature. Anyone trying to imagine a sustainable order for humans can build the image on the foundation of sustainable nutrient cycles.

Next in importance to food is shelter as provided by clothes and housing. As with our biological metabolism, clothing and housing have, for most of our million year history, been composed of materials grown by other living things. As such, their provision can be sustained.

Clothing

Cotton, linen, silk, hemp, wool, leather, woven grasses and other materials used for clothing and bedding have long served our purposes, often, with style. Presently however, cotton, as an extreme example, is produced in such huge quantities and so aggressively that it is among the most destructive of agricultural activities both in terms of soil degradation and pesticide use. Cotton production accounts for one-quarter of all the pesticides used on crops worldwide. Grown in smaller plots, rather than the thousand acre spreads that are so conducive to pest infestations, and using biologically sensitive techniques, cotton can be with us forever. Other fibres — linen, silk, hemp — cause less disruption in their production cycles and could replace cotton for many uses. In addition, since the scenario we are describing has long-term well-being at its core, the overall volume of cloth needed would be reduced substantially by designing clothes for durability rather than to maximize return on investment. The custom of passing clothing to younger siblings and on to other families as children quickly outgrow their clothes, is long-standing and greatly extended through used clothing outlets. In the days before our disposable society, it was a matter of great pride to have items of clothing that our ancestors had worn. Lederhosen, the leather pants of the Swiss Alps, and various ceremonial garments, preserve that attitude. The concept of keeping up with the latest style was a creation of marketing firms employed to get people to keep buying clothing when they already had enough.

Housing

For millennia, housing has been constructed from local materials: rock and mortar for foundations, wood for framing, straw for insulation, thatch or cedar for roofing. Most of these are available almost everywhere. With the exception of mortar, they are either abundant or renewable. The cement and lime in mortar, while abundant, take energy to produce. Such an energy requirement puts mortar into a special category along with glass for windows, polyethylene for vapour barriers, fibreglass as a more durable insulation, and many of the components that enable running water and electricity. Such components can make housing far more comfortable and convenient than if they were not available. The possibilities for having them available over the long-term depends, to a large extent, on whether we come to steady state ways of living by choice or whether we grasp on to the old system until it disintegrates from its own excesses. At many places in-between, energy-intensive housing components could be maintained to some degree if they are given priority within the available energy budget and if they are produced with durability in mind.

If we can stop wasting energy on unnecessary transport, we may be able to reserve enough for use in the production of special items requiring centralized production. Glass is a good example. To be able to see clearly through glass, in addition to requiring a particular quality of sand, both sides must be near perfectly flat and the pane of a consistent thickness. Flatness is a quality that liquids approach when undisturbed. The state of the art in glass making is to melt the component materials and stream them on to a pool of molten tin. Gravity does its job and the molten glass spreads out evenly across the hot fluid bed. The material then floats off one end to cool and be prepared for distribution. Such "Float Glass" operations understandably require large amounts of energy to become operational. Once the molten metal bed is up to operating temperature, however, much of the heat can be retained within an insulated space, and some of the heat coming off the cooling glass can be used to preheat the materials moving on to the float bed. In the end, such large-scale operations require less energy per window than do smaller operations.

Will we want clear windows in the generations ahead? Will it be possible? If we choose an early acceptance of our maturity, as a species, there will be many places where we can balance the advantages of centralized, large-scale production of special goods, with our ability to transport those goods over distances.

A population whose numbers are stabilized through education and old age security will eventually provide a huge opportunity to catch up with housing needs. From that stage, as population numbers slowly recede toward a sustainable level, the lowest quality housing could be recycled, leading, eventually to higher quality overall.

Durability and easy maintenance are important to anything we produce. While we still have abundant energy available, we are well-advised to upgrade the energy efficiency of the housing stock and to establish techniques and facilities for the relatively local provision of as many of the materials needed to maintain those houses as possible.

With food, clothing, shelter, and a variety of tools and utensils, our lives can be maintained in good health and with a positive outlook. Once necessities are assured, we can look at all the other things that we might want in our lives and apply our creativity to seeing how they could be produced in a durable, non-polluting manner. The systems criteria of the Natural Step (Chapter 12) or the basic outline of sustainability inside the front cover, provide design criteria with which to work. Given the experience we have had with human ingenuity to date, once the goal has been legitimized, we can expect wide-spread, creative innovations. There is a huge versatility in the ways that the planet's millions of species use the building blocks of life. We have the ability to expand on those techniques. We can secure long-term well-being by avoiding toxic materials and conscientiously recycling non-biological substances, while maintaining the biological precedent for everything else to be re-absorbed, harmlessly, into the greater cycles of life.

In the City

While the proposals above may be easier to imagine in rural settings where land and sunshine abound, the reality is that most of us live in cities. The main problem for people in cities is their detachment from the source of the goods on which they depend. Obscured by masses of buildings and activity, and supported by mass-market economics, people seldom get a glimpse of the actual supply processes that support them. Nevertheless, there are some advantages in concentrated settlements and there is a great deal that individuals can do to help adapt cities for the times ahead.

The challenge everywhere is to acknowledge that the job needs to be done. Awareness is growing about the material needs of cities and the impacts that they have — their ecological footprint. While the lands needed to support cities are many times greater than the territory upon which the cities are built, those lands need not be as great in volume, nor as far away as they presently tend to be.

Because food is a key necessity, a relationship with soil and nutrient cycles has to be established and maintained. Cities are often built on the planet's best soils. While it has been a huge loss that must not increase, much opportunity exists for cycling nutrients on the remaining spaces between the buildings on urban lands. Rooftop gardens have proven an effective way to grow food locally in cities. They can increase the availability of fresh vegetables, help keep buildings cool and provide personal experience of natural processes. Even when cities are surrounded with marginal soil, such volumes of nutrients are flowing through the population that it would not take long to build up fertility once the critical importance of nutrient cycling is recognized.

The compactness of cities offers some advantages. Efficiencies of scale can work in favour of both nutrient cycling and all manner of enterprises aiming to trade one form of provision for others. People collect in cities for such opportunities. What goods or services might you be able to provide for local trade? What goods and services are available locally that you can draw on? The more local provision there is, the stronger the foundation will be for the post-petroleum age.

If a local currency or trading system can be established, so much the better. Besides freedom from the downward suction of conventional money, local, interest-free money gives local businesses an edge. Huge, remotely run businesses, which send money out of the communities where they operate, have little use for local money. In contrast, local businesses that spend their earnings in the community, find that it can serve many of their purposes. In the event that financial speculators target one's national currency, or there is an unfortunate reckoning in global finance overall, communities with local currencies will already have a medium for continued trading.

Concentrated populations offer more than abundant opportunities for trade. Cities offer all manner of life-based prospects. Whether one is interested in learning, sport, entertainment, creativity or socializing, there are plenty of contacts to be made with people who would share such pursuits.

Possibilities for genuine progress exist in abundance, but the will to move in that direction has to gain priority. Community associations with their newspapers, meeting places and citizens' networks provide channels for raising awareness and sharing ideas. In a sustainable world, politics will be a customary extension of socializing that will provide opportunities for co-intelligence and long-term problem-solving. Aware candidates can inform the electorate. An aware population will elect councilors who can lead the reorientation, and municipal councils can enact significant changes. City taxes are spent, in large part, on environmental services, making municipal government a gateway to environmental adaptation. Water, sewage, air quality, transportation and energy rank high among municipal concerns. While time may yet pass before the general population acknowledges the call, a municipal government can start improving the performance of the local "metabolism" and shift the entire community toward more sustainable living.

A municipal index of well-being is one place to start. Establishing such an index can provide a focus around which a community can identify what they feel is important. Whatever a community chooses, whether it be clean air, clean water, food security, energy security, community cohesion, adequate employment, reduced crime, cultural opportunities or other factors, once the issues are identified, measuring techniques can be established to indicate if they are improving or deteriorating. Such measuring systems are effective at drawing public attention to the issues involved. In turn, municipal councilors, and anyone else making decisions have a much broader perspective upon which to weigh the pros and cons of the decisions they are making.

Individuals can contribute to long-term security through respectful use of water, energy and sewage systems. Conservation saves money and reduces the ecological footprint. Energy-efficient lights, motors and appliances can stretch energy resources to maintain levels of comfort while reducing consumption. The same can be done for water, by using state of the art shower heads, low flow toilets, plus general respect and appreciation for the resource. Keeping toxic substances out of sewage is a critical step requiring only common sense. Planting shade trees for natural air conditioning, and building and renovating houses to take advantage of the Sun for heating and light are one-time efforts that can provide benefits for generations.

Each individual can contribute to meeting the challenge. The vast numbers of individuals in cities constitute a huge creative force for advancing the necessary adaptation.

There are many organizations working on "Green Cities." Do an Internet search and see what is current.

Population

A gradual reduction of the population seems natural wherever societies achieve material security. If the shift from a capital-based to a life-based culture can be made before a crash limits our options, it should be possible for the population to shrink toward sustainable levels through natural attrition. If not, whatever net of sustainable systems can be woven in the meantime will eventually catch the population when its traumatic decline brings it to within the range that can be supported. It cannot be overstated that a willful shift will leave us with far more options than would a crash and recovery approach. Anyone who worries that the population will drop too low does not appreciate the enormity of the present problem, nor the resilient sexuality of people, should a falling population ever become a real problem.

The fossil energy presently available, if carefully managed, could serve us in the same way that the yolk of an egg serves the embryo living from it. It can provide the nourishment to set things up in ways that will enable us to provide for ourselves when the yolk is used up and we "hatch" into the new era. We can use available energy to assure an abundance of nutrients in our food cycles, to produce durable building components and to maintain some reserves for further experimentation within the new system.

Needs and Desires

It is critical, as we recreate mutual provision in a sustainable form, that we keep track of the line between needs and wants. While a permanent place for people on Earth requires that our needs be met, people gathering about themselves quantities of unnecessary goods, while others lack food and shelter, cannot be part of a durable order. A society that oppresses other people to bloat itself will not stop at undermining foreign nations. The ethic will express itself with exploitation at home. While ingenuity and hard work will still lead to improved circumstances as communities increase the effectiveness by which they use local resources, when one's achieved affluence is at the expense of others, much good-will, effort, and resources will be lost to resentment, rebellion and repression. A huge bonus is available for everyone when the focus of development is securing and improving the quality of life for all.

Personal Fulfillment

We can no longer have everything we want,
but we can be more than we ever imagined.
Howard Jerome

Once material necessities are taken care of, the greatest potential for increasing satisfaction with life is in the realm of life itself. Whereas material consumption will always be subject to limitations, what we can gain from life far surpasses anything for which any individual will ever have time. That so many have lost sight of our potential as human beings is a side effect of the largest propaganda machine the world has ever known.

Advertisers emerged with the age of industrialization. Each enterprise took the steps it felt were necessary to sell more of its product. Collectively, it has been an enormous project. Once we passed the stage of enough, people then had to be trained to forget the frugality we had practiced since ancient times. For the industrial world to perpetuate its growth, people had to want things that they would likely never have thought existed, and they had to be convinced to discard what they already had, to make way for new purchases. Advertising evolved from simple notification that goods or services were available, to a sophisticated psychological/social science that, through massive application, implants at the core of our beings the urge to consume.

Advertising will have to become responsible to long-term interests for the new paradigm to find natural receptivity in the popular mind. Whether this is through voluntary measures, legal restrictions, or a toll levied on messages aimed at public persuasion, balance needs to be achieved. To escape from the material consumption trap, we will have to tone down the enormous effort spent convincing people to buy more. Instead, time and creativity could be directed toward introducing the opportunities that living offers for personal fulfillment. Opportunities that don't draw down natural resources, release toxic substances or exploit other people. As described earlier, these life-based pursuits are so easily enjoyed that they often produce little or no financial revenue, hence, there is little profit available to be used for their promotion. A toll on the promotion of non-essential material goods, or simply the elimination of tax exemptions for advertising them (beyond the level of basic notification that they are available), could provide resources to encourage life-based activities. This change would greatly reduce our demands on the material world.

Health and Belonging

Materially, good health depends on good nutrition, sanitation, clean air and adequate shelter. These are products of mutual provision and everyone needs access to them. Beyond gaining material security, participating in mutual provision has a positive effect on psychological health. Being appreciated by one's community is a significant factor contributing to physical and emotional health. Other factors of well-being, which are entirely within the realm of life-based activities, are relative equality, acceptance, peace of mind, and opportunities for personal development.

Local provision can contribute to personal well-being by giving a far greater proportion of the population opportunities to provide service to people they know, and to experience the resulting appreciation in return. Such appreciation fills an inner void that otherwise leaves people seeking something, anything, to fill it. In the "long-arm's-length" world of global trade this void is continuously targeted by advertising, which asserts that buying products will fill it.

The void, however, is a thing of the heart, of life, and it exists on an entirely different plane from anything that can be purchased. Consumer goods can never deliver. They can only distract, and extract our personal resources, leaving us more susceptible to anxiety and disease.

A secure, loving caregiver in the early years of a person's life has been found to be the single largest factor determining the health and well-being of those people in later life. Beyond that, participation in the provision of food and shelter, establishes basic security. Once basic needs are met, and childhood wounds addressed, whether life is personally exhilarating or a struggle is largely a matter of attitude.

When, as a society, we shed the self-centeredness of childhood and assume the confidence of maturity, we will cultivate customs for enabling every individual to work through past traumas and misfortunes, great and small, which inhibit peace of mind. While this would take a great deal of good will, the material cost would be practically nothing. The result would be people largely immune to propaganda and willing to cooperate on the task of maintaining civilization on a sustainable course.

Celebrating Life

A social order capable of spanning the centuries ahead will act on the understanding of human nature that has evolved over time. Upon that understanding we can revitalize the once great mainstay of culture — our ability to find fulfillment through living. Overshadowed by the hype and glitter of mushrooming material production and its accompanying promotion, we can still find within each person a vibrant bud of this ability. Many of us have found satisfaction passing time in creative activities: sports, interpersonal relations, art, music, education and other expressions of these latent qualities. The most fortunate among us have found ways to support ourselves thereby. A convivial society, where people again trade the products of their skills, rather than selling their time into anonymous systems, will offer far more opportunity for exercising these attributes. As the propaganda of consumption diminishes, the satisfaction derived from living will rise. As more and more people find life personally satisfying, they will create a cultural example that will open others up to the possibilities.

Already today, people who want mostly what life offers, and are thereby successful at living the lifestyle of voluntary simplicity, are the envy of those in debt bondage. Imagine, if you are not already doing this, getting all the material stuff you need and want by working halftime, living free from the pressure of debt, and having much of your time available to do whatever it is that you would do if you didn't have to work all the time.

The voluntary simplicity movement will expand as contentment is increasingly realized to be a matter of life-based accomplishments. Within a framework of mutual provision that assures health and well-being without the risk of rebellion, life-based pursuits are the bright light revealing the end of the tunnel of humankind's extended adolescence. Living within the boundaries of planetary ecology will be as logical a precaution as respecting the boundaries that deter us from walking across freeways at rush hour. It is literally as sensible as loving our children.

Adventure

Personal security and satisfaction are sufficient for many people, but what about the drive others feel for adventure and to expand the boundaries of the possible?

Once we have food in our bellies and shelter to return to, the human appetite for adventure, novelty, satisfaction and much else that drives us can be provided within the realm of life's possibilities. Individually, and with others, what happens within and between our hearts and minds has little to do with physical ecological reality.

Much of the urge to expand boundaries can be satisfied by exploring human experience. As long as there are people who are uncomfortable in themselves, there will be a need to further understand human nature and pioneer techniques for sharing that understanding so that life becomes a quality experience for everyone.

Each of our lives is a universe unto itself. Each of us continually integrates everything we sense, feel, and think with every other experience that we have had. Coupled with our genetics, and other circumstances of origin, there is no one else in the world the same as any one of us. More than six billion parallel universes. Furthermore, when two or more of these universes interact as family, friends, lovers, associates, or in organizations, communities and nations, the opportunities for facilitating better outcomes multiply. Better understanding can lead to more effective interaction. For those craving territory to explore, and wishing to help others realize their personal potential, the scope in this realm is practically unlimited.

Material Innovation

Perhaps not as abundant, but still ample, are the opportunities for exploration and innovation in the material world. While this realm has enabled us to disrupt life and threaten the future, it also includes a huge range of sustainable possibilities. As a calling, research and experimentation can provide enormous satisfaction to those drawn to understand the wonders of the world. Such knowledge can also lead to innovations that can improve long-term well-being. As long as we distinguish between innovations that undermine sustainability and those that enhance it, the exploration, discovery and utilization of new material opportunities will remain a viable challenge for the ambitious.

There is a long history of people becoming rich thanks to making material innovations. Discover something useful or interesting for our mass culture, and "the world will beat a path to your door." Significant contributions will, no doubt, be made to our material well-being for eons to come. However, because we all share a single planet, and because we have grown to meet its limits, we have to assure that those who desire to get rich from innovations do not undermine long-term well-being. Vigilance has to be maintained in assessing the safety of such innovations, particularly as we penetrate deeper and deeper into the core structures of matter and life. Much damage has been done in the past by the premature commercialization of chemical innovations. In the future, new chemicals and new forms of life must be proven safe long before they have any chance of disrupting the living world and its cycles.

The institution of well-being measurement is critical. As a society we need to keep all possible senses open for any kind of problem that might arise. As long as our collective sensory system is healthy and unrestrained, we will be able to respond quickly to problematic trends and circumstances. With such sensitivity in place, the search for opportunity can continue.

Exploration often finds ways around perceived barriers. The "atom" was once, by definition, the smallest portion into which matter could be divided. Today, atoms are understood to consist of numerous smaller components. More recently, the possibilities for communications have burst through boundaries previously thought to be impenetrable. I remember being given a floppy disk containing a "hypertext" document. It was a tremendous innovation in communications, but I was told that it required so much information to be directly accessible that it would never be possible to use over the budding electronic mail (email) system. Today, "hypertext" documents flow at the speed of light — millions of billions of bytes daily — through phone lines, cable and microwaves. (Hypertext is what the "ht" stands for in the "http://www" that connects the World Wide Web.)

We need not worry about the goal of sustainability resulting in a lack of opportunities for those who wish to explore. Young activists today are inspiring examples. Since they could first see, pictures of the Earth as a finite ball in empty space have been part of their experience. Much of the design criteria of sustainability is second nature to them. While they are making sense of the world in general (as young humans have always had to do) Spaceship Earth is a given, like gravity, and the Internet. Their inventive exploration starts with the recognition of these design criteria, yet they do not find their lives boring.

Sensitive Transition

At present, society is like a huge tree with numerous limbs representing different sorts of activities. Many of the limbs are sound, filling real needs without causing serious harm. Other limbs represent activities that are endangering long-term well-being, some very seriously. Everywhere there are buds of new activity that receive only enough light to grow a leaf or two. Anyone who has pruned a tree, or watched a tree recover from a lost limb, will recognize the following parallel to social transformation.

When we choose to develop a sustainable order, there will be limbs that have to be pruned back. The need for social stability and ongoing cooperation require that those involved in these areas be assisted in finding new ways to participate. In many communities, there are people working on sustainable enterprises that deal locally with local skills and local resources. Many of these are equivalent to the little twigs setting out their leaves to catch the Sun. When unsustainable branches are removed, the energy they previously absorbed will reach the leaves on those twigs increasing their ability to grow. Replacing fossil energy with conservation and renewable energy would parallel such a case. When the old industries no longer consume the bulk of resources, the new branches of activity will thrive.

If one is pruning a big tree, ridding it of inappropriately positioned or diseased limbs, it is advisable not to remove too much too fast. There has to be sufficient foliage to support the roots and trunk. New growth thrives on the new opportunities and will support further pruning in seasons to come. While trees do not put energy into what has been lost, a broken limb can enable rot to enter. A purposeful cut, because it is clean and dries out quickly after a rain, will have fewer problems than a broken branch. Similarly, when sectors of our present industrial structure have to be replaced by more sustainable alternatives, it is far better to do it with forethought and care than to leave such adjustments to the process of collapse and recovery.

Many of the economic techniques described earlier were designed to accommodate the transition to sustainability. Rather than aggressive pruning jobs, such adaptations would tend, incrementally, to thin out problematic activities and allow resources to flow into the new work that solutions require. Good economic rules can level the playing field sufficiently that opportunity alone is no longer sufficient for a new product to spring past any negative impacts and fill the market. Pollution, excess resource consumption or the exploitation of others would weigh against problematic products and retard dangerous developments before they multiply.

There is nothing new in this sort of moderation. Rules to cover considerations of fairness and ecological health will not stifle innovation any more than do the present rules that disallow bombing competing factories or murdering their executives. Designers would no longer be faced with the choice between making sense and making money. In order to make money, they would have to make sense.

There will probably never be a shortage of opportunities to discover new ways of doing things and to make one's fortune by improving the human condition. This will be particularly true as we shed the caterpillar skin of our material growth oriented form. As we become the "butterfly" of a sustainable culture, there are enormous areas where innovation will be necessary to recreate mutual provision. Those who discover and implement the new components will be heroes and will be rewarded appropriately.

Insights from the new biology point increasingly to the tendency for living things to cooperate as individuals within larger associations of individuals. Experience with co-intelligence shows that when people gather around common interests and express their views with the openness that comes from trusting, no is dismissed and creative solutions emerge. Opinions that, on first expression appear contradictory, come to be seen as different dimensions of the same issue. With the perspective gained from such discussion, solutions arise that take everyone and all of their concerns into account.

We have been enculturated to follow competitive self-interest for so long that we are often disadvantaged by lack of trust and collective vision. Making the shift in priorities is the largest part of the challenge. If we so choose, competitive self-interest can give way to positive feedback and cooperation.

The co-intelligent approach to mutual aid has likely been with us since language first emerged — perhaps before. Rooted in antiquity, techniques for thinking and acting together get recreated when need arises. The use our society makes of our immense collective potential is haphazard at best. As our greatest hope for moving successfully through this time of passage, it is scarcely recognized, let alone tapped.

Forming governments through proportional representation (PR) can be a step toward co-intelligence on the institutional level. In the winner takes all system, used in Canada and the U.S., where political parties see each other as adversaries, each party seeks majority power so that they can ignore the others and do things the way they want. With PR, it is much less likely that any single party would be able to do as they please, ignoring the interests of others. Members of governing bodies, elected proportionally to the public's divergent attitudes, would be forced to cooperate to find solutions that serve a variety of interests. It makes sense that, over time, as governments get used to collaborative problem solving, some of the synergy of co-intelligence will enter the picture. As a central institution, the process followed by government sets an example. Cooperation rather than competition could be expected to influence the internal workings of political parties and private institutions.

Reclaiming Politics

Back in the 1920s we had the capability to serve all human need in the industrialized world. What if we had used that capacity to eliminate need, and shared what we had learned with the developing world? If, rather than expanding the public's appetite for consumption and wild speculation in financial markets, we had followed the other path, the next decade might have begun an extraordinary new age. Had pressing need been abolished at that stage in history, basic security would have been available to all, and the global population would have stabilized at a level that could easily be sustained.

What will it take to choose that route today and overcome the problems that have grown serious since that time? While we are already in for a rough ride, the longer we put off acknowledging the need, the more difficult our challenge becomes. Whatever the fate human kind will enjoy or suffer, we will be well advanced toward that state by the time today's children are raising children of their own.

There are millions of people around the world working on recreating civilization. Collectively, we can achieve sustainable ways to live. Your continued actions, if you are already involved, or, your time, inspiration and patronage, if you take up the challenge today, are important. Given legitimacy and the mechanical strength that is still available to help reorganize material structures in the short-term, the pioneering work underway today could spawn the transformation around the world.

The changes outlined in Chapters 11, 12 and 13 are structural and will multiply the efforts of citizens many times over. Legitimizing indicators to track changes in social, environmental and economic well-being will bring problems to light sooner and will help identify which solutions work best. Full-cost accounting, tax shifting, forms of governance that recognize the need of every person to participate in mutual provision and the right to create local currencies, can turn the entire process toward long-term well-being. Instituting such reforms requires political process. Bad government is the price we pay for not getting involved.

One of the hallmarks of the new era would be a more positive attitude toward politics. There has certainly been enough unfair advantage taken by politicians to make people want to stay away. However, as citizens shy away from the political process, other interests line up to apply pressure. Ordinary citizens, without large financial stakes to advance, make up the vast majority of the population. Our immediate interests tend to be personal livelihood and the well-being of our families and our communities. We have the numbers to set the agenda. Popular involvement in politics will result in far more attention being paid to these concerns. Without clear messages from ordinary citizens, however, politicians have little to base their decisions on besides the urgings of those motivated by, or paid from, expanding wealth.

It has taken more than petty abuse to give politics its bad name. In the Canadian elections of 2004 and 2006, a huge fuss was made about a hundred million dollar patronage fund. Money was passed to companies that were friends of the government in ways that many thought were not in the public's interest. A hundred million dollars is a lot of money, but it is inconsequential in comparison to the interest pay-off for the Canadian Government's use of debt-based money. Presently, each year, this unreported humiliation costs 650 times as much as the patronage fund. Over the years, the total pay-out of taxpayers dollars exceeds five thousand times that of the patronage scandal.

The negative attitudes about government and politics, stimulate a sense of deja vu. Is it not similar to the rebellion against the direct tax on tobacco and the fight against pollution controls on cars? Like the tobacco tax, and automobile emission controls, when issues come up that might diminish profits, the corporate owned media emit messages suggesting that people should oppose such moves. Ever since Samuel Huntington, writing for the Trilateral Commission, suggested that there was an "excess of democracy," rhetoric to discredit government and actions to reduce it, have taken a toll.

Less government means less discussion about what actions to take and less accountability for the impacts of decisions. Even with present shortcomings, government action is the product of different points of view being discussed and compared. It is the primary medium by which public will can become public action. When people become disengaged, moneyed interests have increasingly free reign to consume resources, pollute and to mold our institutions so that they might advance toward the End Game.

Political will ought to be the public's will. Government is an institution appointed by the votes we cast and supported by the taxes we pay. Collective persuasion is indeed the only power available to those without vast fortunes or aggressive weapons. The stakes are high as we are presently directed to turn the Earth into money. Nevertheless, we can still talk with others, share our views and promote a political agenda for taking intelligent steps toward securing the future. Inspired by the changing relationship between people and the Earth, Green Parties have arisen in a hundred countries around the world. They are united by a common vision, recognizing current problems, and creating practical policies for addressing them.

If you are aligned with another political party, see where they stand on these critical issues and use your connection to encourage your party to adapt and implement changes for sustainability. Measuring well-being with a Genuine Progress Index is a good place to start.

Politics need not be a dirty game. It does not need to be about channelling society's wealth toward one community of supporters or another. If we are successful at awakening the public to the need for "full world" responsibilities, governments will turn into cooperative bodies working to coordinate the reorganization of society.

A Shift in Priorities: Local Trading

Monetary reform is a crucial detail. The present system milks us like a herd of dairy cattle and has indentured much of the world. The value extracted by interest, through the present system of money creation, is like a tax. However, for taxes paid to government we get services like education, health care and social security. For the interest "tax" we get nothing that a sovereign people could not provide for themselves at minimal cost. If, rather than complaining about taxes and accepting the costs of debt-based money, we empowered government with our taxes and limited the budget haemorrhage of interest payments to private lenders, government would become cost-effective and could lead the way to sustainability.

Effective monetary reform at the national level will likely require international cooperation, yet, any system of local currency serves the dual purpose of sidestepping the extractive process, and educating participants as to how money functions as the blood of our communities. This could be done at the national level through a national bank, but while we wait for governments to take leadership on this, any community can move forward.

Communities that have set up local exchange systems, whether electronic, such as the LETS programs or with paper currencies like Turkey, Argentina and Ithaca, New York, not only come to understand the advantage of having an exchange system with no interest, they have a system in place that can replace a lot of chaos in the event that international finance succumbs to its own excesses.

Elder Care: A Litmus Test

One indicator that the shift in consciousness has taken place will be seen in how we care for our elders. In the present system, retirement possibilities are, for the most part, based on the assumption that we live on money and the expectation that the economic system will continue expanding. Pension funds are volumes of money invested largely in resource extraction, manufacturing and abstract financial speculation. Pension payments are made from the income generated by those investments as they grow. It is a support system subject to all the dangerous limitations of the old Monopoly Game.

When the perpetual expansion of production and consumption finally snaps, the expectation that our elders (perhaps, ourselves by that time) will be able to draw on expanding financial accounts will be found lacking in substance.

The historical, default precaution against suffering in old age has been to have as many children as possible in expectation that some will survive and care for one when one cannot care for one's self. The problem of an expanding population on our full Earth makes this a self-defeating option.

In a sustainable world, the security of the aging population will be more directly tied into the security of its communities. Economic systems that produce food, and maintain the skills to fashion local materials into shelter, will be able to sustain people while they take care of other aspects of mutual provision. While it is possible for local provision to fail in some areas, such failure would more often be local rather than international. The possibility could remain for neighbouring communities to help.

In the sustainable scenario, a stabilized population will be an asset to security. Assuring that we will not have to suffer in old age removes the need to double and redouble production to serve an expanding population. After a lifetime of mutual provision, individuals will have earned a place in the life supporting process. The space in which they have been living may not be suitable for their final years, but without an expanding population we will have long since caught up with housing needs. Indeed, one of the prime opportunities to make a contribution to mutual provision will be in the maintenance of housing stock. With most nutritional needs being supplied by the cycling of nutrients in nearby areas, all participants in a trading community will have access to the elements of sustenance. Surpluses would likely be shared in a manner reflecting individual contributions.

If this difference in how old age security can be managed is clear, glimpses of a sustainable future are possible. Tapping into the cash flow of an expanding financial system can be replaced with that which comes from stable life-supporting systems, rooted in community and enduring ecological systems.

Closing Thoughts

By definition, any species whose life process is not sustainable, will pass away. Even with the extensive trespassing of our adolescent phase, humans are a prime candidate for a very long stay on Earth.

We are truly extraordinary in our capabilities. We need only break away from the obsolete system of perpetual growth and legitimize the urge to secure well-being for the long-term. We do not need to await our crash on the rocks of destiny to confirm that we are in trouble.

We have a classic "Catch-22" situation. If the life perspective had clear legitimacy, the vast majority of people would join the reformation. If they were to join in, the perspective would clearly be seen as legitimate and the inclination to participate would flow naturally. Instead, we are urged by the perceived legitimacy to press on with expansion. Discomfort and fear for the future grow with the contrast between the external order and the considerations recognized as valid by conscience and reason. After 30 years of working to clarify the goal of sustainability, this book and the work to follow, aim to energize the issue to the point that it will jump the gap between individual recognition and accepted legitimacy.

The signs that this change must take place are all about us. Practically everyone knows, at some level, of the trouble we are in today. Share your feelings with those around you. Break the silence that comes from feeling we are alone with our concerns. If you don't speak up, how will your neighbours know that their concerns are shared? "What's the point?" they might ask, "Everyone else just wants to get ahead." If you don't talk with them, who will? Enough alternatives have been pioneered that, when the popular will becomes apparent, we could move quickly forward. The task at hand is to cultivate and to reveal that popular will.

As a population we have many ways to communicate with each other to demonstrate the new legitimacy. The greatest obstacle is the ability of a very small portion of the population to launch enormous volumes of communications, contradicting the call for change. Without popular participation in advancing the message of transformation, mass media will outweigh our efforts. It is important that we recognize this engine of apparent legitimacy as the minority view that it is.

Those controlling big media are at a disadvantage when it comes to acknowledging the need for change. They have been true to the principles of the "invisible hand" and it has worked well for them, thereby reinforcing their belief in the passing paradigm. Yet, the need for change is irrefutable when observed without bias. While they have the bias of their obvious success, they are also parents, uncles and aunts. The inspiration to do the right thing for the next generation has roots that run far deeper than self-interest. If those in controlling positions are approached person to person in the spirit of cooperation, rather than as adversaries, they will have the opportunity to join in. They should be leaders pointing toward what must be done. If not, their views, even as multiplied by the media, may yet be overruled by the larger population, through democratic means. Eventually, they will be replaced by their own young who will not be able to avoid awareness of Spaceship Earth's limitations.

Not long ago it became obvious that the reasons for invading Iraq in 2003 were mistaken, if not outright lies. Outrage can result when people who believe in justice and the rule of law find that they have been conned on a world-class scale into accommodating the desecration of both. A brutal war inspired by the thirst for oil might be the last straw that leads large numbers of people to realize that the material expansion model is sputtering over its peak and heading for decline. If this round of violence does not shock the belief system, perhaps the next desperate measures taken to feed mushrooming material requirements will. Or, perhaps a series of climate-related disasters, or some other consequence of our accumulating waste will reveal the ecological bankruptcy of the passing order. If popular will can raise the sustainability vision to legitimacy, we can secure the future. We have until the industrial giants begin fighting directly with each other to see which will feed its continued growth on the ruins of the others.

After World War II, specialists were sent to Germany and Japan to assess how long it would take to reconstruct those shattered countries. As vast as the destruction of buildings and infrastructure was, it turned out that the material structures were only a small part of those societies. The people, their knowledge and their skills and access to resources were still largely intact. Once the destruction stopped, and the goal established to rebuild, the work was accomplished in far less time than the experts had predicted.

While the reconstruction funds provided through the Marshall and MacArthur Plans was instrumental because it enabled the people to begin rebuilding and to resume trading their skills in mutual provision, the rekindling of mutual provision could have been accomplished with local currencies had they been allowed and respected. Every part of any society exists thanks to people working with the resources of the land and life. Creativity is a product of being human. An effective currency enables us, by the millions, to merge our creative abilities into a synergetic whole capable of unimaginably huge tasks.

Such potential can be applied to creating a sustainable order, if we choose that goal. With the new legitimacy established we could expect our collective ingenuity to bring the vision about with an elegance never before experienced. Have we the will to set our sights on a mature social order — one where we responsibly apply what we know about the Earth and about human needs? Will you speak to taking such a path? Will you walk upon it?

Appendix: Tapping Our Collective Potential

Tapping our Collective Potential

While "two heads are better than one" is time honoured knowledge, there is a catch.

Co-intelligence requires open, trusting communication. This is not always easy in a world flooded with audiovisual imagery of people taking offense, expressing indignation and getting even. We learn by example, and the television/video/DVD industry now produces a large proportion of what many individuals presently experience as human interaction. Under pressure, we draw rapidly on our mental store of experience, and pseudo-experience, to form the thoughts we express. One careless phrase can change an interaction from one of trust to one of suspicion. From suspicion it is not far to the frustration, anger and obstruction that can paralyze a group that might, otherwise, have worked very effectively together.

Those who dare to look at the challenge of our times can be particularly prone to suspicion. While a solid faith in human potential might enable one to escape paralysis, fear is often not far from the surface. We are in extreme danger, and suspicion is a complement to the fight or flight response by which creatures have escaped danger since long before humans appeared.

It is also the case that those of us who feel that the popular legitimacy must change, have taken a bold step. Having taken issue with the conventional legitimacy once, it is not as hard a second time to challenge the emerging wisdom of our own organizations. Times of change are volatile.

Allies and Spies

At a conference I attended last year, the organizers had every participant draw a slip of paper from a hat. We were told that, according to the note we had each drawn, we were to play the role of either an Ally or a Spy.

We were then divided into groups, and given a topic related to the conference theme. We were asked to seek consensus on the topic. If during the discussion, anyone suspected another participant of being a spy, a vote was initiated. If the majority in that group believed the person to be guilty, he or she was barred from speaking.

After the designated time, eight of the ten groups had censured people. The facilitator then explained that all of the slips of paper from the draw said "Ally." There were no "Spies."

Following the game, we were asked how we felt. Some of the people who had made the accusations were embarrassed to find that they had jumped to a false conclusion, based only on the suspicion that there were spies among them. Those fearing accusation and rejection found the exercise intimidating. Afraid they would be taken for "spies," they had censured themselves from expressing dissenting views. Some of these mentioned feelings of shame at not having had the courage to speak up. Many of those deemed as "spies," even though they were "allies," expressed feelings of betrayal and rejection. Because distrust had run rampant in both directions, many good ideas were lost to the discussion. As a result of the exercise, participants better understood that differing opinions do not necessarily mean people should be distrusted.

It Is From the Clash of Differing Opinions that the Light of Truth Shines

What follows is a procedure that a group can adopt to tap into its greatest potential for its work together. "Consultation" is a recipe for co-intelligent meetings.

Assembling in a circle gives form to the assertion that everyone is equal. In a circle, each person can hear everyone else directly and be heard clearly in return.

Come together with confidence that there are solutions to whatever issues you are going to discuss. Identifying the topics to be discussed in advance enables some premeditation that will help prepare participants for the occasion.

Before getting down to business, it helps to take a few moments to focus attention on the spirit of the gathering, the whole that is greater than all the individuals present. Sometimes joining hands to connect the circle for a few moments of silence is helpful. The mood of the meeting can be further guided by expressing together the wish, silently or verbally, for guidance and inspiration. While focussing on the synergetic potential of the group, or whatever sense of a higher power participants hold, ask for help to make the best possible decisions for the effectiveness of the group, for the well-being of the next seven generations and for all life on Earth.

So met, the gathering is ready to proceed. The four techniques below can guide discussion to more productive ends.

1. When an idea leaves a person's lips, it no longer belongs to the individual but becomes the possession of the circle.
Individuals let go of the ideas they offer, and comments are directed at the ideas and not at the people who happened to introduce them. Ideas can be too important to carry the baggage of individual personalities. Without this precaution good ideas are sometimes neglected for reasons that have no relationship to the idea's content.

Every effort should be made to avoid ridiculing anything that is presented. Intimidation of any sort will discourage people from offering divergent views and the whole group will be poorer for the loss of perspective. The precaution of separating ideas from the people who voice them creates a safe environment that encourages adherence to the second rule.

2. Express everything that comes to heart or mind on the topic being discussed, even if it goes against what you feel yourself or the mood of the meeting.
This is sometimes called brain-storming. The mind in free-association can come up with ideas that have not been considered before. They are worth adding to the process. Even ideas that seem to contradict one's personal views should be expressed. The same person might express both pros and cons to an argument. If they do not, some perspective on the topic might go unexpressed, depriving the group of the broadest possible perspective from which to consider its plans. If the topic of discussion has been researched elsewhere, an effort should be made to include the research findings for consideration as well.

3. When conflicting views do arise, they are not to be avoided.
Differing opinions must come into contact so that the sparks of their confrontation can illuminate the truth of the matter. At these times, however, it

is most important to remember that it is the ideas that are clashing and not the people. There is no harm in this sort of confrontation if the group has been diligent in detaching the ideas from the people; indeed, valuable insights can be gained from the exchange. Recall the wish at the commencement of the meeting for decisions to emerge that are best for all involved. If this wish is sincere, participants can watch the fireworks of the interaction in anticipation that the truth of the matter will emerge when all is said and considered.

4. After all views have been heard and considered, if total agreement is not reached but a significant majority feel they have identified an appropriate course of action, dissenters are asked to go along with the plan.

The purpose of this is to avoid confusion about the decision when it is being implemented. If there is not total cooperation in implementing a decision, and the action fails, it will not be clear whether the failure resulted from a wrong decision or from the lack of cooperation. The distinction is important for guiding future actions.

Since all perspectives are to be given fair consideration at the time of the meeting, any shortcoming arising as the plan unfolds will be viewed in the light of the divergent views. If everyone is trying to make the plan work and it doesn't, it will be clear that something is wrong with the decision, and it can be reconsidered at another meeting.

Attitudes

Attitude can make all the difference. If cultivated, the following attitudes can help the process become increasingly effective.

Courtesy:
Listening with interest to all ideas expressed and speaking the content of one's own mind fully and with clarity.
Aspiration: allowing and encouraging our better selves to dominate our weaknesses.

Detachment:
Allowing equal respect for all views whether they come from our own lips or from someone else's.

Humility:
Removing the obstacle of one's own importance and thereby enabling serious consideration of what others say.

Patience:
Hearing all that is being said before forming judgments.

Service:

Accepting the responsibility of looking for the truth by expressing all that comes to mind related to the topic and in turn listening to all opinions put forward.

Consideration:

Topics of sustainability require that consideration go beyond the interests of the people present. Success requires including the interests of other people, both those alive today, and those who will be living in the future. In addition, the interests of the other living things, with whom we share the Earth, and the Earth as a whole, need to be held respectfully in mind.

When the topic at hand has been fully discussed, the group can then make its decision about what actions to take. Who will do what; what effects are expected from the action; and how will the effects observed be compared to those anticipated? Finally, the information gathered, following an action stage, can provide feedback for subsequent meetings, enabling the group to move forward towards its goals.

Recommended Reading

Adams, Patricia & Solomon, Lawrence. *In the Name of Progress: The Underside of Foreign Aid* (Energy Probe Research Foundation, 1991) ISBN 0919849121

Adler, Mortimer (Ed.). *The Great Ideas,* (Encyclopædia Britannica, 1952) ISBN 0852295316

Arnold, Thurman. *The Folklore of Capitalism,* (Beard Books, 1937) ISBN 1587980258

Atlee, Tom. *The Tao of Democracy* (The Writer's Collective, 2003) ISBN 193213347X

Bacher, John. *Petrotyranny* (Dundurn Press, 2000) ISBN 0888669569

Berger, Janice. *Emotional Fitness: Discovering Our Natural Healing Power* (Prentice Hall, Canada, 2000) ISBN 013018182X

Blewett, Duncan B. *The Frontiers of Being* (Award Books, New York, 1969)

Braden, Gregg. *Walking Between The Worlds: The Science of Compassion* (Radio Bookstore Press, 1997) ISBN 1889071056

Briggs, John & Peat, David. *Seven Life Lessons of Chaos* (Harper Collins Publishers, 1999) ISBN 006093073X

Brown, Lester, *Eco-Economy* (W. W. Norton & Company, 2001) ISBN 0393321932

Bruges, James. *The Little Earth Book* (Alastair Sawday Publishing, 2000) ISBN 190197023X

Brundtland Commission. *Our Common Future* (Oxford University Press, 1987) ISBN 019282080X

Campbell, Joseph. *Myths to Live By* (Penguin Books, 1972) ISBN 0140194614

Canadian Bank Notes. *The Charleton Standard Catalogue of Canadian Bank Notes, 2nd Edition* (The Charlton Press, 1989) ISBN 088968071X

Carmack, Patrick S.J. & Still, Bill. *The Money Masters*, (Video- Royalty Production Company, 1998)

Carson, Rachel. *Silent Spring* (Boston: Houghton Mifflins, 1962) ISBN 0-618-24906-0

Carson, Rachel. *The Sea Around Us* (Oxford University Press, 1951) ISBN 0195069978

Cheveldayoff, Wayne. *The Business Page* (Deneau & Greenberg Publishers, 1977) ISBN 0888790007

Chomsky, Noam, Herman, Edward S. *Manufacturing Consent: The Political Economy of the Mass Media* (Random House, 2002) ISBN 0375714499

Chossudovsky, Michael. *The Globalization of Poverty* (Zed Books, 1997) ISBN 0185569347

Clarke, Tony. *Silent Coup* (Canadian Centre for Policy Alternatives and James Lorimer & Company Ltd., 1997) ISBN 0886279232

Club of Rome. *Limits to Growth* (Universe Books, 1974) ISBN 0876631650

Crooks, Harold. *Giants of Garbage* (James Lorimer & Company, 1993) ISBN 1550283987

Crosby, Alfred W. *Ecological Imperialism: the Biological Expansion of Europe* (Cambridge University Press, 1992) ISBN 0521336139

Czech, Brian. *Shoveling Fuel for a Runaway Train* (U of CA Press, 2000) ISBN 0520225147

Dahrendorf, Ralf (and others). *Report on Wealth Creation and Social Cohesion in a Free Society* (The Commission on Wealth Creation and Social Cohesion, 1995)

Daly, Herman E. & Cobb, John B. Jr. *For the Common Good*, (Beacon Press, 1989, 1994 edition) ISBN 0807047058

de Chardin, Tielhard. *The Phenomenon of Man*, (Harper Torch Books, 1962) ISBN 0061303836

Dillon, John. *Turning the Tide: Confronting the Money Traders* (Canadian Center for Policy Alternatives, 1996) ISBN 088627155X

Dominguez, Joe & Robin, Vicki. *Your Money or Your Life* (Penguin Books, 1992) ISBN 0140286780

Douthwaite, Richard. *Short Circuit* (The Lulliput Press, 1996) ISBN 1874675600

Douthwaite, Richard. *The Growth Illusion: How Economic Growth has Enriched the Few, Impoverished the Many and Endangered the Planet* (Green Books, UK, 1993) ISBN 0933031742

Douthwaite, Richard. *The Ecology of Money* (Green Books for The Schumacher Society, 1999) ISBN 1870098811

Douthwaite, Richard and Jopling, John (Editors). *FEASTA Review: The Foundation for the Economics of Sustainability* (FEASTA, 2001) ISBN 09540151009

Durning, Alan Thein & Bauman, Yoram. *Tax Shift* (Northwest Environment Watch, 1998) ISBN 188609075

Fanfani, Amintore. *Catholicism, Protestantism and Capitalism* (Sheed & Ward, 1935) ISBN 0971489475

Fischer, Louis. *Gandhi: His life and message for the world* (The New American Library of Canada Limited, 1954) ISBN 0451627423

Frum, David. *Dead Right* (New Republic Book Basic Books (Harper Collins, 1994) ISBN 0-465-09825-8

Fuller, Buckminster, *Utopia or Oblivion: The Prospects for Humanity* (Bantam Books, 1969) ISBN 0713901349

Fuller, Buckminster, *Operating Manual for Spaceship Earth* (Pocket Books, NY, 1970) ISBN 671780468

Fuller, Buckminster, *World Resources Inventory; Human Trends and Needs*, (1965-1975) ISBN 0192811673

Galbraith, John Kenneth. *A Life in Our Times: Memoirs* (Houghton Mifflin Company, 1981) ISBN 0-395-30509-8

Gibran, Kahlil. *The Prophet* (Alfred A. Knoff, Inc, 1923) ISBN 0394404289

Gorz, Andre. *Paths To Paradise: on the liberation from work* (Pluto Press, 1985) ISBN 8-86104-762-1

Greco, Thomas H., Jr, *Money and Debt: A Solution to the Global Crisis* (Self Published, 1990) ISBN 0-9625208-1-0

Griffin, G. Edward. *The Creature from Jekyll Island: A Second Look at the Federal Reserve* (American Media, 1998) ISBN 0-912986-21-2

Hamond, M. Jeff, (and others). *Tax Waste, Not Work* (Redefining Progress, 1997)

Hardin, Garrett. *The Ostrich Factor: Our Population Myopia* (Oxford University Press, 1998) ISBN 0195122747

Hardin, Garrett. *Avoiding the Tragedy of the Commons* (Federation for American Immigration Reform [FAIR], 1968) ISBN 093577615

Hartmann, Thom. *The Last Hours of Ancient Sunshine* (Three Rivers Press, 1998) ISBN 0-609-80529-0

Hawken, Paul & Lovins, Hunter & Lovins, Amory, *The Ecology of Commerce: A Declaration of Sustainability* (Harper Business, 1993) ISBN 0887307043

Hawken, Paul. *Natural Capitalism* (Little, Brown, 1999) ISBN 0316353167

Heilbroner, Robert L. *The Making of Economic Society* (Prentice-Hall, Inc., N.J.,1985 ed) ISBN 0135462010

Heilbroner, Robert L. *Twenty-First Century Capitalism* (House of Anansi Press Limited, 1993) ISBN 0887845347

Henderson, Hazel. *Beyond Globalization: Shaping a Sustainable Global Economy* (Kumarian Press, 1999) ISBN 1565491076

Henderson, Hazel and Sethi, Simran. *Ethical Markets: Growing the Green Economy* (Chelsea Green Publishing, 2006) ISBN 1933392231

Hunnicutt, Benjamin Kline. *Work Without End* (Temple University Press, 1998) ISBN 0877225206

Huxley, Aldous. *Brave New World*. (Penguin Books, 1963) ISBN 0060929871

Jackobs, Michael. *The Green Economy* (U. of B.C. Press, 1983) ISBN 0774804742

Jacobs, Jane. *The Nature of Economics* (Random House Canada, 2000) ISBN 0679310363

Jackson, Kevin (Editor). *The Oxford Book of Money* (Oxford University Press, 1995) ISBN 0192142003

Kelly, Marjorie. *The Divine Right of Capital* (Berrett-Koehler Publishers, Inc, San Fran, 2001) ISBN 1576751252

Keynes, John Maynard, Stone, Richard. *The National Income and Expenditure of the United Kingdom, and How to Pay for the War* (Booklet 1939)

Kohn, Alfie. *No Contest: The Case Against Competition* (Houghton Mifflin Company, 1992) ISBN 0395631254

Korten, David. *When Corporations Rule the World* (Berrett- Koehler & Kumarian Press, Inc, 1995) ISBN 1887208003

Korten, David C. *The Post-Corporate World: Life after Capitalism* (Berrett-Koehler Publishers & Kumarian Press, Inc, 1995) ISBN 18872080308

Krehm, William. *A Power Unto Itself: The Bank of Canada* (Stoddart Publishing Co., Limited, 1963) ISBN 0773756213

Krehm, William. *Meltdown: Money, Debt and the Wealth of Nations* (Comer Publications, 1999) ISBN 096806812X

Krehm, William. *Towards a Non-Autistic Economy: A Place at the Table for Society* (Comer Publications, 2002) ISBN 0968068138

Kurtzman, Joel. *The Death of Money* (Little, Brown and Company, 1993) ISBN 0316507377

Lewinsohn, Richard. *The Profits of War* (New York: E. P. Dutton, 1937)

Lietaer, Bernard. *The Future of Money* (Century, 2001) ISBN 0712683992

Lietaer, Bernard, & Belgin, Stephen. *Of Human Wealth: New Currencies For a New World* (Human Wealth Books and Talks, Boulder, CO., 2003)

Lietaer, Bernard. *The Future of Money* (Century, The Random House Group Limited, London, England, 2001) ISBN 0 7126 8399 2

Lipsey, Richard & Sparks, Gordon & Steiner, Peter. *Economics* (Harper & Row Publishers, 1973) ISBN 0060440147

Lovelock, James. *Gaia: A New Look at Life on Earth* (Oxford University Press, 1979) ISBN 019217665X

Lundberg, Ferdinand. *America's Sixty Families* (The Vanquard Press, 1937)

Lundberg, Ferdinand. *The Rich and the Super Rich* (Bantam Books, 1968) ISBN 0553146017

Madron, Roy & Jopling, John. *Gaian Democracies* (Green Books for The Schumacher Society, 2003) ISBN 190399828X

Mankiw, Gregory. "Gas Tax Now," (*Fortune Magazine*, May 24, 1999)

Margulis, Lynn. *Origin of Eukaryotic Cells* (Yale University Press, 1970) ISBN 0300013531

McDonough, William & Braungart, Michael. *Cradle to Cradle: Remaking the Way We Make Things* (North Point Press, 2002)   ISBN 0865475873

McKibben, Bill. *Hope, Human and Wild* (Little, Brown and Company, 1995) ISBN 0316560642

McMurtry, John, *The Cancer Stage of Capitalism* (Pluto Press, 1995) ISBN 0745313523

Michalos, Alex C. *Good Taxes: The Case for Taxing Foreign Currency Exchange and Other Financial Transactions* (Dundurn Press, 1997) ISBN 0888669542

Mumford, Lewis. *The City in History* (Harvest Books, 1968) ISBN 0156180359

Nickerson, Mike. *Bakavi; Change the World, I Want to Stay On* (Bhakti Press, 1977) ISBN 0949970036

Nickerson, Mike. *Planning for Seven Generations; Guideposts for a Sustainable Future* (Voyageur Publishing, 1993) ISBN 0921842279

Odum, Eugene. *Fundamentals of Ecology; Third Edition* (W. B. Saunders Company, 1971) ISBN 0721669417

Orwell, George. *Nineteen Eighty Four* (Penguin Putnam, 1949) ISBN 451518004

Palast, Gregory. "The Other Side of the Fence! IMF's Four Steps to Damnation," (*London Observer,* Apr 29, 2001)

Palast, Gregory. *Armed Madhouse: Dispatches from the Front Lines of the Class War* (Penguin Dutton, June 2006) ISBN 0973940905

Papanek, Victor. *Design for the Real World: Human Ecology and Social Change* (Academy Chicago, 1985, second edition, 1999) ISBN: 0897331532

Porter, John. *The Vertical Mosaic* (University of Toronto Press, 1965) ISBN 0802060552

Price, Weston A. *Nutrition and Physical Degeneration* (The Price-Pottenger Nutrition Foundation, Inc., 1970) ISBN 0916764001

Ralston Saul, John. *The Unconscious Civilization* (Anansi Press, 1995) ISBN 0887845762

Ralston Saul, John. *Voltaire's Bastards: The Dictatorship of Reason in the West* (Penquin Books, 1993) ISBN 014015373X

Redefining Progress. "If the GDP is Up, Why is America Down?" (*Atlantic Monthly,* October 1995)

Roodman, David. *The Natural Wealth of Nations* (W. W. Norton & Company, 1998) ISBN 0393318524

Rosenberg, Marshall B. *Nonviolent Communication: A Language of Life (and companion workbook)* (PuddleDancer Press, 2005) ISBN 1892005034

Rowbotham, Michael. *The Grip of Death* (Jon Carpenter Publishing, 1998) ISBN 1897766408

Rowbotham, Michael. *Goodbye America! Globalization, debt and the dollar empire* (Jon Carpenter Publishing, 2000) ISBNs 1897766564 & 0858811774

Ryan, John C. & Durning, Alan Thein. *Stuff: The Secret Lives of Everyday Things* (Northwest Environment Watch, 1997) ISBN 1886093040

Schumacher, E. F. *Small is Beautiful; A Study of Economics as if People Mattered* (Sphere Books Ltd. 1974) ISBN 0349131384

Sheldrake, Rupert. *The Presence of the Past: Morphic Resonance and the Habits of Nature* (Park Street Press, Rochester, Vermont, 1998) ISBN 089281537X

Sheldrake, Rupert. *Seven Experiments That Could Change the World* (1995) ISBN 1573220140

Smith, Adam. *The Theory of Moral Sentiments* (Liberty Fund, 1759, 1984 edition) ISBN 08659710122

Smith, Adam. *The Wealth of Nations Books 1 - 3* (Prometheus Books, 1776, 1994 ed.) ISBN 0879757051

Steiner, Rudolf. *The Three Fold Social Order* (Anthroposophical Publishing, London, 1923)

Steiner, Rudolf. *The Being of Man and His Future Evolution* (Rudolf Steiner Press, London, 1981) ISBN 0854404058

Steiner, Rudolf. *Toward Social Renewal* Rudolf Steiner Press, Bristol, 1977) ISBN 1855840723

Suzuki, David & Dressel, Holly, *Good News for a Change: Hope for a Troubled Planet* (Stoddart Publishing Co., 2002) ISBN 0773733078

Tawney, R. H. *Religion and the Rise of Capitalism* (Peter Smith Publisher Inc, 1922) ISBN 0844614467

Taylor, Walt. *Waging Peace for a Living: An Action Plan for Survival of Life on Earth* (Trafford Publishing, 1999) ISBN 1552122344

Thompson, Fred G. *Looking Back on the Future: Adventures in the Futures Field* (FutureScan International Inc., 1992) ISBN 0969662408

Townson, Monica. *Health and Wealth; How Social and Economic Factors Affect Our Well Being* (The Canadian Center for Policy Alternatives, 1999) ISBN 1550286587

Vitousek, Peter, et al. "Human Appropriation of the Products of Photosynthesis," (*BioScience* 36: 368-373, 1996)

Waring, Marilyn. *Who's Counting? Sex, Lies and Global Economics,* (National Film Board Video, 2000)

Weber, Max. *The Protestant Ethic and the Spirit of Capitalism* edition, Allen & Unwin, 1917, 1976 edition) ISBN 0043310680

Berry, Wendell, *Citizenship Papers* (Shoemaker & Hoard, 2004) ISBN 1593760000 (HC) 159376037X (PB)

Wright, Ronald. *A Short History of Progress* (House of Anansi Press Limited, 2004) ISBN 0887847064

Index

About the Author

Throughout his adult life, Mike Nickerson has been fascinated by how societies evolve. Even in the early 1970s, when many of today's problems were still projections, Mike sensed that we were beginning what will likely be the greatest transformation of all time. He was motivated early on by the collective vision of voluntary and non-profit citizens' groups. To look at the problems and solutions that stimulate change, and to learn about the ways in which change takes place, he founded the Institute for the Study of Cultural Evolution in 1971.

By assembling common themes from the aspirations and concerns of citizens' groups, the Institute's work culminated with the outline for sustainability presented in *Life, Money & Illusion*. There are abundant solutions, well within our grasp, if we choose to apply them.

Mike's first book, *Bakavi; Change the World I Want to Stay On* (1977) explained the basic goal of sustainability. To take the message into classrooms, living rooms, community halls and institutional offices, he and his associates created an audio-visual discussion kit titled *Guideposts for a Sustainable Future* (1990) and, in 1993, the book from the kit was published in a stand alone edition as *Planning for Seven Generations*.

From 1997 to 2003, Mike coordinated work on the *Canada Well-Being Measurement Act*. He has served on the Board of the Ontario Environmental Network, as a public liaison member on the United Counties of Leeds-Grenville Waste Management Planning Process and on the Governing Council of the Green Party of Canada.

Mike lives in rural Lanark County with his wife, Donna Dillman, and her teenage daughter. He boasts two grown daughters and four grandchildren. To support his studies and writing, Mike designs and builds custom furniture.

Generations from now, parents will tell their children the story of our times. They will tell them about the Great Transformation; the shift that civilization made from its growth phase, which had continued since early times, to a new, mature state where the total volume of material, energy and consequent waste was maintained within steady, sustinable volumes. With human activity already stretching planetary limits, and systems in place to fully double that activity every 20 years, this change will have to have happened.

The story told about our times will be one of praise — telling how well our generation recognized the challenge and rose to meet it, or it will be a tale of great sorrow — telling how those alive today denied that it was our task to find a stable relationship with the Earth. Whether the story the children hear is one of triumph or of sorrow depends on how soon we recognize the challenge and accept the historic responsibility.

Elizabeth May

The greatest obstacle to triumph is pessimism. Many feel that we cannot overcome the forces of greed, or of the institutions now in place that enable greed to serve itself. Yet, to be greedy requires a sense of self. Far older and more firmly rooted than self-awareness is the urge to launch offspring successfully into the world.

There is much cause for hope.

Like many an adolescent, longing to maintain the carefree privilege of childhood, humankind hesitates at the threshold of maturity. Given the enormous scope of knowledge and skills at our command, civilization has no more cause to fear the future than do adolescents viewing adult responsibility. As individuals, almost all of us rise to the challenge. As a species we can do as well.

While we know which way to proceed to secure well-being for generations into the future, we have yet to clearly accept the goal. The Question of Direction focuses on the pivotal choice. You are invited to apply your will to this lever so that, together, we might tip the balance and set our sights clearly on a sustainable future.

The 7th Generation Initiative, a non-profit organization, exists to help accommodate the transformation. If, after considering the story told herein, you want to get involved, please contact us. Your vision, skills, understanding, contacts and financial support can all help to increase the chances that the seventh generation will look back to our generation with gratitude.

The 7th Generation Initiative
RR #3 Lanark, Ontario, K0G 1K0
613-259-9988
http://www.SustainWellBeing.net